Lee Hall

Plays: 2 (Adaptati

A Servant to Two Masters, The Good Hope, Mr Puntila and His Man Matti, Mother Courage and Her Children

A Servant to Two Masters: 'wildly and inventively farcical. More surprisingly still, it also contrives to find passages of deep feeling amid the comic.' *Daily Telegraph*

The Good Hope: 'a theatrical revelation' *Evening Standard*

Mr Puntila and His Man Matti: 'Lee Hall mixes in-your-face contemporary slang with endearing jokes . . . it's not often that you can write "Bertolt Brecht" and "knockabout fun" in the same sentence' *Independent*

Mother Courage and Her Children: 'Clarifies . . . shows we are mad to neglect Brecht' *Guardian*

Lee Hall was born in Newcastle-upon-Tyne and studied English Literature at Cambridge University. His stage plays include *Cooking with Elvis, Bollocks, Wittgenstein on Tyne* and *Two's Company* (Live Theatre Newcastle) and *Genie* (Paines Plough). He has written extensively for radio, including *I Love You, Jimmy Spud* (Sony Award 1996) and *Spoonface Steinberg*, which was filmed for BBC2 and performed as a play starring Kathryn Hunter at the Ambassador's Theatre in January 2000. The award-winning *Child of Our Time* plays were produced by Radio 4 in 2000. He has also written adaptations of Brecht's *Mr Puntila and His Man Matti* (The Right Size/Almeida, Traverse and West End), *Mother Courage and Her Children* (Shared Experience), Goldoni's *A Servant to Two Masters* (RSC and Young Vic) and his adaptation of Herman Heijermans' *The Good Hope* premiered at the Royal National Theatre, London in autumn 2001. His screenplay for *Billy Elliott* was nominated for an Oscar.

LEE HALL

Plays: 2 (Adaptations)

A Servant to Two Masters

by Carlo Goldoni

The Good Hope

by Herman Heijermans

Mr Puntila and His Man Matti

by Bertolt Brecht

Mother Courage and Her Children

by Bertolt Brecht

introduced by Lee Hall

Methuen Drama

METHUEN CONTEMPORARY DRAMATISTS

Published by Methuen 2003

1 3 5 7 9 10 8 6 4 2

First published in 2003 by
Methuen Publishing Limited
215 Vauxhall Bridge Road,
London SW1V 1EJ

Introduction and collective copyright © Lee Hall 2003

A Servant to Two Masters copyright © Lee Hall 1999
The Good Hope copyright © Lee Hall 2001;
song lyrics copyright © John Tams 2001
Mr Puntila and His Man Matti: original work entitled *Herr Puntila und sein Knecht Matti* copyright © 1951 by Suhrkamp Verlag, Berlin; this adaptation copyright © Lee Hall 2003, based on a literal translation by Purni Morell.
Mother Courage and Her Children: original work entitled *Mutter Courage und ihre Kinder* copyright © 1940 by Arvid England Teatreforlag, a.b., renewed June 1967 by Stefan S. Brecht, copyright © 1949 by Suhrkamp Verlag, Frankfurt am Main; based on a literal translation by Jan-Willem van Jen Bosch

A Servant to Two Masters first published in 1999 by Methuen Publishing Ltd
The Good Hope first published in 2001 by Methuen Publishing Ltd

Lee Hall has asserted his rights under the Copyright, Designs and Patents Act, 1988, to be identified as the author of this work

Methuen Publishing Limited Reg. No. 3543167

A CIP catalogue record is available from the British Library

ISBN 0 413 77377 9

Typeset by SX Composing DTP, Rayleigh, Essex
Printed and bound in Great Britain by
Cox & Wyman Ltd, Reading, Berkshire

Contents

to Beeban

Lee Hall:
A Chronology

1992 *Bartleby* (adaptation from Hermann Melville) first performed at Dance City, Newcastle as part of Dance Umbrella season

1995 *I love You, Jimmy Spud* first broadcast on Radio 4

1996 *Blood Sugar* broadcast on Radio 4

Adaptation of *Aunt Julia and the Scriptwriter* by Mario Vargas Llosa broadcast on Radio 4

Bollocks broadcast on Radio 4

January 1997 *Gristle, The Love Letters of Ragie Patel, The Sorrows of Sandra Saint* and *Spoonface Steinberg* broadcast on Radio 4

May 1997 *Wittgenstein on Tyne* first performed at Live Theatre, Newcastle

November 1997 *The Student Prince* broadcast on BBC1

December 1997 *Leonce and Lena* translated from Buchner premiered at The Gate Theatre, London

February 1998 *I Love You, Jimmy Spud* screenplay first read and *Bollocks* first performed at Live Theatre, Newcastle

June 1998 *Spoonface Steinberg* screened on BBC2

August 1998 *Mr Puntila and His Man Matti* (translated from Brecht) first performed by The Right Size opened at the Traverse Theatre before transferring to the West End

October 1998 *Cooking With Elvis* first performed at Live Theatre, Newcastle

March 1999 *Genie* first performed at Live Theatre, Newcastle as a co-production with Paines Plough

December 1999 *The Servant of Two Masters* (adapted from Goldoni) first performed by the Royal Shakespeare Company at Stratford before transferring to the Young Vic

January 2000 *Spoonface Steinberg* first performed at the Ambassador's Theatre

2000 *Mother Courage and Her Children* (translation from Brecht) first performed by Shared Experience Theatre Company and played at The Ambassadors Theatre, London

June 2000 *Children of the Rain* broadcast on Radio 4 as part of the *Child of Our Time* series

October 2000 *Billy Eliott* directed by Stephen Daldry opens in London

November 2000 *The Adventures of Pinocchio* (adapted from Collodi) first performed at the Lyric Theatre, Hammersmith

Two's Company performed at Live Theatre, Newcastle

November 2001 *Gabriel and Me,* directed by Udayan Prasad, opens in London

The Good Hope (adaptation from Herman Heijermans) opens at the Royal National Theatre

Introduction

I suppose the fact that this volume bears my name but is entirely made up of plays by other people deserves some sort of explanation. It strikes me as odd that I've been afforded this anomalous position in the Methuen list but I am entirely grateful, as adapting other people's plays has been central to my working life as a dramatist. Comparing my original plays with these adaptations, I think there is a consistency of theme and tone which makes all this seemingly disparate work of a piece.

During the first few years of writing plays for theatre I was asked to rework various foreign plays for specific productions. The orthodoxy goes that because any translation will bear the imprint of its time, plays written in a foreign tongue require a constant effort of re-evaluation to make an impact: reading eighteenth century versions of the Greeks often tells you more about the eighteenth century than it does about the Greeks. So theatres are keen to have versions which allow an audience a contemporary connection to a foreign play, rather than one via an English idiom that is itself a foreign language.

From my point of view, being asked to work on a play that is already scheduled for production, often with actors and directors already involved, is a huge privilege. So much of one's time as a writer is spent on the periphery of the actual process of 'making' theatre – you write a play in your garret and send it off into the ether. And even if you are involved in the production, you are always slightly apart from the other members of the production team because you've had an enforced headstart as well as a proprietorial interest. Whereas working as an adaptor puts you in the room on an equal footing with everyone else. In a way you can be a more genuine collaborator than you can with your own work as you are an equal partner in the process, as for once all your skills are being used to decipher something someone else has already made, rather than trying to invent it in the first place.

One of the main reasons for my pursuing a career as a dramatist rather than a novelist or poet, for instance, was to work collaboratively. Although I can be single-minded at times, and the process can be endlessly frustrating, the theatre is one place where creativity is essentially a collective act. I am sure that many writers are secretly jealous of their theatrical colleagues who spend virtually all of their creative time together in meetings and rehearsal rooms, so the fact that one could collaborate so closely with actors, directors and musicians, as well as enter into an intimate dialogue with past masters, was an opportunity too good to miss.

I have always been an avid reader of old and foreign plays, and the opportunity to bring some of the more peripheral texts into the 'canon' has been a special privilege. Many of the plays I've worked on have come from socialist traditions and it seems an important thing to remind ourselves that, in an age which is prone to caricature work with a radical stance as somehow naive or outmoded, the mainstream of our theatrical culture was once much more unafraid to speak out from that particular standpoint without being formally unsophisticated. To proselytise on behalf of Brecht's *Puntila* or Heijermans' *Good Hope* seemed a noble use of one's time. The exception in this volume is Goldoni who was a natural reactionary. However, since the war, there have been many celebrated European productions of his work that have found in his examinations of love and commerce a profound illumination of the concerns familiar with politically motivated theatre. Strehler, Fo, Planchon and Fassbinder (to name a few) have all looked to Goldoni to provide material for their leftish concerns.

Once one sets about examining the background to most plays, the question of authorship becomes a complex one. Precisely because theatre is a collective enterprise and a living tradition whose achievements have to be constantly remade, it often becomes very difficult to attribute everything to the 'authorial' voice'. In this volume, *A Servant to Two Masters* was first conceived as a list of scenes nailed behind the set of a certain *commedia dell'arte* company. When Goldoni visited the set he was so appalled by the baroque excesses of the company he wrote a script to prevent their improvisations going any further. Whether he acted as author or amanuensis can never be conclusively determined. Brecht, now notorious for his 'borrowings' from a considerable entourage, clearly mined Goldoni and much of the *commedia* tradition when writing *Puntila and His Man Matti* which is pure *commedia dell'arte* in many respects. To make matters more complicated, his play was a rewrite of a Finnish play by his host of the time, Hella Wuolijoki. His *Mother Courage* is an adaptation of Grimmelshausen's 'novel' of the same name, though clearly Heijermans' *The Good Hope* is such an obvious precursor to Brecht's play it is impossible to know whether these borrowings were conscious or subliminal. What is clear is that nothing is sacred. The reality of play-writing, as in culture as a whole, is that the role of the adaptor is much more central to the heart of the culture than the idea of the inspired genius who magics the whole thing out of the air fully formed and unsullied by another human hand. In post-structuralist theory I believe this is called intertextuality, in polite society it is called plagiarism, but anyone intimate with the practice of making plays knows there is nothing new under the sun. Whether it is deliberate homage or unconscious borrowing even the most original work is a palimpsest on which the influences are indelibly inscribed even if you have to look below the surface. Most of Brecht, most of Shakespeare, most screenplays and most television has been openly stolen from somewhere else. However, I would not be so bold as to claim any of these pieces as my own, and in fact part of my purpose was to restore the particular voices of these long dead writers.

*

I was asked to help create a version of *Mr Puntila and His Man Matti* by Kathryn Hunter for the comedy group, The

Right Size. Doing a Brecht with a team steeped in the popular traditions of music hall and vaudeville seemed a brilliant idea. Obviously Brecht had a very close affinity to the cabaret of his time, living and working in the popular theatre of 1930s Berlin as he did; and Joan Littlewood's work in translating Brecht's discoveries into a British idiom had hewn serious theatre from the deep seam of popular entertainment. Anyway, we set about taking apart the various British versions and discovered something more lithe and playful underneath. Working with the dramaturg Jan van den Bosch, I realised Brecht's German is much more salty, slang and heterogeneous than the existing versions would suggest. His language is highly allusive, coarse, deeply ironical, rhetorical and rude in equal measure and between us we tried to carve out a production that would put these qualities into relief.

The adaptation of *Mother Courage and Her Children* came as a continuation of this process, this time with Kathryn Hunter playing Mother Courage and Nancy Meckler directing for Shared Experience. There are many good versions of this play in English and I add my own slant to the chorus of voices. Without any doubt it is a very partial and particular take on the play.

The adaptation of the Goldoni play *A Servant to Two Masters* came as a suggestion from Simon Reade, the then literary manager of the RSC, who suggested I work on a new version of the play. I had wanted to work on this play for a long time. It has a dizzying architecture whereby chaos is meticulously organised and orchestrated. Although it is a play central to the history of European theatre, there was not a single faithful translation in print. The various versions I could find were either very dated or completely bowdlerised. My intention was to go back to the Italian text and give a straightforward account of the play rather than succumb to the temptation to embellish it.

To produce an English version of *The Good Hope* was a long-held ambition of Bill Bryden's who had directed a Dutch version of the play several years before. I was very keen to work with Bill, whose Cottesloe productions had been a huge influence on me as a teenager. After seeing his *Mysteries* I was certain I had to pursue theatre as a career, as nothing else had excited me so much. Of all the adaptations it is the most radically different from the original. Bill and Trevor Nunn encouraged me to take it out of the single room it was set in and to give it the epic grandeur that the original implies. But my most flagrant infidelity was to soften the original portrayal of the villain of the piece. I decided it was much more interesting to examine the complexities of collusion between oppressor and oppressed and to explore the moral dilemma within the character's conscience than to keep him as a stereotypical moustache-twiddling Victorian 'baddie'. The play was written as a piece of crusading agit-prop rather than as a piece of dramatic literature, but now that we were holding it up to examination long after its usefulness as a direct political corrective had expired, it seemed only fair to Heijermans to allow the character to match the complexity of the dramatic situation he had developed.

At a time when it's harder than ever for a playwright to write for large casts, to get their plays out of the studio spaces and into the West End, writing these adaptations afforded me a chance to work on a scale and with a calibre of colleagues that simply being an 'original' playwright would not have allowed me. I was given an invaluable space to explore the themes and preoccupations that I was working on in my plays – only on a much bigger canvas. Picking the brains of both living and dead and working on a whole volume of plays, which would simply be impossible with original material, was an invaluable experience.

One of the great pleasures of the theatre is that it is a place where there is a real and constant dialogue between the past and the present, where forms of expression are constantly in need of renewal as the world changes, where values and voices need always to be reassessed. I am sure in a few years these versions will all seem as outmoded as the ones I set out to replace, and will inevitably seem more mine than Brecht's, Heijermans' or Goldoni's. All the nuances and mistakes will be mine and I will have no one else to blame. But in the meantime these versions were made inestimably better by the contributions of Kathryn Hunter, Jan van den Bosch, Hamish McColl, John Foley, Chris Larner, Nancy Meckler, Bill Bryden, John Tams, Simon Reade, Tim Supple, Jason Watkins and Dominic Muldowney. The infelicities are all mine.

Lee Hall
September 2003

A Servant to Two Masters

Adaptor's Note

Carlo Goldoni (1707–1793), known as one of the masters of the comic stage, was a failed tragedian. His first works for the stage (although they never actually made it) were in fact tragedies. His first play *Amalasonte – A Lyrical Tragedy* did not, by his own admission, 'make the choice of connoisseurs'. After a few subsequent failures Goldoni pursued a career in law which typically seemed to burgeon by accident. Because of a clerical error he was made a barrister before he'd even completed half of his pupilage. Thrust backwards into the limelight he triumphed with his first case and was a huge success in his profession, unencumbered by training. This is typical of his life, which reads – in his autobiography at least – like an Italian version of *Tom Jones*.

Assailed by bandits, war, *amour fou*, penury and professional catastrophe he limped around Italy pursuing various adventures, throwing out the odd plot now and then for travelling theatre companies until in 1745 he received a commission to devise a play for a famous Harlequin. Thus *A Servant to Two Masters* was born as a scenario, pinned to the side of the stage, from which the *commedia dell'arte* troupe would improvise their play. The production was a huge success but when Goldoni finally came to see it he was appalled by the indulgence of the actors. In a fit of pique he wrote down a text for the players to learn and thus dealt the fatal blow to the centuries-old tradition of *commedia dell'arte*.

Commedia dell'arte, founded in Italy, was a popular theatrical tradition which became a transnational form during the Renaissance. Its improvised plays were performed by a company of actors; each one specialising in a stock character. The most famous of these characters was Harlequin. Harlequin was a *zanni*; a comic character, hailing from the mountains of Bergamo, who was both as thick as a post and sly as a fox and who specialised in all sorts of acrobatics. As the *commedia dell'arte* companies travelled round the different states in Italy they were forced to rely on visual forms of theatre to keep their audiences engaged no matter what language they actually spoke. In fact the companies themselves were sometimes made up of actors who spoke the specific dialects or languages from the various corners of Italy in which they were born. The plays were often (but not exclusively) performed in the open air and the heterogeneous crowd that gathered to watch saw a cross-section of their society which mirrored their own various origins.

Not only were the *commedia* plays a rattlebag of characters from different classes, they were also a jumble of styles. Actors who played the lovers would pride themselves on the beauty of their poesy, whilst the *zanni* would excel in the mechanics of slapstick motion. But the main theme of the plays was desire. Food, sex, love and money were the motors for the absurdly convoluted plots, and the players were never scared to explore the bodily baseness of these motivations. Harlequin frequently mimed eating himself because he was so hungry and is often depicted receiving an enema from a quack doctor. *Commedia*'s roots in the middle ages consistently showed through.

It was precisely this robustness that Goldoni desired to temper. In his opinion the *commedia dell'arte* had become decadent in the sense it was more concerned with the form of presentation than with the reality it represented. Goldoni's instinct was that of a realist, in the way that Ibsen and Chekhov were realists who sought to make the heightened drama of their day bear more resemblance to the reality of the bourgeois world they knew so well. And so for good or bad Goldoni stepped into the fray and attempted to deal with the realistic psychology of the *commedia dell'arte*'s stock of characters. He thus started a journey which led him to abandon the *commedia* conventions altogether, thus opening up a whole new world for the nineteenth century.

A Servant to Two Masters is pivotal to this revolution in the Italian theatre. But it seems crucially torn in its allegiances. The piece sounded the death-knell of *commedia dell'arte* at the same time as it revelled in its stagecraft and absurdities. It ushered in a new 'psychologism' of character whilst never letting the characters themselves escape the traditional trajectories of their comedic fates. In short, Goldoni was trying to serve both the *commedia* tradition and the current dragging him towards a realistic aesthetic more typical of the nineteenth century.

The play is full of *lazzi* – the moments such as Truffaldino serving the food and tearing up the letter – which were bravura flourishes that a skilled *zanni* would develop into a baroque set piece to delight audiences with his improvisatory skill and comic invention. Yet there is a tentative move towards making the crude excesses of the other characters more nuanced. The priapic indulgences of Pantaloon, which the *commedia dell'arte* revelled in, are softened to reveal a man internally torn rather than outwardly driven. (A distended phallus was an oft-used prop in some companies.) Indeed, some of the pathos which informed Goldoni's attempts as a tragedian seems to be embroidered throughout the piece.

Whilst the strengths of the play are so obviously grounded in its delight at theatrical mechanics, the plot rests on darker matter – a murder which has caused real loss and longing. Goldoni is juggling the dual enticements of a glorious confection on one hand and an attempt at emotional truth on the other. Any version of the play must recognise that it is neither a satisfactory *commedia dell'arte* piece nor a fully realised realistic world. It is impossible to realise its true value as a comedy without exploring its melancholy, and its melancholy is not sufficient meat without the sauce of *commedia*. Of the various versions that are played on the English stage none is entirely faithful to Goldoni. The most widely available is the French's version, prepared as a vehicle for Tommy Steele, which is quite simply a travesty. I was attracted to this master and servant play because I adapted Brecht's *Mr Puntila and his Man Matti* and was interested to investigate the genealogy of this relationship in an older play. However, instead of ripping the text apart to find the play anew as I'd done with the Brecht, I realised quite quickly that I would have to restore a work that has been worn down by our preconceptions, appropriations,

additions and meddlings for many years. And so my project
has been to reinstate the actual Goldoni play rather than
create my own riff on it. I am the last to disparage anyone
who wishes to stamp their own design on an old text, but
since the director, Tim Supple, was drawn to the play not as
a gagfest but as a drama, it seemed more appropriate to
reinstate Goldoni than reiterate my own preoccupations.

I hope I haven't made too many claims for what is, and
always was, an entertainment that delights in what
developed later into farce. Disguises, muddled
identifications, someone coming in the wrong door at the
wrong time are all standbys for a simple good night out in
the theatre – well, at least in my book. From Feydeau to
Rix, farce has always been a form that poked fun at the
hypocrisies of the middle classes. Goldoni certainly does that
here, but there is a more unfamiliar drive to his writing. The
comic resolution where all the couples are successfully
paired is not for Goldoni simply a conservative endorsement
of the status quo, or a cheap sentimental conclusion, but
represents a profound longing for some kind of cohesive
community. Goldoni was writing a year after the War of
Austrian Succession and had been dragged into it himself
and badly injured. This was more than a hundred years
before the Risorgimento, and the turbulence of economic
and political life made such happy endings in reality quite a
rare event. I think we may read into what might seem a trite
formula a wistful utopian sentiment where everyday
exigencies of political division, hunger and economic
instability are forgotten.

And so throughout every aspect of the piece Goldoni
seems divided between these twin masters of a love of
tradition and instinct for change. His life seems exemplary
in trying to have one's cake and eat it; wanting to be both a
lawyer and a dramatist, an instinctive conservative whilst
being an accidental reformer. In the end Goldoni, who so
celebrated the real people of Italy, was ironically driven out
and ended his days in exile in Paris. He was condemned by
the aristocratic playwright Carlo Gozzi as a radical for
ruining traditional *commedia dell'arte*. And so he ended his

days in Paris, as he says in his autobiography, with a 'stout stomach and a tender heart'. But the final act was far from uncomplicated. During the revolution he had his state pension discontinued because he was deemed to be an undoubted bourgeois influence. However, in true Goldoni form it was reinstated the very day before he died by the National Convention in recognition of his portrayals of the common man. And so maybe, like Truffaldino in the play, through luck as much as design Goldoni managed to serve conflicting ends simply through a mastery of common stagecraft. And in the process of killing off *commedia dell'arte* he has in fact served to keep it alive to this day.

Lee Hall
December 1999

A Servant to Two Masters, a co-production between the Young Vic Theatre Company and the RSC, was first performed at The Other Place, Stratford-upon-Avon, on 8 December 1999, and at the Young Vic on 4 February 2000. The cast was as follows:

Clarice	Nikki Amuka-Bird
Florindo	Ariyon Bakare
Dr Lombardi/First Waiter	Geoffrey Beevers
Pantaloon/First Porter	Paul Bentall
Smeraldina/Waiter	Michelle Butterly
Beatrice	Claire Cox
Brighella/Second Porter	Kevork Malikyan
Silvio/Second Waiter	Orlando Seale
Truffaldino	Jason Watkins

Director Tim Supple
Designer Robert Innes Hopkins
Lighting Designer Paul Anderson
Sound Andrea J. Cox
Fights Malcolm Ranson
Dramaturg Simon Reade
Assistant Director Dan Milne
Traditional commedia consultant Andrea Cavarra (from Teatro del Vicolo)
Company voice work Andrew Wade
Production Managers Mark Graham/Paul Russell
Costume Supervisor Jenny Alden

Stage Manager Heidi Lennard
Deputy Stage Manager Maddy Grant
Assistant Stage Manager Paul Williams

Characters

Clarice; Florindo; Dr Lombardi; Pantaloon; Smeraldina; Beatrice; Brighella; Silvio; Truffaldino; First Waiter; Second Waiter; First Porter; Second Porter

Act One

Scene One

Pantaloon's *house*.

Pantaloon, **Dr Lombardi**, **Clarice**, **Silvio**, **Brighella**, **Smeraldina**.

Silvio Here is my hand. And with it, I give you all my heart.

Pantaloon Come along, my dove, let's have your hand now, we'll get you properly engaged and have you wed in no time.

Clarice Dearest Silvio, I give you my hand and with it my promise to be your wife.

Silvio And mine to be your husband.

Dr Lombardi Excellent, that's all sorted then. No turning back now.

Smeraldina (*under her breath*) The lucky cow. I wish it was me standing there.

Pantaloon Smeraldina and Mr Brighella, I trust you will stand as witnesses to this betrothal here of Miss Clarice to Mr Silvio, the very distinguished son of our very good friend, Dr Lombardi.

Brighella Indeed, it is an total honour and a privilege, sir.

Pantaloon Well, it's only right and proper. After all I was the best man at your wedding, was I not. I know it's all a bit low-key. But the last thing you want is the relatives round on mass eating you out of house and home. No, we'll just have a nice quiet little meal together. Is that OK with you, my spooning sparrows?

Silvio All I want is to be by your side.

Smeraldina   That's the tastiest dish for sure.

Dr Lombardi   We really don't go in for ceremony either. Do we, Silvio? No we Lombardis are ever vigilant against unnecessary pomp and circumstance et cetera. No, all that matters is that they love each other. And he thinks of nothing else, I can assure you.

Pantaloon   Well, I have to say this is a match made in heaven. If my prospective son-in-law, Federigo Rasponi, hadn't come to such a dreadful demise in Turin, Clarice would have been bound to marry him as I'd so meticulously arranged. As I say we had certain business arrangements together and he was, if I say so myself, quite a fine catch.

Silvio   Believe me, sir, I am fully aware of how fortunate I am. I can only hope that Clarice will say the same.

Clarice   Dearest Silvio, how could you bear to say that, you know I love you and even if I'd been forced to marry Rasponi my heart would always be yours.

Dr Lombardi   God moves in mysterious ways, eh? How did this Rasponi meet his unfortunate end?

Pantaloon   The poor sod was killed defending his sister's honour. Messy business, I understand. He was run through by the girl's lover and that, I'm afraid, was that.

Brighella   In Turin?

Pantaloon   In the very middle.

Brighella   I'm very sorry to hear it.

Pantaloon   Did you know this Federigo Rasponi?

Brighella   Oh, yes indeed. I was in Turin for three years and often saw his sister riding around on her horse. A very spirited young lady. Often dressed like a man to go riding. But Mr Federigo loved her, that's for sure. Who would have thought it?

Pantaloon   Oh well, the world's never short of a tragedy. Best not dwell too much on it. Tell you what, Mr Brighella, why don't you pop down to your kitchen and knock up a few choice specialities?

Brighella   Certainly, sir. An excellent idea. Though I say it myself, eat at Brighella's and you will have a feast fit for kings, today you will climb the summits of the culinary world and taste the finest delicacies known to man.

Pantaloon   Steady on there, just make sure there's something soft I can dip my bread in.

Knocking at the door.

Pantaloon   What's that?

Dr Lombardi   It's a knock on the door.

Pantaloon   Smeraldina. It's a knock on the door.

Smeraldina   I know.

Pantaloon   Could you see who it is, please?

Smeraldina   Keep your hair on.

She goes to the door.

Pantaloon   Let's hope it's not relatives, eh?

Clarice   Daddy, can we go now?

Pantaloon   Just hold your horses, darling, we'll just see who this is, and we'll all come with you.

Enter **Smeraldina**.

Smeraldina   It's a servant with a message, sir. He won't tell me anything and demands to see the master.

Pantaloon   Well, I am the master, send him up at once.

Smeraldina   All right. I'll show him up, sir.

Smeraldina *goes out again.*

Clarice   Please, Daddy, do we really have to stay?

Pantaloon   Where the devil are you thinking of going?

Clarice   I don't know. Anywhere. To my room.

Pantaloon   You must be joking, young lady. I'm not leaving those two lovebirds alone to peck each other into purgatory. Just stay here till we've sorted this out.

Dr Lombardi   Very wise, sir, take no chances.

Scene Two

Enter **Truffaldino** and **Smeraldina**.

Truffaldino   My most humblest salutations to you, ladies and gents. Ah, yes, a very fine company indeed, if you don't mind me saying so. The crème of the crème, if I'm not mistaken.

Pantaloon   And pray who are you, my good man?

Truffaldino   Please tell me who might be this fair young maiden?

Pantaloon   That's my daughter.

Truffaldino   May I offer my congratualtions, sir.

Smeraldina   And what's more she's just been engaged to be married.

Truffaldino   In that case I offer my commiserations. And who might you be, madam?

Smeraldina   I, sir, am my Lady's maid.

Truffaldino   In this case, I offer both my congratulations and commiserations.

Pantaloon   Come, sir, enough of this nonsense. What do you want? Who the devil are you? And who is your master?

Truffaldino   A very good question, sir. Or may I say more correctly a very good set of questions. But given I am a simple man, may I advise you to take them one at a time.

Pantaloon   The man's a total idiot.

Dr Lombardi   Careful, Pantaloon, he might have some trick up his sleeve.

Truffaldino (*to* **Smeraldina**)   I'm sorry, madam, but was it you or your master who was engaged?

Smeraldina   Unfortunately it was my mistress.

Pantaloon   Look. Either tell us who you are or be about your business.

Truffaldino   If you simply wish to know who I am, I can settle the matter in two words, sir. My master's servant (three words, sir). (*Turning back to* **Smeraldina**.) As I was saying . . .

Pantaloon   But who is your master?

Truffaldino   A gentleman, sir. From another town who would like to pay his respects to you.

Pantaloon   But who is this gentleman? What is his name?

Truffaldino   Who, sir?

Pantaloon   Your master.

Truffaldino   For crying out loud. He is Federigo Rasponi of Turin, he sends his salutations, and he is awaiting downstairs to meet you. Satisified? (*To* **Smeraldina**.) Now where was we?

Pantaloon   I beg your pardon, sir, but what the devil are you saying?

Truffaldino   And if you are so interested I am Truffaldino Batocchio from the mountains of Bergamot.

Pantaloon   I don't give a damn if you're from the Quantocks, sir.

Truffaldino   I beg your pardon?

Pantaloon   I want you to repeat your master's name.

Truffaldino   Poor old boy's deaf as worm. (*As if* **Pantaloon** *is deaf.*) My. Master. Is. Federigo. Rasp. Oni. Of. Turin. Sir.

Pantaloon   The man's out of his mind. Federigo Rasponi is dead.

Truffaldino   Dead?

Pantaloon   Dead. Defunct. Deceased. Demised. Kaput. No more, sir.

Truffaldino   Are you sure?

Pantaloon   I can tell you with complete certainty. He is absolutely, incontravertibly dead.

Dr Lombardi   I'm afraid, this is the case. No doubt about it.

Truffaldino   But this is terrible. Something awful must have happened. You'll have to excuse me. (*Aside.*) I better go and see if this is true.

Truffaldino *leaves*.

Pantaloon   What's going on here? Is this fellow playing the fool.

Dr Lombardi   I don't think he has the wit.

Brighella   Well, he is from Bergamot.

They all laugh superciliously.

Smeraldina   Well, I liked him. I thought he was quite attractive.

Pantaloon   It can't really be Federigo Rasponi?

Clarice   If it is, this is the most terrible news.

Pantaloon   This isn't news, sweetheart. You saw the letters. The man's as dead as a door nail.

Silvio   Even if he is alive and here in person. He's too late, anyway.

Enter **Truffaldino**.

Truffaldino   This is an outrage. How I am served. Duped. Cruelly deluded. Is this the behaviour fitting of a gentleman, sir? I demand satisfaction.

Pantaloon   Steady on now. What on earth's the matter?

Truffaldino   You told me my master was dead.

Pantaloon   And so he is.

Truffaldino   'And so he is'? He is downstairs, sir, as fit as a drayman's donkey. Still waiting to pay his respects, thank you very much.

Pantaloon   Mr Federigo?

Truffaldino   Mr Federigo.

Pantaloon   Rasponi?

Truffaldino   Rasponi.

Pantaloon   Of Turin?

Truffaldino   Of Bangalore. Of course, of Turin.

Pantaloon   This is absolutely preposterous. Get out of here at once.

Truffaldino   Hang on a minute, you pox-ridden little twit. (I said 'twit'.) Go and have a butcher's. He's down the stairs.

Pantaloon   I'm not standing for this in my own house.

Truffaldino   Please be seated, your honour.

Dr Lombardi   Wait. Mr Pantaloon, sir. Let's not get embroiled in trivial recriminations. Let's have the fellow bring up this mysterious Rasponi, so we can see him with our own eyes.

Pantaloon   Yes, that'll fox you. Go on then, bring him back from the dead. You big baboon.

Truffaldino   Listen, perhaps he was dead. Perhaps he has been resurrected for all I know. But don't blame me. You can see for yourself. I've got no problem with that. But what I do have a problem with is your attitude, matey. You're lucky I'm from Bergamot where we have strict codes` of honour. So this time I'll overlook it, smart-arse, but if I was you I'd watch your step.

Truffaldino *winks at* **Smeraldina** *as he leaves.*

Clarice   I'm shaking, Silvio.

Silvio   Don't worry, whatever happens you are mine.

Dr Lombardi   I say, it's quite a little mystery, isn't it.

Pantaloon   No doubt it's somebody trying on some sort of extortion.

Brighella   I knew the fella in Turin. I'll tell you if it's him or not.

Smeraldina   Well, I thought that little fella looked all right to me. I think I'll have a word with him. Excuse me, I just have to see a man about a dog in the courtyard, sir.

Smeraldina *leaves.*

Enter **Beatrice** *in man's clothing.*

Beatrice   Mr Pantaloon, it appears the courtesy which I have received in correspondence is not matched by your behaviour in person, having dutifully sent up my servant to gain an audience with you I am left standing this half-hour before you condescend to receive me.

Pantaloon   Sir, I beg your pardon. But may I enquire as to who you are?

Beatrice   Your humble servant, sir. Federigo Rasponi.

Pantaloon   Of Turin?

Beatrice   Of Turin.

General amazement.

Pantaloon   Well, we rejoice to see you alive and well, sir, after the dreadful news we received.

Beatrice   Indeed. It was given out that I was killed in a duel. But thanks be to heaven, I was merely wounded and quickly recovered, as you see. I immediately set out to Venice to meet our previous arrangements.

Pantaloon   I don't know quite what to say, sir, but unless you have concrete evidence to the contrary we have every reason to believe Federigo is dead.

Beatrice   You are quite right to be cautious in these ontological matters. And I am well aware that such arrangements need credentials. Here are four letters of introduction from various correspondents known to you. And one from the director of the bank. I think you will be satisfied.

Clarice   Oh, Silvio, we are lost.

Silvio   No. I will die before I lose you.

Brighella *is staring at* **Beatrice**.

Beatrice   Do I know you, sir?

Brighella   Indeed, sir. Surely you recognise Brighella Cavicchio. From Turin, sir?

Beatrice (*aside*)   Please don't give me away. Oh, yes, of course. What brings you here?

Brighella   I keep an inn, sir. At your service.

Beatrice   Brighella Cavicchio. What excellent luck, I will lodge with you for certain.

Brighella   It'd be a pleasure, sir.

Pantaloon   Well, they certainly appear to be in order. And as you've presented them in person, I have no other option but to accept you.

Beatrice   If you have any lingering doubts I'm sure Mr Brighella can vouch that I am, indeed, a Rasponi.

Brighella   That I can.

Pantaloon   That settles it. I must ask for a pardon, sir, I have done you a great disservice.

Clarice   So this really is Federigo Rasponi?

Pantaloon   The very man.

Clarice   Oh this is terrible.

Silvio   Listen, you are mine and I will let no man tear us asunder.

Pantaloon   Well, that's what I call timing.

Dr Lombardi   *Accidit in puncto, quod non contigit in anno.* Or so they say.

Beatrice   But tell me, sir. Who is this lady?

Pantaloon   This is Clarice, my daughter.

Beatrice   The daughter promised to me in marriage?

Pantaloon   The same, sir.

Beatrice   Ma'am, permit me to say I am honoured.

Clarice   Your most humble servant.

Beatrice   A rather cool reception.

Pantaloon   I'm afraid it's rather par for the course. She's timid by nature.

Beatrice   And this gentleman is also your relation?

Pantaloon   Well, yes. I suppose he is my nephew.

Silvio   No, sir. I am nobody's nephew. I am the husband of his daughter. Miss Clarice.

Dr Lombardi   That's my boy. Say your piece, son, but careful he looks like a bit of a bruiser.

Beatrice   I beg your pardon, sir, but how can you be Clarice's husband when she was promised to me?

Pantaloon   All right, all right. I'll come clean. Dear Mr Rasponi, sir, convinced of your very sad and tragic demise I have given my daughter to Mr Silvio here with the best intentions in the world. But thanks be to God, you arrive in the nick of time, and of course, I am now bound to keep my word. Mr Silvio, I don't know what to say. Surely you can appreciate an old man's predicament and know I mean you no ill will whatsoever.

Silvio   But surely Federigo Rasponi will never consent to marry a lady who has already given her hand?

Beatrice   As long as her dowry's intact, I couldn't care less, sir.

Dr Lombardi   A very fashionable attitude, I must say.

Beatrice   I trust Miss Clarice will not refuse my hand?

Silvio   But you are too late. Clarice is mine and I will never give her up. And should you do me wrong, Mr Pantaloon, I will take my revenge upon you, and anyone who tries to take Clarice from me will reckon with this sword.

Silvio *exits*.

Dr Lombardi   Bravo, by God.

Beatrice   Isn't it a little drastic?

Dr Lombardi   With all due respect, sir, I think you have arrived too late. And I'm afraid Clarice will have to marry my son. The law is quite clear on this point. *Prior in tempore, potior in iure.*

Exit **Dr Lombardi**.

Beatrice   And you, good Lady Bride, haven't you anything to say?

Clarice   Only that you have ruined my entire life.

Exit **Clarice**.

Pantaloon   Oh the insolent little minx!

Pantaloon *goes to pursue her, but is stopped by* **Beatrice**.

Beatrice   Please, sir. This is not the time to reproach her. I have no doubt that in good time I will win her affections but in the meantime I think we should go over the accounts of our business arrangements; which must, you will agree, be sorted out whatever happens.

Pantaloon   Everything is in order, I can assure you, and we can settle up the money I owe you whenever it suits you, sir.

Beatrice   Excellent. I'll call again once I'm settled in. But if you'll excuse me, Mr Brighella and I have a little business we must attend to.

Pantaloon   As you wish, sir, but if you are in need of anything, anything at all, I am at your disposal.

Beatrice   Well, if it's not too much trouble perhaps you could furnish me with a little cash to tide me over, I'd be enormously obliged.

Pantaloon   At once, at once, sir. I'd be delighted. My cashier, Michael Cassio, will be here forthwith and soon as he arrives I'll have some money sent over to Brighella's.

Beatrice   Thank you. But really, I'll have my servant drop by. Don't worry, he's an honourable chap. You can trust him with anything.

Pantaloon   If you say so, sir.

Beatrice   Well, I must be about my business. Until later.

Pantaloon   Your most humble servant, sir.

Scene Three

Beatrice *and* **Brighella** *are alone.*

Brighella   Miss Beatrice, I presume.

Beatrice   For heaven's sake, please, don't undo me now, Brighella. My poor brother has been killed by my lover, Florindo Aretusi. Florindo has fled from justice and now I'm left to wander in misery in the hope of finding him. But knowing Federigo was bound for Venice to marry the young girl, I have borrowed my brother's clothing and some letters of identification, and with the money I will get from Pantaloon I'll be able to track Florindo down. Please, Brighella, please don't give me away. I will reward you generously for your pains.

Brighella   It's all very well but I don't want to be seen as responsible for Mr Pantaloon being swindled out of a fortune.

Beatrice   What do you mean 'swindled'? For God's sake that money is rightfully mine. Am I not my brother's heir?

Brighella   Well, in that case, just tell him who you are.

Beatrice   And end up with nothing? You've seen him. The first thing he'd do is start clucking like a mother hen and have me sent home. No, I will have my freedom as brief as it may be. Please, Brighella, take me as a man.

Brighella   Well, I always said you had a lot of spunk. Trust me. Brighella is at your service. 'Sir.'

Beatrice   Shall we go to your inn?

Brighella   What about your servant?

Beatrice   He's in the street.

Brighella   Where on earth did you happen to meet such an 'interesting' fellow?

Beatrice   I picked him up on the way here. I know he looks a bit stupid, but actually, I think he's rather loyal.

Brighella   Well, at least he's got one good quality. We better go. The things we do for love, Mr Beatrice?

Beatrice   Believe me. Love could drive me to far greater excesses.

Brighella   Please. Don't let me stop you. It's better than a night in the theatre.

They leave.

Scene Four

The street in front of **Brighella**'s *inn*. **Truffaldino**. *His belly rumbles.*

Truffaldino   It's just not on, is it? I'm sick of this for a lark. I've had some stingy swines in my time but this takes the biscuit. I'll be lucky to see a bowl of gruel from one week's end to the next with this fella. It's not even twelve o' clock and I'm on starvation point. I mean the first thing you do when you get into town is put your feet up and get some decent scran down your neck, don't you? But oh no, not Lord Anorexia here. No, he's pissed off down the quay to get his trunk, et cetera, et cetera; I could have passed on for all he cares. If I only had some dosh I'd sod the skinny sod; nip in there and give me gnashers a bit of training out of me own back pocket. But have I seen any wages? Have I buggery. I'm stood round here like one o'clock half struck, and bloody well famished. I could have been somebody, you know. I could have been a contender.

Enter **Florindo** *followed by a* **Porter** *carrying a trunk on his back.*

Porter   I can't go any further. It's killing me.

Florindo   Look, just another few steps, you're nearly there.

Porter   I can't, I can't. It's slipping.

Florindo   I told you you weren't up to it.

Truffaldino   Can I help there, sir?

Florindo   For God's sake grab that end and take it into the inn.

Truffaldino   Right you are, sir.

Truffaldino *grabs the trunk, it's heavier than he thought, but pushes the* **Porter** *out of the way.*

Truffaldino (*to the* **Porter**)   Now bugger off, will you.

Florindo   Bravo, that man.

Truffaldino   There you go, sir, a piece of cake.

Truffaldino *exits into the inn.*

Florindo (*to the* **Porter**)   See. That wasn't very difficult at all.

Porter   But I'm an old man, sir. I wasn't meant to be a porter. I was reduced to it. I was quite respectable in my day, sir.

Florindo   You are a waste of space, man.

Florindo *turns to go in.* **Truffaldino** *comes out.*

Truffaldino   All done and dusted, sir.

Porter   Excuse me.

Florindo *looks at him in amazement.*

Florindo   What now?

Porter   Something for my labour, sir.

Florindo   What labour? I'll give you something 'for your labour, sir'. A good kick up the arse. Now get out of it before you're arrested.

Florindo *gives the* **Porter** *a kick and he goes off terrified.*

Truffaldino   Like I say, sir, you just can't get the staff these days, can you?

Florindo   Have you any idea what this place is like?

Truffaldino   Oh, a top-notch establishment this, sir. Nice comfy beds, an excellent cellar, and, mmm, a delicious smell of food coming from the kitchen. Just mention my name and you and your servant, sir, will be served like aristocracy.

Florindo   And your name is . . . ?

Truffaldino   Truffaldino Battachio.

Florindo   And what line of work are you in?

Truffaldino   Well . . . erm . . . service, sir.

Florindo   Are you indeed. And at this moment, are you gainfully employed?

Truffaldino *looks around.*

Truffaldino   Well, no, not at this moment. (It's not exactly a lie, is it.)

Florindo   So you're without a master?

Truffaldino   Here I stand, sir. I can do no other.

Florindo   Well, do you want to be my servant?

Truffaldino   It's very hard to say, sir. What terms are we talking about?

Florindo   Terms? What do people usually pay?

Truffaldino   Well, my other master, I mean, the one who I am no longer employed by, paid a ducat a day.

Florindo   A ducat a day.

Truffaldino   But, of course, a man of my calibre, and undeniable charm, sir, is always looking to better himself.

Florindo   A ducat a day and a ha'penny's worth of baccy.

Truffaldino   And a nice little ham sandwich of a lunchtime.

Florindo   Done. All your meals will be taken care of.

Truffaldino   It's a pleasure doing business with you.

Florindo   I suppose you can furnish me with the requisite references.

Truffaldino   I beg your pardon, sir?

Florindo   You don't expect me to take you on without someone to vouch for you?

Truffaldino   No problem at all. Just nip up to Bergamot, there's plenty of people know me there, sir.

Florindo   But we're in Venice.

Truffaldino   Ah, I never thought of that. Look, we could forget about the tobacco.

Florindo   OK, I'll give you a go, but listen, any monkey business and you're for the high jump. Understood?

Truffaldino   Indupidipipably, your honour, sir.

Florindo   Just go down to the post office and collect any letters that may have been sent for Florindo Aretusi. And bring them here, toot sweet, understood.

Truffaldino   What about the ham sandwich, sir?

Florindo   When you are gone. I'll order lunch.

Truffaldino   Very good indeed, sir.

As **Florindo** *leaves*.

Florindo (*aside*)   Cheeky little sod, aren't you. We'll see how it goes.

Scene Five

Truffaldino, *then* **Beatrice** *and* **Brighella**.

Truffaldino   Just call me Mr Machiavelli. A ducat a day.
I'd be lucky to escape malnutrition with the other bugger.
Well, seeing Mr Bumfluff is not at hand, I may as well nip
down the old post office and earn a decent living for a
change.

Beatrice   Where are you going? Is this what you call
waiting here patiently for me.

Truffaldino   Terribly sorry, sir. I was just, er, stretching
my legs.

Beatrice   How do you expect me to find you. If you go
walkabout every five minutes.

Truffaldino   I was just trying desperately to stave off my
hunger, sir.

Beatrice   Listen, if you want any lunch at all, you will get
down to the landing stage and bring up my trunk to
Brighella's immediately.

Truffaldino (*of the inn*)   That one there?

Beatrice   That one there. And if I were you, I'd be smart
about it. And while you're at it go to the post office and
enquire if there are any letters for me. Infact enquire if there
are any letters also, for my sister. She was supposed to be
coming with me, then something came up. Anyway, you
never know who might be writing to her expecting an
immediate reply. So away you go, there's a good man. Just
see if there's anything for a Miss Beatrice while you're there.

Brighella (*to* **Beatrice**)   But who will be writing to you
here?

Beatrice   I asked my faithful steward to send me any
news that could help me. (*To* **Truffaldino**.) Look, get a
move on or the place [*city*] will have sunk.

Truffaldino   And who are you?

Brighella   I'm the innkeeper, now off you go and I'll sort you out with a nice bit of lunch when you get back.

Beatrice *and* **Brighella** *go off.*

Truffaldino   Bloody brilliant. There are vast ranks of the unemployed looking in vain for a master and I go and land myself with two of the buggers. What am I going do now? I can't look after both, can I? I suppose I'd get double the pay, and two suppers, and to be quite honest, it's something to be proud of, isn't it. Streamlined efficiency, a sort of downsizing of the service economy. If they'd have thought it up, it'd be called innovation. That settles it. I'm off to the post office. Twice.

Enter **Silvio**.

Silvio   Ah, my good man. Could I have a word with you.

Truffaldino   Bloody hell. Not another one.

Silvio   Where is your master?

Truffaldino   My master?

Silvio   You do have a master, do you not?

Truffaldino   Er, yes, sir. He's in the inn.

Silvio   Well, go tell him, that I want to have a word.

Truffaldino   But, sir –

Silvio (*shouts*)   Tell him I want a word or else.

Truffaldino   But –

Silvio   One more sound and I'll cut that tongue out of your slavering mouth.

Truffaldino   But which master do you want?

Silvio   That's it.

Silvio *lunges at* **Truffaldino** *who escapes.*

Truffaldino (*aside*)   I'll just have to take pot luck.

Truffaldino *goes*.

Silvio   I am not going to stand for any rivals. Federigo may have got off once with his life, but I promise it won't happen again. Either he drops all pretensions to Clarice or I will cut his heart out. Who on earth is this?

Silvio *withdraws as* **Truffaldino** *enters with* **Florindo**.

Truffaldino   There he is, sir. Watch it. He's a nutcase.

Florindo   Who's this? I've never seen the fellow in my life.

Truffaldino   I don't know nothing, sir. And by your leave I will go for those letters, sir. I'm not getting mixed up in this.

Truffaldino *exits*.

Silvio   Where the hell is this Federigo?

Florindo (*to himself*)   Well, here goes. (*To* **Silvio**.) Are you the man who has been calling for me?

Silvio   I'm afraid not, sir. I have not had the honour of your aquaintance.

Florindo   Yet my servant who just left informed me you were issuing threats and provoking me to a challenge.

Silvio   He misunderstood, sir. I wished to speak to his master.

Florindo   Well, I am his master.

Silvio   You, sir?

Florindo   Indeed.

Silvio   Then, I must beg for your pardon, sir, either your man is the double of one I saw this morning, or this man waits on someone else.

Florindo   I can assure you, sir. The man waits on me.

Silvio   In that case please accept my humble apologies and we'll make no more of the matter.

Florindo   No harm done. These things happen.

Silvio   Are you a stranger here, sir?

Florindo   From Turin, actually, at your service.

Silvio   How amazing. The man I would speak to is also from Turin.

Florindo   Maybe I could help you. I may know the man and would only be too happy to see you have satisfaction, sir.

Silvio   Do you know, then, a certain Federigo Rasponi.

Florindo   Only too well.

Silvio   He insolently makes, on some previous pretext with her father, claim to my fiancée who only this morning publicly gave me her hand.

Florindo   Please, let me allay your fears. Federigo cannot take your wife from you, because he is dead.

Silvio   So everyone thought, sir, but this morning he turned up here in Venice, very much alive.

Florindo   Alive! I am dumbstruck.

Silvio   You're not the only one.

Florindo   But I can assure you, sir, he is dead.

Silvio   But I can assure you, sir, he is alive.

Florindo   But you must be mistaken.

Silvio   Master Pantaloon Parsimoni, father of my betrothed, made all possible enquiries to ascertain the man's identity, and he had incontestable proofs, sir.

Florindo (*aside*)   So he wasn't killed after all.

Silvio   And so, he either abandons his claims to Clarice or I will end his life for sure.

Florindo   I came all the way to Venice only to be haunted by him here.

Silvio   I am surprised you haven't met him. He is supposedly lodging in that inn.

Florindo   I haven't seen a soul. I was told there were no other guests here.

Silvio   Maybe he has changed his mind. I'm sorry to have troubled you. But I trust if you come across the scoundrel you will, for his own welfare, persuade him to abandon all claims to my wife. I am Silvio Lombardi, and for ever, your humble servant, sir. And might I discover your name?

Florindo   Oh, er, Fusilli Arrabiata, your obediant servant.

Silvio   Master Arrabiata, I am yours to command.

Silvio *exits.*

Scene Six

Florindo   How is this possible? I felt the sword pierce to the bone with my own hand. With my own eyes I saw him drowned in his blood. How could he have survived? Perhaps I fled too quickly and he was resurrected without my knowledge. And now I have left my beloved Beatrice to die with sorrow at my disappearance. Oh I must go straight back and console her grieving soul.

Scene Seven

Enter **Truffaldino** *and a* **Porter** *carrying* **Beatrice**'s *trunk. They see* **Florindo** *and they jump out of sight.*

Truffaldino   Get down – Christ. There's the other master. Back a bit. Wait here. (*To* **Florindo**.) Wotcha, guv.

Florindo   Truffaldino, we must leave for Turin.

Truffaldino   I beg you pardon, sir?

Florindo   At once, now. We're leaving for Turin.

Truffaldino   But we haven't had dinner.

Florindo   Well, we must eat quickly and be on our way.

Truffaldino   This might cost you a bit extra, you realise.

Florindo   Never mind the expense, this is important. Did you go to the post office?

Truffaldino   Indeed I did, sir.

Florindo   Well?

Truffaldino   I have something for you right here, sir.

Florindo   Where is it?

Truffaldino   I'm just looking.

He pulls out three letters.

Oh flummery. They're all mixed up. I knew I should've learned to read.

Florindo   What are you doing, man. Give me my letters.

Truffaldino   Right away, sir. (*Aside.*) Bollocks. (*To* **Florindo**.) I have to warn you, sir, but not all of the letters are for you.

Florindo   What do you mean?

Truffaldino   On approaching the post, sir, I happened upon another servant who I knew from Bergamot, sir, and he asked me to retrieve some letters for his master, you know, to save him the trouble, sir, as he is a very busy man, the other servant. And, er, his letters are here too.

Florindo   Give them here.

Truffaldino   Terribly sorry.

Florindo (*aside*)   What is this? To Beatrice Rasponi. (*To* **Truffaldino**.) What is this?

Truffaldino   That must be the one for my mate.

Florindo   Who is this 'mate' exactly?

Truffaldino   A servant, sir, name of . . . Pasqual.

Florindo   Pasqual!

Truffaldino   Yes, sir, a very fine friend, sir.

Florindo   Whom does he serve?

Truffaldino   Don't know, sir.

Florindo   But how could you have retrieved the letters without his master's name?

Truffaldino   Very good point, sir. (*Aside.*) Shit!

Florindo   What was the name?

Truffaldino   It's slipped my mind, sir.

Florindo   What mind?

Truffaldino   I had it on a bit of paper, sir.

Florindo   Well, where is the bit of paper?

Truffaldino   At the post office. (*Aside.*) You won't catch me out.

Florindo   Well, where is this Pasqual?

Truffaldino (*aside*)   Bollox. (*To* **Florindo**.) I haven't the foggiest.

Florindo   How on earth did you expect to deliver this letter to him?

Truffaldino   We arranged to meet at the piazza.

Florindo   This is ridiculous.

Truffaldino   And if you'll give me the letter I'll take it there forthwith. (*Aside.*) A beautiful move.

Florindo   No. I think I will open the letter.

Truffaldino   No. Oh, please, please don't open the letter, sir. It is a grevious offence, sir, to open people's letters.

Florindo   I don't care who I offend. This letter is addressed to someone who is dearer to me than my own soul. I have no scruples here.

Truffaldino   Oh Christ.

Florindo (*reading*)   'My Illustrious Milady, news of your departure has set the whole town of a fire and the general consensus is that you have gone abroad after Mr Florindo. The court what have discovered that you are abroad in a man's dress are doing their utmost to have you arrested. I did not send the letter immediately from the suspected place of correspondence but did give this missive to a friend who posted it to you on account of avoiding any such tracings or other such which might inevitably befall you. Any further news and I shall write to you by the same. Your humble, obediant and truly faithful servant, ever yours with everlasting honour, Antonio della Dorio. PS This letter was penned by the chambermaid, Mistress Pantone, on my humble behalf.

Truffaldino   Very well writ if you don't mind me saying so.

Florindo   This is unbelievable. Beatrice abroad. Dressed as a man. To join me. Oh my sweet angel, if only there is a way to find her here in Venice.

(*To* **Truffaldino**.) Truffaldino, you must find this Pasqual and the person he serves, find out where they are lodged, bring him here to me and I will give you more money than you've ever dreamed of.

Truffaldino   Well, thank you very much, sir. And maybe a bit of lunch, eh?

Florindo *gives* **Truffaldino** *the letter.*

Florindo   Here. I am relying on you completely. This matter is of infinite importance to me.

Truffaldino   I can't give it back like this.

Florindo   Tell him there was an accident or something, don't make difficulties, make haste.

Truffaldino   So we're not going to Turin I take it?

Florindo   Stop wasting precious time. (*Aside.*) Beatrice in Venice. Federigo in Venice. If her brother catches me there'll be hell to pay. I'll have to do everything to track her down myself.

Florindo *leaves.*

Scene Eight

Truffaldino (*very pleased with himself*)   I just can't help myself. Seeing how well I'm doing I may as well give this double service thing a proper run round the block. A man of my singular potential, it seems, is up to anything. But I can't get away with giving this thing back in this state. Let's see if I can fold it so they won't notice.

He makes a pig's ear of it.

That's better, but it needs sticking. How the hell do I wangle that? Maybe I could chew up a bit of bread as a sort of mortar, and then stick it like me granny used to do with her false teeth.

He fishes in his pocket and pulls out a bit of bread.

I'll give it a go. Well, there goes the emergency rations, but que sera sera as they say in England.

He chews the bread but inadvertently swallows it.

Oh bugger. There's hardly any left now.

Chews it and swallows some more.

It's just not natural to have to do this. One last go.

He manages not to swallow it and unwillingly removes it from his mouth.

Got you. Now to seal the bastard.

He seals the flap with bread.

Champion. Look at that. Top-notch. Oh Christ. The bloody porter.

He goes to the wing.

Hey, come on with that trunk.

Porter   I thought you'd never ask. Where d'ya want it, guv.

Truffaldino   Quick, get it over there, I'll be in in a mo.

Porter   Hang on a minute, who's going to pay for all this humping?

Scene Nine

Enter **Beatrice** *from the inn.*

Beatrice   Is that my trunk?

Truffaldino   Yes. I think so.

Beatrice   Take it up to my room.

Porter   But which is your room, sir?

Beatrice   I don't know. Ask the waiter.

Porter   Here, wait a minute. There's three and six to pay on this.

Beatrice   Look, just get it upstairs pronto or you'll be getting a kick up the backside.

Porter   Listen, I've been stood round for half a bleeding hour. I want me money before I move another inch.

Beatrice   Look, my good man. This really isn't a good time.

Porter   I've got a good mind to drop this in the middle of the street.

Beatrice *gives him a look of authoritative disdain and the* **Porter** *is chastened. He scuttles off without another word.*

Truffaldino   Charming fellows these Venetians.

Beatrice   Have you been to the post office?

Truffaldino   Indeed I have, sir.

Beatrice   Any letters for me?

Truffaldino   None at all. But there was one for your sister, sir.

Beatrice   Give it here at once.

Truffaldino   Here you go.

Beatrice   This letter's been opened.

Truffaldino   Opened. No, it isn't possible.

Beatrice   Opened and sealed with bread.

Truffaldino   How on earth could that have happened?

Beatrice   You insolent blaggard. Who opened this letter?

Truffaldino   Please, sir. I'll confess. We all make mistakes and there was a letter for me at the post and since I can't read I opened your letter by mistake. It was a dreadful thing and I should be flogged, sir, beaten and flogged and quartered, but please know it was a humble mistake, sir.

Beatrice   Well, I suppose there's been no harm done.

Truffaldino   I'm a very simple man, sir.

Beatrice   Did you read this letter? Do you know what it says?

Truffaldino   Not a word.

Beatrice   Has anyone else seen it?

Truffaldino (*indignant*)   Oh!

Beatrice   Has anyone seen it?

Truffaldino   Perish the very thought, sir.

Beatrice   If you're lying . . . (*She reads the letter.*)

Truffaldino (*aside*)   Well, that didn't go *too* badly.

Beatrice   Antonio, you are no scholar but you are a good man.

(*To* **Truffaldino**.)   Now, Truffaldino, there is a certain matter I must attend to and I want you to go into the inn, open the trunk – here are the keys – unpack my clothes and give them an airing. And then when I get back we'll have lunch.

Truffaldino   Hallelujah.

Beatrice (*to herself*)   I better check up on Pantaloon and that money he owes me.

Beatrice *goes out.*

Scene Ten

Truffaldino   I don't know how I get away with it. I'll have to start putting my fees up.

Enter **Pantaloon**.

Pantaloon   Ah, my good man, is your master at home?

Truffaldino   No, sir. I'm afraid he ain't.

Pantaloon   Have you any idea where he's gone?

Truffaldino   Not the foggiest, sir.

Pantaloon   Well, will he be back for lunch?

Truffaldino   I should bloody well hope so.

Pantaloon   In that case, as soon as he returns make sure he gets this. There's a hundred ducats there. It should tide him over for a couple of days. I'm afraid I can't stop. Make sure he gets it. Good day.

Exit **Pantaloon**.

Scene Eleven

Truffaldino   Hang on a minute. Wait. Bon voyage, then. He never said which master.

Enter **Florindo**.

Florindo   Well, have you found Pasqual?

Truffaldino   No, not exactly, but I met a man who gave me a hundred ducats.

Florindo   A hundred ducats. What the devil for?

Truffaldino   I haven't the foggiest. You weren't expecting a hundred ducats, were you?

Florindo   I don't know. I suppose I did present a letter of credit to a merchant this morning.

Truffaldino   So the money's yours?

Florindo   Well, what did this fellow say?

Truffaldino   He said give it to your master.

Florindo   Well, of course it's my money, you incompetent dolt.

Truffaldino   I was just checking.

Florindo   Now for the love of God stop messing about and go and find Pasqual.

Truffaldino   No, I can't, sir.

Florindo   I beg your pardon.

Truffaldino   Not on an empty stomach. Please, sir, just a tiny little morsel and I'll be off like a bloodhound.

Florindo   All right, all right. I'll order right away.

Florindo *goes in.*

Truffaldino   Bloody hell. At least I've done one thing right today.

Scene Twelve

A room in **Pantaloon**'s *house.*

Pantaloon   It's no use. You're marrying Federigo Rasponi whether you like it or not. I have given him my word and there's the long and the short of it.

Clarice   Please, Daddy. This is absolute tyranny.

Pantaloon   I'll not have you using that sort of language. You were quite happy with the arrangement when it was first proposed, you can't go chopping and changing now whenever it suits you.

Clarice   But the only reason I consented was out of obedience to you.

Pantaloon   So why refuse me now?

Clarice   I simply can't do it.

Pantaloon   What do you mean: 'can't do it'?

Clarice   Nothing will make me take Federigo.

Pantaloon   Nothing? What's the matter with him?

Clarice   I hate him.

Pantaloon   Come on, sweetness. I mean, he has his good points.

Clarice   Daddy, I am sworn to Silvio.

Pantaloon   Please, my little duckling, put Silvio out of your mind and consider Federigo on his own merits.

Clarice   I can't put Silvio out of my mind. All I see, all I think, all I feel is Silvio. My entire world is Silvio and you were the first to approve him.

Pantaloon   Oh my poor lamb. Don't you see? You have to make a virtue out of necessity.

Clarice   How can I 'make' anything? Now I am nothing?

Pantaloon   Please, please, my poor child.

Enter **Smeraldina**.

Smeraldina   Sir, Master Federigo is here and desperate to see you.

Pantaloon   Send him up, I am at his service.

Clarice   Oh this is unbearable.

Smeraldina   You silly thing. What on earth are you upset about? Ma'am. I'd give my right arm to be in your position.

Pantaloon   Come on, my sweet thing, don't let him see you cry.

Clarice   What am I supposed to do? My heart is burst open.

Scene Thirteen

Beatrice   My greatest respects, Mr Pantaloon.

Pantaloon   Ever your humble servant, sir, I trust you received the hundred ducats.

Beatrice   I'm afraid I did not.

Pantaloon   I gave it to your man only just now. You did say he was to be trusted.

Beatrice   No cause for alarm. I just haven't caught up with him yet. Is anything wrong?

Pantaloon   Please, Mr Rasponi, you must understand that the news of your death has affected her greatly. We are sure she'll get over it in time.

Beatrice   Perhaps if I spoke to her alone, I might be able to bring her round.

Pantaloon   Yes, of course, I'll leave you for a moment. Clarice, I'll be back shortly, I want you to try and be nice to your future husband for me. Come on, try to be sensible.

Exit **Pantaloon**.

Scene Fourteen

Beatrice   My dear lady . . .

Clarice   Get away. I don't want you anywhere near me.

Beatrice   Those are cruel words to give your future husband.

Clarice   Even if they drag me screaming and kicking to the altar I will never love you.

Beatrice   Please, just listen and you won't hate me for long.

Clarice   I shall hate you, sir, to the end of eternity.

Beatrice   You don't even know who I am.

Clarice   I know you, sir, you are the destroyer of my life.

Beatrice   But, really, I can console you.

Clarice   Don't flatter yourself. Silvio is my sole consolation.

Beatrice   Look, I'm not saying I can do what Silvio does, but I can make you happy.

Clarice   Are you such a monster you'll ignore everything I say?

Beatrice   Please.

Clarice   I'll scream the place down.

Beatrice   Just let me share a secret.

Clarice   I will share nothing with you.

Beatrice   Oh for God's sake just let me get a word in edgeways.

Clarice   You monstrous egotistical bastard! You've ruined everything.

Beatrice   Listen, you have no desire for me. I have no desire for you. You have given your hand to another, I have to another given my heart.

Clarice   Maybe you're not so bad after all.

Beatrice   That's what I've been trying to tell you since I came in.

Clarice   Is this some kind of joke?

Beatrice   I've never been so serious in my whole life. And if you swear to keep this a secret I can completely put your mind at rest.

Clarice   OK. I swear.

Beatrice   I am not Federigo. I am his sister, Beatrice.

Clarice   What? A woman?

Beatrice   A woman.

Clarice   But what about your brother?

Beatrice   Killed in the fight. The man I love was blamed
for his death and it's him I am desperate to find here. I
thought I'd stand more chance as a man. But please, by all
the sacred laws of love and charity, do not betray me. I
know it was a bit rash to tell you, but you seemed to be
getting hysterical. And to make matters worse, your sweet
Silvio has threatened to slit me navel to chops, which you
will admit is not entirely in my best interests.

Clarice   I'll tell him at once.

Beatrice   No you will not.

Clarice   Won't I?

Beatrice   I'm absolutely counting on you. You mustn't
tell a soul. And to be quite honest, it would make life a lot
easier if you were just a little more civil towards me.

Clarice   Civil. I will be your greatest friend. I'll do
anything you ask.

Beatrice   Look, I pledge my eternal friendship. Give me
your hand.

Clarice   I beg your pardon

Beatrice   Are you afraid I'm lying? I'll give you
incontrovertible proof.

Clarice   This is a dream.

Beatrice   Well, it isn't exactly the kind of thing that
happens every day, is it.

Clarice   Extraordinary. Extraordinary.

Beatrice   Look, I must go. Let's embrace in honest
friendship.

Clarice   I doubt you no longer.

Enter **Pantaloon**.

Scene Fifteen

Pantaloon   Oh, praise the lord. Nice work, there, if you don't mind me saying so. I see you've sharp changed your tune.

Beatrice   Did I not say I'd win her round?

Pantaloon   Well, I take my hat off to you. You've done in four minutes what would've taken me four years. We'll see to the wedding right away then.

Clarice (*aside*)   Oh, this is worse than ever. (*To* **Pantaloon**.) Please, there's no need to hurry, Daddy.

Pantaloon   What? Messing around in here like a couple of polecats. Listen, I'm taking no chances, you're getting hitched tomorrow and that's final.

Beatrice   Of course, it's completely necessary to get all the financial arrangements out of the way first.

Pantaloon   Don't worry, we'll have it sorted out in no time.

Clarice   But Daddy . . .

Pantaloon   I'll pop over and tell Silvio right away.

Clarice   Please, no. He'll go crazy.

Pantaloon   What, are you after both of them?

Clarice   But Daddy . . .

Pantaloon   No more buts. It's decided. I am ever your humble servant, sir.

He starts to leave.

You're man and wife now and that's the end of it.

Clarice   But . . .

Pantaloon   We'll talk about it later.

He exits.

Scene Sixteen

Clarice   Brilliant.

Beatrice   Don't worry. We'll work something out.

Clarice   This is more of a mess than before.

Beatrice   I'll think of something.

Clarice   And what do you want me to do until then?
What about poor Silvio? What do you expect us to do?

Beatrice   Oh, for God's sake, just suffer for a while.

Clarice   I don't think I can bear this.

Beatrice   Well, bear it you must. I can assure you your
present woes will make your future joy the sweeter.

Beatrice *leaves.*

Clarice   How can I think of future happiness when I am
lost in such present pain. Why is life so much endless hoping
and insufferable desire and so little actual joy.

Act Two

Scene One

A courtyard, **Pantaloon**'s *house.*

Silvio   Leave me alone.

Dr Lombardi   Wait. Silvio.

Silvio   I'm warning you.

Dr Lombardi   What do you think you're doing prowling round Pantaloon's courtyard?

Silvio   Either he'll keep his word or I'll force him to reap the consequences.

Dr Lombardi   Silvio, this is the man's own house. You're making a complete fool of yourself.

Silvio   No. He's making a fool of me. He deserves no civility from us.

Dr Lombardi   That might be true – but it's no reason to be running around like some rabid dog. Please, let me have a word with him and perhaps a little reason will remind him where his duties lie. Why don't you just slip off somewhere, out of this courtyard, I'll talk to Pantaloon and be with you forthwith.

Silvio   But . . .

Dr Lombardi   No buts. Just do as I say.

Silvio   This once. I'll be waiting at the coffee bar but if he persists, I swear I'll skewer that fat gut of his.

Silvio *exits.*

Dr Lombardi   Oh my poor boy. How could they do this if there was any doubt about the Turinese gentleman's eschatological status. But what is required here is to deal with this in a completely rational and objective manner.

Enter **Pantaloon**.

Pantaloon   What the devil are you doing here?

Dr Lombardi   Ah, Mr Pantaloon, my greatest respects.

Pantaloon   I was just on my way to see you.

Dr Lombardi   Excellent. I expect you were hurrying with the news that Clarice will indeed marry dear Silvio.

Pantaloon   Well, actually . . .

Dr Lombardi   No need for explantions, I totally appreciate the delicacy of the difficult imbroglio you were placed in. But as we're old friends let's put the matter completely behind us.

Pantaloon   Well, the fact is . . .

Dr Lombardi   I would be the first to admit that you were taken totally by surprise and had no time to consider the obvious and grievous wrong you were to perpetrate on our family name.

Pantaloon   Just a minute, I wouldn't say 'grievous wrong' after all, there was a previous contract . . .

Dr Lombardi   Stop. I know exactly what you are about to say. It appeared, in fact, that the contract with the Turinese was binding a priori. Where as, of course, with greater reflection you realise ours takes precedence by its actual ratification by the tendering of the good lady's hand.

Pantaloon   Yes, but . . .

Dr Lombardi   And as you'd say so yourself, *concensus et non conubitus, facit virum.*

Pantaloon   Look, in plain English . . .

Dr Lombardi   *Ipso facto*, The lady is not for burning. As they say.

Pantaloon   Have you finished?

Dr Lombardi   Yes. Completely. And utterly.

Pantaloon   If you'll allow me to speak . . .

Dr Lombardi   Be my guest.

Pantaloon   Look, I am fully aware of your extensive legal knowledge . . .

Dr Lombardi   Of course, we'd turn a blind eye to the matter of the dowry, you understand. What's a few ducats here and there between friends, eh?

Pantaloon   What do I have to do to get a word in edgeways?

Dr Lombardi   There's no need to take umbrage, sir.

Pantaloon   With the greatest respect. Stuff your legal acumen, sir, there is nothing else I can do.

Dr Lombardi   You mean you are going through with this treacherous arrangement!

Pantaloon   Sir, I had given my word. And now my daughter has agreed to the whole thing – so as much as it pains me – I'm afraid there's nothing I can do. I was just about to come to explain to you and poor Silvio how dreadfully sorry I am for the whole horrid business.

Dr Lombardi   I can't exactly say that I'm surprised at that little minx of daughter, sir, but I am dumbfounded by your dispicable treatment of me. If you hadn't cast-iron concrete proof that that Rasponi was six feet under you should never have given the slightest glimmer of a hope to my son. Well, let me tell you, sir, you've made the arrangement and you should go through with it whatever the cost. Surely the news that he was dead is ample proof for the fellow to withdraw with his name intact. *Coram testibus*, sir, *coram testibus*. Infact, sir, I should simply insist that this arrangement be annulled and Clarice married instantly to my son, but I'd be ashamed to have such a hussy in my household. The daughter of a man who goes back on his word, sir, is no daughter at all. You have not merely injured me, but you have cruelly maimed the whole house of Lombardi. A plague be upon you. You'll live to regret this: *Omnia tempus habent*. Yes, you heard, *omnia tempus habent*.

Scene Two

Pantaloon   Go and fry in hell you overeducated stoat. The wart on the end of my arse is worth more than the entire house of Lombardi. It's not every day you get the chance of a son-in-law so well connected. And cultured. And rich. So stuff you and your petulant little offspring. The marriage has to be.

Enter **Silvio**.

Silvio   Your humble servant, Mr Pantaloon, sir.

Pantaloon   Ah. Good day, sir. (*Aside.*) There's steam coming out of his ears.

Silvio   I couldn't help but overhear, sir, that the marriage to Rasponi still stands. Is that correct?

Pantaloon   Well, I'm afraid it is, sir. Signed, sealed and delivered.

Silvio   Then, sir, you are no man of honour and no gentleman at all.

Pantaloon   I beg your pardon. How dare you insult a man of my standing.

Silvio   I don't care who I insult just count yourself lucky I haven't run you through.

Pantaloon   Don't dare threaten me in my own house.

Silvio   Well, come outside, if you are a man of honour.

Pantaloon   I demand to be treated with the respect and decorum I am due.

Silvio   Very well. You are a villian, a coward and a scavenging dog, sir.

Pantaloon   That's it, you ignorant little frog.

Silvio   I swear to heaven . . .

Silvio *grabs his sword.*

Pantaloon   Help! Help!

Scene Three

Enter **Beatrice***, with sword drawn.*

Beatrice   Ha. I come in your defence.

Pantaloon   My dear son. Thank the heavens.

Silvio   The very man I wish to fight.

Beatrice (*aside*)   Oh, blast.

Silvio   Come, sir.

Pantaloon   Careful, son. He's as high as a kite.

Beatrice   I am no novice in the arts of fighting, sir. Do your worst. I fear nobody.

Pantaloon   Help! Help! Anyone!

Scene Four

Pantaloon *rushes towards the street.* **Beatrice** *and* **Silvio** *fight.* **Silvio** *falls and drops his sword.* **Beatrice** *stands over him, her sword pointing at his chest.*

Enter **Clarice***.*

Clarice   Oh God. Please stop.

Beatrice   Beautiful Clarice, for you alone will I spare him, but in return you will remember your promise.

Exit **Beatrice**.

Clarice   Are you hurt, my love?

Silvio   'My love'? First you scorn me then you call me 'my love'. You perfidious wretch. You cankerous mould. How can you bear to humiliate me like this?

Clarice   No, Silvio. You don't understand. I love you, I adore you, you have my absolute fidelity.

Silvio   Fidelity! Is this your idea of fidelity? Marrying that bloodthirsty beast?

Clarice   But I haven't yet and I never will. I'd rather die than desert you.

Silvio   But you've only just now given your promise.

Clarice   No, the promise is not to marry him.

Silvio   So what exactly is this promise?

Clarice   I can't tell you.

Silvio   Why not?

Clarice   Because it's a promise.

Silvio   This just proves your guilt.

Clarice   No it doesn't. I'm completely innocent.

Silvio   If you're so completely innocent, then why don't you tell me?

Clarice   Because if I told you then I'd be guilty.

Silvio   Oh, for God's sake, at least tell me to whom you have sworn the promise.

Clarice   Federigo.

Silvio   Federigo. Well, that explains it.

Clarice   If I don't keep my word, then I am a liar.

Silvio   And you have the audacity to stand there and tell me you don't love him. You liar, you treacherous whore. Get out of my sight.

Clarice   If I didn't love you, why would I come running to save your life?

Silvio   But what is my life worth when it is weighed by such a miserable wretch?

Clarice   I love you with all my heart.

Silvio   I hate you with all my soul.

Clarice   I'll die if you don't believe me.

Silvio   I would sooner see you dead than unfaithful.

Clarice   Then you shall have that satisfaction.

Clarice *picks up his sword.*

Silvio   Go ahead. You'll be doing me a favour.

Clarice   How can you be so cruel?

Silvio   I have had the finest teacher.

Clarice   Then you want me dead?

Silvio   I don't know what I want any more.

Clarice   Oh but I do.

Clarice *turns the point against her breast.*

Scene Five

Enter **Smeraldina**.

Smeraldina (*to* **Clarice**)   What on earth do you think you're doing? (*To* **Silvio**.) And what are you doing standing there? Oh I expect you're having a whale of a time, aren't you, beautiful young women sacrificing themselves over you left, right and centre. Well, if he doesn't want you, miss,

stuff him. Just tell him to go to hell. There's plenty more fish
in the sea.

She throws down the sword. **Silvio** *picks it up.*

Clarice   You monstrous wretch. Is my death not even
worth a single sigh? Well, I shall die, sir, of sorrow. I shall
die and you shall have your satisfaction. And when it's all
too late you'll realise my innocence and you will weep
boiling tears for what you killed through your own
barbarous cruelty.

Clarice *leaves.*

Smeraldina   I hope you're very pleased with yourself.
She's on the brink of suicide and you just stood there like a
stale panattone.

Silvio   Absolute nonsense. You don't really think she
would have done it, do you?

Smeraldina   If it wasn't for me, mate, she'd already be
dead.

Silvio   It was nowhere near her heart.

Smeraldina   You ignorant pig.

Silvio   See. You women are all hysterics.

Smeraldina   Hysterics! Listen, the only reason we get all
the stick is because we haven't got a dick. Oh yes, a
woman's hysterical but a bloke is full of passion, whereas
I'd be called a slut you'd be a Jack the lad. Well, let me tell
you, the only reason you get to run round like the cock of
the midden is because of the unequal economic relations of
the sexes, matey. If women had a position in this society that
was equal to their tact, intelligence and ability to get things
done you don't think they'd put up with you poncing round
like some superannuated gondolier. They wouldn't give you
a second glance, 'big boy'.

She leaves.

Scene Six

Silvio   You think you can fool me with that ridiculous display of mendacity. You traitorous strumpet. You perfidious whore. Even if he kills me in the trying, I'm going to find that notorious little Rasponi shit and the faithless Clarice shall watch him wallow in his own suppurating blood.

Exit **Silvio**.

Scene Seven

Truffaldino   Just my luck. Two gaffers and neither one of the beggars comes back for their scran, and I've been stood here like an escapee from the catacombs for two bloody hours. The next thing you know they'll both show up and I'll be up the Po without a paddle with terminal malnutrition. Oh hang on. Talk of the devil.

Florindo   Well, did you find that fellow, Pasqual?

Truffaldino   Funnily enough, not yet. I thought I was going to look for him after lunch?

Florindo   I've got no time to waste, it's imperative I get to him as soon as is humanly possible.

Truffaldino   Sir, it's 'imporative' that I get to some lunch as soon as is humanly possible or I'm going to pass away. If we don't order now all will be lost, sir.

Florindo   I'm not even hungry. Look, I'll go back to the post office myself and see what I can find out.

Truffaldino   Just a little bit of advice, sir, here in Venice it's advisable to eat at every mealtime or you can do yourself a mischief. It's the water, you know.

Florindo   What on earth are you on about? I really have to go, if I'm back for dinner, all well and good, if not then we'll just have to eat this evening.

Truffaldino   This evening!?

Florindo   Look, grab something to put you off if you're that desperate. Take this money, it's far too heavy to be trailing round. Put it in my trunk, here's the key.

Truffaldino   On the double, sir. Two ticks and I'll be back down with it.

Florindo   No, no. You hold on to it. I'm going right away. If I don't turn up for dinner then find me in the piazza. I'm going to find this Pasqual if it kills me.

Exit **Florindo**.

Scene Eight

Truffaldino   Thank God for that. If he wants to starve himself senseless that's his pigeon, but I tell you what, I'm buggered if I'm going on a diet for the sake of Pasqual.

Enter **Beatrice**.

Beatrice   Truffaldino.

Truffaldino   Oh my giddy aunt.

Beatrice   Truffaldino, did Mr Pantaloon Parsimoni give you a purse of a hundred ducats.

Truffaldino   Yes, sir, indeed he did.

Beatrice   Then why haven't you given them to me?

Truffaldino   Ah. Was it meant for you, your honour?

Beatrice   Was it meant for me? Well, what did he say when he gave it to you?

Truffaldino   I'm not sure. I think he said give it to your master.

Beatrice   And who is your master?

Truffaldino   You are.

Beatrice   Well, why on earth are you asking such ridiculous questions ?

Truffaldino   Just checking, sir. Can't be too careful.

Beatrice   Well, where is it?

Truffaldino   Where is what, sir?

Beatrice   The bag of ducats.

Truffaldino   I haven't a clue, sir.

Beatrice   What is that then?

Truffaldino   Oh, here it is, sir.

Beatrice   Is it all there?

Truffaldino   Of course it's all there. As if I would mess about with it.

Beatrice   I'm going to count this later.

Truffaldino (*aside*)   So what if it wasn't his. He's never going to notice.

Beatrice   Is that innkeeper about?

Truffaldino   He most certainly is, sir.

Beatrice   Tell him I have a friend joining me for dinner, so he'll need to lay on an extra few dishes.

Truffaldino   What do you mean? An extra few dishes?

Beatrice   I don't know. It's for Mr Pantaloon. I don't think he's much of an eater. I'd say we'd get away with four or five between us, as long as they're tasty.

Truffaldino   Leave it to me, guv.

Beatrice   See what you can do. I'm going to fetch Pantaloon from around the corner, just see that it's all sorted when I get back.

Truffaldino   No problem at all, sir.

Beatrice   Put this paper in my trunk. And be extremely careful with it, it's a bill of exchange for four thousand crowns.

Truffaldino   Rest assured, sir, I will give it singular attention.

Beatrice   Just make sure everything's ready.

Scene Nine

Truffaldino   Right, now this is a great chance to demonstrate my various skills at the ordering of a dinner. I'll just pop the paper . . . oh, bugger the paper, I'll sort it out later. More important matters. Hello. Garçon. Anybody there? Can you please advise Monsewer Brighella that I would like to speak to him toot sweet. Now the secret of a proper dinner is not simply in the selection, but the way it's all laid out. It's your presentation, isn't it.

Enter **Brighella**.

Brighella   Can I be of assistance?

Truffaldino   Indeed you can, my good man. My master is entertaining a very good friend of his and requests you prepare an enormous amount of food for them to eat of, immediately. I trust you have the necessaries on hand in the old kitchen, sir.

Brighella   Oh I always have the necessaries.

Truffaldino   So what would you recommend, then?

Brighella   For two people. A couple of courses maybe four little dishes each.

Truffaldino   Well, just throw a few more in just to be on the safe side.

Brighella   For the first course we have some nice soup, some whitebait, a meat platter and a fricandeau.

Truffaldino   I beg your pardon.

Brighella   A fricandeau. It's French. A sort of ragoût.

Truffaldino   Sounds just the ticket. But be careful with that frigandoo.

Brighella   Then we could do you a roast, a nice salad, a game pie and then follow it all up with a spotted dick.

Truffaldino   There's no need for that, sir. My master is a man of some standing.

Brighella   It's an English dish, sir.

Truffaldino   I don't care where it's from, sir, a dick's a dick in my book. I think we'll have a trifle. Very good. So how will the dishes be laid out, if you please?

Brighella   Well, the waiter will just bring them to the table.

Truffaldino   Ha, ha! That's where you are wrong. No, my friend, the laying of a table is a very special matter, believe me, sir, I am a stickler for the presentation.

Brighella   Well, the soup goes here, the whitebait, here. And there the cold cuts and we'll put the ragoût over there. OK?

Truffaldino   The 'fricandeau'?

Brighella   The fricandeau.

Truffaldino   What about something in the middle?

Brighella   Then you'd need an extra dish, wouldn't you?

Truffaldino   What do you think I am? A skinflint. We're talking about the laying out of a meal, sir. Do an extra dish, for God's sake.

Brighella   Maybe we could do a nice dip for the whitebait?

Truffaldino   A dip. Don't be so ridiculous. Where would the soup go.

Brighella   We could put the soup on one side and the dip on the other.

Truffaldino   No we could not, sir. This is an absolute outrage. You might know how to cook a pimpled dick, sir, but you don't have the first idea how to lay a table. Now, if this is your table, your five dishes must be placed like so, with your soup in the centre.

He tears a bit off the bill of exchange and puts it one one side.

And on the opposite side. The whitebait.

He tears another bit off.

Your sauce. Or 'dip' as you call it, would, of course, go here.

More tearing, etc.

And, here, we'd have the what-do-you-call-it.

Brighella   The fricandeau.

Truffaldino   And bob's your uncle.

Brighella   But isn't the dip too far away from the whitebait?

Truffaldino   Well, move them closer together then. For God's sake.

Scene Ten

Enter **Beatrice** *and* **Pantaloon**.

Beatrice   Excuse me. What are you doing?

Truffaldino   Ah, just a bit of culinary experimentation.

Beatrice   But isn't that my bill of exchange?

Truffaldino   Indeed it is, sir, and we'll have it stuck back together in no time.

Beatrice   You asinine twit. What on earth were you thinking of?

Pantaloon   Look, there's no harm done, I'll write you out another one.

Beatrice   That's not the point. What if it had been irreplaceable? You cretinous halfwit.

Truffaldino   Now hang on a minute, sir. None of this would have happened if he knew how to lay a table.

Brighella   Listen, I've been laying tables all my life.

Truffaldino   Look, don't try and tell your granny how to suck eggs, matey.

Beatrice (*to* **Truffaldino**)   Bugger off, you stupid little man.

Truffaldino   But it's a very important matter . . .

Beatrice   I'm warning you. Go. Away.

Truffaldino   Well, don't blame me if you have to stretch for your dip.

Exit **Truffaldino**.

Brighella   I can't make any sense of him. One minute he's as sharp as a whip, the next he's thick as a baron of beef, sir.

Beatrice   Don't worry about it. The attributes of intelligence are all put on. May we have dinner now?

Brighella   It might take some time if you're wanting five dishes for each course.

Pantaloon   Five dishes. Courses? Listen, a bit of risotto and a few leaves of lettuce will do me fine.

Beatrice   Yes. Whatever he fancies.

Pantaloon   And a couple of rissoles.

Brighella   Coming right up. If you'd like to make yourselves comfortable in your room, sir – lunch will be served in no time at all.

Beatrice   And tell Truffaldino to come and wait on us.

Brighella   It's your funeral, sir.

Scene Eleven

Beatrice, **Pantaloon**, **Waiters** *and* **Truffaldino**.

Beatrice   I hope you don't mind such a meagre meal.

Pantaloon   On the contrary, my dear sir, you are going to far too much trouble. You should be dining at my house, not me prevailing on you. It's just with Clarice at home I think it's more appropriate to keep you two apart till the knot's tied. Anyway, I'm very much obliged for your valiant bravery before, sir.

Beatrice   At least there was no blood spilt.

The **Waiters** *go through to the room* **Brighella** *had indicated, carrying wine, glasses, etc.*

Pantaloon   They're very efficient, aren't they?

Beatrice   This Brighella is a first-rate fellow. Used to serve a gentleman in Turin and I can tell you he hasn't changed his spots.

Pantaloon   There's an excellent little place the other side of the Rialto, you know. Often pop down there with a few friends. You can have quite a feast just sharing a couple of starters. They do a bloody good burgundy, if you'll pardon the French. Very fine indeed.

Beatrice   Yes, to eat in company is one of life's great pleasures. I dare say you have often seen good times, sir.

Pantaloon   And will see many more. I hope.

Truffaldino (*carrying a tureen of soup*)   Dinner is served. If you'd be so kind to take your seats, gents.

Beatrice   For God's sake, just put the soup down on the table.

Truffaldino   At your service, sir.

Pantaloon   He's a queer fish that fellow of yours. You don't think he's er . . . You know?

Beatrice   I beg your pardon?

Pantaloon   Let's go through, eh?

Beatrice (*to* **Truffaldino**)   Less of the acrobatics and a bit more concentration, please.

Truffaldino   Call this a dinner? One dish at a time? I tell you, you don't get much for your ducat in here. Let's a have a taster.

He tries it with a spoon he keeps in his trousers.

Always keep your tools handy. Not bad, actually.

He exits into the room.

Scene Twelve

First Waiter *carrying a dish, then* **Truffaldino**.

First Waiter   When is that tosser coming for the rest?

Truffaldino   Hold your horses. What's this then?

First Waiter   That's your charcuterie.

Truffaldino   I beg your pardon.

First Waiter   Your meat plate, mate. I'll get the next.

Exits.

Truffaldino   Mmm? What's this? Horse meat? Actually, not bad. A nice bit of brisket, that is. Mmm.

Enter **Florindo**.

Florindo   Where are you going with that?

Truffaldino   What, sir?

Florindo   That plate.

Truffaldino   The charcuterie, sir? I was just going to put it on the table.

Florindo   Who for?

Truffaldino   You, sir.

Florindo   But I wasn't even back.

Truffaldino   Ah, always thinking ahead, sir.

Florindo   But what's the idea of starting with the meat before the soup?

Truffaldino   It's an old Venetian custom, sir.

Florindo   It's absolute poppycock. Take it back to the kitchen. I will not have my meat previous to any other course.

Truffaldino   Yes, sir. Very good, sir.

Florindo   I just want to eat something quickly and lie down.

Truffaldino   On the double, sir.

Florindo   Will I ever find Beatrice?

He leaves.

As soon as **Florindo** *has disappeared into the other room,* **Truffaldino** *rushes into* **Beatrice***'s room with the plate.*

First Waiter   For crying out loud. Oi Speedy Gonzales.

Truffaldino   Coming. Quickly go and lay the table in there. That other fellow is screaming for soup.

First Waiter   All right, wind your neck in.

He exits.

Truffaldino   And what have we got here, then. The flickflack?

He tries some.

Absolutely delicious.

He exits to **Beatrice**'s *room.*

The **Waiters** *go through with the things for* **Florindo**.

Truffaldino   Very good, lads. Quick as a rat in a priest's cassock this lot. Right. Two masters, two tables, one very handsome servant. And away we go. If I manage this lot I want a bloody medal never mind a ducat a day.

The **Waiters** *come out of* **Florindo**'s *room and head for the kitchen.*

Truffaldino   Come on, hurry up with that soup, will you?

First Waiter   Look, you worry about that table, we'll see to this one, OK?

He exits.

Truffaldino   Cheeky little bastard.

First Waiter *comes back with the soup.*

Truffaldino   Thank you. I'll deal with that. Go and get the rest of the stuff for room one.

He exits.

First Waiter   If you want to run around like a blue-arsed fly, that's all right with me, mate, as long as I get the same tips as usual.

Truffaldino *comes out of* **Florindo**'s *room.*

Beatrice   Truffaldino.

First Waiter   Hey, look lively.

Truffaldino   Just coming.

Truffaldino *goes into* **Beatrice**'s *room.*

Second Waiter *brings in the boiled meat for* **Florindo**.

First Waiter   Give me that here.

First Waiter *takes it,* **Second Waiter** *goes off.*

Truffaldino *appears with a pile of dirty plates.*

Florindo   Truffaldino.

Truffaldino   Give that to me. (*He wants to take the dish from* **First Waiter**.)

First Waiter   No, I'm taking this.

Truffaldino   Listen, he's shouting for me. (*Takes dish into* **Florindo**.)

First Waiter   Who the hell does he think he is?

Second Waiter *brings in a dish of rissoles, gives it to the* **First Waiter** *and leaves.*

First Waiter   I'm not taking it just to get screamed at.

Truffaldino *comes out of* **Florindo**'s *room with dirty plates.*

First Waiter   Oi, Sancho Panza. Rissoles.

Truffaldino   Don't start.

First Waiter   Your rissoles.

First Waiter *leaves.*

Truffaldino   Who the hell would order rissoles? I could just take potluck, but then if they got eaten by a non-rissole orderer and the rissole orderer called for the rissoles that were ordered but went astray then I'd be right up the rissole. I know. Genius. I'll cut the rissoles in half and each room will have rissoles ordered or not. Four and four and one. Mmm. Who's that going to go to? Fair's fair, no favouritisation. (*He eats the spare rissole.*) Right. Rissoles away.

Enter **First Waiter** *carrying a pudding.*

First Waiter   Truffaldino. Your spotted dick.

Truffaldino   One moment.

Truffaldino *runs into* **Florindo**'s *room with a plate of rissoles.*

First Waiter   But the rissoles were for that room.

Truffaldino   Look, mind your own business. As they were so delicious the rissoles were shared around as a courtesy of one gentleman to another. You can't be too free with your rissoles.

First Waiter   Well, it's perfectly possible that they can all dine together, you know.

Truffaldino   What the hell's this?

First Waiter   Spotted dick.

Truffaldino   Who's it for?

First Waiter   Your master.

Truffaldino   But I ordered trifle.

First Waiter   Look, it's got nothing to do with me.

First Waiter *leaves it with* **Truffaldino**.

Truffaldino   It can't really be dick, can it?

He tastes some with great trepidation.

Very tasty, actually.

Beatrice   Truffaldino.

Truffaldino (*mouthful*)   I'll be right with you.

Florindo   Truffaldino.

Truffaldino (*stuffing more into his mouth*)   Bugger.

Enter **Beatrice**. *She sees* **Truffaldino** *eating*.

Beatrice   Stop that at once. Come in here and wait this table.

Exits into room one.

Truffaldino *puts the plate on the floor and goes into* **Beatrice**'s *room. Enter* **Florindo** *from his room.*

Florindo   Truffaldino. Where the devil's he got to?

Enter **Truffaldino** *from* **Beatrice**'s *room. Sees* **Florindo**.

Truffaldino   Here.

Florindo   Where did you disappear to?

Truffaldino   More dishes, sir.

Florindo   More food?

Truffaldino   Just a mo.

Florindo   Well, get a move on. I want to take this nap.

Truffaldino   Don't worry. Garçon. Is there anything else coming? (*Of the pudding.*) I'll keep this for later. (*Hides pudding.*)

Enter **First Waiter**.

First Waiter   Roast.

Truffaldino   Thank you. Now fruit. Fruit.

First Waiter   Calm down.

He exits.

Truffaldino   Eeny Meeny Miney Mo. (*Takes the roast to* **Florindo**'s *room.*)

Enter **First Waiter** *with the fruit bowl.*

First Waiter   Fruit. Where are you?

Enter **Truffaldino** *from* **Florindo**'s *room.*

Truffaldino   Thank you.

First Waiter   Anything else, your Lordship?

Truffaldino   Stay there. (*Takes fruit into* **Beatrice***'s room.*)

First Waiter   Look at him go.

Truffaldino (*re-emerging*)   No, that's it now. Everybody's happy.

First Waiter   Glad to hear it.

Truffaldino   All we want is a table for me.

First Waiter   Charming.

He leaves.

Truffaldino   Now for me pudding. There you go: two masters, three diners, four courses in all. Everybody's happy. Nobody's any the wiser. I have served to two, now I will eat for four. Thank you.

Scene Thirteen

The street outside **Brighella***'s inn.*

Smeraldina   Charming this. Sending me out at all hours to run messages to a common tavern. I can't make head nor tail of it. One minute she's going to top herself, the next she's sending secret letters to all and sundry. Well, I'm buggered if I'm setting foot in this fetid dump.

First Waiter *comes out.*

First Waiter   Hello, hello, hello. What can I do you for?

Smeraldina (*unimpressed*)   For Christ's sake. (*To him.*) Is there a Federigo Rasponi in residence?

First Waiter   Certainly is. Just finishing his meal.

Smeraldina   Well, is it possible I could have a word. I have something for him.

First Waiter   No problem, gorgeous. Want to come in?

Smeraldina   To that rat-hole. Listen, I'm a Lady's maid, you know.

First Waiter   Come on. You don't expect me to send him out here, do you? Anyway, he's currently engaged with Mr Parsimoni.

Smeraldina   I'm staying put.

First Waiter   Look. I'll send his servant out then.

Smeraldina   The little funny-looking fella?

First Waiter   That's the one.

Smeraldina   Top idea, mate.

First Waiter   Too shy to come in, are you? But you'll talk to any Tom, Dick and Harry on the street corner. I know your type.

First Waiter *exits*.

Smeraldina (*to herself*)   Wanker.

Scene Fourteen

Enter **Truffaldino**, *bottle, glass and napkin*.

Truffaldino   Did somebody call?

Smeraldina   It was me. I'm so sorry to drag you out.

Truffaldino   No trouble at all, miss. At your service.

Smeraldina   I hope I didn't disturb your dinner.

Truffaldino   Not to worry. It won't run away.

Smeraldina   No. Seriously.

Truffaldino   To be quite honest, I've bloody well stuffed meself, and your lovely eyes, miss, are a perfect digestif.

Smeraldina (*aside*)   He's quite sophisticated.

Truffaldino   Oh, yes. (*Burps.*) Hang on a mo, and I'll just go and relieve myself of my accoutrements and be back in a tick.

Smeraldina (*impressed*)   Accoutrements! (*To* **Truffaldino**.) My mistress has sent this letter to Mr Rasponi, and as it wouldn't exactly be decent for a young lady as myself to be seen in an inn on her own. I thought you might deliver it for me.

Truffaldino   It'd be an absolute pleasure. But first, madam, I must deliver a message to you.

Smeraldina   Who from?

Truffaldino   A very distinguished fellow, madam. Are you aquainted with a certain Truffaldino Battocchio?

Smeraldina (*aside*)   Truffaldino Battachio. (*To* **Truffaldino**.) Never heard of him.

Truffaldino   A very handsome fella, if you don't mind me saying so, short, very muscular, a fine turn of phrase and an expert at the laying of tables.

Smeraldina   Well, I don't know anyone of that description.

Truffaldino   Well, he loves you with all his heart.

Smeraldina   You're joking.

Truffaldino   Not at all. If there was any hope that his affections might be reciprocated he would reveal himself to you. I mean make himself known.

Smeraldina   Well, if I had some idea what he looked like, you never know. Maybe I'd fancy him.

Truffaldino   Shall I introduce you, then?

Smeraldina   If you want.

Truffaldino *goes out. Then returns, makes a bow, heaves a sigh and goes back out. Re-enter* **Truffaldino**.

Truffaldino   Did you see him?

Smeraldina   Who?

Truffaldino   The man totally besotted with your beauty.

Smeraldina   I only saw you.

Truffaldino   Oh.

Smeraldina   You're not besotted with my beauty, are you?

Truffaldino   Well, just a little bit.

Smeraldina   Why didn't you say so in the first place?

Truffaldino   I'm . . . rather shy.

Smeraldina (*aside*)   The little tinker.

Truffaldino   Well?

Smeraldina   Well, what?

Truffaldino   What do you say?

Smeraldina   I'm rather shy myself.

Truffaldino   Well, it's a perfect match, isn't it?

Smeraldina   Well, to tell you the truth. You're not bad. On the whole.

Truffaldino   Are you courting, miss?

Smeraldina   What sort of question's that?

Truffaldino   I suppose that means you are, then?

Smeraldina   On the contrary, it means I certainly am not.

Truffaldino   Hard as it may seem, neither am I.

Smeraldina   Of course I could have been married fifty times over, but I've never really met the right sort of man.

Truffaldino   What do you think of this sort of man?

Smeraldina   I don't know. We'd have to see.

Truffaldino   And if this sort of man wished to ask for your hand. How would he do that?

Smeraldina   You don't waste your time. Since both of my parents are dead if a man happened to be interested, I suppose he'd have to ask my master or my mistress.

Truffaldino   And what would they say?

Smeraldina   They'd say 'if it makes her happy'.

Truffaldino   And would it make you happy?

Smeraldina   Only if they were happy about it.

Truffaldino   Bloody hell, you need a degree in philosophy to get anywhere with you. Now give uz the letter and I'll bring you the answer and we'll have ourselves a nice little chinwag.

Smeraldina   OK.

Truffaldino   Have you got any idea what's in it?

Smeraldina   No. But I'm dying to find out.

Truffaldino   Look, I don't want to take him any insults or anything. I get it in the neck every time.

Smeraldina   I think it's a love letter.

Truffaldino   I'm in enough trouble as it is. If I don't know what's in it, I'm not taking it through.

Smeraldina   Couldn't we open it? We'd have to seal it back up though.

Truffaldino   Leave that to me. I know the perfect method. He'll be none the wiser.

Smeraldina   Go on then.

Truffaldino   Can you read?

Smeraldina   A bit. But you can, can't you?

Truffaldino   Well, to a point.

Smeraldina   Let's have a look.

Truffaldino   Now this is a very delicate operation. (*The letter gets torn.*)

Smeraldina   What are you doing!?

Truffaldino   Nothing. We'll soon put that right. There you go. (*It's open.*)

Smeraldina   Well, go on then.

Truffaldino   No. No. Ladies first.

Smeraldina (*looks at it*)   I can't make head nor tail of it.

Truffaldino (*looks at it*)   Me neither. Not a sausage.

Smeraldina   Well, what was the point of opening it?

Truffaldino   Hang on. Let's have another shot. Wait. Here's something.

Smeraldina   Yep. I think I can make out the odd letter.

Truffaldino   Well, let's go through the alphabet and work out which one it is. 'A'.

Smeraldina   That's not an 'A', it's an 'R'.

Truffaldino   Bloody hell they're quite similar, aren't they.

Smeraldina   'Ri, ri, ria.' No I don't think it's an 'R'. It's an 'M'. Mia.

Truffaldino   No, wait. It's 'Mio'. No wonder we can't read it. It's in bloody Italian.

Scene Fifteen

Enter **Beatrice** *and* **Pantaloon**.

Pantaloon   What are you doing here?

Smeraldina (*terrified*)   Nothing, sir. I was just on my way to find you.

Pantaloon   What do you want me for?

Smeraldina   My mistress was asking for you.

Beatrice   What's that you've got there?

Truffaldino   Nothing, sir. It's just a piece of paper.

Beatrice   Give me that here.

Truffaldino *hands her the piece of paper.*

Beatrice   What's this? This letter's addressed to me. Am I ever going to get a letter that hasn't been read by all and sundry.

Truffaldino   It was nothing to do with me.

Beatrice   Look, sir, a note from Lady Clarice warning me of Silvio's insane jealousy and this impudent rascal has the gall to go and open it.

Pantaloon (*to* **Smeraldina**)   And you, you had your grubby hands in this.

Smeraldina   I don't know anything about it, sir.

Beatrice   Well, who opened the letter?

Truffaldino   Not me.

Smeraldina   Not me.

Pantaloon   Well, who the devil brought it?

Smeraldina   Truffaldino. He was taking it to his master.

Beatrice   Is this true?

Truffaldino   Yes. I got it from Smeraldina.

Smeraldina   You little shit.

Pantaloon   You meddling hussy. I knew you'd be at the bottom of this. I've got a good mind to smack your backside.

Smeraldina   I beg your pardon. I have never been 'smacked' by any man, sir. I am outraged.

Pantaloon   'Outraged' are you?

Smeraldina   I'm not standing for this, you rheumatic old git. Goodbye.

Exit **Smeraldina**.

Pantaloon   Rheumatic old git!

Exit **Pantaloon** *in pursuit.*

Scene Sixteen

Beatrice, **Truffaldino**.

Truffaldino   Well, that's another fine mess I've got myself into.

Beatrice (*aside*)   Poor Clarice despairing over Silvio's jealousy. I'll have to uncover myself and put an end to this lunacy.

Truffaldino   I think I better make myself scarce.

Beatrice   Where do you think you're going?

Truffaldino   Nowhere.

Beatrice   Why did you open this letter?

Truffaldino   It was Smeraldina. I had absolutely nothing to do with it.

Beatrice   Smeraldina. This is the second letter today. Come here.

Truffaldino   Have mercy on me, sir.

Beatrice   Here.

Truffaldino   Please, I didn't mean it, sir.

Beatrice *gives him a good thrashing.*

Florindo *appears at the window.*

Florindo   Beat my man, would you?

Truffaldino   Please, stop. Ow.

Beatrice   Never, never open my letters again.

Scene Seventeen

Beatrice *leaves.*

Truffaldino   Thank you. Thank you very much. After everything I've done for that bastard. If you're not happy with your service sack me by all means, but there's no need to go for grievous bodily harm.

Enter **Florindo**.

Florindo   What's that you're saying?

Truffaldino   Oh nothing, sir. Just that beating other people's servants is a disgrace and insult to their master, sir.

Florindo   It is a heinous insult. Who was that man?

Truffaldino   I don't know, sir. I haven't seen him before in my life.

Florindo   This isn't funny. What on earth did he beat you for?

Truffaldino   Really, I don't know. It must have been because I spat on his shoe, sir.

Florindo   Spat on his shoe?

Truffaldino   By mistake, sir.

Florindo   You blithering idiot. Didn't you think to defend yourself. I suppose you thought it was funny to lay your own master open to an insult. Have you any idea how serious that could be. Well, if you like a good thrashing now and again, I'd be happy to oblige.

Florindo *beats* **Truffaldino** *and leaves.*

Truffaldino Well, that's it. I definitely know I've got two masters now, as I've had my wages from each one. I mean two. Or . . . ? Oh, sod it. 'The interval.'

Interval.

Act Three

Scene One

A room in the inn. Enter **Truffaldino**.

Truffaldino (*burps*)   To be quite honest it was worth having two beatings to get two excellent meals. Supper number one was absolutely first class but supper number two was in a second first class all of its own. Bad times look a lot better on a full belly – I'll tell you that much. I'm going to keep this lark up as long as I can still waddle upright without need of assistance. Righty-ho. What's on the agenda? Numero uno is out on the town and numero duo's snoring like a babe in arms, so I reckon it's high time to get these clothes out. So we'll sort these trunks out and have a shufty through to see what's what. I'll need a hand. Garçon!

Enter two **Waiters**.

First Waiter   What?

Truffaldino   I just need a hand getting a couple of trunks out of those rooms here.

First Waiter (*to* **Second Waiter**)   That's your job, mate.

Truffaldino   Come on. I'll make it worth your while.

Truffaldino *goes out with the* **Second Waiter**.

First Waiter (*aside*)   There's a rabbit off somewhere. He seems a bit too keen for my liking.

Truffaldino *comes back.*

Truffaldino   Careful. Put it down here. (*They put a trunk down.*) Right. T'other one. But shh, the guvnor's having a kip.

First Waiter (*aside*)   He's definitely up to something. The servant of two masters. More like the thief of two masters.

Truffaldino (*coming from* **Florindo**'s *room with* **Second Waiter**)   We'll put this one here. Champion. Right, you can piss off now, thank you very much.

First Waiter   Yes, bugger off to the kitchen, like a good lad. (*To* **Truffaldino**, *who's struggling with a case.*) Can I help you at all?

Truffaldino   No, thanks all the same. All under control.

First Waiter   Fair enough, if you want to break your back that's your problem, smart-arse.

Exit **First Waiter**.

Truffaldino   Thank God for that. A bit peace and quiet. (*Takes key from his pocket.*) Which one's this? Let's have a gander. (*Tries it in a trunk. It works.*) Yes, right first time. The Brain of Bergamot strikes again. I suggest that this key, therefore, will open this trunk over here. (*Tries it.*) He puts it in. He turns the key. Yes. Two in a row. There will be riots on the streets tonight. Right, let's be having you.

He takes the clothes out of both trunks; lays them on the table. In each trunk there must be a black jacket, books, papers and various other items.

Let's have a look in these pockets. You very often find the odd biscuit and the like.

He feels in the pocket of **Beatrice**'s *jacket and finds a small photo / miniature*

Look at that. Very nice. Now there's a handsome young fella. I'm sure I know him from somewhere. Who the hell is it? Hey, he looks the spit of my master, except with different clothes and wotnot.

Scene Two

Florindo (*off*)   Truffaldino.

Truffaldino   Oh bloody hell. I've woke the miserable sod up. If he comes out here I'm snookered with these two cases. Get this rubbish back in and deny everything. That's the ticket.

Florindo (*off*)   Truffaldino.

Truffaldino (*shouts*)   Here, sir. (*To himself.*) Shit. Where did this jacket come from?

Florindo (*off*)   Are you coming or do I have to come out there with a stick and get you?

Truffaldino   Coming at once, sir.

Truffaldino *throws everything in the trunks willy-nilly.*

Enter **Florindo** *in a dressing gown.*

Florindo   What the devil are you doing?

Truffaldino   I was just giving your clothes an airing like you asked, sir.

Florindo   Whose is that other trunk?

Truffaldino   What trunk? Oh. Haven't a clue, sir. I've only just noticed it.

Florindo   Give me my black jacket.

Truffaldino   No problem, sir.

He opens **Florindo**'s *trunk, takes out the black jacket. He helps* **Florindo** *try it on.* **Florindo** *finds the miniature.*

Florindo   What's this?

Truffaldino (*aside*)   Balls.

Florindo (*aside*)   There is no mistake. This is my picture. The one I gave to Beatrice. (*To* **Truffaldino**.) How did this get into my jacket pocket?

Truffaldino   Don't panic.

Florindo   Out with it. What is this picture doing in my jacket pocket?

Truffaldino   Please, please, forgive me, sir, but I have taken a great liberty. The picture infact is mine, sir, and I put it there for safekeeping.

Florindo   Safekeeping? How did you come by such a picture?

Truffaldino   I inherited it, sir. From my previous master.

Florindo   Inherited it!

Truffaldino   When he died I was left several things and flogged them all except this exquisite item, sir.

Florindo   When did your master die?

Truffaldino   A week ago. (*Aside.*) You do realise I'm making this up.

Florindo   What was his name?

Truffaldino   I do not know, sir, the man went incognito.

Florindo   Incognito. How long were you in his service?

Truffaldino   Not long at all. Maybe twelve days, sir.

Florindo (*aside*)   This is Beatrice. Fleeing Turin dressed as a man. Oh this is unbearable. (*To* **Truffaldino**.) Was he young, your master?

Truffaldino   Alas, a very young man, sir.

Florindo   Without a beard?

Truffaldino   Not even bumfluff, sir.

Florindo (*to himself*   It was Beatrice. No doubt about it. (*To* **Truffaldino**.) Do you at least know where this master was from?

Truffaldino   I'm trying to remember.

Florindo   Could it have possibly been Turin?

Truffaldino   Exactly. Turin. That's the one.

Florindo (*to himself*)   Every word is a dagger to my heart.
(*To* **Truffaldino**.) And you are certain the man is dead?

Truffaldino   As a dodo, sir. (*Aside.*) Think about it.

Florindo   What did he die of?

Truffaldino   He had a nasty accident and that was that.
(*Aside.*) A very good answer.

Florindo   So where was he buried?

Truffaldino (*aside*)   For crying out loud. (*To* **Florindo**.)
He wasn't buried. Another servant put him in a coffin and
sent him home.

Florindo   And this servant was the man for whom you
collected the letter at the post office.

Truffaldino   Yes. The very same, sir, the infamous
Pasqual.

Florindo   Then Beatrice is dead. The torture of the
journey must have broke her heart and killed her. Beatrice.
This is a living hell.

Florindo *leaves in tears.*

Scene Three

Truffaldino   What have I done now? Poor delicate soul.
It's as if he knew the gentleman in question. Weeping like a
child, and all I was doing was covering up for the bloody
trunks. Right, I'm getting these buggers (*the trunks*) out before
I get in any more trouble.

Enter **Beatrice**.

Beatrice   I assure you, Mr Pantaloon, there are some definite discrepancies in these accounts. I'm sure the last consignment of sun-dried tomatoes has been entered twice.

Pantaloon   Maybe my young men have made some mistake. Don't worry, I'll have it gone through with a fine-tooth comb.

Beatrice   Don't worry, I've a complete list of everything copied into my record book with me, if we sit down with all the figures we'll have it sorted out in no time. Truffaldino.

Truffaldino   Hello.

Beatrice   Have you the key to my trunk?

Truffaldino   Yes. Here you are, sir.

Beatrice   And what's it doing out there?

Truffaldino   I was just going to air your clothes, sir.

Beatrice   And whose is that other trunk?

Truffaldino   Haven't a clue, sir. It must belong to the other geezer what's just arrived.

Beatrice   There is a notebook in my trunk. Can you retrieve it for me so that I can sort out this matter with Mr Pantaloon?

Truffaldino   No problem at all, sir. (*Aside.*) God preserve me.

He opens the trunk and looks for the notebook.

Pantaloon   Of course, if there is any material discrepancy the matter will be reconciled not withstanding, sir.

Beatrice   Just a tick, I've got it all written down.

Truffaldino   Is it this one?

Beatrice   It looks like it. (*Looks in it.*) What in hell's name is this?

Truffaldino   Bollocks.

Beatrice (*aside*)   Here are two of the letters I wrote to Florindo. What's going on?

Pantaloon   Mr Federigo, are you feeling all right?

Beatrice   It will pass, I assure you. (*To* **Truffaldino**.) Truffaldino, how did these get into my trunk?

Truffaldino   I don't really know, sir.

Beatrice   Out with it. The truth, you lying toad.

Truffaldino   Please, sir, that is infact my own book, and I took the liberty of putting them in there myself, sir. Terribly sorry. (*Aside*.) If it worked once . . .

Beatrice   If it's your book how come you gave it to me?

Truffaldino (*aside*)   Clever bastard. (*To* **Beatrice**.) Sir, I haven't had it very long, sir – so it seemed unfamiliar.

Beatrice   So where did it come from?

Truffaldino   I was left it, sir, when my previous master sadly died, sir.

Beatrice   Died? When did this master die?

Truffaldino   Hard to say, sir. Twelve days ago?

Beatrice   But you were in Verona with me twelve days ago. That's exactly when I met you.

Truffaldino   Absolutely right, sir. I had to leave for Verona on account of the grief, sir.

Beatrice   And was this master called Florindo?

Truffaldino   I think he was, sir.

Beatrice   Florindo Aretusi?

Truffaldino   That's the fella.

Beatrice   And he is dead?

Truffaldino   As a door nail, sir.

Beatrice   Oh this is too much. How did he die? Where is he buried?

Truffaldino   He fell into a canal, knocked his head on a gondola, drowned of an instant and was never seen again, sir.

Beatrice   No. No. No. Florindo dead? My hope, my being, my life, my everything is gone. Love has vanished from the world. All my plans, my disguises, the danger, the suffering have all been for nothing. It was torture enough to lose a brother, but now a husband too? If I am the cause of this let heaven tear me limb from limb and rip my heart out of my body as it is useless to me now. Not tears, not medicine, not anything will ever bring it back to life. Florindo is dead. And I am dead with grief. I can't stand this light. I followed you in life, so I shall follow you in death, my dearest love.

She exits.

Pantaloon   Truffaldino!

Truffaldino   Mr Pantaloon, sir.

Pantaloon   A woman!

Truffaldino   And not bad at all if you don't mind me saying so.

Pantaloon   This is extraordinary.

Truffaldino   You can say that again.

Pantaloon   Extraordinary.

Truffaldino   Well, it's certainly a turn-up for the books.

Pantaloon   I must go straight home and tell my daughter.

Exit **Pantaloon**.

Truffaldino   So it's not the servant of two masters any more but the servant of one master and another-master-who-on-revealing-their-true-nature-appears-to-really-have-been-quite-a-good-looking-mistress all along. Not as snappy, is it?

Scene Four

Courtyard, **Pantaloon**'s *house.*

Enter **Dr Lombardi**.

Dr Lombardi   That doddering old clot's going to get it this time. I shall brook the argument no further.

Enter **Pantaloon**.

Pantaloon   Ah, my dear Doctor, how very good to see you.

Dr Lombardi   I'm surprised you even have the gall to speak to me, sir.

Pantaloon   But I have some wonderful news.

Dr Lombardi   Don't tell me. They've married already. I don't give a damn for your news, sir.

Pantaloon   Please, listen . . .

Dr Lombardi   Speak then, you villanous Turk.

Pantaloon (*aside*)   He's asking for it. (*To* **Dr Lombardi**.) Sir, my daughter will marry your son, whenever you wish.

Dr Lombardi   Oh I am very much obliged, but don't put yourself to any inconvenience, sir. I'm afraid it would turn my son's stomach to even contemplate the matter, the man from Turin is perfectly welcome to her.

Pantaloon   But the man from Turin is not a man from Turin.

Dr Lomabardi   I don't care where he's from, sir, she can take the blaggard whatever his provenance.

Pantaloon   But . . .

Dr Lombardi   And I don't want to hear anything further.

Pantaloon   Please, this is important.

Dr Lombardi   We'll see what's important.

Pantaloon   Please, my daughter's reputation is entirely untarnished.

Dr Lombardi   Go to the devil, sir.

Pantaloon   Go to the devil, yourself.

Dr Lombardi   You welching runt.

Pantaloon   I beg your pardon?

Dr Lombardi   I said welching, sir.

Dr Lombardi *storms off.*

Scene Five

Pantaloon   Sod you. The man's a rabid goat. Saints preserve us, here's another one.

Enter **Silvio**.

Silvio   Pantaloon. I would like to rip the innards from your overweight gut.

Pantaloon   Please, Mr Silvio, sir, I have some very good news for you.

Silvio   You malignant worm.

Pantaloon   I want you to know, sir, my daughter's marriage to Mr Federigo is off.

Silvio   Don't even try to make a fool of me.

Pantaloon   It's the God's honest truth. Please, you can have her, sir, she's yours for the taking.

Silvio   Oh thank the heavens. I am ressurrected.

Pantaloon   At least he's a little more civil than his father.

Silvio   But how can I knowingly accept a woman who has been wedded to another for so long?

Pantaloon   Because, sir, that other, that Federigo Rasponi, is no other than Beatrice his sister.

Silvio   I don't understand.

Pantaloon   Don't be an arse. The person we assumed was Federigo was his sister in disguise.

Silvio   Dressed as man?

Pantaloon   No, dressed as the Goddess Athena.

Silvio   Bloody hell. Now there's a turn-up.

Pantaloon   Believe me, no one was more surprised than me.

Silvio   How on earth did this come about?

Pantaloon   Let's go to my house. I haven't even had time to tell Clarice herself, you can hear the whole story together.

Silvio   Oh I must humbly apologise for anything I might have said, sir.

Pantaloon   Let's forget it. I'm quite familiar with the hot passions of love. You come along with me, son.

Exeunt.

Scene Six

Darkness. The inn. **Beatrice** *and* **Florindo** *come out of their rooms, each carrying a rope. Neither sees the other. Each has a picture of their loved ones. They both make careful preparations to hang themselves. They each kiss their picture and jump off the chair. [If this is not possible the method of suicide should need elaborate preparation and be painful to witness.]* **Brighella** *and the* **First Waiter** *come in with a lamp and accidentally see* **Beatrice** *jumping into oblivion.*

Brighella (*to* **First Waiter**)   And then I said to him . . . (*On seeing* **Beatrice**.) Stop in the name of God.

They try to support her. She struggles. The **First Waiter** *tries to cut her down.*

Beatrice   Let me go. Let me die.

First Waiter   This is madness itself.

Florindo *then sees* **Beatrice**.

Florindo (*choking*)   Oh my God.

Beatrice   No one can stop me.

Suddenly **Brighella** *and* **First Waiter** *see* **Florindo**.

Beatrice   Florindo.

The **First Waiter** *has cut her down. They fall in a heap.*

Florindo   My Beatrice.

Beatrice   Alive?

Florindo *is choking.*

Florindo (*choking*)   My dearest love.

Beatrice   Florindo.

Brighella *gets up and rushes to assist* **Florindo**.

Brighella   What are you thinking of? You haven't paid up yet.

They cut down **Florindo**. *He stands staring in astonishment at* **Beatrice**. *She is equally dumbstruck.* **Brighella** *and the* **First Waiter** *watch as* **Beatrice** *and* **Florindo** *are reunited.*

Florindo   Beatrice.

Beatrice   Florindo.

They kiss.

Scene Seven

Florindo   But what drove you to this madness?

Beatrice   News that you were dead.

Florindo   Who said I was dead?

Beatrice   My servant.

Florindo   And my servant told me that you too had passed away.

Beatrice   It was this book that caused me to believe him.

Florindo   But that book was in my trunk. What's going on? Of course, the very same way my picture got into my jacket pocket. The servants.

Beatrice   Those scheming little rascals. Lord knows what they've been up to.

Florindo   Where the hell are they? Let's sort this out once and for all. (*To* **Brighella**.) Where are our servants, sir?

Brighella   I'm afraid I have no idea, whatsoever, Would you like me to find them by any chance?

Florindo   Of course I want someone to find them. Have them grabbed by the scruff of the neck and dragged here at once.

Brighella   I'm afraid I've only ever seen one of them, but Charlie here will sort them out. Just a little word in your ear, sir, but it is customary to mention any suicides, maimings or sundry self-mutilation when you check in, sir, as all such activities are subject to a little service charge as they often result in us having to get in a cleaner. Nothing personal, you understand. Just something to bear in mind for the future, sir.

Exit **Brighella**.

Scene Eight

Florindo   So you came to Venice too?

Beatrice   I arrived this morning.

Florindo   But I arrived this morning too. How did we miss each other?

Beatrice   Fate has enjoyed tormenting us a little.

Florindo   But, Beatrice, is Federigo really dead?

Beatrice   You know he is. He died instantly.

Florindo   But I was told he was alive and well and here in Venice.

Beatrice   My dearest Florindo. It was me. I followed you using his name and clothing.

Florindo   Yes, yes, I know about the disguise from the letter your steward sent you.

Beatrice   From the letter my steward sent me?

Florindo   My servant gave it to me by mistake.

Beatrice   And you opened it?

Florindo   I had to. It had your name on it.

Beatrice   Exactly.

Florindo   Beatrice, the whole of Turin was buzzing with your flight. How can you go back there now.

Beatrice   Quite easily, as your 'wife'.

Florindo   But, sweetheart, I can never go back there. I am wanted for murder.

Beatrice   I've collected sufficient funds from Federigo's business ventures here in Venice to pay off whatever fine they throw at you. (You'd not believe what you can make out of sun-dried tomatoes.) Oh Florindo. I think everything is going to be all right, believe me. Where are those blessed servants?

Florindo   Look, here's one of them now.

Beatrice   Looking guilty if you ask me.

Scene Nine

Truffaldino *is frogmarched in between* **Brighella** *and the* **First Waiter**.

Florindo   Come on, here, there's nothing to be scared of.

Beatrice   We're not going to harm you.

Truffaldino (*aside*)   A likely story, I'm still recovering from the last lot.

Brighella   Well, that's one found. We'll soon have the other one.

Florindo   Excellent. We must have both blaggards together.

Brighella (*to* **First Waiter**)   You do know what he looks like, don't you?

First Waiter   I haven't a monkey's. He's the only one I've seen.

Brighella   Someone must have seen him.

Exit **Brighella**.

First Waiter   Listen, if he'd so much as put his nose round the door I'd've clocked him.

Exit **First Waiter**.

Florindo   Right. Now you can explain how this picture got in this pocket and how this book was miraculously switched around. And why you and the other rascal plotted to drive us into despair.

Truffaldino (*to* **Florindo**)   Please. I can explain everything. May I just have a moment. It is all that will be needed.

He draws **Florindo** *aside.*

I have to point out none of this is my fault, sir. It's all down to that Pasqual, the lady's servant, sir. He twuddled all the stuff up, and put it back without telling me anything about it. And then he begged me and prayed and pleaded for me, sir, to take the blame on myself on account of his deep family troubles, sir, and since I am the sweetest and kind-hearted soul, who'd have himself hung, drawn and quartered rather than see another man in trouble, sir, I have indeed kept you from the truth. Had I known the picture was of you and you'd be caused such intolerable distress I would immediately have had myself flogged. And that's the God's honest truth, sir.

Beatrice   What on earth's going on?

Florindo   So the man who asked you to collect the letter from the post office was Pasqual?

Truffaldino   Yes, the very man, sir.

Florindo   Why didn't you tell me this. You knew how anxious I was to find this Pasqual.

Truffaldino   He begged me on his very life, sir, not to give him away.

Florindo   But am I not your master?

Truffaldino   But I promised poor Pasqual, sir. To protect him from a hiding.

Florindo   I've got a good mind to give you both a good hiding.

Beatrice   What's going on?

Florindo   The fool was explaining that –

Truffaldino   For the love of God above, please don't give poor Pasqual away. Say it was me, sir, beat me if you like, sir, but please save poor Pasqual from a pasting.

Florindo   You're very loyal, aren't you.

Truffaldino   I love him like a brother. Now let me go to the lady and take the blame, sir, no doubt she'll scold me as is her right, but you'll see I'll take it as a man of honour.

Florindo   What a loyal and upright fellow you've turned out to be.

Truffaldino (*taking* **Beatrice** *to one side*)   Sorry, madam.

Beatrice   You were over there a very long time.

Truffaldino   You see, the gentleman has a servant, a one Pasqual, ma'am. And a more dim-witted nonce you have never encountered. Having mixed all of his accoutrements up, he was sure to be expelled from service only to end up starving with him and his five children on the side of the road. And so, to get him out of this tight spot, I, quick as a flash, conjured the story of the book, the dead master who hit his head and was drowned and whatnot, in a desperate effort to save the man from penury, or worse. And thus I was allowing Mr Florindo to believe I was to blame.

Beatrice   But why take the blame if you don't have to?

Truffaldino   To save Pasqual, ma'am.

Florindo   You're taking your time, aren't you.

Truffaldino   Ma'am, please, I beg you, please don't let the man get into trouble.

Beatrice   Which man?

Truffaldino   Pasqual, ma'am.

Beatrice   You and this Pasqual are a right pair of rascals.

Truffaldino   But we share a common humanity, ma'am.

Florindo   For God's sake, Beatrice, let's put an end to this matter before it drags on into the new millennium, why don't we just forget about this as an 'expression of our current good fortune'.

Beatrice   But surely, your servant . . .

Truffaldino   Don't mention Pasqual.

Beatrice   You're right, but I ought to settle everything with Mr Parsimoni right away. Will you come with me?

Florindo   Of course, but I have an appointment here with my banker. Go on ahead and I'll join you presently.

Beatrice   I'll wait for you at Pantaloon's, and please, darling, don't be long.

Florindo   Wait a minute. I don't even know where he lives.

Truffaldino   Don't worry, I'll show you.

Beatrice   Very well, I'll just go and sort myself out then.

Truffaldino   Excellent. Don't worry, I'll be with you anon.

Beatrice   Oh Florindo. What torture I've been through because of you.

Exit **Beatrice**.

Scene Ten

Florindo   And mine was no less severe, my angel.

Truffaldino   Sir, I've realised without Pasqual Miss Beatrice has no one to help her get ready. Perhaps it's best to allow me to be at her service, sir?

Florindo   Yes, of course, an excellent observation, but only if she is served with exemplary diligence.

Truffaldino   Oh yes indeed, sir. She'll get double attention. A masterpiece of timing. The sheer effrontery, the pirouettes of logic, the fine balance of nuance. They are cheering in the gallery. This is the crowning and most astonishing of all Truffaldino's bravura performances. Can the man do anything wrong?

Florindo   How many strange things can happen in one day. Tears, anguish, sheer despair and yet in the end such resolution and incalcuable joy. When we move from pleasure to pain we miss our former state so keenly, but when our fortunes move the other way round, one feels as if there was never an unhappy moment in one's entire life.

Beatrice   I'm back. That was quick, wasn't it?

Florindo   I thought you were going to change those damn clothes?

Beatrice   I think they rather suit me.

Florindo   Please, darling, pop yourself into a blouse and bodice. You shouldn't hide your figure from me for a moment longer.

Beatrice   Nonsense, I'll wait for you at Pantaloon's, get Truffy to bring you there as soon as poss.

Florindo   Don't worry. If this banker doesn't show up soon, I'll just come along anyway.

Beatrice   Good, if you really love me you'll not waste a second.

Truffaldino   So you wish me to stay here with Mr Florindo?

Beatrice   Yes, show him over to Pantaloon's.

Truffaldino   What a good idea seeing as Pasqual is not here.

Beatrice   Do whatever he bids you to, I love him more than I love myself.

Beatrice *exits*.

Scene Eleven

Truffaldino   I can't believe he'd run off like that, just when his mistress needed to be dressed.

Florindo   I'm sorry?

Truffaldino   Pasqual. I swear I love his funny scrunched-up face and pity his terrible bad luck, but what a lazy little sod he's turned out to be. Where as I pride myself, sir, on doing the work of two men.

Florindo   Well, come and help me dress, will you. Sod the bloody banker.

Truffaldino   And then we'll nip over to Pantaloon's?

Florindo   Yes. What about it?

Truffaldino   Well, I hope it's not too much to ask, sir, but I hoped to ask you a favour.

Florindo   A favour. After everything you've put me through!

Truffaldino   I must ask you to remember, sir, that any trouble was Pasqual's doing not mine.

Florindo   But where is this blessed Pasqual? What is he? Invisible?

Truffaldino   He'll show up, the ungracious cad, and I'll put paid to him. But about this favour, sir.

Florindo   What is it?

Truffaldino   I am in love, sir.

Florindo   You?

Truffaldino   With a girl, sir, and she's a servant of Mr Parsimoni, sir.

Florindo   What on earth has any of this to do with me?

Truffaldino   I just hoped you could, put a word in, sir.

Florindo   Well, the girl mightn't even like you.

Truffaldino   Oh she wants me, sir, no mistake. All I ask is a kind word, sir. It'd make all the difference.

Florindo   But how could you afford a wife?

Truffaldino   Don't worry about that, sir, I'm very versatile. I'll get some advice from Pasqual.

Florindo   If I was you I'd ask someone with a little more sense.

Exit **Florindo**.

Truffaldino   Well, if I don't start having a bit of sense now, I think I never will.

Exit **Truffaldino** *(walking into a door)*.

Scene Twelve

A room in **Pantaloon**'s *house*.

Pantaloon   Come, dear Clarice, let bygones be bygones. You can see Silvio has repented and is begging for forgiveness. Admittedly the poor lad behaved a bit badly, et cetera, but it was all out of love. If I can forgive him for his little indiscretions, I'm sure you can, sweetpea.

Silvio   If what you have suffered, Clarice, is the tiniest measure of the torment I have felt, you'll know how the fear of losing you drove me to such mad despair. I love you more than life itself. Surely, heaven demands that we be happy. Please don't let revenge darken what should be the brightest day of our lives.

Dr Lombardi   I beseech you, my dear, dear daughter-in-law, try to understand the poor child. He was on the very brink of lunacy.

Smeraldina   Come on, miss, there's nothing to gain by moping round. All men are bastards to some degree or other. But you'll have to have one one day, so if you're forced to take your medicine, I'd get it over with.

Pantaloon   You see. Smeraldina likens marriage to medicine. Not poison, dear. (*Aside*.) We have to try and cheer her up.

Dr Lomabardi   Certainly. Marriage is a confection, a sherbet fountain, a bag of bonbons.

Silvio   Clarice, not a word from your sweet lips. I know I am a wretch but at least punish me with words. This silence is too much for me. Look, I'm at your feet, please have mercy on me.

Clarice (*to* **Silvio**)   Oh Silvio.

Pantaloon   Did you hear? A sigh. A very good sign.

Dr Lombardi (*to* **Silvio**)   Go on. Follow it up.

Smeraldina   They reckon a sigh is like lightning, there's bound to be rain sooner or later.

Silvio   If my blood could wash that wicked stain of cruelty from you, believe me, I would cut open these veins. But since it can't, let these tears wash away my mistakes.

Clarice *sighs again.*

Pantaloon   Bravo!

Dr Lombardi   Excellent. Excellent.

Pantaloon (*takes* **Silvio**'s *hand*)   Up with you. (*Takes* **Clarice**'s.) You too. Now take each other's hands and make peace. We'll have no more tears, only love and laughter and happiness, let heaven bless you both.

They hold hands.

Dr Lombardi   That's more like it.

Smeraldina   They've done it. They've done it.

Silvio (*holding her hand*)   My darling. I beg you.

Clarice   You ungrateful wretch.

Silvio   My darling.

Clarice   You uncircumcised dog.

Silvio   My sugarplum.

Clarice   You rat. You canker.

Silvio   My sweet angel.

Clarice   Ah! (*Sighs.*)

Pantaloon   Going, going . . .

Silvio   Forgive me. For the love of heaven.

Pantaloon   Gone.

Clarice   I forgive you.

Dr Lombardi   Thank the Lord that's over.

Smeraldina   The patient is prepared, give her her medicine.

Scene Thirteen

Enter **Brighella**.

Brighella   Ah, Mr Pantaloon, sir, hope I haven't come at a bad time.

Pantaloon   Quite the reverse, my good friend. It was you, was it not, who told me all those fine tales and assured me that this was Mr Federigo, did you not?

Brighella   My dear sir, who would not have been mistaken. Especially with young women these days.

Pantaloon   Whatever, whatever, what's done is done. Let us ask, instead, what is new?

Brighella   Well, the good Lady Beatrice is here to pay her respects, sir.

Pantaloon   Show her in. Show her in.

Clarice   Poor, poor Lady Beatrice. I am so delighted her troubles are over.

Pantaloon   You were sorry for her?

Clarice   Of course.

Silvio   But what about me?

Scene Fourteen

Enter **Beatrice**.

Beatrice   I have come to beg your forgiveness and implore you all to pardon the terrible confusion I have caused.

Clarice   Not another word, my friend. (*Embraces her.*)

Silvio   Hang on a minute.

Beatrice   What's wrong with her embracing another woman?

Silvio (*aside*)   It's the clothes.

Pantaloon   Well, I must say for such a young woman you certainly don't lack any get-up-and-go, do you?

Dr Lombardi   You've got rather too much, if you ask me.

Beatrice   Love can make us do extraordinary things.

Pantaloon   And you have found your young gentleman?

Beatrice   Yes, it seems that the heavens are smiling on us.

Dr Lombardi   I think you've gained yourself quite a reputation, young lady.

Beatrice   My reputation is no business of yours, sir.

Silvio   Father, please leave everyone to their own business and stop moralising. All I want now is that everyone in the world be as happy as I am. If they want to get married, let them all get married, for God's sake.

Smeraldina (*to* **Silvio**)   Well, infact, I'd like to get married, actually.

Silvio   Who the devil to?

Smeraldina   Anyone really.

Silvio   Well, go on then. Find somebody. I'll be here for you.

Clarice   Here for what?

Silvio   A dowry.

Clarice   A dowry!

Silvio (*aside*)   Charming, I see she's not going to give anyone else a nibble of her cake.

Scene Fifteen

Truffaldino   Hello there. Respects to the company.

Beatrice (*to* **Truffaldino**)   Where is Mr Florindo?

Truffaldino   He's awaiting downstairs for permission to come in.

Pantaloon   Is that your young gentleman?

Beatrice   Indeed. The man I will marry.

Pantaloon   I'd be delighted to be aquainted.

Beatrice   Show him in.

Truffaldino (*to* **Smeraldina**)   Hello again.

Smeraldina (*to* **Truffaldino**)   Hello there.

Truffaldino (*to* **Smeraldina**)   Let's keep this till later, eh?

Smeraldina   What for?

Truffaldino   Nothing. Just you be patient.

Smeraldina (*to* **Truffaldino**)   Patient! Hang on a minute, (*To* **Clarice**.) Madam. May I ask of you a little favour?

Truffaldino *goes out.*

Clarice   What on earth is it now?

Smeraldina (*to* **Clarice**)   Mr Beatrice's servant has proposed to me and I thought maybe you could have a quiet little word with his mistress and get her to give it the OK and I'd be made for life, Miss.

Clarice   Oh, all right, if I get the chance.

Pantaloon   What's going on here?

Clarice   Nothing, sir. Women's business.

Silvio (*aside to* **Clarice**)   Go on, let me in on it.

Clarice (*to* **Silvio**)   Buzz off. It's a secret.

Enter **Florindo** *with* **Truffaldino**.

Florindo   Ladies and gentlemen. Your most humble servant. Are you the master of this house, sir?

Pantaloon   Yours to command.

Florindo   No, allow me the honour, sir. I present myself at Beatrice's instigation. I am sure you are acquainted with our various travails.

Pantaloon   But I have to say, I am delighted it's all worked out in the end.

Silvio   Do you remember me, sir?

Florindo   Indeed I do. You provoked me to a duel.

Silvio   Well, I got my come-uppance. This is the opponent (**Beatrice**) who disarmed me and could have easily taken my life.

Beatrice   But gave it you instead.

Silvio   True.

Clarice   Only because I pleaded for you.

Pantaloon   All's well that ends well, eh.

Truffaldino (*to* **Florindo**)   Mr Florindo, sir. Don't forget that word, I mentioned.

Florindo   What word?

Truffaldino   The word, sir. What you promised.

Florindo   I don't remember promising you anything.

Truffaldino   But, sir, to ask Mr Pantaloon for the girl.

Florindo   Oh, all right then. Mr Pantaloon, I really shouldn't be troubling you right now with this . . .

Pantaloon   Please, go right ahead.

Florindo   My servant wishes to marry your maid. Any objections?

Smeraldina (*aside*)   Bloody hell, another one! It's my lucky day!

Pantaloon   Can't see why not. If he's decent and honest man. What do you say?

Smeraldina   Well, it depends on what he looks like, doesn't it. A girl in my position has to be choosy.

Florindo   For the short time I've known him he has been a beacon of trustworthiness and intelligence.

Clarice   Mr Florindo, I'm afraid you have anticipated me in something I was going to do. You see, I was about to speak for my maid and ask Miss Beatrice if Smeraldina could have permission to marry his servant.

Florindo   Well, in that case I must immediately withdraw my request and leave it up to the good lady in question.

Clarice   But I could never put my interests above yours, sir.

Florindo   Consider the matter closed. I refuse to let him marry her.

Clarice   Well, rather than slight you, sir, neither man shall have her.

Truffaldino   Fantastic. Falling over themselves to do me out of a wife.

Smeraldina   One minute I've got two. The next minute I've got bugger-all.

Pantaloon   For God's sake, if the poor lass wants a husband, at least let her have one or the other.

Truffaldino   Excuse me. If I could be so bold. Mr Florindo, have you or have you not asked that Smeraldina marry your servant?

Florindo   You heard me ask yourself. Did you not?

Truffaldino   And Miss Clarice, were you or were you not intending Smeraldina to marry Miss Beatrice's manservant?

Clarice   That's what I intended.

Truffaldino   In that case give me your hand.

Pantaloon   Hang on a minute.

Truffaldino   You see, I am servant to both Florindo and Miss Beatrice.

Florindo   I beg your pardon.

Beatrice   What exactly are you saying?

Truffaldino   Everybody stay calm. Mr Florindo, sir. Who asked you to ask Mr Pantaloon for Smeraldina?

Florindo   You.

Truffaldino   And Miss Clarice, who was it you thought Smeraldina wanted to marry?

Clarice   Well, you.

Truffaldino   Therefore, ipto fatso, Smeraldina is mine.

Florindo   But Beatrice, where is your servant?

Beatrice   Here. Truffaldino.

Florindo   Truffaldino is my servant.

Beatrice   But isn't your servant Pasqual?

Florindo   No, Pasqual is your servant.

Beatrice   What?

Florindo   You deceitful little arse.

Truffaldino   But, sir, don't you see, this is a miracle of time management, sir, a thing to be applauded not condemned. There was nothing except a good honest day's graft and had I not fell in love, sir, you would never have known at all. It's all right for you running round with your banker's bonds and your fancy costumes. We've got to fit our love life in between forty years' hard labour. Look, I didn't mean any harm. I've served you both and give or take a few complications when you might have killed yourself and that, it's worked out pretty well, I mean everybody's happy, aren't they.
All I ask now is :
you forgive the faults of my performance what I didn't get right,
so I can serve Smeraldina, and bid you all good night.

The Good Hope

Adaptor's Note

The Good Hope is one of those few plays that actually changed things. Heijermans wrote with such campaigning zeal about the deceit and corruption which allowed a fishing ship to go out in an unfit state that nine years later the Dutch actually passed an act that outlawed the practices which caused the play's central tragedy. So my problem was how to make a play that had so efficiently served its purpose speak with a freshness and urgency when everything appears to have changed.

The play is seemingly old-fashioned in its fiercely felt emotion and its unstinting quarry of injustice. But I quickly realised the key to understanding the work was to see how much Heijermans steers the play away from the melodrama of its time. A typical act of restraint is the central storm scene which is really just a conversation by a hearth but which vividly allows us to feel the enormity of what is happening to the men offstage. Heijermans creates a storm in the audience's mind rather than pursuing the spectacle that characterised popular theatre at the turn of the century. (Drury Lane, for instance, was famous for its earthquakes and shipwrecks at precisely this point.)

However, unlike other theatrical 'Realists' he resolutely chose to focus attention on the working classes. (Ibsen's *The Pillars of the Community* – almost identical in theme – opens in the shipowner's drawing room, for instance, whereas almost all of Heijermans' original play takes place in a fisherwoman's hovel.) *The Good Hope* is powerful as a piece of agitprop in direct proportion to its complexity at examining complicity and consensus. Heijermans' examination of the emotional and psychological economies at work in the community is just as acute as his sketches of the political and fiscal realities that underpin them. And it seems to me in this way *The Good Hope* is very much a precursor of Brecht's *Mother Courage* – another character who sends her sons to their doom but inspires pity as much as opprobrium.

So in the 'European Theatre' the play has gained an iconic status as a piece about resistance and the maintenance of dignity amidst the injustices of fate. In Truffaut's *The Last Metro*, as Catherine Deneuve nightly descends the cellar steps of her theatre to bring sustenance to her Jewish husband as he hides from the Nazis beneath the stage, it is no accident that she passes a poster for 'La Bonne Esperance'.

However, even knowing its history, I was still daunted about finding a contemporary relevance for a piece largely about outdated shipping laws in a small Dutch village at the turn of the last century. But within days of first reading the play a train was derailed at Hatfield and the emergent story of our railways seemed a sad, poetic repetition of the events of the play. Economic expediency had again lead directly to people's deaths. Then, as I embarked on the first draft, hospital workers in Dudley, striking over their concerns at PFI (Private Finance Initiative) in the Health Service, were writing to me for support. And it swiftly became clear that I did not have to worry about a contemporary resonance. In the 100 years since it was first written we are no further forward in solving the manifest problems that underlie the tragedy of *The Good Hope*. The issues about commerce and the common good, responsibility for our collective safety, and the public and private ownership of the fruits of our labour and the means by which we produce them are as contentious as ever.

But as much as the play is a powerful piece of political writing, throwing up many more questions than it answers, it is also a play about loss. The catastrophe of *The Good Hope* is always placed in the context of common mortality. Death, in the play, is inevitable and everyday but nevertheless this is a play of mourning. As we started rehearsals the World Trade Centre was destroyed and, as I am writing this, war-like reprisal seems imminent. I think everyone involved in the production feels the subject of mourning is about to gain an unfortunate pertinence, although none of us know exactly how.

The only thing for certain seems that the incremental progress people like Heijermans have gained in the past is not something we can rely upon for the future. The checks to tragedy, inequality or injustice are as fragile as ever and they must be vigilantly kept and fought for. I believe the strength of Heijermans' play is in its probing at the supposed consolations of compromise and spelling out the cost of the consensus politics the Makepeace character so eloquently elaborates. These problems are no less urgent because they are knotty. Although he is unequivocal about tracing the mechanisms of disaster he seems uneasy about 'working out' everything in the drama. His method is not didacticism, melodrama or agitprop. There is a cyclical pattern in the play which, although a concession to the strength of community to rejuvenate, is also a call to our conscience that here is a cycle as destructive as it is cohesive.

But even as a play of mourning it is still full of vibrancy, humour and life, although not of the sentimental kind. It is precisely the sentimental calls to community or to trite ideology to which the play raises its eyebrow. It is our everyday culpability that Heijermans is concerned most about. He sees it is in the small negotiations of common experience that our larger fate is sealed. It is in these small matters of course and conscience that he asks us to be most vigilant.

Lee Hall
September 2001

The Good Hope was first performed at the Cottesloe Theatre, Royal National Theatre, London, on 2 November 2001. The cast was as follows:

Kitty Fitzgerald, a fisherman's widow	Frances de la Tour
James, her son	Steve Nicolson
Ben, her younger son	Iain Robertson
Jo, her niece	Diane Beck
William, her older brother	John Normington
Christopher Makepeace, a shipowner	Tom Georgeson
Clementine, his daughter	Charlotte Emmerson
Arthur, his bookkeeper	Howard Ward
Simon, the drunken shipwright	John Tams
Mary, his daughter	Emma Bird
Michael, her fiancé	William Macbain
Dan, an old seaman	Trevor Ray
Susan, a fishwife	Linda Thompson
Sarah, a fisherman's widow	Sheila Reid
Harry, the barman of the Compass	Robert Oates
First Copper	Edward Clayton
Second Copper	Kenneth Anderson
Jed & **Trudger**, the village musicians	Alan Dunn & Graeme Taylor
Musicians	Christine Coe & Keith Thompson

Director Bill Bryden
Designer Hayden Griffin
Lighting Designer Rory Dempster
Music and lyrics John Tams
Sound Designer Ed Clarke

Act One

Whitby. 1900. A late blaze of summer. Rows of masts and sails blow
in the gentle wind. The whole stage seems to move as if the audience
were at sea, the winds whip up and blow harder, so the sails flap over
one another. Through the forest of boats and the flap of canvas we
glimpse a panorama of a thriving fishing port. All as if from the
photographs of Frank Meadow Sutcliffe. The bustling quay fringed
with stout Victorian rows of pubs, the Fisherman's Rest and the
Compass, and shops, Braithwaite's General Store; and perched above it
all the office of Makepeace Shipping. The stern line of buildings all
intently focused on the quay, give way to the gentle incline of back
gardens, which lead to the fishermen's cottages which ascend terrace
after terrace up the steep banks of the town. At the very foot of the quay
is a sandy beach where a few old rowing boats lie upturned, derelict
among the old nets and detritus of the town. And leading offstage is the
stone pier festooned with lobster nets and broken fish barrels. At every
point in the play we are aware of the proximity of the sea. It is always
lapping up to the action.

For the moment we catch only the vaguest glimpse of this panorama and
the almost-dance to the hornpipe of the late summer breeze. Suddenly,
they seem to have been blown together and somehow form an iris of a
camera lens. The population of the town gather, facing the audience, as
if posing for a group photograph. They sing.

> I dreamed a dream the other night
> Lowlands – Lowlands away, my John,
> I dreamed a dream the other night
> Lowlands away
>
> I dreamed I saw my own true love
> Lowlands – Lowlands away my John
> Lowlands
>   Away
>
> I dreamed I saw my own true love
> Lowlands away.

And as the song ends and there is a blinding flash, the company freezes, as if a camera has caught them.

The quayside.

As we get used to the light after the blinding flash, the people seem to disappear, fading away into history. On the stage, **Clementine**, *the shipowner's daughter of a patronising but philanthropic bent, is adjusting an enormous camera on a tripod.* **William**, *a once statuesque sea dog, now bent with old age, and his decrepit friend,* **Dan**, *a sickly curmudgeon, are posing for the camera in a most unnatural manner.*

Clementine *adjusts the old men's poses and looks through the lens. A puff of smoke goes up as she takes a picture just as the old boys decide to adjust their position.* **Clementine** *is less than pleased.*

Clementine   Bugger.

She changes a plate, disgruntledly.

Can't you stand still?

William   I was standing still.

Clementine   You moved your leg.

William   What d'ya expect, it's gone to sleep.

Clementine   Now you've moved completely!

William   Well, it were a bloody ridiculous position int' first place.

Clementine   It is not a ridiculous position. It's picturesque.

William   I'd never stand like that.

Clementine   You just did.

William   Aye, cos I were put. I thought this were supposed to be 'real life'.

Dan *has steadfastly maintained his ridiculous pose. Still frozen, he moves his eyes to catch* **Clemetine**'s *attention.*

Dan   Can I go yet?

Clementine   Stay where you are.

She arranges **William**.

Just look over your shoulder – like so.

Dan   I'll be late for tea, Miss.

Clementine   Just be quiet.

Clementine *rearranges their poses.*

Dan   Think I'm going to faint, Miss. You better hurry up or there'll be nowt left.

Clementine   Right now, keep quite still.

Dan   Why's he pulling that stupid face?

William   What d'ya mean a stupid face?

Clementine   Be quiet, the pair of you.

Dan   I don't see the point in this posing around.

Clementine   I'm just trying to capture a moment of truth.

Dan   Look, truth is it's teatime.

Clementine   You can't just photograph 'real life' willy nilly. Real life can be rather boring.

The two fishermen look at one another. It's the most natural pose they've made so far.

Don't move. That's perfect.

She fiddles with the camera.

Dan   But Matron'll kill us if we're late. You don't know what it's like down there.

Clementine   Well, at least somebody's got you two in check. Anyway, if I was in your shoes I'd thank God I was provided for in my old age.

Dan   I thank nobody, God included. I've served me time on deep water. I was a deckie when I was twelve years of age. I shouldn't have to put up with the bloody Matron. If I was a bit taller I'd bite the bugger's nose off.

Clementine   You're not in the 'Sailor's Rest' now, Daniel.

Dan   More's the pity. They'll've closed the bugger down at this rate. She threw me out last week. Just cos I were sick ont' floor. Tweren't my fault. Banned for three days. Had to sleep on the quay – in my condition. Wish I'd been finished by sharks years ago.

William   What shark's gonna touch you?

Clementine *laughs.*

Dan   You might laugh – I saw George Braithwaite bit clean in half and he were nowt but bag o' bones.

Clementine   A shark? In the North Sea?

Dan   *Six* of the buggers. Sea boiled beetroot.

Clementine   I wish I'd seen something really shocking like that. Did he scream?

Dan   No, just took his cap off and waved at Skipper.

William   Of course he screamed. You'd scream with a shark's set in your arse.

The sound of music starts to drift on to the stage – 'Clara's Waltz' from two itinerant musicians.

Clementine   The light's gone. Forget it. We'll try again tomorrow.

William   Thank Christ for that, I'm stiff as a parson's elbow.

Then **Jed** *and* **Trudger**, *the itinerant musicians, emerge from over a bank.* **Jed** *leads* **Trudger**, *blind as a bat, in an eccentric progress.* **Trudger** *is a fully kitted one-man band,* **Jed** *plays the banjo.*

Dan   Look, bugger off. You know we've got nowt to gi' ye.

William   Aye, away with you. We've been doing 'real life'. You want to try it some time.

Clementine   Don't be cruel. Here.

Clementine *throws a penny at them. It misses the bag on* **Trudger***'s accordion and rolls away off the end of the quay and on to the beach.*

Dan   Charming. We've stood here for past half-hour and now she's throwing money at this lot.

Jed *immediately stops playing and climbs down on to the beach to find the penny. As he is tied to* **Trudger** *this causes havoc.* **Trudger** *exclaims as he is pulled about. Tangled chaos. They both fall on to the beach.*

The beach.

Dan   It's behind you.

More chaos.

William   Here.

They all struggle to find the penny.

Dan   Christ, you've buried it, you daft git.

Dan *and* **William***'s assistance only adds to the tangle. They are all scrabbling on the ground. The inadvertent music of the one-man band adding to the chaos.*

Dan (*to* **Clementine**)   You and your grand ideas of charity.

As the hopeless crew attempt to discover the penny a lone figure ambles along the beach with a few meagre scraps of driftwood. **Ben** *is in his late teens, frail with a sensitive demeanour. He looks at the chaotic scrabbling with wry amusement.*

Clementine   Look, it has to be somewhere.

Ben joins the group and whispers into **Clementine**'s *ear. He speaks with a pronounced stutter . . .*

Ben   M- m- maybes you should give 'em another one. I'm sure you can stretch to a p- p- penny.

Clementine   It was a ha'penny, actually.

Jed   A ha'penny!?

He considers giving up, but then thinks better of it.

Ben (*to* **Clementine**)   Christsake, just p- pretend you've f- found it.

Clementine *smiles at* **Ben**.

Clementine   Oh. Here it is.

She puts it in **Trudger**'s *bag.*

William   And count yourselves lucky.

Jed *and* **Trudger** *go off, noisily.*

Ben   Best not t- throw money about in future. They'll only drink it.

William   Hark at him. You'd best think about earning yerself a crust than worrying 'bout t' other folks' welfare.

Ben   D . . . d . . . don't start.

William   Oh, you've got a gob as wide as t' Humber when it suits – but it's tight as a skate's arse when work's mentioned. The big man, eh? Least I don't shit me pants every time I see a trawler.

Dan   Come on, get us teas.

Clementine   Ten o'clock sharp, tomorrow.

Dan   We can't, Miss Makepeace. We're scrubbing stones int' morning.

Clementine   What's this? Another ancient custom?

Dan   That's right. Called cleaning the steps of the Seaman's Mission.

Clementine   Well, it'll have to be the afternoon.

William   So be it. We'll be here. See you, Miss. Ta-ta, Shite Pants.

William *and* **Dan** *go off.*

Clementine   He's got a sophisticated sense of humour, your uncle.

She dismantles the camera. **Ben** *says nothing.*

See you've been beachcombing.

Ben *nods.*

Clementine   Find much?

Ben   N- not much, twere neap tide – what we need's a storm. I found this, though . . .

He gives **Clementine** *a heart-shaped stone.*

Weird, in't it? Turn it round. It's a heart.

Clementine   It's quite beautiful. You're not really scared to go to sea, are you? Everybody does it.

Ben   Aye, but not everybody comes back.

Ben *helps* **Clementine** *with the camera and tripod.*

Clementine   So you are scared.

Ben   No. I just have a preference for d- d- dry land.

Clementine   How old are you?

Ben   Old enough.

Clementine   Really. I thought a strong lad like you'd be off in the Navy or something.

Ben   I were r- rejected.

Clementine   Why's that then?

Ben   I . . I . . . I . . . I don't know, Miss . . .

Clementine   Maybe they took you for a coward. You're not scared of me, by any chance, are you?

Ben   I'm not scared of anything on dry land. I'd stick one in anybody if I had to.

Clementine   Are you sure about that?

Ben   No offence, Miss.

Clementine *sits on one of the upturned boats,* **Ben** *sits down next to her.*

Clementine   Don't worry. I don't scare that easily. Is your brother still in jail?

Ben   What's it to y- you?

Clementine   I expect you're ashamed of him. Getting done for insubordination. A bit too red-blooded for your liking?

Ben   W . . . what do you mean by that?

Clementine   Or maybe there's more to you than meets the eye?

She looks at him closely.

No, you're not the type to take advantage, are you?

Ben *stumbles over his answer.*

Ben   Y- you never know.

Clementine *is lying against the boat. She looks at* **Ben**. **Ben** *hesitates. She enjoys his discomfort.*

Clementine   Prove it?

Ben *might be about to make a move, when . . .*

Backyard of house.

There is a shout from inside the house (offstage).

Kitty (*off*)   Benjamin! Benjamin!

A chicken flies out of the door and into the yard.

What the hell's going on here?

Kitty, *a stately but harried fisherwoman in her fifties, bursts through the door into the back garden of her cottage. The weight of her experience has done nothing to diminish her vigour. She immediately begins to give chase to the chicken.*

Kitty   Benjamin!!

Ben *looks up to the yard where* **Kitty** *is running around.*

Ben   S . . . s . . . shit.

Ben *looks at* **Clementine** *apologetically, scrambles up the bank and climbs over the fence to* **Kitty**.

Kitty   How the hell did they get out?

They both chase chickens.

Ben   It's not end of w- w- world, Mam.

Kitty   It was in the bloody stewpot, you daft bloater. The sooner I'm shot of you the better.

She plonks a chicken into his hands.

Ben   H- h- honest, Mam . . . I . . .

Suddenly, **Jo**'*s head appears from a trench in the garden.* **Jo** *is an unsentimental but intensely warm young woman in her twenties. She has a wit and vital directness that give her an edge of sexual danger. She is covered from head to toe in mud.*

Jo   For Christsakes, Kitty. I let them out myself.

Kitty   What the hell did you do that for?

Jo   I couldn't stand the bloody clamour of them cooped up all day.

Kitty   So you'd sooner they were plodging int' stew.

Jo   Listen, I'm t' one stuck down here digging the spuds out while you two are swanning . . .

Kitty   I've been working all morning.

Jo   What about Captain Cook, then?

Ben   I've b- been collecting driftwood.

Jo   I'll give you driftwood straight up your arse. Scared of the spuds, 'nall, are you?

Ben   Oh, s . . . s . . . shut up.

Jo   Look at this one. Aaaaagghghg!!??

She throws a potato at **Ben** *as if it were some terrifying beast. She points to it on the ground.*

(*Mock horror.*) Look out! Look out. It's c- c- c- coming for you. Oh my God, you're surrounded by vegetables.

Ben   B- b- b- GET LOST, will yous.

Ben *storms off.* **Jo** *and* **Kitty** *laugh, then they spot* **Clementine** *looking over the fence.*

Kitty   Oh, good afternoon, Miss.

Clementine   He's a little sensitive.

Kitty   He's a little layabout. Can I help you, Miss?

Clementine   He dropped this.

Clementine *gives her the heart-shaped stone.*

Jo   He wants it chucking at him. I've been up since the crack of dawn and he's been pissing about collecting pebbles. Look at this lot, they're rotten.

Kitty   It's all the bloody rain. This is the first fine day we've had all week. Oh, the lot of the poor, Miss. God knows how we're going to get through winter if it keeps going like this.

Jo   Here we go – the Lamentations! Look on the bright side for once in your life. Least James'll be back.

Kitty   What good's that gonna do?

Jo   You might just break into a smile for five minutes. Look, I caught a rabbit.

Jo *brings a rabbit from her trench.*

Clementine   Were you poaching?

Jo   Poaching? No, it had a taste for manky spuds – so I brayed it with t' spade. Worth a tanner, I reckon.

Clementine   I say, well aimed. Anyway, tell Ben I'll be on the quay in the morning. I best be going.

She turns to go but at the door is **Mr Makepeace**, *the shipowner. He has the charm and confidence that affluence makes easy, but there is a rough edge which tells us it was hard won. He stands with a chicken in his hands.*

Makepeace   Afternoon. (*To* **Kitty**.) I think this might be yours.

Kitty   Oh my goodness, Mr Makepeace.

Makepeace (*to* **Clementine**)   I thought I might find you here. (*Of the chicken.*) It was in the front room.

The chicken shits on **Makepeace**'*s jacket.*

Kitty   I'm so sorry about the chicken, sir.

Kitty *fusses over him.*

Makepeace   Don't worry about that, Kit, a little muck never hurt anybody. Hello there.

Jo   Hello.

Kitty   You remember Jo, sir, my niece.

Jo   I won't . . . er . . . [shake your hand].

She shows her filthy hands in explanation.

Makepeace   Going somewhere posh, are you?

Jo   A tea dance int' Scarborough.

Makepeace   A proper cheeky piccaninny? (*To* **Clementine**.) Well, come on, sweetheart, take me picture. 'The Shipowner visits the Cottages.'

Clementine   Certainly not.

Makepeace   Oh go on. (*To* **Jo**.) Come over here. They'll think I was in darkest Africa.

Clementine   Shut up, Father. You don't know anything about photography.

Makepeace   Oh, that's very nice, in't it. You spend a fortune ont' camera and she won't even take your own picture.

Clementine   I don't find you an interesting subject, Father.

Makepeace   Two years at boarding school and she thinks she's Lady Muck. You'll end up like your mother.

Ben *comes in and stops dead when he sees* **Makepeace**.

Makepeace   Ah, little Benjamin – just the fella.

Ben   M- m- me, sir?

Makepeace   The one and only. How long have you been out o' work, son?

Ben   Nine month.

Kitty   You little sod. More than a year, sir.

Ben   N- n- no it's not . . .

Jo   What are you? Stupid as well as lily-livered.

Makepeace   All right, all right, children. Now then, Benji – what would you say to forty-seven?

Ben   Forty-seven, sir?

Makepeace The *Good Hope*.

Clementine The *Good Hope*?

Makepeace You keep out of this.

Clementine But . . .

Makepeace I've warned you. I'm in the middle of a business arrangement here. Now bugger off home.

Clementine Do you realise how vulgar you are, Father?

Makepeace Thank you, Clementine. I'll see you at home.

Makepeace *looks sternly at* **Clementine** *and she, reluctantly, leaves.*

Makepeace I've got a fleet of eight luggers on my mind. You didn't think I had time for compliments, did you? Anyway, what about it, son?

They all look at **Ben**.

Kitty Say something.

Ben I- I- I'd rather . . .

Kitty 'Rather'!

Makepeace Now, now, children. It's up to you. She was only out four times last year and made four thousand. She's just been int' dock, fully insured, Adams is skipper, we're looking for a deckie. Take it or leave it, son.

Ben I- I- I- I . . .

Jo For Christsake, get it out.

Ben I . . . don't know, sir.

Kitty You obstinate little shit. I should drag you on by the scruff of your neck.

Makepeace What's up, little man? You've got one trip behind you?

Ben   Just a day trip, sir. As cabin boy.

Jo (*with contempt*)   You don't understand. He don't like the sea, sir.

Makepeace   Do you think anyone likes it? I used to go with your grandfather when we were half your age – oh yes, I'd've rather been tied to me mammy's apron sooner than stood out with fists like clods of ice – I'd've rather been home wi' a nice warm plate of soup rather than biting the heads off mackerel. But that's not how things work, son. Is it? What would your father say?

Ben   My father drowned, sir. And my brother Joseph and my brother Henry, sir. I just c- can't, sir.

Makepeace   Fine. If that's how you want it. No one's trying to force you. Sorry, Kit. I sympathise, son. My dad didn't die in his bed neither. But if we were all as sentimental as you, we'd be living off seaweed and field mice.

Kitty   I could tan your hide for you.

Makepeace   Whoa, calm down, lass. Can't catch a herring with a pitchfork.

Jo   Give me a pitchfork and I'll sort the bugger out.

Makepeace   You'll get more from a trout if you tickle its tummy.

Kitty   What are you trying to say, anyway? That *I've* forgotten. How dare you even bring up their names. Have you any idea what I went through?

Kitty *breaks down.*

Jo   You see.

Makepeace   Come on, Kitty.

Kitty   Twelve year next month.

Makepeace   I know. It was September eighty-eight.

Kitty   He were only six. You can't even remember them.

Ben   It's not my f- f- fault.

Makepeace   Well, what are you getting yourself worked up for?

Ben   I just want a different t- trade.

Makepeace   What were you thinking of? You can't read or write.

Ben   I'll do anything, sir. I'll d- dig, plant things, s- s- salt down, anything. I'll be a b- bricklayer, a carpenter . . .

Jo   Or Lord Mayor. Or the bloody Chief Constable. You could crawl around at night arresting smugglers.

Ben   I- I don't care what you say. Did I come c- crying when the salt cracked me hand open . . .

Kitty   What makes you think you'd be any better off as a brickie. They're dropping off ladders left right and centre.

Makepeace   She's right. Do you think you'd be any safer down a mine? Or in a factory? Do you think you're going to be safe racing round in a train? Accidents happen. It's a fact of life, son. You might walk out of here and get run down by a pony and trap.

Kitty   We haven't got a choice, Ben. God knows what winter'll bring, potatoes are rotten already.

Makepeace   All over Yorkshire.

Ben   I- I- I just can't, sir.

Kitty   Well, get out.

Ben   P- p- please, Mam.

Kitty (*with real anger*)   Now!

Makepeace   Kitty . . .

Ben *looks at his mother, turns and leaves.*

Makepeace   I suppose that's a no, then.

Jo   I'll talk to him. It's a good job James isn't here. He'd murder the little sod.

Jo *goes out.*

Makepeace   James. Six months, wasn't it?

Kitty   That's right.

Makepeace   Insubordination?

Kitty   He's fiery b' nature, sir.

Makepeace   He's a fool.

Kitty   He was provoked, sir.

Makepeace   Nobody 'provokes' in the Navy. If there weren't discipline the officers'd be shark bait.

Kitty   But . . .

Makepeace   And she's got her eye on him, I take it.

Kitty   He's a good-looking lad.

Makepeace   He's from a handsome family, Kitty.

Kitty   He's a decent man, sir. Been to India twice. He's just proud. God knows what he'll do when he gets out. I'll have to put him up here. It's a waste, sir – a strong lad like him.

Makepeace   He's a Red Flagger, Kitty.

Kitty   But he's known the sea since . . .

Makepeace   Forget it, Kit. I can't take a bloody red on. All the same those lads from the Navy.

Kitty   But you don't understand . . .

Makepeace   Look, I'll not have anyone trying to steal me bloody boats off me. I worked my way up from nowt. You know what I put into this. What's wrong with that? I keep half of Whitby in a job. Am I unfair, Kitty? Tell me, am I unfair with anybody?

Kitty   No.

Makepeace *and* **Kitty** *look at each other. We sense there is a long, unrequited history there.*

Makepeace   Tell him to keep his gob shut and I'll send him out on the *Hope*.

Kitty   You're a good man, Christopher.

Makepeace   It's just business. He knows how it works.

Kitty   Will I tell him to go to the docks or your office?

Makepeace   Just tell him one word of socialism and he'll never work again. Understand?

Kitty   Yes, sir.

There is the sound of a trawler whistle. Suddenly, **Susan**, *an older woman full of hope and compassion, bursts through the back door of an adjacent cottage and runs into her garden.*

Susan   Kitty, d'ye hear? Great news. It's the *Anna*.

Susan *does not stop and runs from her garden down to the quay and off along the pier.* **Kitty** *and* **Makepeace** *immediately rush to catch sight of the boat returning.* **Kitty**'s *expectant look suddenly grows grim with trepidation.*

Makepeace   She's flying a black flag.

Kitty   A death on board.

Makepeace   Not another crewman. This is a blow. I best go down.

Kitty   I'll come with you.

Kitty *and* **Makepeace** *follow* **Susan** *down the bank with urgency. Other people run along the quay in the direction of the ship, and soon disappear offstage.*

The stage is bare, then centre stage a figure appears carrying a meagre bundle. **James**, **Kitty**'s *son, is in his early twenties, normally rugged, handsome and self-possessed. But when we look closer we see he*

*is filthy and haggard. There is a frailty under his pride and swagger
that tells us every movement is fought against great pain. He emerges
into the street which leads to* **Kitty**'s *garden. He is perplexed that no
one is around. He makes his way, with some effort, to the garden. As
no one is there he climbs over the fence and looks through the doorway to
the inside of the cottage.*

James (*shouting*)   Mam?

He comes out. He starts to walk down towards the quay. **Ben** *is
coming up the other way. He stops and stares in disbelief.*

James   I don't bite, you know.

Ben *runs up the bank and hugs him.*

Ben   J- James.

James   Where's Mam?

Ben   I d- d- don't know, she . . .

James   What's the matter with you?

Ben   N- nowt . . .

James   What do you mean nowt?

Ben   You look . . . pale.

James   What did ya expect. A suntan?

Ben   I hardly recognised you.

They sit in the garden.

James   Is there owt to drink?

Ben   I d- d- don't think so.

James   Well, go and bloody fetch summat.

Ben   I haven't got any money.

James   For Christsakes.

He throws **Ben** *some money.*

Ben   Where did you get that?

James   It's got bugger all to do with you. Just get uz summat to eat, will you.

He calls after **Ben**.

Benny. Is she all right? Me mam?

Ben *doesn't reply*.

James   And Jo? Is she angry?

Ben   W- w- what about?

James   Don't be a twat, Benny.

Ben   I'm just . . . I'm a bit surprised. I don't know.

James   Piss off out of it, will you.

Ben *slips out. We hear* **Jo** *singing*.

Jo
    If I had the wings of Noah's dove
    Jimmy where are you bound to
    I'd fly back home to the one I love
    Across the Western Ocean

She appears, carrying the dead rabbit. She sees **James** *and drops it. She flies over to him and kisses him – then bursts into tears.*

James   Stop it! Stop howling.

Jo   Jim. Jim.

James   Come on. Shush. Stop crying now.

Jo   I can't help it, Jim.

James   Get off. You'll smother uz. Just give uz a bit of space.

Jo *backs off.*

Jo   What happened to your beard?

James   Confiscated by Her Majesty. Apparently she took a liking to it. What do you reckon?

Jo You look great.

James I look like shit.

Jo No. Not to me, Jim.

James I'm *fucked*, Jo. Look at uz.

Jo No, James.

James I've been lying in me own shit for six months.

Jo *is crying.* **James** *gives her no comfort.*

James What did you expect?

Ben *comes back. He approaches* **James** *tentatively.*

Ben Some of Harry's gin.

Jo That moonshine!

Ben For him.

Jo Ben . . .

James Mind your own business, will you. Get a glass. Sod it.

He drinks the gin from the bottle.

That's better. What's the time?

Ben Half four.

Jo Please. Eat some bread, won't you?

Jo *starts to go inside,* **James** *stops her.*

James I don't want bread. Can't keep anything down.

He drinks some more gin and coughs.

Jo Please, James. That's enough, you can't take it.

James Enough! I haven't even started. (*He drinks more.*) There. (*And more.*) And another fathom. Yeah, that'll put a bit of colour in me cheeks. What's the matter? You never seen anyone drink before?

He drinks more. Coughs.

Where the hell did you get this?

He drinks some more. Burps.

Is there anything to eat?

Jo   Look. Caught it myself. It's not been dead an hour.

She shows him the rabbit.

James   It'll do for the morrow. Here, go and get some brawn or something.

James *throws* **Ben** *some money.*

Jo   What you doing? You can't go wasting that on cooked meat. I'll make you something . . .

James   Look, I've had nowt but gruel for six months, woman. If I want meat I'll have it. And get some cheese while you're on.

Ben *exits.* **James** *reaches for the bottle.*

Jo   Stop it, Jim. Stop it.

James *drinks too much. He coughs violently and retches.* **Jo** *takes the bottle off him. He spits out bile.*

Jo   Sit down, pet.

James   So who have you been going with since I've been inside then?

James *stares aggressively at* **Jo**. *She stares back through the insult.*

Jo   Who do you think? Uncle Willie and his mate, Dan.

James *stares at her angrily, then his face bursts into a smile.*

James   You daft hap'o'rth.

Jo *laughs.* **Kitty** *comes on from the quay and starts up the hill. She is obviously upset at the death. She relays the news with some urgency to* **Jo**.

Kitty   Jo. Jo. Terrible news. It's Susan's bloke, Stephen. He collapsed two days ago . . .

As **Kitty** *approaches the cottage she sees* **James** *and falls silent. They stare at one another.*

James   Mam.

Kitty   Jesus.

James   No. It's just me – James.

Kitty   Oh, you'll give me a bloody heart attack.

James   It'll take more than that to see *you* off.

James *goes to embrace her.*

Kitty   What the hell were you thinking of?

James   Oh, Jesus Christ, don't start, will you.

Kitty   Don't Jesus Christ me, young man.

James   I didn't come back to be got at.

Kitty   What did you expect, you ignorant sod?

James   What do you want me to do? Stand int' corner?

Kitty   The whole of t' harbour talking. I couldn't even go to t' quay without people . . .

James   Look, if anybody's got stuff to say they can say it to me face.

Kitty   So you can punch their lights out.

James   He deserved what he got, Mam.

Kitty   He was your skipper, bloody fool.

James   He was a bastard. I should have done him proper when I had the chance.

Kitty   Have you any idea what you've done to us, James?

She starts crying.

James   First they lock you up like a dog, then send you home to this!

He looks at **Kitty** *who is staring at him with immense anger and disappointment, tears streaming down her cheeks.*

Mam.

Jo   Kitty.

Kitty   Did you think once of your poor father?

James   Dad's dead, Mam.

Kitty   Have you any idea what he put up with?

James   Well, you should be glad that I won't let them kick me around.

Kitty   No. But you'll let them bang you up in jail.

James   If it happened again tomorrow, I'd still break his jaw for him.

Kitty   If *what* happened?

Jo   Sit yourself down, Jim, take it easy.

James   Take it easy? I've been sat on me arse for six months, for Christsake. So you just think I should just stand there like a lass while people slag off me family.

Jo   You've got thicker skin than that?

James   He called you a hoor.

Jo   A what!

James   You heard.

Jo   The bastard!!

Kitty   Language!

James   So I waited till graveyard watch and gave him 'good hiding. Sorted him out. 'Cept five minutes later I was straight down t' hatch. Six months in solitary. A ban for ten year.

Kitty   Why didn't you explain to the commanding officer? You can't go round calling people like that.

James   The commanding officer!?

Kitty   He could have sorted it out. There are rules.

James   And do you think they're made for us, Mam?

Kitty   If you'd've just gone to the captain for a quiet word.

James   Oh for Christsake, Mam. A quiet word! I was lucky they didn't have uz flogged. You don't think they locked uz up because I had a barney with the quartermaster? They locked uz up cos of *what I was reading*. Otherwise I'd still be swinging on me bunk in Bay of Biscay.

Kitty   What were you reading? Not that socialist rubbish?

James   It's not rubbish, Mam.

Kitty   I thought I brought you up decent.

James   Decent? So I could be treated like a slave. So I can spend my life licking some bloke's boots so he can toss his scraps at uz like a dog. Have you any idea what it's like in t' Navy?

Kitty   Of course I know what it's like.

James   I fought in a war, Mam. I stuck a knife in somebody's head. I stabbed a fella in the bloody heart. I killed people. I was a hero. Look at me now.

He takes off his shirt. We see in his face it is painful. His body is covered in scabs, sores and bruises. It is both shocking and disgusting. He stretches out his arms offering his wounds in some sort of supplication.

Look at me. That's what they does to uz heroes. A quiet word!?

Kitty *stares at him.*

Kitty   What have they done to you, son? I hardly recognise you.

James *stands in speechless anger.*

Kitty Your anger, son.

James I know – why should I be angry? Just because they took a bairn who couldn't read nor write and drilled the life out of him so he could barely stand up straight. Just so they made him cut other blokes into horse meat to save his own skin. Just to end up in a cell, lying in his own piss, sweating like a dying pig in his own shit and vomit . . .

Jo Stop it. Stop it. Don't say any more.

He takes some more drink.

Kitty James. James.

James Let uz finish. Hallucinating. Shitting himself. Drinking water from a slop can. Screaming for dear life. Getting beaten for t' privilege. Just because I read a few pamphlets about the dignity of man. No, why the hell should I be angry?

Silence. **Jo** *approaches him.*

Jo James.

Ben *stands looking at him.*

James Anyway, let's not make a meal of it.

He holds back tears.

Have you got a light?

He puts his shirt back on. He tends to **Kitty**.

Now, come on, Mam. Take the weight off your feet. I see the chickens got out again.

Pause.

With a bit of luck I'll be out again in no time. Two days. That'd be all. Two days out and I'll be right as rain.

A bell starts to ring from the direction of the quay.

What's going on?

Kitty   It's the *Anna*. Brought back Stephen Kemp. Died yesturday. He'd been bad for a while.

James   Stephen Kemp. What the hell was he doing out at his age?

Kitty   You can't live ont' wind.

James   We should go down, Mam.

Kitty   Yes, we should go down, son, we should.

James *takes* **Kitty**'s *hand and they head off down the bank and along the quay, followed by* **Jo**.

Along the pier, **Dan** *appears with a rackety fish-cart on which a boy is wrapped in a shroud. The women of the town have gathered and, with great dignity, they bear the body off.*

As the body is carried back to the town the piped lament, which follows the procession, turns into a hornpipe and the stage transforms into the outside of The Compass.

Act Two

Dusk. Early autumn.

The set is almost a cross-section, cutting a line from the back of a huge quayside pub, on to the street which leads to the quay, which falls down into the harbour lined with the masts and sails of a myriad vessels. We are outside in the courtyard of the Compass. It is decked with lights and streamers for a party, there is a serving hatch and a cellar door. This leads to a covered alley which runs the whole length of the pub, and leads on to the cobbled street, lined with gas lamps, which in turn gives way to the quayside studded with moorings. The sails flap gently in the September breeze. The feel is of summer's very last night.

The sun is setting and through the act, the light gradually fades to darkness. The courtyard is lit by the lamps decked out for **Kitty**'s *party, and the quay by gas lamps, lit by an old lighter meandering along the harbour.*

Harry, *the barman, comes through the courtyard and drops an empty keg into the cellar and shuts the wooden hatch.*

Jed *and* **Trudger** *are tuning up whilst* **Kitty** *and* **Jo** *are fussing at a trestle table that contains their spread of food. Perhaps tying a sign wishing* **Ben** *farewell. However,* **Kitty** *sees something's missing . . .*

Kitty   Harry. Where are the pickled onions? I ordered pickled onions.

Harry   No one said owt to me about pickled onions.

Kitty   You have to have pickled onions. You can't eat all this potted meat without a pickled onion.

Jo   Anyway, they were paid for.

Harry   Look, nobody's paid for any onions pickled or otherwise to my knowledge. If they have I'll knock it off t' reckoning.

Kitty   I don't want it knocked off, I want me pickled onions.

Harry   Tough, I haven't got any pickled onions. Look, have a pint on the house, Kitty, and calm down.

Kitty   This would never happen in the Sailor's.

Harry   The Sailor's! You'd be lucky to get out alive, eating owt in there.

He presents two foaming pints of ale.

Here's to t' young un.

Simon *and* **Mary** *come along the quayside and down the alley to the party.* **Simon** *is rather the worse for wear.*

Mary   Helloooo!

Jo   Hello, Mary.

Mary *stops.*

Mary   There's no one here.

Jo   We're here!

Kitty   The lad's are upt' house getting ready.

Simon   I was told there were a party.

Harry   Simon.

Simon *ignores him and heads straight for the spread.*

Simon   What? No pickled onions.

Mary   Oh for God's sake, Dad, sit down.

Simon   Call this a party. I'm off to t' Sailor's.

Simon *leaves.*

Jo   One down . . .

Mary   Dad! Dad!

Simon *heads up the quay.*

Simon   Leave uz alone.

Mary   It's that way.

She indicates the correct way to the Sailor's Rest. **Simon** *proudly turns round without acknowledging* **Mary** *and heads off out of view.*

He's at it as soon as cock crows.

Jo   He's doing no harm.

Kitty (*to herself*)   It's a bloody disgrace. I'm going to Braithwaite's.

Jo *and* **Mary** *watch* **Kitty** *go off in a tizzy.*

Mary   Should've seen him yesturday. Came out of t' Sailor's – fell straight int' harbour. Took five of them to drag him out – then he was back in t' Sailor's suppin' brandy without even drying off. Me mam would've killed him. I don't know what to do. If he carries on at this rate, I'll have to stick a bloody cork down his neck.

Harry   What can I get you?

Mary (*to* **Harry**)   Pint of ale, lover. (*To* **Jo**.) When are they off, then?

Jo   Bout eight to catch tide. Anyways, did you get owt sorted with Michael?

Mary   Did I heck. Tried to wangle summat wi' magistrate. But soonest we can get t' licence is a fortnight, and he'll be ten mile off the Hook of Holland. We'll have to wait till he gets back. Jo, I'll be showing.

Jo   Ach, nobody'll notice. Not with your figure.

Mary   What's that supposed to mean?

Jo   James's agreed to December. Soon as he's back.

Mary (*screams*)   No.

Jo   Yes.

Mary   You as well! Come on, spill the beans then.

Jo   Shhh. Haven't told Kitty yet, she'll kill uz.

Enter **Kitty**, *with a huge jar of pickled onions.* **Jo** *shuts up.*

Kitty (*to* **Harry**)   Was that difficult? It's the last time I'm booking here. Those pasties must be a week old. Onion, anyone?

Jo   Stop fussing, Kitty, and sit down.

Kitty   Mary. Look what I've got for our Benji. What do you think?

She holds up some earrings.

Jo   I still think you should give them to James.

Kitty   No, it's only fair. Now he's come to his senses.

Mary   Where did you buy them?

Kitty   Buy them. Do you think I'm made of money? (*Pointedly to* **Harry**.) This spread just about ruined us. They used to be Jack's.

Mary   Look, they've got little ships on them and everything.

Jo   I still say James is t' one takes after his father. I tell you what I'd give Benji, a good slapping.

Kitty   Leave the poor bugger alone for once in his life. Fair dos. He took his time. But he signed, didn't he. I just want to give him a proper send-off, after everything he went through with Jack and everything.

Jo   Christ. One minute you're wanting to crucify him and t' next he's up for t' sainthood.

Kitty   All right, all right. He might have been a little bugger but let bygones be bygones. Never part in anger. Come on, Mary, would you like a bit of beetroot? I'd get stuck in before those greedy beggars get here.

William, *smoking a pipe, comes along the corridor with* **Dan**.

Kitty   Talk of the devil.

William   Three young lasses and not a single fella in sight. Looks like we've come at right time, Dan.

William *surveys the sandwiches, takes a drag of his pipe and coughs – all over the spread.*

Kitty   And you can put that filthy pipe out. I'm not having you stinking the place out.

William   Great party this is gonna be.

Dan   We're not stopping . . . Oh, sandwiches!

Jo   So you'll not be wanting a drink then, Bill?

William   I'll write you out me will.

Jo   Dan?

Dan   Just a drop of brandy, love. Just to wet me whistle. Make that a double.

Kitty   Hey, I'm not made of money.

Harry *supplies the booze.*

William   Where's the lads, then?

He carefully knocks back the drink in one. **Dan** *is stuffing his face.*

Dan   Nice bit of pasty, is that?

Kitty   Would you like a onion?

Dan   No thanks, love. Doesn't agree.

Dan *continues to stuff his face as if food was going out of fashion. Then sits down, exhausted. He yawns.*

Mary   You're not sleepy already, are you?

Dan   I'm proper poorly. It's all that chewing.

Jo   There's beds upstairs. Get yoursel a lie-down.

Dan   No. I'll just have a nice sit by here.

William   He'd be up like a whippet if you went with him.

Jo   I think he'd be better off with hot-water bottle.

William   Well, I'm available.

Kitty   You! Matron has to help you on with your breeches.

William   Exactly – cos I'm irresistible.

Kitty   That's not what she told me about your breeches.

William   Unlike Matron, we fellas mature like a good wine.

Jo   An old cheese.

Enter **Sarah**.

Sarah   Cooee!

William   Hello, hello, me luck's in.

Sarah   Hello there, Danny. Hello there, Mary. Hello, Kitty, Jo . . .

William   How do?

Sarah *ignores him*.

Jo   Drink, Sair?

Sarah   No, not for me. Go on then, a small one.

Jo   Ale?

Sarah   Make it a pint. What a lovely spread.

Kitty   Pickled onion?

Sarah   Not for me. (*She is handed the drink.*) Bless you. To the lads . . . where are . . . ?

Kitty   They'll be down shortly. Ben's loading the oilskins with James. They're off at eight.

Sarah *has finished her pint*.

Sarah   Nice drop, that. Where were you the other day, Kitty? At Eileen's wedding?

Kitty   Was busy.

Sarah   Oh, very superior spread, proper bit of class.
Mind, the bride was bladdered, five gins, seven whiskies and
a quart of that Madeira.

William   I bet those sweet lips were sticky that night, eh,
Dan?

Dan *is asleep and wakes with a jolt.*

Dan (*muttering*)   No, Matron, not . . . Oh!

Kitty   Oh, leave him be. He only comes out for a nap.

William *gets his pipe out and starts to stuff it.*

Kitty   William.

Chastised, he puts it away. **Jed** *and* **Trudger** *arrive.*

Kitty   All right, lads.

Jed   We'll just set ourselves up over here [i.e., by the food].

He starts eating.

Kitty   Go steady on wi' those sandwiches. You're the
'turns'.

Jo   Will you take another, Sair?

Sarah   Oh no. I'm not stopping. Oh, go on then. One for
the road.

Kitty   Come on, you two. Sing for your supper.

Kitty *notices that* **Jed** *and* **Trudger** *(the band) are stuffing their
faces. She rushes over snatching a sandwich out of their hands.*

Kitty   Cut that out you two. Sing for your supper.

Jed *and* **Trudger** *start playing a hornpipe.* **Sarah** *starts dancing
and everyone claps her on. As the music gets wilder* **Michael** *runs up
the quay and grabs* **Mary**. *He spins her round high in the air, kissing
her with gusto and passion. Everyone cheers,* **Mary** *squeals with
exhilaration and delight.* **Michael** *reels her round and round, down
the alleyway, and he ends exhausted on the quay. In the courtyard, the
band are on to another hornpipe and there is less energetic dancing. By*

now the quay is in half light. **Michael** *kisses* **Mary***, their hearts obviously pounding. As they snog they try to converse.*

Mary   You should be more careful. A lass in my condition.

Michael   I think you can take more than a bit of dancing.

Mary   It's all sorted for when ye get back. Maybe *we* could have a do in the Compass?

Michael   What with those sandwiches?

Mary   I'll be showing you know. I don't know what Dad'll say.

Michael   He'll be grateful you've not married some infertile.

Michael *smothers her with kisses. Suddenly,* **Simon** *staggers past them and dances into the pub, doing his own version of a hornpipe.*

Mary   Dad!

They follow him into the pub.

Storm (*drunk*)   Wey hey.

Simon*'s increasingly energetic dance causes him to fall over. Everyone cheers.* **Michael** *picks him up.*

Michael   Come on, Big Man

He props him up against the wall.

Kitty   Hello Simon.

Simon *looks up at* **Kitty** *and burps loudly.*

Simon   Don't mind me.

William   Would you like a drop of ale, son?

Mary   No – he would not.

Simon   What do you mean – he would not?

Michael   He's not doing any harm.

Mary   You've had quite sufficient.

Simon   I haven't even started.

Kitty   Have you seen James, Simon?

Simon   James-Simon?

William   For Christsake, give him one for the gangplank.

Mary   No. No. Don't give him anything.

Simon   Hard lines. Carries his own supplies.

Simon *gets a little bottle out of his pocket and takes a swig.*

Sarah *finishes off her second pint, a prodigious feat.*

Sarah   Well, I best be off then.

Jo   Are you sure you don't want to wait? They'll be down any minute.

Sarah   I don't want to be an imposition. Maybe I'll have a little whisky and be on me way. (*To* **Harry**.) No, make that another pint, love.

James *arrives. A cheer.*

James   It's all hands on deck. Hello there, Si, not pissed again, are you, lad?

Simon   Haven't touched a drop.

Mary   Wait till you get home, Dad.

James   Oh, let the bugger be. Harry – drinks on me. We'll have to be sharpish, it's half seven already.

Drinks are distributed. **James** *kisses* **Jo**. *Then raises his glass.*

To Benji . . .

He realises he is missing.

Where is he?

Kitty   I thought he was with you.

James   No, he went off in a huff.

Kitty   He's not been whinging already, has he?

James   He's just a bit nervous. Budge up.

James *sits next to* **Dan** *who is asleep.*

William   I'd watch yourself next to him. He pissed himself last night. Matron had to scrub him down.

Jo   Charming, that is, dropping your only pal in it.

William   It's a natural bodily function. But the last thing the lad wants for a send-off.

James   Poor sod. I hope I never get that old.

Jo   We're not even married and he wants to make uz a widow.

James   Let's sing him a lullaby.

He sings a sweet song.

> Where have all the fishees gone?
> Sleeping on the Ocean bed
> Hush now go to sleep
> Sailing on the ocean deep

Then he shouts the last line.

FISHEES IT IS MORNING!!!

Dan *wakes up with a fright.*

William   Careful. He'll piss himself again.

Jo   Bill!

Dan   Stuff the lot of yous. You'll not be laughing at my age.

Kitty   This is supposed to be a civilised send-off.

Dan *goes back to sleep.*

Jo   Oh, calm down, Kitty.

Sarah *finishes her third pint.*

Sarah   Well, I'm away then.

Jo   For Christsake, sit down. Here, have Dan's.

Jo *gives* **Dan***'s pint to* **Sarah***.* *Sarah sits next to* **William***. They all have to move along the bench.* **William** *complains.*

William   Hey, steady on, I'm nearly ont' floor here.

Sarah   Anyway, to the lads! And the *Hope*.

General toasting. Suddenly, **Simon** *stands up, takes a drink of his bottle.*

Simon   The *Hope*. The *Hope*. The ribs. James, Michael, where's Benji? Wait there, I have to find him.

He leaves looking for **Ben***.*

Everybody laughs. **James** *raises his glass in a mock toast.*

James   To Harry's gin and all who sail in her.

Kitty   Where the hell is he?

Michael   He'll be saying his bye-byes to his favourite photographer.

Jo   Benji!? She wouldn't touch him with a tripod.

Michael   Come on then Molly, give us a dance then.

Molly *demurs but the crowd egg her on. The band start up and the Clog dance is done. The women sing:*

> I went down to dig some tatters
> Dig some tatters for me tea
> I tripped up and dropped me bucket
> A Deckie lad come kissing me
>
> My Mother says I shouldn't marry a Deckie
> If I do he'll break my heart
> I don't care what me mother tells me
> I'll have a Deckie for my sweetheart.

Scarbro lads earn gold and silver
Whitby lads earn nowt but brass
Filey lads are not so choosy
They'll go a-courtin' an owner's lass

Tell me skipper is it right
Come tell me skipper is it true
You're not going out tonight
No bugger wants to sail with you.

The dance ends to uproarious applause.

Kitty   Where the hell's he got to?

Michael   He'll be down shortly. Drink, anyone?

William   I'm all right, son.

Sarah   Pint of same, please, Michael.

Michael   He's not going to miss his own party.

Michael *passes the drinks out.*

Kitty   You've got me worried sick now.

Jo   Calm down. He's got half an hour.

Kitty   He'll be the death of me. I've taken an advance, you know. How'd you think I paid for this?

James   What you worried about? He's signed up, hasn't he. Howay, Michael, give us a song.

Jed
Bound together through the land
Keep the spirit keep the way
Brothers sisters make a stand
Unity will win the day.

Jo *and* **Kitty** *boo* **Michael***'s song.* **Sarah** *laughs at its sentiment.*

Michael   You won't be laughing come the revolution.

Jo   Revolution, my arse.

James   Ah, you load of old reactionary bastards. Keep going.

(*Sings.*)
> Bound together through the land
> Keep the spirit keep the way
> Brothers sisters make a stand
> Unity will win the day.
>
> Raise your banners high
> Strength to strength and line by line
> Unity must never die
> Raise your banner high.

James *sings the song with real passion. As he is singing we see* **Makepeace** *come along the quay. He stops and slowly comes up the corridor to watch* **James** *singing. The others are so engrossed in his song, no one notices* **Makepeace** *is there. Suddenly,* **Jed** *sees* **Makepeace** *looking on and stops. Everybody looks at* **Makepeace**.

Makepeace   Get yourself on board. You'll miss the tide!

Makepeace *turns and leaves.*

Kitty   Oh my God. Now you've done it.

Jo   What's the matter with him?

Michael   Where the hell did he come from?

Sarah   You idiot. Fancy squealing like a stuck pig when his nibs is just up the street.

Mary   He was none too chuffed, was he?

William   You'll not be singing at his table, that's for sure.

Kitty   Why on earth do you have to sing such upsetting songs?

James   For Christsake, it's my party. He's lucky I didn't plant him one. 'Get yourself on board'! Who does he think he is?

Kitty   You're just asking for trouble.

James   Oh, I'm banned from singing in me own pub, am I? Nobody tells me what to do.

Sarah   Fair's fair. If you were Makepeace you'd not want your lads preaching revolution.

James   Oh, shut up, Sarah.

Kitty   He knows how dependent I am.

James   Dependent! What are you on about. You skivvy for the fella. He's t' one dependent on you.

Jo   Give it a rest, James!

Kitty   Don't you realise – I'm going to get a right dressing down on Saturday.

James   A dressing down! Me dad and two brothers drowned so he could afford to get his house skivvied. If you weren't so bloody servile it'd be you doing t' dressing down.

Kitty   You've no idea what he's done for us.

James   He's kept your nose to the grindstone's what he's done.

Jed *reprises the first anthem.*

James
  Though the struggle brings you pain
  Though the struggle brings you tears
  Yours will be the final gain
  You shall hear the victory cheers.

Kitty   Stop it, James, Please.

James (*shouting*)   You shall hear the victory cheers.

Jo   Stop it! For God's sake, stop it!

Jo *slaps* **James** *across the face.*

The music stops dead. Everyone is silent. **James** *is furious but chastened.*

Tense silence.

Michael   Better be getting off, then.

Sarah   My goodness, is that the time!

She finishes her last pint.

Sarah, **Simon**, **Mary** *and* **Michael** *go off embarrassed.* **Jed** *realises the party's over. He puts a load of food in* **Trudger**'s *bag and leaves, leading* **Trudger** *out.* **Kitty** *is left mortified.* **James** *stares at* **Jo**. **Jo** *stands defiant.* **Kitty** *is almost in tears.* **Makepeace** *appears from the pub.*

Makepeace   Decided to stay, have you?

James   Talking to me?

Makepeace   Aye, I'm talking to you. You work for me now. So let's be having you.

James   I'm coming, calm yerself down.

Makepeace   Harbour police have been informed.

James   I couldn't care if you've informed the Queen. I'm just saying bye to me mam.

Kitty   It's true, sir, he's . . .

Makepeace   Where the hell's that other dunce of yours.

Kitty   We don't . . .

James   He'll be along with me.

Makepeace   I warned you once. Get going.

James   I'm not on your boat yet. I'm saying my goodbyes.

Makepeace *calmly walks across.*

Makepeace   If I were you I'd watch my tone, mister.

James   No, you watch my tone . . . Bugger off!

Makepeace *is still cool as a cucumber.*

Kitty   James. Please, don't take offence, sir – he's angry with his brother . . .

Makepeace *breaks into a smile – perhaps recognising* **James***'s hot head.*

Makepeace   Well, there's gratitude for you. You do folk a favour and they throw it in your face. Have it your way, son, but if you're not ont' ship in five minutes I'll have the whole constabulary out to fetch you.

James   Have me fetched, will you? Who do you think I am?

Jo   James.

Makepeace   Are there any more little favours you'd like to ask, Kitty?

James   Oh, I'm a little favour, am I? Listen. You pay wages – I give my labour – I'm nobody's favour.

Makepeace   If it wasn't for your mother, I wouldn't give you time of day.

James   If it wasn't for me mam I'd knock you flat on your back. Now get to fuck.

Kitty   James, James!

A long silence.

Makepeace   Quite a party this has turned out to be. Good evening.

He turns and walks out to the quay. **Kitty** *follows him to the street, now lit by gas lamps.*

Kitty   Please, sir . . . Christopher.

Makepeace   I hope you know what you're doing, Kitty. I paid that advance in good faith.

Kitty   I know, sir.

Makepeace   Have I ever treated you badly?

Kitty   Never.

James *has followed them out. He pulls* **Kitty** *away to stop her begging.*

James   For God's sake.

Makepeace *looks at* **Kitty**.

Makepeace   I'm very sorry, Kitty.

Makepeace *walks away.* **James** *goes after him. He grabs him and swings him round.*

James   Who the fuck do you think you are?

Kitty   James.

James (*shouting back to* **Kitty**)   Get inside.

Makepeace   Any reasonable bloke about to get wed would be crawling up my arse. You've got a ten-year ban, son. I'm warning you now, you're trying my patience. Look at my grey hair, son. Think about your father.

James   The 'deep six', my dad is.

Makepeace   And mine too. Do you think you've got the monopoly on pain? Do you think you were the only fella born with a chip on his shoulder? Listen, your mother used to watch me as a bairn waiting by the bins – biting the heads off bait I was that hungry.

James   Oh, me poor heart bleeds. You weren't waiting by the bait bins when I came looking for news of me dad. You were sat in a nice warm office, counting your piles of money when I came in from t' cold.

Makepeace   Don't start, son. I'm trying to help you. I've been out in winds that would cut your ears off. I've seen things that'd have you blubbering on the floor. I got where I am by hard graft. I've been out more times than you've had cold suppers. You're young, strong, full of fire, so *use* it. Make something of yourself.

James   So I can be like you and sell every fucker else down the river . . .

Makepeace   What century are you from, son? Listen, I'm saying this as a friend. You have a mother. You have a mind to get married. All right, you might have done six months – I'm not making a song and dance about that – you might have barked at me in a unseemly manner – but as I say, you're young and stupid. So, I'll tell you this once only. Treat me fair and I'll look after you – play silly buggers on t' *Hope*, I'll throw the fucking book at you. Understood?

James *and* **Makepeace** *are face-to-face on the quayside.*

James   That's right, you go off to your fucking office with your big safe and your tot of rum.

Makepeace   And my troubles, son. Do you think fleets run themselves? I've got a hundred men to worry about. Who do you think feeds you?

Jo *comes along the alley and watches from a distance.*

James   The fellas who tek fish out of sea. Fellas who risk life and limb every second they're out. Who don't change clothes for six weeks in a row? Whose hands are raw with salt? Who have no water to wash themselves clean? Who sleeps caged like beasts? Who leaves his wife and mother to go begging for alms? Twelve of us go out tonight. What will we get for our labour? What will you get? For rubbing your hands raw while you fester by the fire.

Makepeace   For taking the risks. Who coughs up if you lose a net or if there's a poor catch or if lightning strikes the mast or you run the ship aground or God knows what else? I make my money because I look after the lot. I don't see you dipping in your pocket when there's storm damage. Yet you go home with a full packet. I'm not a bad man, I'm not a greedy man, I am a businessman. I'm not after the shirt off your back. Everybody gets their due. If I do well – you do well. If you do well – I do well. That's how it works. That's how it *should* work. There isn't us and them. My business is making sure you can do yours. It's not a fucking fight. We're all in this together. This isn't the nineteenth century any more. Wake up, lad. I didn't just wax my moustache and tie someone tot' railway. But there are people's livelihoods at stake here and if you make an agreement you have to bide by it. So if I were you I'd spend less time shouting at folks trying to help you, and more time looking for your brother.

Kitty   I can't . . .

Makepeace   It's past eight already. If you two aren't there in five minutes, I'll invoke article sixteen, and that's a five-quid fine before you'll've left port.

James   Go on then, fucking fine me.

Makepeace *looks at him, does not rise to the bait, turns and walks off towards the dock.* **Kitty** *chases after him.*

Kitty   Please, please, forgive him, sir.

Makepeace   I've never been spoken to like that in my life.

Kitty   He doesn't know what he's saying.

Makepeace   And you can forget coming on Saturday. We have no other use for you.

Kitty   But, sir, it's nowt to do wi' me.

Makepeace   You brought them up.

Makepeace *walks off.* **Kitty** *shouts after him.*

Kitty   Christopher!

James *is watching from under the light outside the pub.* **Kitty** *slowly walks up to him with dignity and starts to lash out at* **James**. *She thumps at him, more out of frustration and humiliation than anger. He takes the blows, then grabs her. She is crying. She continues to lash out. He hugs her, until she calms down. She is sobbing.*

Kitty   What a send-off this's turned into.

Jo *comes up to* **James** *and takes* **Kitty**, *pushing* **James** *away.*

Jo   It's all right, Kitty. James was right what he said.

Kitty   Right? What's use in being right?

Kitty *pulls herself together and pushes* **Jo** *away.*

James   You're not going after him.

Kitty   I'm going to look for Ben. They'll have him in jail.

Kitty *heads back to the pub.*

James   Aren't you going t' say goodbye?

Kitty   I'll come t' harbour.

Kitty *goes back along the alley into the pub courtyard to collect her things.* **Jo** *and* **James** *stand under the gaslight. There is an awkward pause between them.*

James   Best be off.

Jo   Be careful, won't you?

They kiss.

I'll come down with you.

James *and* **Jo** *disappear into the darkness.* **Kitty** *puts on her hat in the pub courtyard, and walks down the alley towards the quay. Suddenly, the cellar shutter opens, and a figure peeps out. It is* **Ben***. He drops the shutter which makes a noise.* **Kitty** *turns to look and sees* **Ben** *emerging from the cellar.* **Ben** *sees that* **Kitty** *is about to shout at him. He tries to keep her silent.*

Ben   Shhhh.

Kitty *storms into the courtyard.*

Kitty   You stupid little . . .

Ben   Shhh.

Kitty *clouts him around the head.*

Kitty   Don't bloody well shush me. I'll scream the place down if you don't get after your James this minute.

Ben   M- M- Mam, go. Catch him. Stop him, M- M-
Mam. S- s- stop him.

Kitty   What's the matter with you?

Ben   *Hope*'s rotten, Mam – the r- ribs are rotten. Whole
bulkhead's rotten.

Kitty   Get on that boat. Now!

Ben   P- please, Mam.

Kitty   I'll take your face off . . .

Ben   H- hit uz, h- hit uz. I don't care. Stop James. Simon
says . . .

Kitty   That pisshead.

Kitty *grabs him by the ear and is pulling him towards the quay.*

Ben   N- no. I won't. Even if you thrash me.

Kitty   It's just been int' dock.

Ben   It w- were past saving.

Kitty   I'm warning you.

Ben   I can't. You'll have to kill me. It's full o' water, Mam.

Kitty   It's bilge, you stupid idiot. Every boat's got that.

Ben *wrests himself away from his mother and runs back into the
courtyard.* **Kitty** *follows him.*

Ben   P- please, Mam, please don't make me go!

Kitty   Michael's going. Your own bloody brother's going.
I've taken money. They'll drag you through the streets.

On the quay two **Coppers***, looking for* **Ben***, almost stop by the
pub, but carry on towards the dock.*

Ben   I'll r- run away.

Kitty   You're not running anywhere.

Ben *tries to get past, but* **Kitty***'s too fast for him.*

Ben   Let uz past. I w- warning you . . .

Kitty   Oh, you're brave enough now you're faced with a sixty-one-year-old woman.

Ben *collapses on to the floor.*

Ben (*shouts*)   No, no, no. You'll never see me again.

The two **Coppers** *are now far along the quay. They hear* **Ben**'s *shout. They turn.*

Kitty   Get up.

She helps him to his feet. He is shaking. **Kitty** *pulls the earrings out of her pocket.*

Look, I brought you these. They were your father's.

She puts the earrings into his ears. **Ben** *is still, like a child, as she puts them in his ears. She steps back to proudly admire them. But he is weeping.*

Ben   Hide me, Mam. I'm going to drown.

Kitty   It's all right, lover. You'll get used to it.

Two **Coppers** *arrive.*

First Copper   Come on, let's be having you.

Ben *tries to make a run for it, he tries to get down the cellar, but the* **Coppers** *grab him.*

Ben   I'm not going. I'm not going. The ship's rotten.

Second Copper   Should have thought about that before you signed up then.

Ben   G- get off, get off.

They struggle with him.

Second Copper   Don't make us put cuffs on, lad.

Ben   Mam. Help me. H- help m- me.

The **Coppers** *drag* **Ben** *away but he hangs on to a wooden pillar for dear life.*

First Copper   Let go of the post.

Ben   You'll have to cut me hands off.

Kitty   Stop! Please! The lad's scared to death.

First Copper   Let go.

Both men struggle to loosen **Ben***'s grip but can't budge him.*

Kitty   Come on, son.

To wrench **Ben** *away* **Kitty** *is forced to join in. She wrenches* **Ben***'s hands from the post.*

Ben   Mam.

The **Coppers** *drag* **Ben** *out.* **Kitty** *is left standing.* **Harry** *emerges from the bar.*

Harry   What the hell's going on out here?

Kitty   They had to drag Ben out. I can't go down t' docks now.

She looks bereft.

The shame of it.

Harry   Never mind. There's plenty food left.

Kitty *takes no notice.* **Harry** *helps himself to a sandwich.* **Kitty** *looks towards the quay, shaken and upset.*

Harry   You all right, love?

Kitty *takes no notice.*

Harry   Pickled onion?

Kitty *does not react.* **Harry** *shrugs, pops an onion in his mouth, collects some glasses and disappears into the pub.* **Kitty** *is left devastated. In the distance we hear the noise of a horn signalling the* Good Hope*'s departure. Slowly the pier fills with townsfolk who watch the ship gradually disappear into the darkness.*

Act Three

Night. A storm is raging.

Kitty's *tiny house is set centre stage against a panorama of the harbour. It is dwarfed by the masts and sails of scores of vessels blowing violently in the gale that is sweeping through the town.*

The noise of the storm is tremendous, the masts jolt about perilously. Lights come up on the inside of **Kitty**'s *parlour, a frail oasis of light and warmth in the turbulent pitch of the town.*

Every time the door opens, the storm shrieks and breaks into the tiny cottage, but for now, inside, it is relatively calm, with the sound of a storm as if observed from inside.

Kitty *is asleep, covered in a blanket.* **Jo** *is reading. There is a knock at the door.* **Jo** *tiptoes to answer it. She opens it and we hear the shriek of wind outside. Enter* **Clementine** *and* **Arthur**, *the bookkeeper, carrying a tureen. The door closes.* **Kitty** *wakes with a start.*

Kitty   What is it?

Clementine   It's only us. I've never seen such weather.

Kitty *coughs and tries to get up.*

Jo   You sit down.

Clementine   How are you feeling? I've brought some soup and a few eggs. Arthur, Arthur.

Arthur   Beg your pardon?

Clementine   The eggs.

Arthur   The what?

Clementine   He's an absolute trial – deaf as a post. The EGGS.

Arthur   No need to shout.

Kitty   Has it calmed down yet?

Clementine   If anything it's getting worse. I've brought you a chicken broth, Kitty. It's delicious.

Clementine *gestures to* **Arthur** *to give* **Kitty** *the chicken broth. He puts it down.* **Clementine** *takes off the lid and looks in dismay.*

Clementine   For crying out loud, there's hardly any left.

Arthur   You try keeping pan o' soup steady int' force-nine gale.

Clementine   When we set out there was half a chicken in here.

Arthur   Beg your pardon, Miss, can't hear a thing with t' wind.

Kitty   Thank you, Miss.

Arthur *puts the eggs on the table too.*

Clementine   Arthur, there are only four eggs here.

Arthur   That's all you gave me.

Arthur *is setting up the food, much to* **Clementine**'s *consternation.*

Clementine   Get out of the way.

Clementine *pushes* **Arthur** *out of the way, as she does so, we hear a crack. They all look.*

Arthur   Oh buggery.

Arthur *puts his hand in his pocket and retrieves his keys dripping with yolk. He accidentally brings out a chicken drumstick, also covered with yolk.*

Clementine   You thieving scoundrel. Taking food from a sick woman.

Arthur   But there were too much for one.

Arthur *seems more perturbed about the mess than being told off.*

Jo   I expect you fancied a nice chicken omelette, when you got home.

Arthur   You'd never've known if you hadn't pushed me.

Clementine   I'll make sure Daddy knows about this. Now get lost.

Arthur   You're not sending me back out right away.

Kitty   Let him stay. It's no crime being hungry.

Clementine   It serves him right.

Arthur   But I might slip.

Clementine   You'll just have to be careful.

Arthur *looks put upon and reluctantly leaves. Again, the gale howls through the house as the door is opened.*

Clementine   You have to count your fingers every time he shakes your hand. How is the soup?

Kitty   Delicious, Miss, I don't know how to thank you. Does your father know you're here?

Clementine   No. And I think it's best he doesn't. He's still apoplectic over James. He'll get over it. Come on, Jo, come look at the sea with me. It's astounding.

Jo   That all right, Kitty?

Kitty   You can't go t' beach in this.

There is a huge cracking sound.

Jo   What the hell was that?

Enter **William**.

William   Bloody hell.

Jo   William!?

William   Nearly killed me.

Kitty   What was it?

William   Tree, smashed right down on next door. Near took my neck off.

Kitty   I hope they're not in.

Jo   What the hell are you doing running around in this?

William   Fetching doctor. Dan's sick.

Clementine   What's the matter?

Jo   Sit down, will you.

Jo gives him a cup of tea.

William   Can't keep owt down – brought up bacon and beans all over t' show.

Clementine   What on earth are you feeding him bacon and beans for!?

William   Unfortunately, Matron had run out of caviar. He's talking weird – stuff about putting out lines – I'm scared, Kitty. I told her to get doctor this morning, but she wouldn't listen. I've told Simon to get cart and take uz down.

Jo   Simon?

William   He's on his way.

Clementine   You'll end up off a cliff with him driving.

William   No, no, he's sober.

Jo   And I'm a Dutchman. You might be daft enough to get on his cart but doctor'll think twice.

There is a howling and cracking from outside.

William   Christ . . . listen to it. He's in a bad way. He's terrified he won't pull through.

Clementine   Who wouldn't be?

William   I dunno. If it were my turn tomorrow, I'd say: *so be it.* We all have to go some time. Don't see what there is to

be scared on. Death's not a 'thing', it's not summat out
there you can fight or flee from; it can't rip you apart or tear
your heart out. It's life does that. Death's not a 'thing' you
can touch or feel or hear or take a look at. Death's nothing.
Nothing. You don't get scared 'bout before you was born.
What's there to fear of t' other end? . . . don't laugh . . . God
takes us, we take the fishes. That's the order. There's
nothing more to know. Nothing to be feared on. Many's the
time, I've been on deck gutting herring, there's few as fast as
I, and you push the knife in and you look int' eye of that
creature, an eye full of fear and . . . intelligence . . .
flickering, asking, am I less blessed than thee? And I think,
maybe in ten year, maybe in fifty, not one of us out there
will still be here. Say in ninety year not one of us on t' entire
globe, that's now living, will be here. No, we are all as
blessed as each other. We take the fishes, God takes us. One
barrel tips int' other. There's no chance about it. That's the
order, there's none escape – men nor fishes. Tis only time
that separates us one from other. Sooner or later we will all
be one. Returned to nothing, from whence we came. That's
the facts, lass. Nay, you're not scared of death – death is
nowt, so there is nought to be scared on. No, lass, it's *life*
you're scared on.

Pause.

Kitty   Have you been drinking?

William   I'm lucky to get cuppa tea round here.

Kitty   I'm worried about next door. Best see they're all
right.

Jo   Sit down, will you. I'll go.

Kitty   No, no. I'm feeling better.

She's up and off.

Jo   You stubborn old cow. Yous stay here.

Kitty *leaves.* **Jo** *follows. The wind howls through.*

William   Careful of the lamp.

Clementine   I'll thank the Lord when the *Hope*'s back.

William   No ship'll be safe tonight. Least *Hope*'s old – old ships are last to go down.

Clementine   You think so?

William   Tis known fact, Miss.

He takes the opportunity to pour himself a dram.

Will you take a drop?

Clementine   No, no. (*Pause.*) But I'll pray for the *Hope* tonight.

William   Good luck to you, but the *Jacob*'s out, and t' *Expectation* . . . you'll be praying for a lot of ships, love.

Clementine   But the *Hope*'s rotten . . .

Clementine *stops dead.* **William** *looks at her.*

William   Who said that?

Clementine   No one. I mean . . . it was in dock, wasn't it.

William   Who said it's rotten?

Clementine   No one. I was letting my imagination get the better of me.

Jo *and* **Kitty** *come back.*

Clementine   Anyway, let's stop dwelling on all this. How was it, Kitty?

Kitty   Went straight through their window. They must be down at their Tony's.

Jo   Lucky they were out.

Kitty   What a night. My poor boys . . . Benji will be terrified . . . so nearly home.

Jo   Here, get warm, Kitty. Will you have a cup, Miss?

Enter **Simon** *and* **Mary**.

Simon   What a blasted gale.

Mary *comes in. She is very distressed, crying.*

Kitty   Are you all right, pet?

Mary   I'm thinking of Michael.

Kitty   Come on, sweetheart. Look at Jo . . . her man's a seaman too . . . seamen's wives don't cry . . . silly lass . . . give her a cup of something.

Mary   But it's the sixth week . . .

William   Stop wailing 'fore you've been hit, lass. Is the coach ready, driver?

Simon   I'm not doing this for fun, you know . . . if it wasn't for Dan . . .

Jo   It'll do you good, Simon.

Simon   Listen, it were a night like this I lost Katherine. She were pregnant and I were taking her down t' road to doctor. The wind were howling and we hit t' rock and whole thing came off road. She were lying there. There were nowt I could do. By t' time I got doctor she were gone. Just lying there by the road. Anyway. We best go, Billy.

Kitty   Go easy, Simon.

Simon   Don't worry.

William   Night, all.

Kitty   Take care.

William *and* **Simon** *wrap up and leave. The relentless wind howls through the cottage. A long silence.*

Mary   Last night. I thought I saw Michael. I don't know if I was awake or asleep. I was just lying and there was a knock – at the window – and I sat bolt upright – and I looked about but there was nothing – then it came again (*She* *knocks.*) – so I got up and slowly went to the window – and looked – nothing – there was nothing there. Then just as I was going to lie down – knock – and I spun round and there was Michael's face – at the window – pale as milk – then there was nothing – just darkness . . .

Kitty *is spooked.*

Kitty   Three knocks?

Mary   That's right.

Jo   Oh for Christsake. The pair of you.

There is a sudden knocking. They all jump.

Enter **Susan** *and* **Sarah**. *Another gust bursts through. The old women struggle to shut the door against the massive gale.*

Susan   It's only us.

Sarah   You look like you've seen a ghost.

Jo   Thank the Lord you've arrived. It's like a morgue in here.

Sarah   What a night. I've got sand blowing down my bloomers.

Susan   I couldn't stand it at home with no one to talk to. Two mooring posts gave way . . .

Kitty   Two mooring posts?

Sarah   It's a terrible night. And you two with sons out.

Susan   Aye, young Toby's a good un – barely twelve – you should have seen him two months ago – when the *Anna* brought back Stephen – what a comfort he was to me – a proper little man – we stayed up right through the night talking – I swear that laddie's wiser than I am.

Sarah   Did you know if you wear red spectacles you don't get seasick.

Jo   Here we go.

Sarah   It's a known fact.

Jo   Oh aye, like you've tried.

Sarah   Listen, I've been out plenty.

Jo   When?

Sarah   When my Ian were alive.

Clementine   You were married!?

Sarah   I know I'm no oil painting but I have my charms. (*She winks.*) Yes, I were married. And a fine head of hair he had too. Fair dos, he smashed the house up most days. But beggars can't be choosers, eh.

Jo   Tell us about the penknife, Sair.

Sarah   You don't want to hear that old yarn.

Jo   Drink anybody?

Sarah   You've twisted me arm. I bought my hubby a penknife – cost a fortune it did, leather sheaf, the lot – he goes off – comes back five week later – so I says where's penknife – it cost a fortune, that did. He says – you never bought me a effin' penknife – I says I did – it was in an effin' sheath – 'scuse my French. So I says – you've lost the effin' penknife, haven't you – he says he's never seen it in his life. Any rate, one thing leads to another, he goes mental, smashes the place up. Plates all over. I thumped him with the poker, et cetera, et cetera. So things quieten down. He takes his boots off to go to bed. Bang. He looks down. There's the effin' penknife. Been stuck in his shoe for six weeks and he never even noticed. But a fine head of hair for a Welshman.

Clementine   He kept his boots on for six weeks.

Sarah   Oh aye. Had to scrub him with soda. Covered in lice, he were.

Clementine   How disgusting.

Sarah   Any rate, temper got the better of him. He slipped on the *Expedition* trying to hit the skipper with a herring rake. Straight over the side. Never heard of again. Still don't understand why I can't remarry.

Clementine   Whoever's stopping you?

Jo   The entire male population of the British Isles.

Sarah   Thank you. Whoever makes up these effin' regulations. You've got to put three ads in t' paper – just in case he managed to swim a hundred miles to dry land and start up a new life in Bridlington. If no one comes forward, you're in the clear. Where am I going to get the money for three adverts?

Jo   Where you going to get another husband.

They all laugh except **Mary**.

Mary   Listen to the wind.

Jo   Look, put Michael out of your mind.

Mary   I'm not thinking about Michael . . . Tony, my brother.

She sobs.

Clementine   Your brother?

Jo   Can we not change the subject.

Clementine   It's all right. You can tell us.

Jo   For God's sake . . .

Mary   It was his second trip – it was a stormy night – and he were hit by the jib – suddenly he was overboard – he were t' cableman. The skipper held out a herring rake and he grabbed it. But it was too slippy – his hand slid off – and he fell back into t' sea, so bosun gets a broom and he grabbed on to that while three of them pulled him – just as he got to t' side the head came off – they threw out a line –

and that snapped 'nall – and that was it. Couldn't see him in t' dark. They went round and round for hours.

Clementine   That's terrible –

Mary   Said he knew it was coming – he sat up crying the night afore. They thought it was because of Mam, but he said no – he just felt something bad coming.

Clementine   Oh, Mary.

Mary   That's what drove me dad to drink.

No one says a word. They listen to the wind howling.

Jo   I really think we should talk about something else.

Clementine   No. You tell us something, Kit. You've been through so much, haven't you?

Kitty   These aren't just tales, sweetheart. These are people's lives. It isn't some big adventure story. Those boys out there are separated from eternity by a plank the thickness of your thumb. It's all right for some. I passed the Mayor's house last night and they were all sat down to big plates of shellfish all steaming – livers on t' side – children with their hands together. And God forgive me – I thought it were wrong – I thought it were wrong for the Mayor to be sitting there – with the wind howling – and the fish coming from the same water as t' dead – I know it's daft – but you know what I mean.

And it made me think of Jack. You see, my husband was a one in a million. Could taste the sand they brought up for depth readings and tell exactly where they were. If he said fifty-sixth latitude, sure as eggs is eggs, it were the fifty-sixth. Once, he drifted for a week with a ship full of men. Fog so thick, they couldn't see floats on the long line. Nowt to eat or drink. Finally, the hull broke up – you should have heard him tell it – he swam with with his mate George to bit of floating hull. Three more nights he hung there – said he'd never forget it. But George were too weak to hang on and started to slip, so Jack stuck his knife int' hull so's George

had summat to grip to – near cut three fingers off – and
each time George fell Jack swam out and pulled him back.
Three days int' water. And he said on t' third George went
mad – he didn't know whether it were from loss of blood or
fear – but his eyes went like cat's eyes – and he was
screaming Satan was in him – and the blood was gushing
over the bit of boat – even the waves couldn't wash it away
– and just as dawn broke George swam away – and Jack
tried to go after but George just disappeared – just like that
– Jack were picked up by a cargo vessel. He was a one in a
million, my Jack. Three years later he went out on t'
Clementine – and never came back. Not a word. Not a
hatch nor a buoy were found. My Jack and two eldest. And
every day when the kids shouted: 'There's a ball up, there's
a ball up,' I'd run down to t' quay, and the ship would come
in, and I'd walk back alone. And you do that for weeks, and
then it's been months. And every time you hope as if it was
the first time. But then one time you hear it. And you don't
go down. And you can't live with yourself for not going
down. But you can't bear living if you do. And every day
that's all you think about. Then gradually you catch yourself
thinking about something else. And soon you're used to it.
And after a few years you can't even remember their face
too well. Yes, you feel guilty, but soon you're thanking God.
For having forgot. No one should be haunted . . . Well,
that's my story. Same as every seaman's wife – it's a high
price to pay for fish, that's for sure.

Clementine   Please God – don't let any ships perish
tonight!

Jo (*screams*)   For God's sake. Shut up! Shut up! Shut up!
You're driving me mad!

Clementine   Jo – is anything the matter?

Jo   Ships go down. We all know that. We all know about
her husband, and her brother, and uncle Tom Cobley and
all – we all know your damned stories. Let me tell you a
story. My dad drowned. He drowned, he drowned, he

drowned, he drowned, he drowned. (*Screaming at* **Clementine**.) What have you got to say to that? . . . Go to hell.

She leaves wearing only her skirt and blouse. The rain pours in for a second before she slams the door behind her.

Clementine   Perhaps I should go?

Kitty   No, love. She'll calm herself down – she's been under a lot of strain.

Clementine   No, it's getting late, Kit – and to be quite honest I don't think your niece appreciates my company – not that I mind, but. . . is anybody going my way?

Sarah   If one goes we all go. Less chance of being blown away.

Kitty   Please, don't.

Mary   No, Kitty. You get some sleep.

Clementine   Bye, Kitty.

Mary   Bye, Aunt Kit . . .

They all get up and go to the door.

Kitty   Thank you again, Miss, for the soup and eggs.

Clementine   Really, it's nothing.

Kitty   Bye, Miss. Bye, Mary. Bye, Sarah – if you see Jo send her in, won't you?

They go. She clears up the cups. The wind howls around the house. She looks anxiously out of the window. She starts to clean the house, but after some time is overcome with the futility of it all. She moves her chair closer to the hearth, and sits uncomfortably, moving around trying to be comfortable. She finally stares into the fire, with a morose torpor. She almost subconsciously starts to mutter a rosary.

Suddenly, the door bursts open. **Jo** *enters, she is soaked to the skin. Exhausted, freezing and blasted by the storm – she seems physically* *shocked.* **Kitty** *tries not to be alarmed by her presence.* **Jo** *shivers and starts to undress.*

Pause.

Kitty   It was good of the girl to bring eggs and chicken through that wind.

Pause.

Jo   Your sons are out in ten times worse.

Kitty   She didn't have to.

Jo   They're out for *her* father.

Kitty   And us.

Jo   It's *wild*, Kitty.

Kitty   You seen it?

Jo   Half the parade's gone . . . I hate those stories, Kit.

Kitty   Were you like this when he was in the Navy? A seaman's wife can't be weak, love. In a week or so there'll be more storms and more after that.

Jo   We shouldn't have sent Ben – I taunted him till the end.

Jo *is naked. She goes to the window and opens it letting the gale blow against her. She roars in anger into the storm. The wind causes havoc, blowing the whole contents of the house into a maelstrom. The light goes out.* **Kitty** *rushes to her and pulls her away and closes the window. She relights the lamp.* **Jo** *is on the floor.*

Kitty   What are you doing?

Jo   I don't know.

Kitty *covers her with a blanket, and helps her up to sit at the table.* **Jo** *is sobbing.* **Kitty** *sits back down allowing her space.*

Pause.

Jo   Kitty. I'm . . .

Kitty   I know. You should have told me, he's my son. Let us pray.

Jo   I don't want to pray.

Kitty   You have to, child.

Jo   What will be will be.

Kitty   Listen. Nothing's going to happen.

Jo *bangs her head on the table, repeatedly. Slowly at first then really smashing her head.* **Kitty** *watches her till she stops.* **Jo** *is crying.*

Jo   The wind.

Kitty *sits, opens a bible . . .*

Kitty

> They that go down to the sea in ships,
>   that do business in great waters;

> Those see the work of the LORD,
>   and his wonders in the deep.

> For he commandeth and raiseth the stormy wind
>   which lifteth up the waves thereof.

> They mount up to the heaven, they go down again to the depths;
>   their soul is melted because of trouble.

> They reel to and fro, and stagger like a drunken man
>   and are at their wits' end.

> Then they cry unto the LORD in their trouble,
>   and he bringeth them out of their distress.

As **Kitty** *reads, the wind blows stronger round the house. The storm whips up and rips through the town. We hear glass breaking. The sails are battered by the wind and the chaos overwhelms the little house, which seems to recede into the distance as the storm engulfs the stage. The high-pitched whining of the storm turns into an eerie small air on the pipes. The light goes out. Blackness, calm.*

Act Four

Morning. Winter.

Whitby Town Square. The cobbled street is covered in snow. In the foreground is **Makepeace***'s office, cut away so we can see inside. It is raised up with windows that survey the whole dockside. It is reached by a wooden staircase that goes down to the quay. Through the windows, and to the rear we see the dockside, endless rows of masts, all covered in snow.*

Snow is falling. The small air merges into The Whitby Carol. In the distance we see a huddle of carol singers, we hear them singing.

> Hark, Hark what news the angels bring
> Glad tidings of a newborn king
> Born of a maid, a virgin pure
> Born without sin, from guilt secure.
>
> Behold he comes and leaves the skies
> Awake ye slumbering, mortals rise
> Awake to joy and hail the morn
> A saviour of this world was born.

Inside **Makepeace***'s office a fire is blazing. There is a rail behind which a bench forms a sort of waiting room by the door.* **Arthur** *is putting up Christmas decorations. When he is done he looks out of the window and, seeing the coast is clear, he sneaks over to the cigar box on* **Makepeace***'s desk and takes a couple, pushing them in his pocket, then takes a whisky bottle from behind some books on* **Makepeace***'s bookshelf. He has a nip, then another, then sees that it is evident someone has been drinking so fills it to the right level with some water and secretly puts it back.*

We hear someone trudging through the snow. We see it is **Simon***. He walks to the office, comes up the steps and through the door.*

Simon   Where's Makepeace?

Arthur   Born in a barn?

Simon *shuts the door and comes into the room.*

Arthur   Behind that gate, thank you.

Simon   Where is he?

Arthur   Out.

Simon   Well, tell me. What's news?

Arthur   What's what news?

Simon   The *Hope*.

Arthur   For Christsake, not that malarkey. As soon as we hear . . .

Simon   So . . . nothing.

Arthur   Nothing.

Simon   It's nine weeks tomorrow.

Arthur   The *Jacob* came back with 190 barrels after fifty-nine days . . .

Simon   You know something.

Arthur   Don't be daft, Simon.

Simon   You know something.

Arthur   You been boozing?

Simon   Not a drop.

Arthur   Well, it's high time you did. What do you mean I know something? Do you think I keep fleet on t' end of string? Look, they've been gone eight weeks. His nibs is sick to death wi' worry. What do you want me to do about it?

Simon   I told you when it was int' dock.

Arthur   You told me a load of drunken horseshit so's you could get yourself the price of a drink.

Simon   You were there – with him and his daughter. It were plain as day. It were rotten. You saw with your own eyes.

Arthur   You could barely stand up. Do you really expect us to take you serious.

Simon   Bastard.

Simon *goes for him.*

Arthur   Get behind that gate. Even if you weren't 'pallatic'. You're not even a qualified shipwright. Are you seriously telling me cos you had a shufty down below afore knocking off t' Sailor's we should've had her int' scrapyard? Look. A certificate of seaworthiness. Know where that come from? The insurers. The insurers, Simon.

Simon   It's got nowt to do with it. I don't care who's been paid off. If they don't come back it's *murder*. There's blood ont' all your hands.

Arthur   If I were you, I'd have meself a jar before you get in trouble. It's Christmas.

Mary *comes in.*

Simon   I thought I told you to stay home. There's nowt.

Mary   No news then?

Simon   Just murder. (*To* **Arthur**.) You hear me.

Mary *and* **Simon** *leave.* **Arthur** *sneaks another nip of whisky.* **Sarah** *comes along the quay.*

The telephone rings. **Arthur** *jumps with fright. It rings and rings.* **Arthur** *looks at it nervously. Finally, he plucks up the courage to answer it.*

Arthur   Hello. Hello. Sorry, can you speak up? What? No. No. This is Arthur Sedgwick speaking. Sorry, can you speak up? No, this is his bookkeeper. I'm afraid he is currently incommoded . . . No, no . . . Sorry, can you please call back, please? That's right, ten minutes. Yes. Thank you.

As **Arthur** *is on the phone,* **Sarah** *comes in.* **Arthur** *finishes the call and slams the earpiece down with relief. He is clearly terrified of the phone.*

Sarah   Morning, handsome.

Arthur   What do *you* want?

Sarah   Me hands are cold. I thought you could warm them up.

Arthur   Stay behind that gate.

Sarah   Oh, a proper tease. Don't fret, lover, I won't take no for an answer.

Arthur   I'm warning you. Stay behind that gate. Or there'll be trouble.

Sarah   No news, I take it.

Arthur   No. There's nothing, funnily enough.

Sarah   No need to jump down me throat. Seven families, lucky most were single lads.

Arthur   Can we get to t' point?

Just as **Sarah** *is launching into her speech.* **William** *comes running along the dock. He is in very bad shape. He slips and hurts himself on the icy cobbles, but gets up and makes great haste towards the office.*

Sarah   Well, as you no doubt know I am currently engaged in a relationship with a certain bargemaster from Saltburn who is currently here with a cargo of manure. However, on account of my husband being deemed neither alive nor dead I am unable to make an honest woman of myself.

Arthur   What's this got to do with *me*?

Sarah   I need an official statement.

Arthur   Look, I can't help you. All you have to do is put three notices in t' paper . . .

William *is rushing up the stairs.*

Sarah   How'm I supposed to do that? I can't even get a widow's pension.

Arthur   Look, it's not my fault. You need to go into town and . . .

*Enter **William**, worn and exhausted. He speaks with great urgency.*

William   What news of the *Hope*? What news of the boys?

Arthur   There is no news.

William   No, there's news . . . You must have heard.

Arthur   There isn't any news. It doesn't matter how many times a day you come in here. There. Is. Nothing. To tell you.

William   No. We've heard . . . The Commissioner . . . a telegram. Please, Arthur . . . We're demented . . .

Arthur   Really, Bill . . . there's nothing.

William   M' niece is home – cleaning up for t' priest . . . I know there's news . . . even if you won't . . .

Arthur   Who's been filling your head with this rubbish?

William   Commissioner's clerk . . . saw telegram be delivered.

William *looks at* **Arthur**.

Arthur   I'm sorry, William.

William *realises* **Arthur** *is telling the truth. He looks at* **Sarah** *and* **Arthur**. *He is lost and broken. He turns and leaves in silence.*

Sarah   What d'ya think?

Arthur   Anything's possible.

Sarah   What does Makepeace reckon 'bout *Hope*?

Outside, **William** *passes* **Clementine** *without acknowledgement.*

Arthur   What's anyone reckon? Nine weeks. After that storm. Rations for a month. If they'd landed abroad we'd've heard. No. Not a snowball's chance in hell.

Enter **Clementine**, *carrying her camera.*

Clementine   Was that William just in here? I almost didn't recognise him. He's aged twenty years.

Sarah   Took it bad when Dan died . . . he's no one to argue with no more.

Clementine   Oh, it's freezing. But the view over the harbour is quite breathtaking.

She warms her hands on the fire as she takes her coat off.

The phone rings. No one answers it. **Clementine** *looks up at* **Arthur***.*

Arthur   It'll be for your dad. They called a while ago.

It rings.

Clementine   Well, aren't you going to answer it?

Arthur   Couldn't you get it, Miss?

Clementine   Oh, for goodness sake.

She answers it.

Hello. Yes. No . . . Yes. I'm afraid he's not here. No, this is his daughter.

Arthur   He'll just be a few minutes.

Clementine *tries to shush him up.*

Clementine   Sorry, what did you say? You'll have to speak up . . . sorry, a hatch . . .

She screams and drops the phone.

Arthur   What's wrong, Miss?

Clementine   I can't listen.

Arthur   What is it, Miss? The Commissioner?

Clementine   Ben has been washed up. It's over.

Sarah   Ben? Ben?

Clementine   A telegram from Berwick. Just a hatch and a body.

Makepeace *comes through the door.*

Makepeace   What is it?

Arthur   The *Hope.*

Makepeace *blanches.*

Arthur   Commissioner's on the line.

Makepeace   The Shipping Commissioner?! (*To* **Sarah**.) What on earth is she doing here? Get out.

Sarah   I . . . I . . .

Makepeace *is mortified.*

Makepeace   Get out, woman.

Sarah *leaves.* **Makepeace** *picks up the phone, clearly shaken.*

Makepeace   Hello? Who is this? Yes, it's me. A telegram . . . from . . . I see . . . You'll have to speak up . . . Oh, this is a blow . . . this is a real blow . . . how did they recognise him? . . . Earrings? . . . skipper of the *Expectation* . . . What was the *Expectation* doing up there?. . . I see . . . no, no . . . This is an awful business . . . so we don't need to send someone . . . no . . . thank you . . . thank you . . . this is awful for us all . . . yes, I'd appreciate the official report as soon as . . . God bless you.

He hangs up the receiver.

Twelve men. This is a real blow.

Arthur   It's a miracle young Ben was washed up at all. With the *Clementine* . . .

Makepeace   Yes, yes. We know!

He is visibly shaken. He takes his secret bottle and pours a drink to calm his nerves.

What were you thinking of taking the call with that woman around.

Arthur   We didn't know.

Makepeace   Half the town'll be here in five minutes. This is a real blow.

Clementine   This is your fault. Why didn't you listen?

Makepeace   Listen?

Clementine   To Simon. The shipwright.

Makepeace   He's a drunk.

Clementine   He wasn't drunk when he warned us.

Makepeace   He couldn't stand up straight.

Clementine   I was there, God save me, I'm guilty too.

Makepeace   Guilty? Guilty! What sort of language is that? It was an accident.

Clementine   You heard him. He said it was a floating coffin. You said in any event it would be the last trip for the *Hope*.

Makepeace   This is nothing to do with you.

Clementine   It's to do with all of us. There's blood on all our hands.

Makepeace   Oh, that damned boarding school. That damned expensive liberal claptrap. You can hang around the quay and fraternise with every drunken beggar you see but don't stick your nose in matters that you don't understand. He was no shipwright. The only thing he's expert at is the drinking of gin. A floating coffin? For crying out loud – the *Victory*, the *King Billy*, the *Expedition*, the *Explorer* – I could go on all day – the entire fishing fleet of the North Sea are 'floating coffins'. The whole merchant navy's a floating coffin. The trouble with you pampered philanthropists is none of you want to deal with hard fact.

Why do you think the underwriters inspect ships once a year? Do you think when I ring up the insurer and ask for seven thousand pounds he's going to write me a cheque for an unseaworthy vessel? You don't understand what you're saying.

Clementine   Well, if I was shipowner . . .

Makepeace   Oh, God help the shipping industry when we get owners crying over scuffed knuckles and taking portraits of the crew every time they set sail. Look, I am a father at the head of a hundred families. I am responsible for the livelihoods of most of this town. There is a system. Look, there is a certificate. The *Hope* was seaworthy. Seaworthy. I've been to Greenland in worse-looking vessels. This is *business*. There's no time to be sentimental – we've too much responsibility to get hysterical. I will not have that language used in this office. This is a tragedy, for all of us.

Clementine *stands chastened.*

Clementine   I won't say another word.

Arthur   I've found the ship's roll. William Hest – thirty-seven, married four children, Henry Adams – thirty-five.

Makepeace *takes the roll from* **Arthur** *and continues reading it.*

Makepeace   Married four children. Stephen Pine – twenty-five, married one child – Geoffery Littleton – single, twenty-six. Neil Bloom – thirty-five, married seven children. George Wainwright, twenty-four, married no children –

As he is reading his litany **Susan** *comes into the office, followed by* **Mary**. *They are confronted with* **Makepeace** *reading the roll. He is obviously upset and they stand dumbstruck as he reads out the names.*

Solomon Berg – twenty-five, one child, Peter Jeffries – twenty-five, two children. Michael Staines, nineteen. James Fitzgerald – twenty-five. Benjamin Fitzgerald – nineteen.

He looks at **Susan**.

Toby Kemp – twelve.

Long devastated silence.

I'm so sorry, Mrs Kemp.

Mary   No. It can't be.

Makepeace   The Commissioner of Wrecks at Berwick telegraphed our Commissioner this morning. Benjamin Fitzgerald was washed ashore.

Susan   Oh Mary mother of Jesus . . .

Mary *bursts into hysterical laughter.* **Clementine** *goes to comfort her but* **Mary** *lashes out.*

Mary   Get off. Get off me.

Makepeace   I'm so sorry. It is God's will. We haven't had such a disaster in years. Please, I know it's no comfort but I'll pay your son's wages in full. Today, if you want it.

He realises this is no comfort. **Susan** *is bereft.*

I think it's best if you went home – this is no place to grieve. Try to rest and accept the inevitable.

Mary   I don't want to go home. I want to die.

Clementine   Cry, Mary, it will do you good. Just cry, my poor love . . .

Mary *shakes her head.*

Mary   No, no, not in front of you. I'll do that on my own.

Mary *looks* **Clementine** *in the eye, then she takes* **Susan** *and leaves.*

Arthur *looks at* **Makepeace**.

Makepeace   What's the matter with you? Are you going to sit on your arse all day? Get the Widows and Orphans' fund.

Arthur   It's locked away, sir.

Makepeace   For good reason.

Makepeace *throws him the keys.*

Arthur   Thank you, sir.

Arthur *opens a safe and takes out a large cash box.*

Makepeace   How many's on already?

Arthur   Twenty-five widows – and thirty-five children.
The fund'll never stand it. We'll have to put out an appeal.

Makepeace *crumples on his desk.*

Clementine   I'll never get over this.

Arthur   You will, Miss. There's plenty ships lost at sea. In
year or two the *Hope*'ll seem irrelevant.

He looks out to sea.

Just look at it now – smooth as a mill pond – who would
think it could take all those souls?

Jo *and* **William** *enter.* **Jo** *is extremely distraught.*

Clementine   Jo.

William   We had to get out of house.

Makepeace   Please, take this seat.

He places her by the fire.

Come by t' fire. You've heard.

Jo   Ben. But what 'bout James? Maybe . . .

Makepeace   Hush child, there's no comfort.

Jo   Maybe it isn't Benji – how can they tell?

Makepeace   His earrings. The skipper of *Expectation* . . .

Jo   What if they're wrong? Please, sir, give me some
money. I'll go up to Berwick myself, sir.

Makepeace   This is madness. Please, my sweet thing . . .

Jo   But if it is Benji, he'll need to be buried.

Makepeace   Please, it's all taken care of.

Under this conversation, **Simon** *has made a drunken progress through the streets and haphazardly comes up the stairs. He bursts in and stands swaying in the door. He is drunk, confused, with a wild look in his eye and a knife in his hand. The room stops dead at his arrival.*

Simon   I . . . I . . . heard . . .

Makepeace   Get out of here. You're drunk!

Simon   I . . . I . . . won't kill anyone . . . I don't mean you any harm . . .

Makepeace   Arthur, fetch a constable . . .

Simon   Stay there. I'll go of my own accord. I just came to say . . . I were right, weren't I? . . . I were right 'bout the *Hope.*

Makepeace   Get him out!

Simon   Don't come near me . . . (*He brandishes his knife.*) . . . I just came to say . . . to say that I were right . . . I warned you . . . admit it, I warned you when she was int' dock.

Makepeace   The man's raving.

Simon   Well, ask t' bookkeeper and daughter. They was there.

Makepeace   The man's a liar and a drunk. This is not the place, there are people grieving. Arthur, did you hear me?

Simon (*to* **Arthur**)   You were there. I showed you.

Arthur   No, I wasn't. Even if I were I wouldn't've heard owt, would I?

Makepeace   Did you hear this derelict warn us, darling?

Clementine   Father . . .

Makepeace   Come on, tell everybody. As my daughter, tell us what you heard.

Long pause.

Clementine   I can't remember.

Simon   Oh, you are so low. I told you it were rotten. Rotten!

Makepeace   You asked my daughter and my bookkeeper to bear witness. You heard what they said. Now be on your way.

William   Wait . . .

Makepeace   What the dickens is it now? Did you warn me too?

William   No, no . . . I remember . . . She knew. She might deny it . . . But she knew. . . night of storm. At Kit's . . .

Clementine   No, I . . .

William   Yes. Yes, you did . . . and I said: 'Miss, you're making it up *cos if your father knew* . . . knew *Hope* were rotten . . .

Jo   You started to cry – you were afraid the ship'd go down – I was there – Susan was there. Oh, you nest of vipers.

Makepeace   Vipers, is it? We who feed you year in, year out. Have you lost your mind? Surely you believe us before some drunken lunatic.

Jo   Believe YOU!? She's a liar but you are worse.

Makepeace   Get out.

Jo   You had Benji dragged on by police. You bastard. You murdering bastard. No need to show us out. James was too big a man to be pushed around. If I stayed here I would spit in your face, sir.

Makepeace   For Kitty's sake I'll assume the news got the better of you. The *Hope* was completely seaworthy.

'Seaworthy' – do you hear? Have I not lost too? Have you any idea what this'll cost me? And what if the drunk *had* warned me? What responsible businessman is expected to take decisions on the whims of an inebriate who can't get work anywhere up the coast cos he's too pissed to handle a mallet?

Simon   I told you . . . It was a floating coffin . . . It was the truth.

Makepeace   It was an accident. There was a storm.

Jo   Just give me some money. I'll go to Berwick – please, I won't say anything more.

Makepeace   You'll not have a penny. Not after what you've said, young lady.

Jo   I didn't know what I was saying – I don't – I don't know anything.

Makepeace (*softly, with great compassion*)   Please. Go home.

Simon   You're worse than the devil.

Simon *leaves, the others follow.*

Makepeace (*to* **Clementine**)   And you. Never set foot in this office again.

Clementine   How could I? . . . How could I ever respect you . . . or myself?

She leaves.

Makepeace   This is insanity.

Outside we hear **Trudger**'*s one-man band singing a carol.*

Makepeace   Oh, for Christsake . . .

He goes to the window.

Get lost, will you.

He sits down exhausted. He drinks some whisky and starts to read the roll of dead men.

Makepeace   'William Hest – thirty-seven . . .'

Tears well up in his eyes. He can no longer continue. He crumples the paper up and throws it away. He grabs the bottle and throws that across the room. He sweeps everything from his desk. He picks up a chair and smashes it into a cabinet. He thrashes and flails around, smashing up the whole room until all his anger, upset and frustration are spent. **Arthur** *cowers in the corner, not moving. This is* **Makepeace**'s *gig. He sits numb at his ruined desk.*

After time to gather himself, he picks up the phone and dials a number. As he is calling, **Kitty** *slowly walks from the dock, along the street and up the steps to the office.*

Makepeace   Hello. Taylor, please. Taylor – the insurer. Hello . . . Yes. Yes . . . The *Good Hope* . . . They found a hatch. And a sailor . . . What's that . . . no, we're not surprised either. What are the odds after sixty-odd days . . . yes, that's right . . . never a pleasant business . . . yes, I'll wait for you at my office. Thank you . . . Goodbye.

Kitty *comes in. She stands still at the door.* **Makepeace** *has his back to her and doesn't see she's there.*

Kitty   . . . I . . .

Eventually, the door falls shut, with a slam, as **Makepeace** *turns . . .*

Makepeace   Can't you knock?

He sees **Kitty** *and freezes.*

Kitty   I . . .

Makepeace   You're too late. They've gone.

He looks at her.

Kitty   Is it true . . . is it true . . . ?

Makepeace *looks at her.* **Kitty** *collapses.* **Makepeace** *runs to her and cradles her.*

Makepeace   Kitty. Kitty. Damn this awful business.

Arthur   Shall I get a doctor, sir?

Makepeace   No. Stay where you are. She's coming round.

Kitty *sobs for a long time in* **Makepeace**'s *arms.*

Arthur   Mrs Fitz . . .

Makepeace   Let her cry.

Makepeace *pushes* **Arthur** *away. He holds her tightly as she cries. It is an intensely personal moment between them.* **Makepeace** *is holding on to her for dear life.*

Kitty   He didn't even want to go. I had to prise him off t' doorpost.

Makepeace   You did nothing wrong.

Kitty   And I put on his dad's earrings – like a lamb to the slaughter.

Makepeace   Sssshh. Shh.

Kitty   And I never even saw my eldest go –

Makepeace (*deeply moved*)   Please. Stop.

Kitty   You know he could've been yours.

Makepeace   I'm sorry, Kitty.

Kitty   He might have been yours.

Makepeace   O God, I wish it were different.

Kitty   You loved me, Christopher.

Makepeace   It were a long time ago, Kitty.

Enter **Clementine**. *She looks in horror at the destruction.*

Kitty   You loved me.

Clementine   Kitty.

Kitty   Four sons. And a husband.

Clementine   Please, don't worry about anything. I've set up an appeal. It will be in the papers tomorrow. Arthur. (*She gives him a sheet of paper.*)

Makepeace *gestures for* **Clementine** *to leave.* **Clementine** *takes no notice and tends to* **Kitty**.

Clementine   Please, Dad, let me stay with her. I'll bring some hot soup. And you must come back to clean for us. You won't object, Dad? We'll look after you. Really.

Clementine *leaves hurriedly.*

Kitty   My only hope is James's bairn.

Makepeace   Bairn?

Kitty   Another accident. Jo.

She laughs.

Accident? It's no accident . . .

Makepeace   Please, you mustn't tell anyone about this. Please, it's for your own good. You know the rules of the fund, Kitty. You know they won't pay up with bastards in the house.

Kitty   Is that how you see it?

Makepeace   Kitty. It's nowt to do with me. You know that committee. Please, think about this. Your son in jail – your niece. I'll do my best but for God's sake don't mention this yet . . . there are seven families – sixteen orphans.

He stands and paces around.

Oh, Kitty.

Kitty   Is that all you can say?

Clementine *has arrived at the door with some hot soup. She is holding it in both hands and calls to* **Arthur** *to open the door.*

Clementine   Arthur. Arthur.

Arthur *opens the door and* **Clementine** *comes in with the tureen of soup.* **Makepeace** *stands at one end of the room, unable to say anything.* **Kitty** *is at the other frozen.* **Clementine** *goes to* **Kitty**.

Clementine (*very gently*)   Here.

Kitty *doesn't respond.*

Clementine   If you don't want it here – take it home. You can bring the bowl back whenever.

Kitty *stares ahead.* **Clementine** *puts the dish into her inanimate hands. A pause.* **Kitty** *is motionless with pain. She carefully puts down the tureen and walks out of the office. We hear her footfalls as she walks away. It is a long, devastating walk through the town, through the sails.* **Makepeace**'s *office disappears and she is alone walking through the endless sails, slowly getting smaller. We hear the footfall of clogs echo as she makes her lonely, proud walk down the quay until she is a tiny figure in the vast distance. She descends the steps down to the fish dock and disappears.*

The stage is empty. Distant voices quietly singing. The snow stops falling.

Epilogue

Spring 1901.

The snow miraculously disappears. It is a bright spring morning. The tattered sails of winter seem brand new and flapping resplendently in the breeze. From the back of the stage we hear a chorus of voices stridently singing.

Chorus
Raise your banners high
Strength to strength and line by line
Unity must never die
Raise your banners high.

Slowly, from the rear of the stage the townsfolk march forward in unison across the stage. In the centre, leading the progress is

Makepeace *with* **Clementine** *close to his side. They move as one towards the audience, resolute and hopeful.*

Raise your banners high
Strength to strength and line by line

They reach the very front of the stage. The line stretches from wing to wing. The entire community, except the men lost during the play, are gathered in an ensemble that echoes the opening image. They sing with strength and purpose.

Unity must never die
Raise your banners high.

As the anthem comes to its natural conclusion **Makepeace** *turns and through the crowd he brings* **Kitty** *carrying a wreath bearing the legend: 'The Good Hope'.* **Kitty** *throws it into the pit / the sea. The tableau freezes. A huge flash as if from a camera.*

Blackout.

Mr Puntila and His Man Matti

Adaptor's Note

'There are bad people who would be less dangerous if they had no good in them.'

La Rochefoucauld

Puntila and His Man Matti is a play riven with ambivalence. Puntila is constitutionally ambivalent about his role as capitalist as soon as he's had a drink, Matti is ambivalent about the virtues of buying into the good life, and it seems Brecht himself was ambivalent about the whole enterprise of the play. He wrote in his journal of 16 September 1940:

> puntila means hardly anything to me, the war is everything. about puntila I can write virtually anything, about the war nothing

Brecht had escaped Hitler and, whilst waiting for a passage to America (and the horrors of Hollywood) he had ended up in Finland as guest of Hella Wuolijoki. Hella was a gargantuan playwright specialising in people's folktales and Brecht came under her spell as a magnificent story-teller. He devoured her stories of everyday Finnish life and agreed that they should work on a play together based on the story of a Finnish landowner and his chauffeur, for a playwriting competition. Hella's original treatment of the tale was a conventional comedy focusing on the chauffeur's travails in love; but Brecht was dissatisfied with Hella's work and decided to write a version of his own and in the process turned the original premise on its head. Rather than being a simple allegory about class conflict with the comic resolution in marriage, the play is an uneasy essay on the difficulties of patronage and the dangers of being bought off. Brecht inverts the comic form and the final marriage is thwarted, leaving Matti to go off on his self-imposed exile from the Eden-like fecundity of the Puntila estate.

It is difficult not to think that Brecht was in some way writing about himself. The picture of an autocrat split between a determined and deterministic vision of how things must run and the Bacchanalian visionary driven by lust and sentimental overflowings of fraternity could easily be that of the contradictory playwright. There seems to be too much good in Puntila for Brecht to be simply preparing a little Marxist parable. Puntila's schizophrenic vacillations between monstrous sobriety and utopian dissipation seem to me to be an essay in self-criticism.

The famous caricature of Brecht at this time is of a philandering patriarch exploiting a harem of beautiful and talented women who were all doing the donkey work in creating the Brechtian canon. Ironists have been quick to point out Brecht's perversion of this communal endeavour. And whilst his collaborators have been famously overlooked (and in his lifetime grievously underpaid), it is still Brecht's plays we put on and not the works of Hella Wuolijoki. Brecht's relationship with his women and his work was difficult. But I don't think Brecht was unaware of the contradictions. The dilemma of the boss, the visionary who relies on others to manifest his projects, is very much at the heart of Puntila. And whilst we have our proletarian hero in Matti, it is Puntila who is the tragic figure, and Matti the one who almost buys into the whole corruption of Puntila Hall just as Puntila is seeking a way out. I think there is an element of self-disgust, impotence and loneliness in Puntila that must certainly have come from Brecht's own despair as he wrote to the sound of the Battle of Britain playing on his radio.

But the play is equally about Matti, his deep ambivalence towards Puntila and his increasing compromise as the story unfolds. I think it is a mistake to read Matti as simply a Harlequin-like prole who exposes the fatuity of his capitalist masters. Surely Brecht is examining everyone's capacity to buy into the paternalistic capitalism which Puntila represents. And in this way the play is about transition: growing self-awareness and discontent and its setting, as a long summer comes to a close, gives a powerful undercurrent. It is not until the very end that Matti finally realises how compromised he has been. I feel his ultimate dissatisfaction with the empty cant of paternalism is a

healthy challenge to the supine tolerance of our Blairite
version. And in this way I think the play is especially
relevant. To me Puntila's rhetoric is in the end as vapid and
as dangerous as Tony Blair's.

But as much as the play is a call to intellectual resolve, it
also punctures the sentimental wallowing in commutarian
cant. Puntila's final exhortations of the Brotherhood of Man
are so close to National Socialist jingoism that we can't
leave the theatre with an untroubled message. And in this
way I think the play is about the politics of our everyday
negotiations and not those of a programmatic kind. Brecht
is interrogating our ability to be bought off, by congenial
rhetoric or by personal promotion when those around us are
hungry, exploited or dissatisfied. It is about the everyday
machinations through which our soul, pride and good sense
are taken from us by tiny compromises. So, far from being
crude and schematic, Brecht is as far away from his parables
as we can imagine. He is domestic and full of melancholia.

But Brecht, to confuse matters, has written a knockabout
comedy purporting to be a class-war diatribe. And it is
precisely this ambivalence which makes it worth reviving.
Because, in an age where his vision is deemed anachronistic,
his sexual politics reviled and his aesthetic principles almost
irrelevant, I think there might be just enough good in him to
still be dangerous.

Lee Hall
1998

The original production of *Mr Puntila and His Man Matti* by the Almeida Theatre and the Right Size was first performed on 7 August 1998 at Malvern Theatres. The cast was as follows:

Puntila	Hamish McColl
Eva	Hayley Carmichael
Matti	Sean Foley
Waiter	Chris Larner
Judge	Mick Barnfather
Attache	Harry Gostelow
Vet	Jim Findley
Moonshine Emma*	Joy Richardson
Chemist's Assistant*	Samantha McDonald
Milkmaid – Lisu*	Hayley Carmichael
Telephonist – Sandra*	Golda John
Fat Man	Samantha McDonald
Labourer	Harry Gostelow
Red Hair	Chris Larner
Cripple	Jim Findley
Red Surkkala	Mick Barnfather
Laina	Golda John
Fina	Joy Richardson
Lawyer	Jim Findley
Parson	Chris Larner
Parson's Wife	Samantha McDonald

*Women of Kurgela
(*Additional Labourers to be played by company*)

Director Kathryn Hunter
Designer Tim Hatley
Associate Costume Design Johanna Coe
Lighting Ian Sommerville
Music and lyrics Chris Larner
Choreography Ryan François
Sound John A. Leonard
Assistant Director Jan-Willem van den Bosch
Lyrics Chris Larner

Prologue

(spoken to the audience by the actors playing Puntila and Matti.)

Before we start
This evening's art
We'd like to take you through a bit of theory
It's conceptual stuff
And it's short enough
But even so we are going to sing it so's to stop it getting
dreary.

(Sung.)

For here comes Bertolt Brecht
And we expecht
Your essays to be handed in b' Friday.
Karl Marx was a German fella
In 1867 he wrote a real bestseller
It's a Capital book packed with wit and wisdom
Concerning economics in a capitalist system
Where the rich get fat
And surplus value is expropriated
From the proletariat
The very hands in which ironic'ly that value is first
created.

Matti   Which means that cash is made by nicking it from
those who generate it.

Puntila *(aside)*   It's a bit political, isn't it?

Matti *(aside)*   It's a political play.

Puntila *(aside)*   No one told me.

Matti *(aside)*   Stick around, you might learn something.

Puntila *(aside)*   My mum is in.

Matti *(aside)*   She might learn something too.

Bert Brecht is a name that's dear to
Any Joe who dips his toe in socialist theatre.

No one ever did more than big bad Bertie Brecht did
In dramatic applications of a Marxist dialectic
Where he recreates
The historic struggle of the working classes
In such a way that alienates
And so denies the viewing public Aristotelian catharsis.

Matti   Which means that you lot have to get up off your theatre-going arses. (*Aside.*) Fat chance of that.

Puntila (*aside*)   What d'you mean?

Matti (*aside*)   Her in the third row, she's no stranger to sherry.

Puntila (*aside*)   She's paying your wages, sunshine.

And so to Puntila and Matti
Matti is a working man, Puntila is a fatty.
And it features some scenes of humorous behaviour
Performed against a backdrop of a mythic Scandinavia
Where the pine trees throng
With hardly room to cram another tree in.
Summer evenings are so long
And in Scene One Mr Puntila discovers a human being.

(*shouted by an actor, preferably through a megaphone*)   **Scene One. Mr Puntila discovers a human being.**

Puntila   Garçon, garçon. How long have we been here?

Waiter   Er, two days, Mr Puntila.

Puntila   What? Only a couple of days. Did you hear the bastard? (*To* **Judge**.) And you've collapsed already. For God's sake man, I'm just getting strong, ready to discourse life, love and the loneliness of man, and the lot of you fold like a deck of cards. Freddie, you have to set an example: subsciousness at any cost, Freddie. We are leaders of men, for Christ's sake. Garçon, what day is it?

Waiter   Saturday, Mr Puntila.

Puntila   That can't be right, it's got to be Friday.

Waiter   I beg your pardon, sir, but I'm afraid it's Saturday.

Puntila   I beg your pardon, sir, but it's Friday. Listen carefully. I want another aquavit and I want it on Friday. Capiche?

Waiter   Certainly, Mr Puntila, sir.

The **Waiter** *retires and* **Puntila** *addresses his sleeping companions.*

Puntila   Oi. You can't leave me alone like this. You've hardly even sniffed this stuff. While I am sailing across vast seas of liquor, the wind in my sails, coursing endlessly over the brine, master of mine own vessel, you are skulking in the keel, queasy before you've even left dry land. I have vast oceans in this belly of mine but do I drown, sirs? Do I drown?

Enter **Matti**, *watching from the door.*

Puntila   Who the fuck are you?

Matti   I'm your chauffeur, Mr Puntila.

Puntila   I beg your pardon?

Matti   Your driver.

Puntila   I don't know you from Adam.

Matti   Perhaps you just haven't noticed me. I've only been with you five weeks.

Puntila   Well, where the hell have you been hiding?

Matti   I've been outside in the car. For the last two days.

Puntila   Car?

Matti   The Studebaker.

Puntila   Absolutely preposterous.

Matti   Look, I've had it sitting out there freezing my bollocks off. You can't go round treating people like that. I'm just an ordinary human being.

Puntila   You just said you were a driver. A bit of a contradiction in terms, eh?

Matti   I'm not going to stand here like one of your cows. I'll take what you owe me and call at the hall for my reference.

Puntila   Wait a minute. I recognise that voice, that's a voice of humanity speaking, that is. Sit yourself down and have a drink. I'd like to get to know you.

Waiter   Your aquavit, sir. And today is Friday.

Puntila   Excellent. I'd like you to meet a friend of mine.

Waiter   Yes, sir, your driver.

Puntila   You meet the finest fellows on the road. Salut.

Matti   Hang on a minute. Hang on a minute. Hang on a minute. What's your game?

Puntila   Worried that you'll only flake out pissed and be robbed blind? I am Puntila of Lami, landowner, gentleman and man of honour. You're all right drinking with me, brother.

Matti   Matti Altonen. Pleased to meet you.

Puntila   I've got a heart of gold, me. I'd stop the car if I thought a cockroach was going to get run over − so I could put the bastard up a twig where it belongs. And I can see, Matti, you're like me. Selfless, Matti. Me, me, me. That's all people bloody think about. They want horsewhipping, Matti, because I ask you, what are we, Matti? We're all human beings, aren't we? At the end of the day we've all got hunger in our hearts and sadness in our bellies. Do you understand?

Matti   Absolutely.

Puntila   I can't believe I left you out in the road, Matti. Listen, next time, listen, just take the jack handle out of the boot and brain my fucking head in. Understand? (*Before* **Matti** *can reply.*) No. I'm serious. Friends?

Matti   No.

Puntila   Matti. Look into my eyes. What do you see?

Matti   A sad fat bastard pissed as an arse.

Puntila   Oh Matti, there is more to me than meets the eye. Beneath this jovial, avuncular exterior, Matti, I am a sick man.

Matti   Sick?

Puntila   I get attacks.

Matti   Really?

Puntila   Of sobriety, Matti. It'll be the death of me. You have no idea of the depravities I am sunk to when sober. I am traduced to a state of responsibility. Can you imagine being responsible for your own actions? Why, a responsible person knows no bounds. Goodbye friendship, goodbye humanity, goodbye basic human decency. A responsible person has only his own interests at heart, by definition. He'd trample over his own dead body to be responsible.

Matti   Isn't there anything you can do?

Puntila   I do everything that's humanly possible. (*Gets a glass.*) But what is this small draft against the vast desert of sobriety? Look at how I have misused you. Get this down your neck. And tell me what wind of fortune blew you my way.

Matti   Actually, I was driven on the wings of unemployment.

Puntila   A fine fellow like you?

Matti   Yes, I complained about the food, so they fired me for being a Marxist.

Puntila   Ah, the devils, skimping on a workman's diet.
Should I hold it against you if you are a Marxist, so long as
you drive in a straight line? Oh I can see we're going to get
along like a house on fire. Just render to Puntila what is
Puntila's and there'll be enough for everybody.

(*Sings.*)

> Oh Tavastland, oh Tavastland
> Let thy name ring clear
> No mountains that across the heavens stand
> No crystal lakes, no foaming strand.

I would love to chop down the birch trees with you, dig the
earth with my own hands, the sweat of our brows are
tributaries to a common river. But do they let me? 'It's
simply not done, Daddy.' No, Puntila has to sit like a
complete prog in a stiff starched shirt. Well fuck that. I'm
getting my daughter married off to an attaché by the name
of Eino Silakka. She's up at his aunt's place now. Listen,
together we'll sort it out. Then I'll be free to drink with my
men, Matti, in shirtsleeves, in fucking overalls. And
everybody'll get a rise.

Matti   You better keep it down or this one will have you
locked up.

Puntila   Matti, we're brothers you and me. Joined at the
hip. Tell me, Matti, that there is no gulf between us. Just say
it.

Matti   Mr Puntila, there is no gulf between us.

Puntila   Hear, hear. We must talk money, brother.

Matti   Absolutely.

Puntila   But we can't talk about money. It's degrading.

Matti   OK, forget it.

Puntila   But why shouldn't we talk about money? It's a
free country.

Matti   No it's not.

Puntila   There you are then. What we have to do, Matti, is drum up a little dowry for my dear daughter, Eva, to marry her off to the attaché.

Judge (*wakes up*)   Silence in court. (*Goes for his gavel and falls over.*)

Puntila   That settles it. We are off, brother. Here, take my money. I won't have it sully me any longer. Oh, I wish I had nothing. To be unencumbered, naked, wandering free, across the fields of Finland, just you and me. We have no need for money, common humanity would meet our every need. Every pub would fuel the ardour of our journey, every drink would be a sacrament to the world of man. Simple and undivided. Tell me, Matti. You like a drop or two. Don't you? Don't you?

Puntila *looks at* **Matti**.

All   (*sing* 'The Puntila Song')
Puntila, Puntila
Spent a week a-drinking in a hotel bar.
The waiter's dead
Three days late for bed
'I never noticed him' says Puntila
'And waiters are for waiting, that's the way things are.'

Puntila, Puntila
Thought that he'd befriend the bloke what drove his car.
'Take my purse
Cash is such a curse
We'll wander naked 'neath a lucky star
And talk about equality,' says Puntila

(*shouted seductively*)   **Scene Two. Eva.**

Eva *is waiting up patiently, the* **Attaché** *comes on bleary-eyed.*

Attaché   Eva, my darling, I've just received a frightful call from the village that a carload of screaming inebriates are heading in our direction.

Eva   That sounds like Daddy.

Noises off.

Eva   That must be him now. Where are you going?

Attaché   I simply have to avoid any unsightly scenes. Any sniff of scandal and my career's ruined. Take the German ambassador, he had eight brandies and called Madam Catrumple a whore. The poor fellow now works out of Ulan Bator. So you'll excuse me if I go to bed, my pumpkin.

Exit **Attaché**. *Enter* **Puntila**, **Judge** *and* **Matti**. *Crash through the door.*

Puntila   Eva. Here we are now. Don't worry, no need to wake anyone up. We'll just have a quick snifter and piss off to bed. Are you all right, dear?

Eva   We expected you three days ago.

Puntila   A little hiccup on the way, darling. But we've got everything we need. Matti, get the bag.

Judge   Anyway, congratulations, little Eva.

Eva   Daddy, this is an absolute outrage. I've been sitting here for a week in a strange house with a senile aunt, nearly driven to tears with boredom.

Puntila   My darling, it hasn't been easy for us either, but we persevered. At least you had the attaché for company. (*Nudge, nudge, wink, wink.*) Matti, watch that case for God's sake.

Judge   I trust you've not been quarrelling with the attaché already, Miss Eva.

Eva   Unfortunately one can't quarrel with a diplomat, even if one wants to.

Judge   Harry, the girl doesn't seem all that keen if you ask me.

Puntila (*opening the case of booze*)   Ta ta tatara ta. Mission accomplished. Listen, all I care about is whether you're happy, darling, if you're not then dump the bastard.

Eva   All I inferred was he's a little serious.

Puntila   Well, you should have Matti, here. He's a frivolous git, if ever there was one.

Eva   Daddy. (*To* **Matti**.) Take that upstairs.

Puntila   What about a toast to celebrate the engagement. Matti, wait a minute.

Eva   Daddy, he hasn't even proposed yet. Shut the case, at once.

Puntila   Not proposed? After three days? What the devil have you two been up to? Matti, the aquavit.

Eva   Daddy! (*To* **Matti**.) No more drinking.

Puntila   Well, what about old Aunt Klinkman, she's always gagging for a stiff one.

Eva   You will go to bed at once. She's furious enough as it is.

Puntila   You don't understand. I'll knock her up and straighten things out.

Eva   I understand perfectly well that no one wants to see you in this condition. (*To* **Matti**.) Take that upstairs. And that's final.

Puntila   Eva, what about the housekeeper with the big . . .

Eva   Don't push it or the crate goes down the stairs.

Puntila   Oh how I am used. Even the prodigal calf got his fatted son. Come on, Freddie, we're buggering off.

Judge   But we'll not find a drink anywhere at this time of night.

Puntila   We'll see about that.

Eva   Daddy, come back at once.

Puntila   You should honour thy father and mother, not hang them up to dry like a pair of old longjohns. I'm not over yet, Miss Eva Puntila. I'm off to find me a woman. You and that frigid bint upstairs can both go to hell. I will drive the winds with my passion and be the terror of the earth.

Puntila *exits*.

Eva   Stop him, do you hear?

Matti   Too late, Miss Eva.

Judge   Oh well, think I'll pop off to bed.

Eva   Now we'll have to wait up for him. He'll only come back and wake up the servants.

Matti   I wouldn't worry about it too much if I was you. They could always resign you know.

Eva   You don't understand. They'll only take advantage of him.

Matti   Miss Eva. The advantage will be all his. He can sit amongst rats and mistake them for kings.

Eva   I'd appreciate you keeping your aphoristic speculations to yourself. And I trust you'll be discreet regarding my comments on the attaché.

Matti   Far be it from me to mention his limitations as a human being, Miss Eva.

Eva   What exactly are you implying?

Matti   I'm not implying anything.

Eva   The attaché is very well respected in his field. With excellent prospects. He's one of the service's most prominent members. It's just, well, I'm more the vivacious type.

Matti   Not getting cold feet, are you?

Eva   Oh, I don't know what I'm trying to say. Anyway, why am I talking to you? Why aren't you in bed?

Matti   I'm keeping you company.

Eva   Well, there's absolutely no need. I just wanted to tell you Mr Silakka shouldn't be judged by appearances or what he says or does, he's intelligent and kind and never inclined to parade any vulgar masculinity . . .

Matti *yawns.*

Eva   Are you tired?

Matti   Not at all. I was only closing my eyes so I could concentrate better.

(*whispered by the cast*)   **Scene Three. Puntila engages the early risers.**

Puntila *runs the Studebaker into a pole.*

Puntila   What the hell is going on here? Out of the way! You pile of piss. Call yourself a telecommunication system. Have you got a forest? Have you got cows? Eh? Eh? Don't look so fagging clever now, do you?

He meets **Moonshine Emma**.

Puntila   Good morrow, my kind lady. I am one Puntila of Lami, farmer, landowner and forever your most humble servant, and I am extremely perturbed on account of the fact that I must obtain sufficient alcohol for my seventy-plus fevered cows.

Moonshine Emma   Jesus H. Christ. Look, the vet's over there, man. But if it's a little drink you are after, I might have a drop or two.

Puntila   How dare you try to palm me off with your illicit moonshine. I drink legit or not at all.

Moonshine Emma   I hope you choke on your legit, sir.

Puntila *knocks on the* **Vet***'s door.*

Puntila   Oh, vet, vet, oh salvation. I am Puntila of Lami, owner of approaching ninety cows, each one of them sick with the scarlet fever.

Vet (*deaf as a post*)   Charles the beaver.

Puntila   What?! Scarlet fever! Sir, I'm not coming to you with some flannel about glanders or consumption. Sir, I am talking full-blown scarlet fever.

Vet   The beaver has a fever?

Puntila   Scarlet fever. They've got red patches – they've got black fucking patches. They've got fucking eye-patches. They can't sleep for thinking of their sins.

Vet   Well, I suppose you better have some of these.

He writes out a prescription.

Puntila   What's this?

Vet   A prescription.

Puntila   Ah, you are the very Hippocrates of veterinary practice. Send the bill to Puntila Hall.

Moonshine Emma (*sings*)
   Got me a man
   The best I have ever had
   Good enough to drive you mad
   Sweet and simple sugar-dad.
   Ooh you're sexy and you're strong
   And I need a man to treat me wrong wrong, wrong, wrong.

Puntila *goes to the chemist and rings the bell.*

Chemist's Assistant   Hey, wait a minute, you'll bust the blooming bell.

Puntila   I'll bust your fat head if you take any longer. This is a dire emergency. I need alcohol for ninety cows.

Chemist's Assistant   Look, I'll call a policeman (if you . . .).

Puntila   A policeman. In my current state you'd need half the local constabulary. But here, my skylark, here's propriety for you.

He offers the prescription.

Cut the crap and get the booze.

She goes into her shop to get the alcohol.

Chemist's Assistant   I hope them cows have plenty herrings for the morning after, that's a fair size bottle you've got there.

Puntila   Glug, glug, glug. Oh melodious music. Finland's fair anthem. The loveliest sound in the world. Give me surfeit of it. But here am I with alcohol and no lady. Oh sweet pharmacist, will you marry me?

Chemist's Assistant   Well, I'd need a ring.

Puntila   A ring! You can have a ring for every digit. You can have a sack full of the buggers. Oh my sweet angel. Just tell me. What sort of life do you lead?

Chemist's Assistant   Me?

Puntila   Yes, my sweetheart, what sort of life do you lead?

Chemist's Assistant   I don't know. Well, I did four years at pharmacy school. And now I work here. They charge me room and board, so I end up coming out with less than the cook. I send half to Mum. She's not too grand. Dodgy ticker. Runs in the family. The chemist's always trying to touch me up, so his wife's got it in for me. But I'm quite good at my job – except the prescriptions. I often get the prescriptions muddled, it's the doctor's writing, it's like an incontinent spider. But nobody's died or anything, except for Miss Blethyn but she was on her way out with the palsy. I'm single, I suppose it goes without saying. I used to go out with the postman but he ran off with Vera from number twelve. So. Here I am, I suppose. On the shelf. It's quite a sad life really.

Puntila   My sweet dove. Come to Puntila. Here, sip the milk of human kindness.

Chemist's Assistant   What about the ring?

Puntila   This is an emergency. Don't you have any curtain rings?

Chemist's Assistant   I imagine. How many do you need?

Puntila   As many as you can spare. I must have lots of everything. One engagement is not nearly enough. I'll marry the whole of Finland.

Moonshine Emma (*sings*)
Got me a man
He's courteous and polite
Comes back home to me at night
Sober as a stalagite.
Ooh, I hope you understand this song
'Cos I need a man to treat me wrong, wrong, wrong.

Puntila   Come up to Puntila Hall on Sunday. There'll be a huge engagement party. (*Walks on and sees the* **Milkmaid**) Woah, my little pigeon. Where are you off to so early?

Milkmaid   I'm off to milk the cows.

Puntila   Sitting there with nowt except a bucket between your legs. Don't you want a husband? What kind of life do you call that? Eh, my little popinjay, what sort of life do you lead then?

Milkmaid   Life? I wouldn't exactly call it a life. I'm up at half three mucking out the cows. Then there's milking, and

sterilising the pails. I'm always burning my hand on that
bloody caustic. Then I have a cup of that cheap blinkin'
coffee and I'm mucking out the stalls again. For dinner I'm
lucky if I get a few slices of toast and a bit of butter.
Although of a weekend I can sometimes cadge the odd
potato but I never see a slice of meat from one month's end
to the next. I get one Sunday off in five and I go dancing –
but you have to be careful, one foxtrot too many and you'd
be up the stick before you can say Tavastland Dairies. I've
got two nice frocks and a bike.

Puntila   Oh my tiny sparrow. I have a farm and a mill and
a forest and one hundred cows and no woman to see me
through the days. Take this ring, come up to Puntila Hall on
Sunday, and Bob's your uncle.

Milkmaid   You're on, mate.

Puntila   Who'd have thought there'd be so many of them
up by dawn? They're irresistibly callow in the young
morning dew. Good morrow, little starling. Aren't you the
telephonist I so often speak with?

Telephonist   Indeed I am, Mr Puntila.

Puntila   Tell me what kind of life is it that you lead?

Telephonist   I'll tell you what kind of life I lead. Fifty
marks for being at the switchboard eighteen hours a day.
For the last thirty years. I've not had a single day off since
1904. I have one meal a day, that's usually gruel and water,
I'm so poor I have to grow my own turnips in the few
moments I have before bedtime. My father was a cobbler
who went blind through lead poisoning and my mother died
when I was a child of bovine influenza so I had to bring up
my seven brothers and encephalitic sister single-handed.
Working my fingers to the bone and growing dud turnips,
that's my life, buster.

Puntila   Well, it's time you had a new one, my poor little
finch. Ring through to the area manager. Tell him you are

about to be married. Here's a ring, some liquor. See you at Puntila Hall on Sunday. Oh life is sweet.

Telephonist   Mr Puntila, aren't you celebrating your daughter's engagement on Sunday?

Puntila   Indeed I am, ma'am. This is going to be the engagement party of the century.

He gives another ring to **Moonshine Emma**.

I trust you will be there too.

Moonshine Emma (*sings*)
> Got me a man
> So damn good to me
> All he drinks is herbal tea
> Treats me like a deity.
> Ooh, I'm sure we'll get along
> 'Cos I need a man to treat me wrong, wrong, wrong.

Puntila   And now to the hiring fair where I will hire only the most humane of workers. Oh you country girls, up so early year after year. Oh now Puntila has come. Come to all you stove lighters and kitchen maids, to you chicken feeders and apothecaries' slaves, women of sturdy thighs and honest toil. Oh how I am moved by the pity of your lives and the spark of your smiles. How I come to adore you. How I am come to raise you up. (*Collapses.*)

(*shouted by the cast*)   **Scene Four. The hiring fair. Fairground music.**

Puntila (*now sobered up*)   I can't believe you allowed me to go off driving in that state. I've got your number. You're no better than the disciples on the Mount of Olives. Taking advantage of an inebriated man. It's not on.

Matti   Of course not, Mr Puntila.

Puntila I'm not prepared to argue with you. I've been hurt enough as it is. Keep yourself to yourself, understand? That's how you stay employed, sunshine. You want someone who pulls his weight not a precocious little twat, who'd rather be bunking off, shovelling fillet steaks down his neck. Know thy place. Be unassuming. Understood?

Matti Be unassuming, Mr Puntila. But perhaps we should get cracking, sir, before they're all gone?

Puntila They've got to be strong. (*Examining.*) Not bad, not bad, quite a big boy. But look at his feet, for Christ's sake. Look at those shoes. The lazy bastard. Can you cut peat?

Man Excuse me, I happened to be here first.

Puntila Look, do me a favour and piss off, will you? Half a mark a metre. Start Monday.

Man This is outrageous, I'm in the middle of negotiating a contract.

Puntila Look, stop interfering, you overweight baboon.

Man I'm not standing here to be insulted.

Puntila Well, go over there and I'll throw my voice. (*To the* **Labourer**.) Have you got a family, mate?

Labourer Yes.

Puntila Okeydoke. I'll hire the lot of them. That's what I call negotiations.

Labourer But where will we lodge?

Puntila Lodge. You'll live like princes. Now I want to see a nice line when I turn round. Where's the nice line? (*Inspects the workmen.*) You'd think this fellow here was ideal to look at him. But if you note the arse of his pants, you see a different story. This bastard's been sat down most of his working life. No. Nothing gets past Puntila. Get them old – so they work like dogs in case you lay them off. Yes. Puntila goes by the man himself, not the outward appearances. No slackers, no men of intelligence. Then we'll all get along like a house on fire. Sort out a few more hands, will you? I just have to pop inside to . . . make a phone call.

Puntila *goes inside and quickly downs a vast quantity of alcohol while* **Matti** *hires more men.*

Matti   Excuse me. Would you be interested in cutting peat up at Puntila Hall?

Surkhala   Listen, if you are gonna work for him make sure he signs the contracts.

Matti   Leave it to me, I'll sort it out.

Puntila   Ah Matt, my fine fellow.

Matti   What do you think, sir?

Puntila   Oh a very fine fellow. Full of vigour. What about this one? I like the look in his eye.

Matti   I don't want to speak out of turn, but the man's a cripple, Mr Puntila.

Cripple   I'll have you know, I'm as fit as the next man. (*The next man is a little girl.*)

Matti   Look, keep schtum, hopalong. As soon as he's sober you'll be out on your ear for the winter picking berries.

Puntila   Gentlemen, I have made a surprise decision. I'm gonna hire the lot of you. Come into the bar and we'll discuss the matter further. Ah madam. Drinks all round. (*To* **Matti**.) Matti, just a little word. I must apologise for my rather fractious behaviour before, old boy. I was unfortunately on the verge of an attack of sobriety. Matti, Matti, say you will forgive me.

Matti   Let's let sleeping dogs lie but you must sort it out properly. The fair'll be over shortly and these blokes will never find anything else. Let's get these contracts settled.

Puntila Come on, Matti, don't be an officious arse. Salut. (*They drink.*) Same again. (*Of the Waitress.*) Fit as a butcher's dog. (*Bites her.*) I am a butcher's dog. Oh how I hate these fairs. One can buy and sell pigs or cattle. But human beings, Matti, how can one sell human beings? It's just not right, Matt. What do you reckon?

Cripple You're absolutely correct, Mr Puntila

Matti But you're not buying or selling people, Mr Puntila. You need workers, they need work. You have to do it somehow. The important thing is to honour the contract.

Puntila Matti, Matti. I am Puntila of Lami. I am a man of the people. A man of honour. We just need to have a natter to see if we get on. To see if they like me. That's the question, isn't it? What kind of man am I?

Matti Mr Puntila, nobody's interested. They want contracts. So please sign them.

Puntila Isn't that Surkhala? I thought he worked for me already.

Matti You fired him because the parson said he was a communist.

Puntila Surkhala! The one intelligent man on the estate. The man has four children. Fuck the parson. Give him ten marks and we'll take him back in the Studebaker.

Red Hair Please. Could you just write out the contracts or I'll have to go.

Puntila Look, (*To* **Matti**.) this is all your doing. Sir, Puntila does not sign contracts. Puntila gives a man a place to live on his estate, food in his belly, work to be proud of, simply in return for a little trust.

Red Hair That's it. I'm off.

Puntila Wait. Sir. Oh he was a good man whatever the condition of his trousers. I say bugger a man's trousers. I

look deeper than that. It's what's inside a man's trousers
that matters to me. To the human being.

All   To the human being.

Puntila
Oh Tavastland, oh Tavastland
Oh country of . . .

What was I saying? You're coming, aren't you?

Cripple   Oh yes, of course, sir.

Matti   Bugger off now before he sobers up.

Puntila   Come on, let's off to Puntila Hall. And bring that
Surkhala, an excellent worker and a first rate mind. Oh
happy days. I tell you what, I tell you what, why don't we all
go and sort out that fat git from before, the capitalist
bastard.

All (*sing*)
Pun-til-a, Pun-til-a
Contractual formality was his *bête noire*
Let's get pissed
I am practically a communist
'Come on and work for me,' says Puntila
'We'll get along like brothers, that's the way things are.'

But have a care, he's a strange one
When he's pissed he's rinky-dinky
As a day trip to Helsinki
But beware, there's a change on
Careful there
After several cups of coffee
He is an archetypal toff, he's
An incorrigable twat
So what d'you make of that?

Puntila, Puntila
La di da di da di da di
Blah blah blaaah.

(*shouted by an actor*)   **Scene Five. Scandal at Puntila Hall.**

Laina *and* **Fina** *nail a sign saying 'Welcome to the Engagement Party' across the stage.*

Laina   Ah, welcome home, Mr Puntila. Miss Eva and the attaché arrived an hour ago.

Puntila   Home sweet home. Now Mr Surkhala, sir, I must, before we go on any further, apologise to you and your wife and all your family, with the deepest regret for the fear and insecurity I have caused you. (*Falsely stopping his interjections.*) No. No. No. No. It was a terrible thing. Laina, these gentlemen are staying to work the forest.

Laina   But I thought you were selling the forest for Miss Eva's dowry.

Puntila   For God's sake, Miss Eva's dowry is between her legs, is it not? I'm off to the sauna.

Fina *hands him coffee.*

Laina   Maybe we should settle the contracts up so we can all relax.

Puntila   Bollocks to the contracts. Laina, get these men an aquavit and a nice strong coffee for me.

Puntila *goes into the sauna.*

Matti   The best thing you lot can do now is bugger off and come back when he's on another bender.

Puntila   Matti, tell Laina about the fat man. Fina, you couldn't just pop a drop of brandy in there for me?

Laina   Mr Puntila, what's the point of having coffee if you're going to put brandy in it?

Puntila   All right, all right. But tell her about the fat man.

Matti   Mr Puntila met a fat man at the fair.

Puntila   One of them fat, blotchy, capitalist pigs. Tell them what he was doing.

Matti   We were going to the car and we saw this fella whipping his horse.

Puntila   If there's one thing I can't abide it's cruelty to animals. Matti, carry on.

Matti   So Mr P grabbed the poor creature's reins and calmed it down and then he gave the fat man a piece of his mind. I thought we were going to get horse-whipped but the fat bastard mumbled something about 'uneducated scum'. So Mr P said at least he had enough education not to be so fat.

Puntila   You forgot to say he went as red as a beetroot.

Matti   He went as red as a baboon's arse and Mr P said don't get excited, mate, or you'll give yourself a stroke but at least his family could donate his body to medical science, and everybody was wetting themselves. You know, I knew a man who donated his body to medical science because of his especially long . . . thigh.

Laughter.

Laina   I think it's terrible hitting animals.

Puntila   Absolutely right. Have yourself a liqueur, Fina.

Matti (*to* **Puntila**)   Do you feel any better now?

Puntila   I feel worse. It's this stinking coffee.

Matti   Anyway, I thought it was very brave. A lot of people would have thought twice, especially him being such a good customer and Mrs Klinkman's brother-in-law.

Fina   You didn't know he was Mrs Klinkman's brother-in-law?

Matti   No. That was the best part. You were slagging her off left, right and centre. What did you say again?

Puntila   I don't remember.

Matti   It was something witty. About her and a saveloy.

Laina   More coffee, Mr Puntila?

Puntila   Don't ask stupid questions. Of course I need more coffee. What are you doing loafing round here telling stories? Take the piss out of me once more, you'll be getting your reference. Understood.

Puntila *storms out darkly.*

Laina   What did you let him go and insult the brother-in-law for?

Matti   It's a free country, isn't it?

Puntila *returns.*

Puntila   Listen. I've decided, I might have taken this one here. At least he can stand upright. But I'm taking no one at all. I'm selling the forest. And you can all blame him. Give me your jacket. (**Matti** *hands him his jacket.*) Bingo. What this then?

Matti   Your wallet, Mr Puntila.

Puntila   I can't hear you.

Matti   Your wallet, Mr Puntila.

Puntila   I beg your pardon?

Matti   Your wallet. Mr Puntila

Puntila   Exactly! Fina, call the police. On second thoughts, I'm not doing you that kind of favour. It'd suit you down to the ground lounging around on taxpayers' money. No, you're not going to a nice warm cell, sunshine. I'm going to have you out driving the tractor. See what a bit of real work does for you.

Cripple   What about me, Mr Puntila?

Puntila   What about you? You're a cripple. You can take a hike as well.

Cripple   But the hiring fair . . .

Puntila   You should have thought about that before trying to take advantage of me. (*He storms off.*)

Cripple   I'll report you.

Matti   Who to?

Labourer   No problem, Matti, we'll just walk the ten miles home. Typical. (*The men leave.*)

Eva   We all know he'd give his wallet to anybody when he's drinking. Why didn't you stick up for yourself?

Matti   What good would it've done me? Surely the last thing you lot want is a worker defending himself.

Eva   For God's sake, don't be so pathetic. I'm not in the mood.

Matti   Of course not, you're about to marry the attaché.

Eva   Don't get smart. He's a terribly sweet man – just not to get married to. Maybe there's a way of getting him to back out of his own accord.

Matti   You need someone to help who has refined the arts of crudity.

Eva   What on earth could you do?

Matti   Well, just suppose I was encouraged by your father's kind suggestion that you take me as your husband. And you felt the certain lure of my crude passion. The attaché interrupts us. And Bob's your uncle. The sniff of scandal and he'd be away like the clappers.

Eva   Goodness, that would be far too much to ask.

Matti   All part of the service, ma'am. It'd take fifteen minutes, tops. Of course, we will have to adopt terms of intimacy. Your blouse is undone, Eva.

Eva   Really? Oh, you were acting. Oh goodness, he's not that easily offended. You see, he's awfully in debt and desperate for the dowry.

Matti   Well, I could pull a pair of your knickers out my pocket.

Eva   You could have taken them in my absence. But, I say, you've got an awfully good imagination.

Matti   In fact, it's running riot.

Eva   Well, you can stop it at once.

Matti   Look if he's that hard up, we'll just have to get caught in the sauna together.

Eva   You're joking.

Matti   I'm dead serious.

Eva   I hope you're not up to something.

Matti   Like what?

Eva   I'm never sure when you're sending me up.

Matti   I quite like making women unsure.

Eva   I can imagine.

Matti   Oh well. (*Walks away.*)

Eva   Oooooooooh, all right. They'll be coming any minute. We better get in there right away.

Matti   Off you go, I'll get the cards.

Eva   Cards?

Matti   How did you think we were going to pass the time?

Laina   Are you OK, Miss Eva?

Eva   I'm just going to the sauna, I have a terrible headache.

Eva *goes into the sauna. Enter* **Attaché** *and* **Puntila**.

Attaché   I wonder where Eva has got to. I was thinking about driving her down to Monte to see if we could borrow Baron Smegma's Rolls. I know she'd make an awfully good impression.

Puntila   Laina, has anyone seen Eva?

Laina   She's in the sauna. She's got a headache.

Puntila   The sauna. With a headache?

Attaché   It's a terribly original idea. I believe we don't make enough of our Finnish saunas. Why isn't there a sauna in the Houses of Parliament, for instance?

Puntila (*bewildered*)   I hope that the minister's still coming to the party.

Attaché   Yes, of course. The old boy's got a soft spot for me. He says I'd make an excellent ambassador, as politics don't interest me in the slightest.

Puntila   Just make sure he turns up.

Attaché   He'll be here as sure as eggs is eggs, Mr Puntila.

Matti *comes through.*

Puntila   What the devil are you up to? Do you think I pay you to loaf about carrying towels around?

Matti   Certainly not, Mr Puntila. I'm just off to the sauna.

Matti *gets into the sauna.* **Puntila** *suddenly realises.*

Puntila   Exactly how well are you getting on with Eva?

Attaché   Terribly well, I'd say. Not unlike our position vis-à-vis Russia. She's sometimes a little frosty, but as we say in the diplomatic corps, relations are correct. Come, I shall pick her some flowers.

Puntila   That's not a bad idea.

Exit **Puntila** *and the* **Attaché**.

Matti   It's all going according to plan.

Eva Didn't he try to stop you?

Matti He's so hung over he hardly knew what was happening.

Eva I'm not sure this will work. What if they don't think dirty thoughts? After all, it's only mid-morning.

Matti All the better. A sign of exceptional passion. Gin rummy? Phew, it's hot. Take something off? I don't mind. Clubs are trumps.

Eva You have no respect, have you?

Matti No.

Eva Actually, I'm used to rather refined conversation. I went to school in Brussels, you know.

Matti Refined or the raw material, stupidity is still stupidity, Miss Eva. Your deal.

Enter **Puntila** *and* **Attaché** *carrying roses.*

Attaché And I said to her, 'Madam, if you weren't so rich you'd be perfect.' And she said, 'I wouldn't be perfect unless I was rich.' Absolutely marvellous, don't you think? Just like the time the Baroness Blackthorn threw the retort at the minister for housing . . .

Matti I think you should moan a bit (*A bored moan from* **Eva**.) as if I'm massaging you. (*A timid moan.*) Try and sound as if you're enjoying it. (*She howls.*)

Attaché I say. Wasn't that Eva?

Puntila Certainly not, it must've been someone else.

Matti Is that good for you, dear?

Attaché What was that?

Moaning.

Matti Not quite so enthusiastic.

Puntila   Oh it must be my chauffeur, Matti, he's in the sauna. He lives there. Why don't we go inside?

Eva   Yes, yes. That's it.

Matti   Don't peak too early.

Eva   Don't stop. (*Very loud moaning.*)

Attaché   That sounds awfully like Eva.

Puntila   Don't be absurd.

In the hut.

Eva   What do I do now?

Matti   Just sound as if you're having a good time.

Eva   Aaaahh! Aaaaaaaah! What now?

Matti   Keep going.

Eva (*excited*)   Matti, Matti.

Puntila   I'm sure there is nothing untoward.

(*Bursts in.*) Eva!

Eva *and* **Matti** *are in a compromising position.*

Attaché   Oh dear.

Puntila   Eva.

Eva   Daddy. Did you call?

Puntila   What the devil are you up to?

Attaché   No need to get upset now. We've just heard some noises and thought you may have been in distress.

Eva   Oh no. It was nothing. (**Matti** *appears.*)

Matti   Ah, Mr P.

Puntila   Do you call that nothing?

Matti   Eva and I were just playing poker. And she got a royal flush.

Puntila You're fired.

Attaché I say, I always get frightfully caught up in cards myself. I once got so excited over a game of pinocle at Mme Binoche's I wet myself. Hideously embarrassing, Eva, I've brought you some roses. And here's one for you. Anyone for billiards?

Puntila (*to* **Matti**) And as for you, if you so much as look at my daughter again, I'll kick you so hard you'll be using your bollocks as tonsils.

Attaché Excellent, carry on.

Puntila *storms off after the* **Attaché**.

Eva Hopeless.

Matti His debts must be bigger than we thought.

The cast sing.

Puntila, Puntila
Introduced his daughter to some caviar
Luxury engenders such ennui
'I'm getting shot of you' says Puntila.
'The wedding's fixed for Tuesday
That's the way things are.'

(*an actor announces*) **Scene Six. A conversation about crabs.**

Farm kitchen at Puntila Hall. **Matti** *is reading the paper whilst music plays outside.*

Fina Matti. Miss Eva wants a word.

Matti Tell her I'm drinking my coffee.

Fina You don't fool me. You're gagging for a bit of posh, aren't you?

Matti   Well, maybe if you'd've had a stroll with me down the river, thoughts of social advantage wouldn't cross my mind.

Fina   I'm not sure I can be bothered.

Matti   It's that school teacher, isn't it?

Fina   You must be joking, all he ever does is read me poetry.

Matti   That's the trouble with educated people. They take their jobs too seriously. Why don't you come and sit over here, Fina?

Fina *goes over and lies down on the table.* **Matti** *mounts her just as the* **Judge** *and* **Lawyer** *arrive.*

Judge   I say, you wouldn't happen to have a glass of buttermilk?

Fina *and* **Matti** *fall off the table and cover with:*

Matti   Oh, here's the needle.

Lawyer   We're not interrupting anything?

Fina   Not at all.

Judge   I'm glad to hear it. This weather is causing me nothing but trouble. There are more paternity cases than I can shake a stick at. Dreadful business. They shag all summer because it's too short, and shag all winter because it's too long. That's all they think of, shag shag shag.

Lawyer   It's non-stop fructification. Absolutely marvellous.

A bell rings.

Judge   I say, shouldn't you get that? Or will we tell them you are working to rule?

Exit **Judge** *and* **Lawyer**. **Eva** *comes in.*

Eva   Didn't you hear me?

Matti   Look. I'm not on until six o'clock.

Eva   I know. That's why I wondered if you'd like to row over the lake with me? To catch crabs for the party.

Matti   Isn't it past your bedtime?

Eva   I'm not a bit tired. Could you sleep if you went to bed now?

Matti   Yes.

Eva   Well, you have an enviable disposition. I'll just have to go on my own.

Matti   OK. I'll row you, if you insist.

Eva   But aren't you tired?

Matti   I've woken up all of a sudden. You weren't thinking of going like that though, were you?

Eva *undresses revealing her shorts.*

Eva   Of course not. Where are the nets?

Matti   Why take nets when we could use our hands?

Eva   No net?

Matti   I'm pretty good with my hands.

Eva   But Daddy likes a lot of crabs.

Matti   We don't want to ruin such a beautiful evening humping all that equipment. I know a real nice spot. Ten minutes and we'd be done. Then we could just lie and watch the moon.

Eva   Anybody would think you didn't want to get your hands dirty.

Matti   On the contrary. (*Long pause.*) But I do have to be up at six to fetch the minister. So . . .

Eva   I see.

Eva *goes out then comes back wearing her coat ready to leave.*

Eva   Take me to the station.

Matti   OK.

Eva   Aren't you going to ask me.why?

Matti   I should think you're catching the 11.10 to Helsinki.

Eva   Doesn't that surprise you?

Matti   What difference does a chauffeur's surprise make?

Eva   I just thought you might be intrigued that I am off to Brussels to stay with a school friend. You'll have to lend me two thousand marks until I get it back off Daddy.

Matti   Sure. No problem.

Eva   I hope Daddy won't be too upset. Him being in debt – to you – so to speak.

Matti   I'd have thought you were more likely to incur his wrath. He's buying you a life of Riley. Ambassadress to Paris, or Estonia, or Berlin. Oh, yes, Miss Eva.

Eva   So you think I should marry the attaché now.

Matti   I suggest you're in no position to do otherwise.

Eva   So you won't lend me two thousand marks, because you don't want to risk your money.

Matti   Or my job.

Eva   Oh, you're really quite a materialist, aren't you, Mr Altonen? I see the love of money is no preserve of the affluent.

Matti   I'm sorry to disappoint you, Miss Eva.

Eva   Well, I'm not going to marry him.

Matti   I don't know why you're so choosy. They're all the same. Public school. University. Breeding. That's what they've got. They have been trained to smell a good ripe vintage. Haven't they, Miss Eva?

Eva   I want you.

Matti   Me?

Eva   Daddy'll give us a sawmill.

Matti   He wouldn't give me flu.

Eva   But if we were married.

Matti   I'd be packed off fishing whenever the parson came round. But at least I'd be able to drive the kids to school. 'Come on now, Daddy, faster in the front, I say.' No thank you.

Eva   Of course not. You'd have to be boss, wouldn't you? I can imagine how I'd be treated.

Matti   Been thinking about it?

Eva   Don't flatter yourself. I'm sick of hearing you talk about nothing but yourself the whole time. What *you* like, what *you've* heard, what *you* think. Well, let me tell you, I can't stand the sight of you any longer. You're just like the rest of them. A tedious pontificating egoist. I hate you.

She goes out. **Matti** *sits down slowly and takes out his paper.*

(*an actor announces*)   **Scene Seven. Union of Mr Puntila's Fiancées.**

Sunday morning. **Puntila** *is arguing with* **Eva**.

Puntila   Look, you're marrying the attaché and that's that. You're not getting a penny otherwise.

Eva   But yesterday you said I should marry the man I love.

Puntila   Yesterday I was pissed. Look, if you so much as go near that stinking chauffeur again I'll murder the pair of you. What were you thinking of? Cavorting. In the sauna! (*Shouting off.*) Get that horse out of the living room. The whole place is going to rack and ruin. I'm not having you lot ruining my estate . . .

Eva   Nobody's ruining anything

Puntila   It's costing me a forest, a whole bleeding forest, to marry you into something decent, and you're in the sauna messing about with every Tom, Dick and Harry who can steer a tractor. You didn't get a posh education in Brussels to end up shagging some jumped-up cabbie.

Telephonist *arrives, with the other three women of Kurgela who wait at the gate.*

Telephonist   Good morning. Is Mr Puntila around?

Matti   I don't think he's taking visitors. He's not feeling too grand.

Telephonist   But he will see his fiancée, I wager.

Matti   Fiancée?! You're engaged to Mr Puntila?

Telephonist   As far as I'm aware.

Puntila (*overheard*)   I've killed a pig, for Christ's sake, I can't just ask it to get up and trot off to its sty because she has changed her mind.

Telephonist   Who is that?

Matti   Your fiancé.

Telephonist   He didn't sound like that in Kurgela.

Matti   Kurgela?

Telephonist   Maybe I need to see his big, kind, smiling face, rosy from the dawn.

Matti   Please. Take my advice and go home.

Moonshine Emma *enters the yard.*

Moonshine Emma   I'd like to see Mr Puntila. Immediately.

Matti   I'm afraid he's indisposed, but perhaps you'd like to meet his fiancée.

Telephonist   Excuse me, but aren't you Moonshine Emma, purveyor of cheap liquor?

Moonshine Emma   I'll have you know my alcohol is used by the stationmaster to pickle his cherries.

Milkmaid and Chemist's Assistant   Excuse me, could we see Mr Puntila?

Matti   Who the hell are you?

Milkmaid   We're from Kurgela.

Matti   For Christ's sake, how many fiancées has he got in Kurgela? Go away. You're not engaged to the same Mr Puntila who is currently upstairs.

Chemist's Assistant and Others   But we are engaged to him. I can prove it. And so can I.

Moonshine Emma   We can all prove it.

Matti   All right, all right, sisters. This is more like it. Strength in numbers. Sisters, listen, I propose to you the formation of a confederation of fiancées. C.O.F. in short. Collective bargaining. That's the way to do it. What are your demands?

Telephonist   To be let into the party.

Matti   That might not be as simple as you might think, sister.

Moonshine Emma   He invited us. It was a personal invitation.

Matti   All I'm saying is we have to pick our moment so Puntila recognises you for the brides you are.

Moonshine Emma   All we're after is a dance and a bit of how's your father.

Matti   Don't worry, sisters, this confederation recognises that those demands are reasonable and must be met. Expenses have been incurred. Have they not?

All   You bet!

Matti   You do realise you'll be sitting with judges and lawyers and doctors. What do you say to that?

Milkmaid   Smell that cheese!

Moonshine Emma   I would say to his honour the judge: 'Your honour, we demand that our conjugal rights as fiancées be satisfied, even if Mr Puntila has changed his mind. A contract's a contract. And if you fail to sort this out the Court of Viborg will have no legitimacy.'

Telephonist   Hear, hear. And I would say to the doctor: 'Doctor, doctor, I demand that you see to my back, which is out again. And I demand you take pains over it because my husband, Mr Puntila, will be paying the bill.'

The slaughtered pig is carried past.

Women   Look at that. Fantastic! Don't forget a bit of marjoram.

Moonshine Emma   Bloody hell, did you see all that champagne go in? Do you think anyone would mind if I slackened my skirt off?

Telephonist   I think they'd be over the moon. Especially our fiancé, Mr Puntila.

Matti   And sisters, I would say to the parson: 'Your reverence, this must truly be a day to celebrate, the sight of Lisu the milkmaid eating off bone china, the fact that we are all at the table together, sharing our lives, celebrating the coming together of good people under the vast umbrella of God.'

Puntila   Just let me know when you're finished. Who is this?

Telephonist   Your fiancées, Mr Puntila.

Puntila   I've never set eyes on you in my life.

Moonshine Emma   Well, what about these? (*The rings.*)

Matti   They were wondering how they might contribute to the party. They've formed a union of fiancées.

Puntila   Why not set up a bloody soviet while you're on about it? It's all your fault. I know what paper you read.

Moonshine Emma   We're only having a laugh.

Puntila   Laugh. You've come here to blackmail me, you bunch of scrubbers.

Moonshine Emma   No, no, no.

Puntila   Well, you'll be laughing on the other side of your faces when I've spoken to your bosses this afternoon. Don't worry, I'll find out who you are. Now sod off back to Kurgela before I have you arrested.

Moonshine Emma   We understand, Mr Puntila. We came up here for old times' sake. To see Puntila, landowner of Lami. Owner of twenty sheep. All we wanted was to sit on your promised land, and I think I will, just so I can tell my grandchildren – yes, I was at Puntila's, yes, I was invited. No, I wasn't on no chair but on the bare soil of Tavastland, our rich inheritance, what the school books say is hard to work but oh how the work's worthwhile. Well. What it doesn't say is who does the work, or whose while it's worth. (*Sings.*)

Oh Tavastland, oh Tavastland,
Oh country of the free.
Oh Tavastlland, oh Tavastland,
How I would die for thee.

Get me up, girls. Don't leave me in this historic position.

Puntila   Tell them to get off my land!

Matti (*shouts*)   Get off his land!

Scene Eight   Tale from Finland

Moonshine Emma   Remember Athi from Viborg. He was locked up for being a communist. 1918. He was so starving, he was eating grass off the ground. They were virtually dying of hunger. So his old mum, who was a tenant and had nothing, went to the farmer's wife and got a fish and a pound of butter, started to walk the fifty miles to see him. And everyone she met she told: 'I got this fish and pound of butter off the rich farmer's wife, who out of the goodness of her heart gave it me to take to my son, who's in a camp for being a communist.' So she gets to the prison camp and sees as she walks inside that there's no grass left because the prisoners have eaten it. And then she sees Athi, her son, and he's like a spelk of wood. And she says: 'Here is a fish and a pound of butter I got from the farmer's wife, who gave it out of the goodness of her heart.' And Athi looked at his mother with sadness in his eyes. He hadn't seen her for two years and he said: 'Did you beg for the fish?' And the mum said: 'Yes.' And Athi said: 'Take it back. I'll eat nothing from those bastards.' And she packed it up – and he was still starving – and she walked back and everyone she met she told: 'I've got this fish and butter that I took to my son in a prison camp, from the farmer's wife, but I am taking it back to her, because even though he is starving he won't take anything from those bastards.' And that was fifty miles.

Milkmaid   Do you really think there are blokes like that?

Moonshine Emma   Yes. But not enough.

They get up and go on in silence.

(*the cast announce*)   **Scene Nine. Puntila betroths his daughter to a human being.**

Parson   They never go near a church. I don't understand it. They've all got bikes.

Lawyer   They lack any moral fibre.

Judge   You can take a horse to water.

Parson   I was giving a man the last rites last week explaining the mysteries of the great hereafter and all he could say was: 'Do you think the potatoes will be ruined in the drought?' What is the point I ask myself? What is the point?

The **Attaché** *and the* **Parson's Wife** *dance in.*

Attaché   Oh you really should be in there. The minister asked our good reverence's wife what she thought of the jazz players. I was absolutely beside myself wondering what on earth she'd say. But she simply said I don't really mind what they use as long as you can dance to it. Well, the minister laughed himself hoarse. What do you say to that, Puntila?

Puntila   Not a lot, as I try not to offend my guests. Freddie, what do you make of this git?

Judge   Who?

Puntila   Who do you think? A straight answer.

Judge   Easy on the punch, old boy.

Attaché (*starts dancing*)   Gets into the old legs, what?

Puntila   Freddie, the truth. It's costing me a forest.

Attaché   I say, I was never any good at calculus but I have rhythm in my bones.

Lawyer   Perhaps we should all move to the drawing room.

Attaché   Oh yes, you just have to see me cakewalk.

Lazzo of the cakewalk, the **Attaché** *is a crazy dancer.*

Puntila   Freddie.

Judge   Did you hear about the one-legged Jew and the lesbian? They come across a coon in an alleyway and the lesbian says: 'Will you smack the cow or will I?'

Everybody laughs hysterically. The **Attaché** *joins in not having understood.*

Attaché   Excellent, so she wasn't really a lesbian at all!

Judge   I think you missed the point.

Attaché   But I thought . . . Oh?

Puntila   Well, what were you laughing at then?

Attaché   I wasn't sure.

Puntila   That's it. I don't care what anyone else thinks. But a man with no sense of humour is no fucking man at all. Out! Yes, you. Get out of my house.

Judge   Hang on a minute, Harry.

Attaché   Please, gentleman. I beg of you, please let's forget this whole business. A man in my position simply can't be seen to cause a scene. I would lose my agrément with the diplomatic corps. The Russian ambassador was fired simply because his mistress hit him with an umbrella.

Puntila   You're a gobbling little grasshopper in tails.

Attaché   You see it wasn't the mistress or the public beating, but the umbrella that did it. Unspeakably vulgar. Diplomacy is a question of nuance.

Puntila   Swallowing whole forests.

Lawyer   Steady on, Harry. You're messing about with his career.

Judge   You're just a bit pissed.

Puntila   I don't think you realise how serious this is.

Parson   Anna, perhaps we should retire to the drawing room.

Puntila   Stay exactly where you are. I am not pissed. I am not losing control. Everything's just fine except that humourless hoop-stretcher's putrid face.

Attaché   Sir, I would warn you to be careful of out-and-out insults. From now on every word must be meticulously weighed. Actually, my sense of humour was recently commended by the lady mayoress of Bilbao.

Puntila   For fuck's sake.

Attaché   Listen, I'll do anything. As long as no names are mentioned then there's been no irreparable damage.

Puntila   Oh, Freddie, what is the bastard's name? Is it Charles? Is it Spencer? Is it Jeremy? Shit. I know, I've got it, Mr Eino Silakka, you little money-grabbing arsehole. Out of my house. You're not marrying my daughter. You little grasshopper. You're not fit to lick the shit off the feet of my bullocks. *I said bullocks, madam.* Do I make myself clear?

Attaché   Manifestly. Well, sir, I must, in that case, humbly take my leave. (*Farewell riff.*)

Puntila   Go on, you fetid weasel, you uncircumcised dog. (*He chases the* **Attaché** *out.*)

Parson's Wife   This is an outrage.

Eva *dances in.*

Eva   Everything all right?

Parson's Wife   My poor child, something terrible has occurred.

Eva   Really?

Judge (*fetching a glass of sherry*)   Your father drank a whole bowl of punch and is currently chasing your fiancé off the estate.

Eva   What did he say exactly?

Parson's Wife   Don't you feel a little shaken, dear?

Eva   Yes of course. (*Shimmy.*)

Parson (*coming in*)   Monstrous.

Parson's Wife   What is it, dear?

Parson   Puntila has him cornered in the yard and is pelting him with manure.

Eva   Has he managed to hit him?

Parson   No.

Eva   Well. You can't have everything.

Parson's Wife   Eva!

Enter **Puntila** *followed by* **Matti**.

Puntila   Oh I have seen the sad depravity of the world. How I have been fooled, blinded and cruelly duped by a leech and a scavenging dog. But I ask no one to worry further as the damned swine has been stoned off the premises. Forget about him and let us now rejoice, as I am betrothing my daughter to a far better fate; I have decided that I am giving her to a real human being, to one of my finest friends, to my chauffeur Mr Matti Altonen. Let's hear it for Mr Matti Altonen. Dance with me, Matti.

Matti   Mr Puntila – perhaps we should talk this over in the kitchen?

Puntila   The kitchen. Man, we have to celebrate your engagement in the bosom of your family. Get the drinks out. Everybody, dance.

Eva (*to* **Matti**)   Don't look at me like that. You seemed quite keen last night.

Matti   It was just a bit of fun.

Eva   Fun.

Matti   Listen, marriage wasn't exactly what I had in mind.

Puntila   Sit down. Sit down, everyone.

They all sit in silence.

I have something I wish to say to my future son-in-law, Mr Matti, here. Matti, I saw your face as I cruelly spurned those good women this morning. And oh how that look cut me to the bone! Oh my Matti. Please can you forgive me? I beg of you.

Matti   Count it forgotten, Mr Puntila. But please tell your daughter she can't marry a chauffeur.

Eva (*tipsy*)   Matti dearest, I beseech you, make me your wife, so I can have an honest husband just like the other girls, we'd catch crabs bare-handed and be so happy – even if we had to go short on a few things.

Puntila   Bravo!

Matti   Mr Parson, describe to Miss Eva a pauper's kitchen.

Parson   Extremely impoverished indeed.

Eva   I don't want it described. I shall see it myself. I will make it my home.

Matti   We haven't even got a bath.

Eva   Well, we can use the public sauna.

Matti   On my wages? You have to use the public stream. Eva, you need a sawmill owner, which Mr P will realise when he's sober tomorrow morning.

Puntila   Say no more that Puntila is our common enemy, an exploiter of the poor, a yolk on the working classes; that evil monster has been drowned in a bowl of punch, and from those dregs has risen a human being. Look at me, I'm a human being. Look at me, I am a human being. To humanity, fraternity and fraternity again.

Matti   Look, Eva, as a wife, I wouldn't touch you with a bargepole.

Eva   Oh Matti.

Puntila The girl's right, you've gone too far now. She'll end up a bit on the fat side like her mother but right now . . .

Matti I'm not talking about how fat she is. I mean, she's totally unpractical. (*They are amazed.*)

Eva Don't be ridiculous.

Matti You haven't got a clue.

Eva All right then. Let's try it. You're the chauffeur – I'm your wife. What am I supposed to do?

Puntila That's my girl. Get the sandwiches, Fina. This is going to be a knockout.

Matti Hang on a minute. We don't have servants so you'll have to go. I wonder what'll be in the larder?

Eva (*thinks*) Herring.

Everyone cheers.

Matti Bring on the herring.

Eva Won't be a moment.

Puntila Don't forget the butter. Matti, I like the way you know who's boss. Very good.

Eva Voilà. But no butter in our kitchen, I'm afraid.

Matti Ah, there he is. How I know his little face. Like his brother I saw yesterday and his cousin the day before that. How many times have we eaten herring this week, dear?

Eva Er? Three.

Laina *laughs.*

Matti Surely you have miscounted, dear, for we have it every day. Oh herring, you wondrous creature, you sustainer of the poor. Oh fishy dynamo, by your power the forests are cut, with your sustenance the fields are sown, from your fuel all those machines called farm hands achieve perpetual happy motion. Oh herring, you are my provider,

my morning, noon and night. Oh sacred fish, how you save
us from meat's sweet corruption.

Matti *gives everyone a piece.*

Puntila   Beautiful. It tastes like caviar to me. Let there be
no inequality any longer. You know, if it was up to me I'd
get all the money from the estate and put it in a big fucking
pot and if anybody wanted any, they'd just come up to the
pot and take what they wanted. Good idea, eh?

Matti   You'd be ruined in a week.

Puntila   That's because you're a cynic, whereas I am an
egalitarian, Matti. In fact, I'm practically a communist, me.
On with the test.

Matti   OK. I come in from work.

Eva *rushes to him kissing him. He pushes her away.*

Matti   The last thing I need is you slavering like a dog.
I've been working since six this morning.

Matt *sits down. He picks up a newspaper. He indicates his shoes.*
Eva *pulls them off with great difficulty.*

Puntila   Oh look. A hole in my sock. What are you going
to do about that?

Eva *looks blankly. Then has an inspiration.*

Eva   Buy a new pair.

Puntila   They don't do that, darling.

Eva   Darn it.

Everyone cheers. **Eva** *is delighted. She drunkenly tries to darn the sock,
she is very pissed and the crowd follows her every move. She finishes
triumphantly and then tries to put the sock back on* **Matti**. *She is a
complete drunken mess. Eventually it hangs limply from his foot.* **Eva**
stands expectantly.

Eva   Well?

Matti   Why didn't you use a darning egg?

Eva   A what?

Matti   A little wooden mushroom-shaped . . . Oh never mind. On with the test.

Matti (*putting his paper down*)   Look, this is hopeless. OK, imagine it's the middle of the night. The old man from the hall arrives and says: 'Matti, Matti you're a real human being but drive me to Kurgela.' What do you do?

Eva   OK. (*Stops and thinks, somewhat beleaguered. She goes to the window.*) What time do you call this? It's the middle of the night. He's been working for eighteen hours as it is.

The others encourage her and to **Matti***'s amusement she gets more and more emboldened throughout the speech.*

When are you going to let the man sleep? He comes home half dead and you want him up again. You wouldn't treat a dog like that. I'd rather he was dead drunk in a ditch than working for you. So you can arse off the lot of you. And you can tell my fat fool of a father to fuck right off. I'll burn Matti's breeches before he leaves here tonight.

Puntila   Bravo!

Matti   Excellent. That's telling them. I'd get sacked in the morning but at least my mother would love you.

Matti *mauls* **Eva** *and feels her arse in his drunken over-enthusiasm.*

Eva   Stop it. Stop that at once.

Matti   What's the matter?

Eva   How dare you?

Matti   You're not offended just because I felt your arse?

Eva   Daddy, this isn't going to work.

Parson   Hallelujah!

Puntila   What do you mean?

Eva   I got it all wrong, Daddy. I'm going upstairs.

Puntila   Sit down at once, Eva.

Eva Daddy, I'm sorry.

Eva *runs off.*

Puntila I fix her up with a first class human being like you. She should be grovelling at our feet, Matti. That's it – you're out of the will, Eva. You can get your rags and piss off out of my house for ever. I disown you, wretch. You are no daughter of mine.

Judge You've gone too far, Puntila. I'm washing my hands of the entire matter.

Puntila That's right, just leave me a father broken by shame and sorrow. Oh what did I do? I ask you, what did I do to bring such a daughter into this world? One who buggers about with a scavenging diplomat, but doesn't know what her arse is for. The Lord above made her arse from the very sweat of his brow to be fondled and felt.

Parson Mr Puntila!

Puntila Oh fuck off, you self-righteous shithead.

Parson Mr Puntila, we bid you goodnight.

Puntila They are not human beings. You can't look at them as human beings.

Matti (*pissed*) No, when you see someone beating a horse you should say: 'He's treating it like a human being.' 'Like an animal' gives the wrong impression.

Puntila That's very profound, Matti. I'll drink to that.

Matti (*drinks*) Sorry to have felt your daughter's arse – it wasn't supposed to be part of the test. More of a little reward. But there lay the gulf between us.

Puntila Matti, fret no more. I have no daughter.

Matti Oh Mr P, don't be too unforgiving.

Puntila Where have these sandwiches gone to?

Scene Ten   Puntila and his man, Matti, climb Mount Hatelma

Library at **Puntila***'s.* **Puntila** *groaning.* **Laina** *with basin and towel.*

Lawyer   A night of misunderstandings, so to speak.

Puntila   If you are inquiring about the attaché, I have spoken to him at length. He has apologised and that's that.

Lawyer   My dear fellow, your family arrangements are your own affair.

Parson   To put it bluntly we've come about the Surkhala problem.

Puntila   Surkhala?

Parson   We were given to understand he'd been dismissed as an undesirable influence.

Puntila   Yes.

Parson   But, Mr Puntila, he was there with his family in church this morning.

Puntila   But Laina, wasn't Surkhala given his marching orders?

Laina   No.

Puntila   Well, why the devil not?

Laina   You met him at the hiring fair and brought him back, and gave him a ten mark note.

Puntila   How dare he take ten marks off me. Get me Surkhala right away. Oh my head.

Lawyer   Coffee.

Puntila   I must have been paralytic, Pekka. The fellow should be in gaol, never mind in full employment.

Parson   Don't apologise, Mr Puntila. It was obviously the alcohol. We all know your true nature.

Puntila   Oh this is a disaster. What if it gets out? I'll be blacklisted. The National Guard will boycott my milk. It's all that driver's fault. He knows I can't stand that red bastard.

Parson   It's all right, Mr Puntila, these things happen.

Puntila   If they don't stop happening I'll have myself arrested. Someone do something. I'll be ruined, the National Guard will boycott my milk. Make a donation.

Lawyer   So you will get rid of him quickly.

Puntila   Absolutely. At once. Thank you so much for coming.

Parson   It was nothing.

Lawyer   But you might find it an idea to check on that chauffeur of yours. Shifty looking fellow if you ask me.

They leave.

Puntila   Laina.

Laina   Yes, Mr Puntila.

Puntila   Never will another drop of alcohol pass these lips again. I've made a resolution. In the cow shed. Fetch the bottles. Bring me all the alcohol in the house and we'll smash every last one. Bugger the cost. we must think of the estate, Laina.

Laina   If you're absolutely sure, Mr Puntila. (*Exits.*)

Puntila   Oh this is a terrible lesson. And tell Altonen I want a word. Immediately. The man's a jinx.

Enter **Surkhala** *with his kids.*

Puntila   Hah. Did I ask you to bring your brats?

Surkhala   No, but I thought it would do them no harm to hear you, Mr Puntila.

Enter **Matti**.

Matti   Morning. How's the head?

Puntila   Here's the bastard. Didn't I warn you only yesterday – any more nonsense and you'd be out on your ear?

Matti   Yes, Mr Puntila.

Puntila   Shut up, smart arse. I'm on to you, matey. How much did he (*indicates* **Surkhala**) pay you?

Matti   I've no idea what you're talking about.

Puntila   You're as thick as thieves. You're a bloody commie, yourself, you little Bolshevik.

Laina *brings in the booze.*

Ah! Here we are. This time it's for real. This is the kind of man I am. The whole lot's going for a burton. Sobriety is the new world order.

Matti   Shall I take them out and smash them, sir?

Puntila   You must think I was born yesterday. You'll get rid of it by drinking it.

Laina   Don't look at it for too long, Mr Puntila, throw it out of the window.

Puntila   Quite right. (*To* **Matti**.) You'll never drink my liquor again. You manipulating little shit. I know you hate me. You're not fooling me with your 'Yes, Mr Puntila.'

Puntila *has unconsciously poured a drink and is about to drink it.*

Laina   Mr Puntila.

Puntila   It's nothing to worry about. Just checking whether those thieving bastards actually sold me proper liquor. And, of course, to celebrate my inflexible resolve.

Laina   Mr Puntila. You're drinking again.

Puntila   Call this drinking? I haven't even started.
Anyway, it's his fault. Destroy this at once. (*Hands her an
empty bottle and she tries to prevent him from taking a full one and
fails.*) What do you expect me to do here? Tot up the cattle
in the field? Count the eggs in the morning? You're a load
of moral pygmies. So sod off. You've got no imagination.
(To **Surkhala**'s *kids.*) Listen, rob, steal, borrow, become
fucking Bolsheviks, but never, ever become a moral pygmy.
Understand? (*To* **Surkhala**.) Sorry to be meddling with the
kids' education. But you understand. Another bottle. I
propose a toast. To red Surkhala.

Matti   Does that mean he's staying, Mr Puntila?

Puntila   That means he's going. Surkhala is going not
because he isn't welcome, hell no, he's got the run of the
place. No, I know he's going because Puntila Hall is too
small for him. And who can blame him? Who can blame
him for hating me? A filthy capitalist bastard. They should
send me down a salt mine. Isn't that right. Surkhala? No
need to be polite.

Surkhala's Daughter   But we want to stay, Mr Puntila.

Puntila   No, no, my little chicks. Your father's made up
his mind and wild horses won't stop him. Look, take this.
(*He gives them money.*) Minus the ten you owe me. Oh my tiny
ducklings, be proud. Your father is a giant amongst men. I
bid you a sad farewell.

Surkhala   Come on. Let's get out of here.

Puntila   See, my hand is not good enough for him. No, I
should cut it off. At least you and me, Matti, at least we have
each other. How much do I pay you?

Matti   Three hundred a month.

Puntila   Make it three fifty? Four hundred? Oh Matti,
one day we will climb Mount Hatelma together. Oh and

you will see what a glorious nation we live in, Matti. Shall we do it, Matti? Right now.

Matti   If it takes your fancy.

Puntila   But do you have the imagination, Matti?

Matti *is silent.*

Puntila   Make me a mountain, Matti, make it enormous, Matti, or we'll have no real view.

Matti   Your wish is my command, Mr Puntila.

Matti *starts smashing the furniture and builds a mountain for* **Puntila** *to climb.*

Puntila   This is all my idea. You won't get a proper Mount Hatelma unless you do exactly as I say. I know what's needed. That's my responsibility. I have the vision. (*As he climbs.*) Christ, I'm going to break my neck.

Matti   Don't worry.

Puntila   Matti, you are going to see the beautiful country which bore you. Without which you'd just be a little turd floating in the Baltic. So be grateful, Matti.

Matti   Unto death, Mr Puntila.

Puntila   We're climbing, Matti. Oh blessed Tavastland. One more drop and all your beauty will be manifest.

Matti   Here, have a swig.

Puntila   Oh can you see the wonder? Are you a Tavastlander, Matti?

Matti   Yes.

Puntila   Then tell me. Where else is a sky so blue? Where else do the clouds glide so delicately? Where are the winds kinder? Where do the swans fly so free? Forget all other places, Matti. That's my advice.

Matti   Of course, Mr Puntila.

Puntila   Matti, just the lakes for instance. Forget the forests – even the magnificent one over there I'm going to cut down. Just the lakes, just one of them. Just the lake itself, forget the fucking fish inside it. In the morning take a look at one single lake, Matti, and you'll never leave, you'll never travel another mile again. That's just one of the buggers and we've got eight thousand.

Matti   Let's just stick with one then.

Puntila   I like it best when it all goes hazy, like those little moments in love when you close your eyes and there's a glow over everything. I don't think you ever really get that outside of Finland, do you, Matti?

Matti   Probably not, Mr Puntila.

Puntila   Look, look. There are some cows swimming across the lake.

Matti   I see. There must be fifty of them.

Puntila   Sixty at least. And over here, Matti, what do you see?

Matti   What do I see?

Puntila   Fields, Matti, as far as the eye can see. My fields. Soil so rich the wheat grows past your chin, Matti.

　　Oh Tavastland, oh Tavastland,
　　Oh country of the free.

Enter **Fina** *and* **Laina**.

Fina   Jesus.

Matti   We're up Mount Hatelma. Enjoying the view.

Puntila   Come on, sing with me. (**Fina** *and* **Laina** *join in.* **Matti** *doesn't.*)

　　Oh Tavastland, oh Tavastland,
　　How I would die for thee.

Where's your feeling for your country, Matti? Tell me your heart swells, Matti. Oh Tavastland thy sky, thy lakes, thy forest, thy people. Tell me your heart swells at it all, Matti.

Matti   My heart swells at the sight of your forests, Mr Puntila.

Scene Eleven   Matti turns his back on Puntila

Fina   Matti. Your lunch. I don't understand why you're going now. Won't you wait until he gets up?

Matti   When he wakes up and remembers what we were up to he'll call out the National Guard.

Fina   But if you leave without a reference, you'll be ruined.

Matti   And what would he write? That I'm a communist, or worse, that I'm just your average human being. Where will that get me?

Laina   But how will he manage, Matti?

Matti   He'll just have to muddle through. I've had it, Fina. Thanks for lunch. Goodbye.

Laina   Matti. Look after yourself.

(*The actor playing* **Matti** *comes forward for his final song in a spotlight. Ukelele in hand. Sings.*)

I'm off – I think that's where we leave it
Puntila wants friendship but it's tricky to achieve it
When you hop between power and sentimental boozing
Unable to acknowledge that the privilege of choosing
all depends on cash.
And face it – if you're loaded then you're laughing
All the rest is balderdash
To talk of misty-eyed utopia
When half of the world is starving.

And as for Matti
The fact of the matter is that he
Finds another job and drives
Some other bloke's Bugatti
But he will only find a boss who actually cares
When he becomes the master of his own affairs.

Mother Courage and Her Children

Adaptor's Note

The cliché about Brecht is that we know him more through
his theories than through his plays, and that his plays baulk
at the simplicity of the theories laid on them. However, even
the most cursory look at his theoretical writings show that
they are as complex and contradictory as anything in his
drama. If my experience is even slightly typical, I suggest we
know Brecht more through hearsay and received opinion
than by directly confronting his work in the way we might
with almost any other 'great' dramatist (think Chekhov or
Shakespeare). I grew up in awe of all that great seventies
work and I imagined there wasn't a rehearsal room in
Britain that didn't have a stringy group of actors smoking
Golden Virginia and discussing *verfremdung*. For me Brecht
had a mystical aura – no one, it seemed, had influenced our
idea of drama more in the last fifty years. And so for years I
trotted out the cant about Brecht's beliefs and his
contradictions with all the confidence of someone who
actually knows very little.

It wasn't until I was asked to adapt *Mr Puntila* for The
Right Size that I suddenly realised I didn't really know
anything about Brecht other than what I had gleaned from
a few cursory readings of the great plays in sixth form and a
glance at the back of *The Messingkauf Dialogues* in a pub on
Tyneside. And so I started actually reading and working –
and discovered, amazingly, that all the hearsay was true.
Brecht is as truculent, as ambivalent, difficult and
completely straightforward as all the banalities had led me
to believe. But there was something more which I was
unprepared for: a real, instinctive sense of fun.

I had always equated Brecht's 'populism' with what I
thought of as rather ascetic German cabarets, or some
rather dry aesthetic of Weimar circuses I'd picked up from
the Lulu plays or suchlike, all of which sent a shiver of dread
through me; nothing seemed so aridly formal as a German
cabaret. But in reading Mr Puntila I was suddenly seeing
glimpses of the time-honoured routines which I knew
through watching Max Wall and Morecambe and Wise.

Soon I was not just seeing vaudeville but *commedia dell'arte* as well, and a whole history of comic stagecraft. (*Puntila* is at heart a classic *commedia dell'arte* piece). And thus I was transported back in time, past all the university crib sheets and O-level essays, to what Joan Littlewood must have seen in the fifties: Brecht's simple and complete connection with British working-class art forms. Brecht could be hilariously funny.

So having got comic Brecht under my belt I was thrilled to be asked to work on *Mother Courage*. How exciting it would be to go on the same journey again, this time with one of the great tragedies of the century. And so I began reading the play. However, what I read disconcerted all my expectations about this 'great tragedy'. It opened with a double act of whingeing men, like something out of *Godot*, making ridiculous claims like 'war is good for people'. Then on comes an Old Mother Riley figure who does a musical number and then mercilessly takes the piss out of the soldiers. Like sitcom, the rest of the play seemed to consist of people sitting around chatting whilst some calamity was about to descend. There were dead chickens, atheist vicars, traders who would sell their own souls rather than lose a consignment of linen, and soldiers who made up a regiment of human venality and ignorance. I was amazed at the final scene where Kattrin is killed. The soldiers who finally shoot her could be straight out of *Dad's Army*. There was even a line: 'Permission to suggest an idea, sir', which I'm convinced was used in every single episode of the *Home Guard* sitcom. These were all old gags; why hadn't anybody told me they were there before? But of course this wasn't vaudeville or sitcom; this was still a tragedy. The banana skins were the scraps of pride, logic or common sense that have no currency in war and were just lying round to slip our characters up. The pratfalls weren't funny; they meant someone was killed, or disfigured or raped. And soon the play seemed so much more awful and so much more familiar than I had ever expected. It was the world of Beckett and Jan Kott's existentialist pantomime *Lear*. It was grave in its humour and unstintingly hilarious in its cruelty, without every losing sight of the impossible contradiction humanity possesses – not because of some abstract 'condition' – but because of the contingent ideological and economic circumstances that we labour under.

So my task appeared clear. It was to clean the rust from the irony and humour in order that they would pierce like a stiletto. All the old debates about whether we should or shouldn't feel empathy seemed much less relevant than if we should laugh or not. To make that decision you have to know what you are trying to achieve, both overall and for the moment, and surely the humour in the script is a crucial indication to any reading. After working on the play I believe there is nothing more central to Brecht's dramaturgy than this element of remaining objective, of being able to watch these sad creatures with their fates and foibles and be moved, disgusted and entertained by the whole process without losing one's head. So I have striven everywhere to allow that sense of objectivity, as it seems to be the whole point; and, as every playwright will tell you, there is nothing more objective in a theatre than a laugh.

Lee Hall
2003

Mother Courage and Her Children was presented by arrangement with Guildford's Yvonne Arnaud Theatre, Guildford. The first performance was at The Yvonne Arnaud Theatre on 9 March 2000. The cast was as follows:

Eilif	Nicholas R. Bailey
Kattrin	Hayley Carmichael
The Chaplain	David Fielder
Mother Courage	Kathryn Hunter
Swiss Cheese/Angry Soldier/ Young Farmer	Francis Lee
Cook	Marcello Magni
Recruiting Officer/Old Colonel/ Farmer	Clive Mendus
Accordion Player	Phuong Nguyen
Yvette/Farmer	Rachel Sanders
Sergeant/Swedish General/ Regimental Clerk	Simon Walter
Soldier/Peasant Boy/ Yvette's Servant	Maurice Yeoman

Director Nancy Meckler
Design Angela Davies
Company Movement Liz Ranken
Music Dominic Muldowney
Lighting Tina Machugh
Ensemble Work Marcello Magni
Dramaturg Jan Van Den Bosch

Scene One

1624. The Swedish Army is recruiting for the Polish Campaign. A Canteen woman known as **Mother Courage** *loses a son.*

A country road by a town. A **Sergeant** *and a* **Recruiting Officer** *stand shivering.*

Recruiting Officer   How the fuck's anybody supposed to recruit an army round here? I'm supposed to have four units together before Friday. I may as well top myself. Even when I do get my hands on one of the pigeon-chested runts and turn a blind eye to their peg legs and wotnot, just when I've got them pissed enough to sign on the dotted line, I'll be paying up for the liquor and these bastards are off out the lavvy window like a flea off a parson's arse. No respect, no loyalty, no basic fucking human dignity. I've lost my faith in humanity down here, sergeant.

Sergeant   The problem with this lot is they haven't had a war for too long. Where're they supposed to get their standards from? Peace is total chaos, isn't it? It's your war what brings people order. They don't even know how many people live down here. They've never even been counted. Why? Because in peacetime all they can think about is stuffing their faces. I've been places where there's not been a war on for seventy years and they don't even know what their own fucking names are. Whereas when there's a war you get decent lists, registers, you get your boots heeled and yer dead counted. That's because war and order go hand in hand. Don't they?

Recruiting Officer   You've hit the nail on the head.

Sergeant   Mind you, it takes a while to get a good war going but once you're started it goes like shit off a shovel. People are bound to be a bit windy at first as the cabin boy said to the bosun. But you sharp get used to it.

Receruiting Officer   Hey up! Look at this lot. Two strapping lads and a couple of slappers. You just keep the old bird talking, I'll see to the fellas 'cos I'm fucked if I'm standing here much longer.

Sound of a Jew's harp. Two young lads pull on a cart. **Mother Courage** *is on top with her dumb daughter,* **Kattrin**.

Mother Courage   Good morning, sergeant!

Sergeant   Morning all. And who are you then?

Mother Courage   Business people.

Mother Courage (*sings*)
Hello, Top Brass, put away your blues
And let your drumbeats rest.
Mother Courage has come with shoes
So men can do their best.
Weighed down by lice they rattle
With guns through snow and sleet
As you march them into battle
They need shoes upon their feet.
  Spring is coming, Christian men arise!
  Snow is melting. (The) Dead are gone.
  And if you've not met your demise
  You should be moving on.

No one will march unto their death
Without a bite of sausage.
Let Mother Courage give them breath
With wine and meat and pottage.
Cannons on an empty gut?!
They'll not do very well.
In their bellies some grub put
And you'll march them down to hell.
  Spring is coming, Christian men arise.
  Snow is melting. (The) Dead are gone.
  And if you've not met your demise
  You should be moving on.

Sergeant   And where are you arseholes going, then?

Eilif   Following the Second Finnish Regiment.

Sergeant   Let's see your papers, then?

Mother Courage   Papers?

Swisscheese   Surely you know Mother Courage?

Sergeant   Never heard of her. What's so courageous about you, then?

Mother Courage   I am called Courage, sergeant, because I drove across the battlefield of Riga to flog a wagonload of bread. Mind, I had no choice, it had started going mouldy. I wouldn't call it an act of bravery myself, more common sense if you ask me.

Sergeant   Watch your lip, lady. Where's your papers?

Mother Courage   You want papers? I'll give you papers. There. Most of a German Bible, very good for the wrapping of gherkins, a nice map of Moravia, God knows when we'll ever get there at this rate, and a very fine certificate proving my horse doesn't have the glanders, pity the poor thing's dead, cost fifteen guilders, not that I paid for the mangy old thing. There's plenty more where that came from.

Sergeant   Pull the other one. You know you need a licence.

Mother Courage   How dare you, sergeant. Let me tell you, I will be pulling nothing of yours with the children present. Besides, you're not my type. My licence with the Second Regiment is my honest face and if you can't read it, matey, that's your problem, I'm not going to have it stamped for no one.

Recruiting Officer   We've got a right one here, sergeant. What you need is a bit of respect, love.

Mother Courage   What you need is a bit of sausage.

Recruiting Officer   What's your name?

Mother Courage   Anna Frieling.

Sergeant   So you're all Frielings?

Mother Courage   No. I'm the only Frieling round here.

Sergeant   But I thought you said they were yours.

Mother Courage   But that doesn't say they've all got to be called the same name, does it? That one's called Eilif Nojokey. Why? 'Cos his dad was called Nojoki. He remembers him very well, don't you? Except he actually remembers somebody else actually, a Frenchman with a little goatee. Nevertheless, he inherited the wit off his old man, who could talk the pants off a farmer's arse and get paid for the privilege. Oh, yes, we've all got our own names, you know. It's common practice.

Sergeant   I suppose he's Chinese, then?

Mother Courage   Hard lines. He's a Switzer.

Sergeant   So you had him after the Frenchman?

Mother Courage   What Frenchman? For Christ's sake, try and keep up. A Switzer who went by the name of Julian Oscar Cebellos, which is nothing to do with his father, who you'd call something else entirely, who pickled himself before he was thirty.

Swisscheese *nods with a smile. Even* **Kattrin** *finds it funny.*

Sergeant   Well, how can he be a Cebellos then?

Mother Courage   Do I have to insult you? He is, of course, so called because at the time I was with a Hungarian who didn't give a monkey's snout, on account of a bloated kidney even though he was teetotal. A very nice fella who the lad takes after.

Sergeant   Hang on. But he wasn't his father?

Mother Courage   Well, he still takes after him. I call him Swisscheese. 'Why?' I hear you ask. Because he is good at pulling carts. And this is Kattrin Haupt. Half German. And that's all you need to know about her.

Sergeant   It's a fucking league of nations.

Mother Courage   Oh yes, darling, I've seen the whole world through my cart.

Sergeant   I'm writing all this down, you know. (*He writes.*) If you're from Bamberg what are you doing here?

Mother Courage   You think I'm just going to wait in Bamberg till the war gets there?

Sergeant   They should have called you two Jacob and bleeding Esau, pulling that cart.

Eilif   Mam, can I smack him in the gob?

Mother Courage   No, you may not. For Christ's sake. You don't go hitting customers. Now, gentlemen, howzabout a few nice pistols or a smart leather belt. I see yours is on its last legs, Mr Sergeant.

Sergeant   I think you've got something better to offer. Look. These two are built like brick shit houses. What's wrong with a bit of military service, gentlemen?

Courage   Leave it out, my boys aren't fodder for your war machine.

Recruiting Officer   Is that right? There's good money in it. Fame and fortune. Or maybe you're quite happy selling footwear. (*To* **Eilif**.) Come here, are they real muscles or just puppy fat?

Mother Courage   That's right. A terrified little puppy. Honestly, if someone looks at him too hard he'd fall over.

Recruiting Officer   Yeah. And knock out the odd bull that's nearby.

Mother Courage   Leave him alone. He's got nothing to do with you.

Recruiting Officer   Well, he should have thought about that before he started promising to 'smack my gob' for me. I think we should just go into that field over there and sort this out like real men.

Eilif Don't worry. I'll fix him, ma.

Mother Courage Stay there, you pillock, you'd stab your own shadow. I'm warning you, he's got a knife in his boot.

Recruiting Officer I'll sharp pull that out like a milk tooth. Come on then, sunshine.

Mother Courage Mr Sergeant, I'll have words with your colonel and have you both in the nick in no time. The lieutenant happens to be the lover of my daughter, you know.

Sergeant You better calm down, mate. (*To* **Courage**.) Anyway, what's wrong with the army? His father was a soldier, wasn't he? He died a decent enough death, didn't he? You said so yourself.

Mother Courage He is a child. You want to take him off me straight to the slaughterhouse. What for? Five guilders. Is that what you'll get for him?

Recruiting Officer He'd get a nice smart hat and a top pair of boots.

Eilif Is that right?

Mother Courage 'Let's go fishing,' said the angler to the worm. (*To* **Swisscheese**.) Go, scream the place down, they're stealing your brother. (*She draws a knife.*) Just try it and I'll cut your liver out. I'll give you a fucking war. We're just honest business people. Selling ham and linen.

Sergeant I can see your business clear enough. Put it away, you daft slag, you want to be ashamed of yourself. You just said yourself you live off the war. How the hell's there going to be a war if there's not any soldiers? Eh? Thought about that one?

Mother Courage They don't need to be mine.

Sergeant So the war should eat the pit and spit out the cherry. Oh, yes, it's all right for you to get fat on the back of other people's labour just as long as you don't have to put in your pennorth. Courage, my arse. What are you scared of?

Eilif   I'm not afraid of anything.

Sergeant   Exactly. There's no need to be. Look at me. It never did me any harm. I joined up when I was seventeen.

Mother Courage   You haven't reached seventy yet.

Sergeant   Don't worry, I'll see seventy.

Mother Courage   Looking up from six feet under.

Sergeant   Oh, I'm terrified. Do you really not think I'm going to make it?

Mother Courage   Listen. You're a marked man, matey.

Swisscheese   She can tell the future, you know.

Recruiting Officer   Go on, then. Tell him his fortune. That'll be good for a laugh.

Sergeant   Fuck that. I don't believe in all that stuff.

Mother Courage   Give me your helmet.

He gives her his helmet.

Sergeant   I'm only doing this to keep him happy. All this hocus-pocus means less to me than a shite in the grass.

Mother Courage *takes some paper and tears it up.*

Mother Courage   Swisscheese, Kattrin, this is what'll happen to you if you mess about with the war. (*To the* **Sergeant**.) For once I'll make an exception and do this for free. But only out of pity. I draw a little black cross on one bit of paper. Black – for death.

Swisscheese   She leaves the other ones blank, you see.

Mother Courage   Then I fold them up and throw them together, like we're all tossed together from birth till Doomsday. Go on, take a dip and so ye shall know.

The **Sergeant** *hesitates.*

Recruiting Officer (*to* **Eilif**)   I don't just take anybody,
you know, but you've got a certain spark.

The **Sergeant** *fishes in the helmet.*

Sergeant   I just want to say this is a load of old crap. Just
so you know.

He draws a paper.

Swisscheese   He got a cross. He's a goner.

Recruiting Officer   He looks like you've shot him.
They're just having you on.

Sergeant   This is a fucking swizz.

Mother Courage   You did it to yourself the day you
became a soldier. Anyway, have to get going, it's not every
day there's a war on.

Sergeant   Bastards. You're not getting away with this.
We're taking that shit of yours to be a soldier.

Eilif   Mam. I want to go.

Mother Courage   Shut up, you Finnish oaf.

Eilif   And Swisscheese. He wants to go too.

Mother Courage   That's news to me. Well, I think you
all better draw lots as well, then.

She walks to the back drawing crosses on bits of paper.

Recruiting Officer (*to* **Eilif**)   I know they say it's a bit
puritan in the Swedish Army, but that's all bollocks. OK,
you have to sing hymns once in a while but all I do is mime.

Mother Courage *returns with scraps of paper in the*
Sergeant's *helmet.*

Mother Courage   So you'd run away from your mother,
like cows to the salt lick. Let's consult the paper and we'll
soon see the world's no Shangri-La with 'Come along, son,

we still need a few generals', sergeant. I'm scared none of them will get through alive, you see they've all got their fatal characteristics.

She offers **Eilif** *the helmet.*

Dig for your destiny. Fish for your fate.

Eilif *dips in, unfolds his paper. She tears it away from him.*

Mother Courage   A cross! What a miserable plight is motherhood. Wasn't childbirth enough to suffer? Dead? In the full bloom of his youth. Who could believe it. It's because you're too enthusiastic, like your dad. There's your proof, if you don't come to your senses you'll go the way of all flesh, son. (*She barks.*) Well, have you come to your senses?

Eilif   Senses?

Mother Courage   What's sensible is staying with your mother, and if they're taking the piss and calling you chicken just laugh in their faces.

Recruiting Officer   Look, if you're shitting your pants, mate, we can easy take your brother.

Mother Courage   Laugh! Laugh I said! (*To* **Swisscheese**.) Go on, Swisscheese, I'm less worried about you, at least you're honest.

Swisscheese *dips into the helmet.*

Mother Courage   What's the matter? There isn't a cross on it, is there? A cross! You as well. Maybe it's because he's so backward. You see, Swisscheese, you're finished if you don't stay honest like I taught you. Go on, you tell me, sergeant, that's a black cross, isn't it?

Sergeant   Yes, it's a bloody cross. But I don't understand. How come I got one? I always keep to the back. (*To the* **Recruiting Officer**.) It must be real, it gets her own as well.

Swisschesse I know. But at least I'll do what I'm told now.

Mother Courage (*to* **Kattrin**) And now you're the only one still all right. I suppose you're my cross, but at least you have a good heart.

Mother Courage *holds up the helmet but takes the paper out herself.*

Oh I'm gobsmacked. It's too much. Maybe I mucked up the shuffling. Oh Kattrin, please stop being so soft. You see it isn't worth it. There's a cross even for you. So best keep quiet in the background, eh? It shouldn't be too difficult, seeing you're dumb. So there you go, there's fate for you, we best be off now.

Recruiting Officer (*to* **Sergeant**) Do something.

Sergeant I feel sick.

Recruiting Officer Maybe you've caught yourself a chill running around without your helmet for too long. Get her talking business. (*Out loud.*) You could at least have a look at a belt. These are good business-people, are they not? Hey, serge here wants to buy a belt.

Mother Courage Half a dollar. It's worth at least double.

She climbs down.

Sergeant But it isn't even new. Look, I need to have a proper look at this somewhere out of this wind.

He goes behind the cart.

Mother Courage It's not that draughty, is it?

Sergeant I suppose it might be worth half a dollar. It is silver, isn't it?

Mother Courage Six solid ounces of silver.

Recruiting Officer   Come on, we'll have a little drink together. I've got some change on me.

Eilif *stands indecisive.*

Mother Courage   Half a guilder then?

Sergeant   I don't understand. I always keep to the rear. There's no safer place for a sergeant. Let the rest charge up front to get the glory. I tell you, it's put me right off. I'll not be able to eat a thing now.

Mother Courage   I wouldn't let it put you off your grub, pal, just keep to the back. Here, have yourself some brandy.

She gives him a drink.

The **Recruiting Officer** *has taken* **Eilif** *by the arm and pulls him to the back.*

Recruiting Officer   Ten guilders cash in hand. You'll be a real man, fighting for the king, girls are going to be all over you. And you can 'smack me in the gob' for what I said before.

Kattrin *makes noises.*

Mother Courage   Hold your horses, Kattrin. The sergeant hasn't finished paying. (*Bites into the coin.*) Never trust coinage, I've been burned once too often. But this is OK. Well, off we go. Where's Eilif?

Swisscheese   He went with the Recruiter.

Mother Courage (*stands absolutely still*)   You idiot. (*To* **Kattrin**.) It's all right, I know you couldn't have said anything. I'm not blaming you.

Sergeant   You better have a swig yourself, ma. C'est la vie, as they say. There's worse things you could be. You want to live off the war but keep your lot out of it. Eh?

Mother Courage   Kattrin, you're going to have to pull with your brother.

Both of them, brother and sister, get themselves into the harness and start pulling. **Mother Courage** *goes alongside. The cart rolls on. The* **Sergeant** *shouts after them.*

Sergeant Listen.

> If from war you want to live.
> You have to be prepared to give.

Scene Two

1626. Poland. **Mother Courage** *meets her son and sells a capon.*

The **General**'s *tent, next to the kitchen. The thunder of cannons. The* **Cook** *is arguing with* **Mother Courage** *who is trying to sell him a capon.*

Cook Sixty shilling? It's a bit of gristle!

Mother Courage Gristle, my arse. This rotund little beauty! You're trying to tell me that that fat greedy twat of a general, with nowt on his stomach, won't pay sixty shilling?

Cook Listen. I can get four for a penny round the corner.

Mother Courage What? A capon of this quality! People are starving, they're eating their young. You'd be lucky to get a field rat for this price. Listen, yesterday I saw five men and a dog chasing a mouse round for the whole afternoon. And this gargantuan beast could be yours for fifty shilling. We're in the middle of a siege, for Christ's sake.

Cook We're not under siege. We're doing the besieging!

Mother Courage And what have they left us? Sweet Fanny Adams. While they're in there stuffing themselves senseless. I've been round all the farmers. They haven't got a sausage.

Cook Don't you believe it. They've got plenty. They just hide it all when they see you coming.

Mother Courage   Don't be ridiculous. They're ruined. They're boiling up the roots of trees. They're salivating over a boiled leather belt. And you expect me to part with this fat capon for forty shilling.

Cook   Thirty. I said thirty.

Mother Courage   This isn't any old capon. This was a bird of refinement. It would only eat to music. It had its own march. It could do fucking calculus, for God's sake. Is forty shilling too much to ask for an intellectual collossus of the poultry world? You'll get it in the neck if his nibs goes hungry.

Cook   You see this. (*He takes a bit of meat.*) That's a nice bit of brisket that is. And that's what he's getting for his dinner if you're not careful.

Mother Courage   Go on then. Poison the overweight sturgeon for all I care. It's at least a year old.

Cook   Actually I saw the bull only last night. Jumping about like a young roebuck.

Mother Courage   Well, its arse must have already started rotting.

Cook   Look, I'll cook it all bloody day if I have to.

Mother Courage   I'd stick in plenty of paprika or the poor sod'll asphyxiate with that pong.

The **General**, *the* **Chaplain** *and* **Eilif** *step into the tent.*

General (*slapping* **Eilif** *on the back*)   Come on, my dear boy, you will sit in here by me. We'll have you a medal just as soon as the siege is over. Don't think it's passed me by that you are serving God like a man possessed, my boy. We come down here to save their papist souls and the ungrateful bastards bugger off with their cattle in the other direction, so they can stuff their stinking priests with fillet steaks from arse to eyeball. But you taught them a little lesson, eh? I've got a nice bottle of red here, we'll soon knock that back. (*They drink.*) Padre's getting none of it, all for being a pious twat. So what do you fancy for dinner, old boy?

Eilif   I wouldn't mind a nice bit of chicken.

General   A first rate idea. Cook! Meat! Meat!

Cook   Typical, there's nothing to eat and now he's inviting guests.

Mother Courage *shuts him up because she wants to listen.*

Eilif   It's hungry work killing peasants.

Mother Courage   Jesus, it's Eilif.

Cook   Who?

Mother Courage   My eldest son. I haven't seen him in two years. They stole him from me when we were on the road. He must be doing all right, having dinner with the general. And what have you got to give him? Bugger all! You heard what the honourable guest wants? Take my advice, mate, buy the capon while you can still afford it, a hundred shillings.

*The **General** has seated himself with **Eilif** and the **Chaplain**.*

General   Cook! Food, I say, or I'll cut your pods off.

Cook   This is extortion. Give me it, for God's sake.

Mother Courage   What this 'bit of gristle'?

Cook   Yes, that bit of gristle. Fifty shilling.

Mother Courage   A hundred. Nothing but the best for my eldest.

Cook *gives her the money.*

Cook   You'll burn in hell, you know that? At least pluck it, till I get the fire started.

Mother Courage *seats herself to pluck the capon.*

Mother Courage   Wait till he sees me. My clever little
darling. I've got another one as well, a bit thick, but at least
he's honest. The girl's nothing to write home about. She's
dumb as a worm, but I suppose that's a blessing really.

General   Get that down you, that's my best Falerner,
there's only a barrel or two left, but stuff it, at least there's
still a true believer amongst my men. And the 'Shepherd of
souls' here just sits there like a eunuch at a Borgia's birthday
because all he knows is preaching. Now, come on, my son,
give us the gory details. How the hell did you nail those
stinking peasants and get your hands on twenty head of
cattle. When will they be here?

Eilif   A day or two at most.

Mother Courage   How considerate of him not to bring
the cows till I've sold my chicken.

Eilif   Well, I cottoned on to where the farmers were taking
the cattle so they could meet up with the others and sell
them of a night. So I just bided my time, I let them round
them up, saved me doing all the work, and staked out the
place ready for them coming. Of course, I'd near starved
my blokes for a day or two just to give them an added little
incentive and Bob's your uncle . . .

General   Genius. Complete genius.

Eilif   The rest was a piece of cake. On they came like
clockwork, we jumped out and we had them ambushed. But
then all of a sudden we realised that there was more of them
than we expected and we were outnumbered three to one
and they started charging us with clubs and four of them
had me in the bushes and knocked the sword out of my
hand. Well, I thought I was a goner, didn't I?

General   So what did you do?

Eilif   I just laughed. Didn't I?

General   Laughed?!

Eilif   Diversionary tactic. That got them talking. So I said, 'Twenty guilders! I wouldn't give you fifteen for that mangy thing.' So being a bit confused by the mathematics and the sudden entry of commerce into the proceedings, I grabbed the old sword back and cut them into little pieces. Necessity's the mother of invention, isn't it?

General   What do you say to that then, padre?

Chaplain   Strictly speaking it's not a tenet of the Christian faith, but I suppose our Lord did feed the five thousand, although that wasn't strictly a 'necessity', there wasn't a war on for a start. In those days you could ask them to love their fellow man because they'd had a bit of bread and herring. Not so simple now.

General (*laughs*)   Maybe you will get a sip after all, you old Pharisee. (*To* **Eilif**.) Cut them to pieces, did you? Quite right, if it saves my men from starvation. What do they say? 'What you do to the least of my children, you do unto me.' And what you did was give them a damn fine feast of oxen. No mouldy old bread for my soldiers, oh no, they fill their bellies with fillet steak and wine before they go off to die for God.

Eilif   So as I was saying, as I started slicing them to pieces . . .

General   A veritable young Caesar. They should present you to the king, you know.

Eilif   Actually, I have seen the king. From a distance. Very impressive actually. I see him as sort of a role model.

General   It's completely obvious. You've no idea what it means to have a valiant young soldier like you by my side, you're like a son to me.

He shows **Eilif** *a map.*

General   Look at this, Eilif, not exactly plain sailing, is it?

Mother Courage, *who has been listening, plucks her capon angrily.*

Mother Courage   There you go. A useless tactician.

Cook   The General?! What are you saying?

Mother Courage   Listen, if he was any good he wouldn't need valiant men, would he? He'd get away with normal ones, wouldn't he? Believe me, wherever there is a heroic deed there's a fuck up gone on somewhere.

Cook   And I thought it was something to be proud of.

Mother Courage   Think about it. It's only when your general or what-have-you sends his army up shit creek that the poor bastards have to be valiant. Is that what you call a virtue? It's when they don't recruit enough men that your squaddie has to fight like bloody Hercules, while your general's sat on his fat arse eating capons. That's not heroics. That's blind terror that's the motivation there. The only reason he values loyalty is 'cos he asks too much of people. If he was any good he wouldn't need loyalty, just ordinary, average people, you could get away with a troop of cowards for that matter.

General   I wager your father was a soldier.

Eilif   Yeah. And a good one. You should have heard my old mum go on about him. Do you want to hear a song?

General   Absolutely! (*Shouting.*) And get a bloody move on with that food.

Eilif   'Soldier and the Young Girl.' (*Sings, dancing a sabre dance.*)

> The shotgun shoots, the sabre slits
> The foolish are the bolder.
> 'What can you do 'gainst guns and knives?'
> Said the young girl to the soldier
> But the soldier grabbed his gun
> 'It can't hurt to have some fun

We'll all live till we're older.
Any danger will be brief
I'll catch the bullets in my teeth'
So said the brave, young soldier.

Sweet sorrow that you ignore
What anyone would have told ya
'Take care it doesn't end in woe'
Said the fishwife to the soldier.
But the soldier grabbed his belt
And crossed the river at full pelt
The water to his shoulder
And the moon was in his hair
'If you're worried, just say a prayer'
Said the brave, young soldier.

Mother Courage (*starts singing from the kitchen, banging on a pot*)

And the soldier with his belt
Was pulled under the water
It was his gun that dragged him down
A poor lamb to the slaughter.

Eilif   What's that?

Mother Courage (*sings*)
And still the moon shone calmly down
As the men began to drown
And the night grew colder
And your hot words were cold as ice
'Why did you not heed my advice?'
Said the young girl to the soldier.

General   They think they can get away with blue murder in that kitchen.

Eilif *goes into the kitchen. He embraces his mother.*

Eilif   Mother. I don't believe it. Where are the others? Are they all right?

Mother Courage (*in his arms*)   They're all fine. Kattrin's still trundling along. And Swisscheese is a paymaster in the Second Regiment, I couldn't keep him out altogether, but at least he's out of the thick of it.

Eilif   And how are your feet?

Mother Courage   Well, it's a bit tricky getting into my boots in the morning.

The **General** *has joined them.*

General   So you're the mother, are you? I hope you've more like this one for me.

Eilif   I can't believe it. You sitting here listening while I'm getting commended by the general.

Mother Courage   Yes. I heard everything.

Mother Courage *hits him.*

Eilif   What's that for? For stealing cattle?

Mother Courage   No. Because you didn't surrender when you had the chance, you little Finnish prick. Didn't I teach you nothing?

The **General** *and the* **Chaplain** *stand laughing at the door.*

Scene Three

1629. **Mother Courage** *is imprisoned with part of the Finnish Army. She saves her daughter and her cart, and her honest son dies.*

Afternoon. A Camp. A flagpole flies a regimental flag. **Mother Courage** *has tied a washing line from her richly burdened cart to a cannon and she is folding washing with* **Kattrin**, *whilst haggling with the* **Quartermaster** *about a sack of bullets.*
Swisscheese, *now in his paymaster's uniform, is watching.*
Yvette Pottier, *an attractive young woman, is sewing a hat and swigging brandy. Her red shoes are laid by her stockinged feet.*

Quartermaster   OK. Tell you what, love, you can have the bullets for a guilder. But only 'cos the colonel here's on a bender and we'll be needing the cash.

Mother Courage   But it's army ammunition. If I get caught with that I'll be up against the wall. You can't sell your own ammunition, you'll have nothing to fight with.

Quartermaster   Don't be so fucking righteous. You scratch my back, I'll scratch yours.

Mother Courage   I refuse to have anything to do with army property. Well, not at that price.

Quartermaster   You could have this sold for five guilders before teatime. Listen, take it down to the quartermaster on the fourth, give him a receipt for twelve, and he'll give you eight guilders for it, no problem. He's out of ammunition altogether.

Mother Courage   Why don't you do it?

Quartermaster   I don't trust the bastard. We're good friends.

Mother Courage *takes the sack of bullets.*

Mother Courage (*to* **Kattrin**)   Take this and give the man a dollar and a half. (*Responding to the protests of the* **Quartermaster**.) That's my final offer.

Kattrin *drags the bag.*

Mother Courage (*to* **Swisscheese**)   Swisscheese, here's your underpants back. Now I want you to look after them this time, 'cos it's October and in all probability winter'll be cutting in shortly. You can't be totally sure 'cos nothing's definite these days, but you want to get yourself sorted. And I hope that cashbox is all in order, 'cos that's got to be done whatever the weather.

Swisscheese   Yes, Mam.

Mother Courage   And no smartarse ideas about running away with it. Just remember they only made you the paymaster 'cos you're honest. And remember: you are too simple to run away with the money. Now go and get it sorted and don't lose those underpants.

Swisscheese   No, I'll put them under the mattress, Mam.

He starts to leave.

Quartermaster   I'll come with you.

Mother Courage   And don't you go teaching him none of your tricks. Understood.

The **Quartermaster** *leaves without acknowledging* **Mother Courage**.

Yvette   Not even a goodbye from Mr Quartermaster.

Mother Courage   I hate seeing them two together. He'll be the ruin of that lad. But look on the bright side, things aren't so bad, are they? Another four or five years and the whole of Europe'll be dragged in this bloody mess and we'll make ourselves a tidy fortune. You know you shouldn't be drinking in the afternoon with your condition.

Yvette   I beg your pardon. Who on earth has said anything about 'a condition'?

Mother Courage   More or less the whole Second Regiment.

Yvette   Lying bastards. I'm ruined. No one'll come near me because of these disgusting rumours. As if I was an open sewer. That's why I drink in the afternoon. I never used to. It ruins your complexion. But what does that matter now? Now the whole of the Third Cavalry's been through me. I only ended up here out of pride. I only left home because my first fella did the dirty on me. No point in being proud now, is there? Either you eat shit or you drown in it.

Mother Courage   Oh for God's sake, don't start about Pete the Pipe again. Not in front of the young 'un.

Yvette   She should hear every word of it. It'll prepare her for the sorrows of the heart.

Mother Courage   I don't think anyone's prepared for the sorrows of the heart, love.

Yvette   Well, I'm going to tell you anyway. A cook he was, met him in Flanders where I was born. Ever so handsome – blond, Dutch and skinny. Just watch, Kattrin, it's the skinny ones you have to watch out for, not that I knew that at the time, nor about the other women, neither. Nor that they called him Peter Piper because he kept puffing away even when he was on the job. Right Mr Sensitive he was . . .

> I was only seventeen
> When they first came into town
> He reached out a friendly hand
> And put his sabre down
>> And in the festive season
>> Late one festive evening
>> The regiment, you won't be surprised
>> Gathered for the kill
>> And took us up the hill
>> And we fraternised.

> There were so many enemies
> Mine was a cook by trade
> I hated him by daylight
> But I loved him in the shade
>> And in the festive season
>> Every festive evening
>> The regiment, you won't be surprised
>> Gathered for the kill
>> And took us up the hill
>> And we fraternised.

> My feelings for him were profound
> As if they came from up above
> But no one really understood
> It wasn't hate but love.

Then one hazy morning
Completely without warning
The regiment, you won't be surprised
Stood as if for drill
Then marched up the hill
And they vaporised.

Oh I tried to find him, but what chance did I have? That was five years ago and here I am

She walks unsteadily behind the cart.

Mother Courage   Yvette, you forgot your hat.

Yvette   Fuck the hat.

Mother Courage   Let that learn you, Kattrin. Promise me you'll never start anything with a soldier. Love is a gift from heaven, so avoid it like the plague. Even if they're civilians it's no bed of roses. One minute he'll be thanking the Lord you were ever put here, the next he'll be thanking heavens that you can't complain when he's shaggin' every skullery maid from here to Baden-Baden. Being dumb – now that's a real gift from God. Talk of the devil, here's the general's cook. What do you want?

Enter the **Cook** *and the* **Chaplain**.

Chaplain   I come with a message from your son. Unfortunately I couldn't stop him from coming. I think you've made quite an impression.

Cook   Actually, I only came for a bit of fresh air.

Mother Courage   Well, you're welcome to it. But any monkey business and you're for the high jump, understood? Now what does Eilif want? I haven't got cash to throw around.

Chaplain   Actually, the message is for his brother. The paymaster.

Mother Courage   Well, he isn't here and he isn't anywhere else either. His brother isn't his paymaster, so he can forget trying to wangle anything out of him.

She gives him some money out of a purse she carries round her neck.

Give him that. He should be ashamed of himself exploiting his mother's love.

Cook   Give him a bit more than that. He's going off to the front. He might die for all you know. You'll be sorry for your penny-pinching then. At least give him the money for a brandy before the poor sod's six feet under.

Chaplain   But don't forget, cook, to fall in this war is a blessing not an inconvenience. This is a religious war not an ordinary one. A war of faith.

Cook   Oh yes. It might seem like an ordinary war with all the burning and stabbing and looting and odd rape now and again. But actually it's totally different, because it's got God's blessing.

Chaplain (*to* **Mother Courage**, *pointing to the* **Cook**)   I tried to stop him coming, but he's a bit pussy-struck. He says he dreams about you.

The **Cook** *lights himself a pipe.*

Cook   Only of receiving a sweet drop of brandy from your dainty little hand. Anyway you can talk, what about that story you were just telling me about the nun and the sauerkraut.

Mother Courage   And you a man of the cloth. Well, before you make any improper advances out of sheer Protestant fervour, I better give you something to drink.

Chaplain   Now there's a temptation as the bishop said to the actress. (*Sees* **Kattrin**.) And who is this charming person?

Mother Courage   That is not a charming person. That is Kattrin. She's my daughter.

The **Chaplain** *and the* **Cook** *go with* **Mother Courage** *behind the cart.* **Kattrin** *watches them go and then leaves the washing and heads for the hat. She puts it on along with the red shoes. From behind the cart we hear* **Mother Courage** *discussing politics with the* **Chaplain** *and the* **Cook**.

Mother Courage   I don't know why these Poles are complaining, they started fighting us in the first place. Admittedly we invaded them, but we were about to leave, weren't we? It's their own bloody faults if they get slaughtered.

Chaplain   After all, it was our king that liberated them from the Emperor.

Cook   Absolutely. Delicious brandy. And after all, it's been a terrible time for our poor king. All he wants to do is liberate a few people and lo and behold, they don't even have the good sense to want to be liberated so he has to lock half of them up and kill the rest of them, and on top of that, lay on a special salt tax at home to pay for it all. Poor man. But at least he's got God on his side. Which just goes to show it can't be for money or power or preserving his name for posterity. No, he's a man with a completely clean conscience.

Mother Courage   Well, it's obvious you're not a Swede, talking about our illustrious hero like that.

Chaplain   After all, you are eating his bread.

Cook   I don't eat his bread, mate. I bake it.

Mother Courage   You know why people fight for him, don't you? Not for God or Right or Justice. No, it's for a much higher purpose. People fight for Profit. Why the hell else would we do it?

Cook   I don't know.

Chaplain   If I was a Dutchman in Poland I'd look to see what flag was flying before I shouted my mouth off.

Mother Courage   Don't fret. We're all good Protestants here!

Kattrin *has started to parade around with* **Yvette**'s *hat on her head, imitating* **Yvette**'s *walk. Suddenly there are cannon shots. Drums.* **Mother Courage**, *the* **Cook** *and the* **Chaplain** *leap from behind the cart with their glasses in their hands. The* **Quartermaster** *and a* **Soldier** *walk up to the cannon and try to push it away.*

Mother Courage   What's going on? Let me get my washing off.

Quartermaster   It's the Catholics. It's a surprise attack. I think it's too late. (*To the* **Solider**.) Grab that gun.

They run off.

Cook   For God's sake I better get to the general. But I'll drop by for a proper chat as soon as I get the time.

Cook *rushes off.*

Mother Courage   Wait. Your pipe.

Cook   Take care of it. I'll be needing that.

He winks at **Mother Courage**.

Mother Courage   Just when we were starting to make a bit of money.

Chaplain   Well, I better be off too. It could be dangerous. I know they say, 'Blessed are the peacemakers' and all that, but I could really do with a top coat.

Mother Courage   I'm not lending out coats even if it is a matter of life and death. I've had some very bad experiences lending out overcoats.

Chaplain   But if they realise I'm a Protestant chaplain . . .

Mother Courage   This is against my better judgement. Run for it.

Chaplain   Thank you, but maybe it's better just to lay low. It might seem suspicious, me running round in a top coat.

Mother Courage (*to the* **Soldier**)   Leave it, you idiot. Run. Do you want to die or something?

Soldier   Just don't say I deserted my post or anything.

Mother Courage   Just go. I'll vouch for you (*Sees* **Kattrin** *with the hat.*) What are you doing in a slag's hat? Are you out of your mind? (*She pulls the hat off* **Kattrin***'s head.*) They'll have you on the game for real when they get here. And the shoes as well. Who do you think you are? The whore of Babylon. Get them off! (*She tries to take the shoes off her.*) Please, Mr Chaplain, get these shoes off her. I'll be right back.

Yvette *arrives powdering her face.*

Yvette   Who'd've thought, eh? Where's my hat? Who's been pissing about with it? I can't go round in this state in front of Catholics, what'll they take me for? And typical, no bloody mirror at a time like this. (*To the* **Chaplain**.) What do you think, luv? Not too much powder?

Chaplain   You look absolutely splendid.

Yvette   Where's my bleeding shoes?

She can't find them because **Kattrin** *hides her feet under her skirt.*

Yvette   They were just there a moment ago. Now I'll have to drum up business in my sockinged feet.

She goes out. **Swisschesse** *comes running in carrying a small box.* **Mother Courage** *comes in with her hands full of ash.*

Mother Courage   Here's some ash. (*To* **Swisscheese**.) What are you doing?

Swisschesse   It's the bank box.

Mother Courage   Throw it away. The Catholics are coming. No more paymaster now. We've put paid to that.

Swisschesse   But they gave me it to look after.

Mother Courage (*to the* **Chaplain**)   For Christ's sake, get that cassock off, they're going to recognise you, coat or not. (*She rubs* **Kattrin***'s face with ash.*) Stay still. A little bit of dirt won't hurt. Hide your light under a bushel, sweetheart. With these Catholics one clean face and a whore is made. Give me a look. Very good. Looks like you've been rolling around in shit all day. Stop shaking, darling. Nothing's going to happen to you now. (*To* **Swisscheese**.) What did you do with the bank box?

Swisscheese   I put it in the cart.

Mother Courage   In the cart! You fucking idiot. They'll hang all three of us.

Swisscheese   I'll put it somewhere else. I'll run away with it.

Mother Courage   Stay here, it's too late.

Chaplain   For God's sake, the flag!

Mother Courage *takes the regiment's flag down.*

Mother Courage   Oh fucking hell.

The roar of the cannons gets louder.

Early afternoon three days later. The cannon is gone. **Mother Courage**, **Kattrin**, *the* **Chaplain** *and* **Swisscheese** *sit huddled together over a meal.*

Swisscheese   But I've been here three days. The sergeant will be wondering where I am.

Mother Courage   Nobody will be wondering where you are. Just count your lucky stars you're alive.

Chaplain   Anyway. What about me? My heart's busting open, yet I daren't even risk a prayer without tempting fate.

Mother Courage   Christ. One with a bank box, the other with religion. I don't know which is worse.

Chaplain   We're all in God's hands now.

Mother Courage   Christ it's not that bad, even if I can't sleep at night with the worry. Life'd be a lot easier if you weren't running round with a death warrant round your neck. I've put them off the scent for the time being. I dropped a few Hail Marys into the conversation and enquired as to where I might buy some votive candles, God knows whether they bought it but they need a canteen, don't they? We might be prisoners but so are the flies on a cow's arse.

Chaplain   Excellent milk. But I'm afraid we'll have to cut down our Swedish appetites now we've been conquered.

Mother Courage   Conquered?! For some, defeat can actually be a victory. It depends where you are in the pecking order. What have we lost? 'Honour.' That's sweet F.A. as far as I'm concerned. When we suffered the so-called defeat of Livonia I managed to get myself a spare piebald horse, pulled my cart for seven months it did, until we won again and they collected it back in. Safe to say either way, victory or defeat, it's a catastrophe for ordinary people. No, what you want is things to get totally bogged down in a drawn-out war of attrition, that's when you're laughing. Eat!

Swisscheese   I'm not hungry. How will the sergeant pay all the wages?

Mother Courage   They're not interested in bloody wages, they're fleeing for their lives.

Swisscheese   But that's their money. If they don't get paid why should they retreat?

Mother Courage   Sometimes you scare me. I told you to be honest because you're as thick as a parson's arse but this takes the biscuit. I'm going with the chaplain to buy a Catholic flag and some meat. He could spot a chop at one hundred yards. Just thank the Lord we're still trading. You don't ask a businessman his religion. You ask him, 'How much?'.

Mother Courage *goes into the cart.*

Chaplain   I think she's still worried about that bank box.

Swisschesse   I'm going to get rid of it.

Chaplain   You can't do that. They've got spies everywhere. I was answering a call of nature yesterday, one popped up out of the midden with a patch on his eye. It was all I could do to stop myself breaking into prayer. No, they'd sniff your shit to see if you're a Protestant and enjoy the privilege.

Mother Courage *climbs with a basket out of the cart.*

Mother Courage   And what do you think these are, you little hussy? (*She holds up* **Yvette**'s *red shoes.*) Yvette's boots. Well, they're going straight back. At least she ruined herself for money. I've warned you. No soldiers. You'll just have to wait till it's peacetime before you start parading yourself around.

Chaplain   She was hardly 'parading' round.

Mother Courage   Even a tiptoe's too much. She's got to be invisible, she has to be pig ugly, so people don't notice her. (*To* **Swisscheese**.) You leave the bank box where it is, you hear, and look after your sister. You two'll be the death of me. It's easier looking after a bag of fleas.

She goes off with the **Chaplain**. **Kattrin** *clears away the dishes.*

Swisscheese   We won't be able to sit out here like this for much longer.

Kattrin *points at a tree.*

Swisscheese   Everything's going brown.

Kattrin *asks him with gestures if he wants something to drink.*

Swisscheese   I've been thinking. If Mam can't sleep, maybe I should get rid of it. That's it; I'll hide it. Yes, I will have one.

Kattrin *goes behind the cart.*

Swisscheese   I'll stick it down a rat-hole, and then I could get up very early one morning and take it to the sergeant and he'll say, 'You may be an idiot, but at least you're an idiot with a bank box.'

Kattrin *returns with a full glass from behind the cart and is confronted by two men. One of them is a* **Sergeant***, the other takes his hat off for her. He has an eye-patch.*

Eye-patch   God be with you, miss. Have you anyone here from the Finnish Regiment?

Kattrin *is very frightened. She runs away spilling the brandy. Both men look at each other and withdraw after seeing* **Swisscheese***.*

Swisscheese   You've spilled half of it. What are you pulling faces for? Have you got something in your eye? I don't know what you're saying. I can't sit round waiting for you to wink to death, I've got the bank box to think about. Don't hold me up or I'll get angry.

He gets up. **Kattrin** *tries to point out the danger to him, but he shrugs her off.*

I would like to know what you are saying and everything. It's not your fault you're dumb. But if it's the brandy, just forget it, I'll have some more another time.

He takes the bank box from the cart and hides it under his coat.

See you later.

She tries to stop him but he kisses her and tears himself away. He goes off. She is devastated, she walks up and down uttering little noises. **Mother Courage** *and the* **Chaplain** *return.* **Kattrin** *storms up to her mother.*

Mother Courage   What's the matter? What's the matter? Did somebody hurt you? Where's Swisscheese? Kattrin, calm down. What, he went off with the bank box? I'll cripple the stupid bastard. Take your time. Use your hands. Really, please don't howl, you'll scare the padre. (**Kattrin** *mimes.*) There was a one-eyed man?

Chaplain　The spy. Have they got Swisscheese?

Kattrin *shakes her head and shrugs her shoulders.*

Chaplain　We're done for.

Mother Courage *takes a Catholic flag from her basket which the* **Chaplain** *fixes to the flagpole.*

Chaplain　God save the Pope.

Voices from behind. The two men bring in **Swisscheese**.

Swisscheese　Get off, I haven't got anything. Ah, my arm. I haven't done nothing.

Sergeant　This one belongs here. You know each other, don't you?

Mother Courage　Us? Where from?

Swisscheese　I've never seen them before. I just bought my tea here and it cost me a fortune. You probably saw me sitting here with my dinner. Which was too salty.

Sergeant　Who are you then?

Mother Courage　Respectable business people. Yes, he bought a meal here. Yes, maybe it was too salty. What do you expect, there's a war on.

Sergeant　So you're going to pretend you don't know each other.

Mother Courage　Why should I know him? Do you expect me to know everybody. I don't ask if they're Protestants. I ask for their money. Are you Protestant by any chance?

Swisscheese　No I am not.

Chaplain　He just sat down quietly and didn't open his mouth. Well, except to eat.

Sergeant   Who the hell are you?

Mother Courage   He's the barboy. I expect you gentlemen are thirsty, maybe you'd fancy a nice glass of brandy for your labours.

Sergeant   Not while we're on duty, ma'am. (*To* **Swisscheese**.) You had something with you. You've hidden it down the river, haven't you? We saw it under your jacket.

Mother Courage   You sure it was him?

Swisscheese   You must have mixed me up for somebody else. There was this other bloke what had a bulge in his jacket. It must have been him.

Mother Courage   Yes, obviously a little misunderstanding. Easily done. Oh yes, I know a thing or two about people, Mother Courage, that's me, I'm sure you're familiar with the name, everybody's heard of Mother Courage. And that's an honest face if ever I saw one.

Sergeant   Listen. We're after the bank box of the Second Finnish Regiment. And we know who looks after it. And we know what he looks like. And he happens to be you.

Swisscheese   No. It isn't.

Sergeant   And if you don't cough it up now, you're a goner, matey. Where is it?

Mother Courage   There you go. If it were him then he'd give it up, wouldn't he? Unless you'd kill him. He'd say where it was straight away, wouldn't he? You've got the upper hand. He couldn't be that stupid. Tell them, you stupid cunt, the sergeant's giving you a chance.

Swisscheese   But I haven't got it.

Sergeant   Come with us then, we'll help you remember where you put it.

Mother Courage (*shouts after them*)   He'd have told you if it was him. He's not an idiot. Watch his shoulder.

She runs after them.

Later. The same evening. The **Chaplain** *and* **Kattrin** *wash glasses and polish knives.*

Chaplain   The history of religion's full of people getting caught like that. It's not dissimilar to what happened to our Lord. As the song goes . . .
In the first hour of the day
The Lord, without reason
Was summoned as a murderer
To Pilate, the heathen.

He declared him innocent
The crime he could not pin
So they sent him on his weary way
To Herod the king.

Then at three the son of God
Was marked by flaggellation
They placed on him a crown of thorns
As if for coronation.

They stripped him down, and then they mocked
They spat, they tore his hair
They put a cross upon his back
That he was made to bear.

At six they stripped him of his clothes
And nailed him to a cross
And there they drained him of his blood
Still praying for his loss.

And crowds came round the men that hung
And still they shouted out
Their vile abuse across the world
Until the sun went out.

And at the ninth hour, Jesus wept
That now he was forsaken

Bitter gall did fill his mouth
Now all else was taken.

And when our Lord gave up the ghost
The earth began to shake
The temple opened as a book
The stones began to break.

Then at vespers, men were sent
To break him bone from bone
They pierced his body with a spear
And left him there alone.

And from the wound blood ran out
While people mocked and cried
That's what they did to the people's son
They laughed until he died.

Mother Courage *comes back agitated.*

Mother Courage   I think it's life or death, but we might
be able to bribe the sergeant, just as long as we're related or
we'll all be for it. I think it's only a matter of money.
Where's Yvette? She's gone to get her fat little colonel, she
thinks he'll buy a business for her.

Chaplain   Are you really going to sell up?

Mother Courage   Where else am I going to get this kind
of money?

Chaplain   But where will you live?

Mother Courage   I don't know.

Yvette *arrives with a very old* **Colonel** *and embraces* **Mother
Courage**.

Yvette   My dear Courage. What a surprise! (*Whispering.*) I
think he might bite. (*Loud.*) This is my good friend who
advises me in all matters of business. I hear perchance that
you'd like to sell your cart.

Mother Courage   Pawn it. Not sell it. Such a cart as this isn't easily come by in times of war.

Yvette (*disappointed*)   I thought you wanted rid of it. It's a lot less interesting if you merely want to pawn it. (*To the* **Colonel**.) What do you reckon?

Colonel   I quite agree, sweetie.

Mother Courage   It's only for pawn.

Yvette   I thought you were in desperate need of money.

Mother Courage   Yes, I need money but I'd rather cut my feet off than sell it to you straightaway. This is my life. And this is a golden opportunity for you, Yvette, Lord knows when you'll find another one and have such an excellent financial adviser to help you make up your mind.

Yvette   My adviser thinks I should take it, but I'm not so sure if it's only for pawn. You think I should buy it outright, don't you, darling?

Colonel   I most certainly do.

Mother Courage   Well, keep looking, maybe you might find something in a year or two, if your financial friend here's still around to go with you.

Yvette   When would you pay back?

Mother Courage   A fortnight. Maybe less.

Yvette   I don't know. Freddie, my little sweetpea, help me, darling.

She takes the **Colonel** *aside.*

Yvette   Look, take no notice of her, I know she's got to sell up. The blond lieutenant will certainly lend me the dosh. He's crazy about me, says I remind him of someone. What do you think, sweetheart?

Colonel   The blond lieutenant! I've told you about that scoundrel, he'll only be trying to take advantage, I said I'd get you something, didn't I, my little partridge? Why don't I buy it for you?

Yvette   I couldn't take that from you! Do you really think that lieutenant's taking liberties?

Colonel   No doubt about it.

Yvette   You're not thinking of taking liberties, are you?

Colonel   Absolutely.

Yvette (*to* **Mother Courage**)   My friend's advice is to accept. Write me a receipt and I'll bring you two hundred guilders shortly. (*To the* **Colonel**.) You go back to the barracks, sweetheart, I'll just take stock in case anything goes missing.

She kisses him. She goes. She climbs on to the cart.

There aren't many boots, are there?

Mother Courage   What are you doing? A fucking inventory. You said you'd talk to the sergeant for us. He'll be in front of the court martial in an hour.

Yvette   I just want to check the shirts.

Mother Courage   You fucking vulture. What about Swisscheese? Look, not a word where the money's coming from or we're all for it.

Yvette   I've arranged to meet One-eye in the bushes. He'll be there now.

Chaplain   And don't offer the whole two hundred. Start off with one-fifty. I'd say that's enough.

Mother Courage   You keep out of this. It's not even your money. Yvette, go. Don't haggle. It's life or death here.

She pushes **Yvette** *away.*

Chaplain   I'm not trying to be funny. But how are we going to live? She's not exactly a career girl, is she?

Mother Courage   I'm counting on the bank box, smartarse. There's at least two hundred in there.

Chaplain   Are you sure she's up to this?

Mother Courage   Of course, she's got a vested interest, hasn't she? If I shell out the money for Swisscheese, she gets the cart. She'll not have the colonel to lean on for much longer by the looks of him. Make yourself useful instead of standing round like Jesus on the Mount of Olives. Wash those glasses, there's going to be fifty horsemen here tonight. Don't worry, we'll get him back. Thank God for bribery. Corruption is to people what mercy is to God. As long as there's corruption, there will be tolerance and justice and the innocent will walk free.

Yvette *enters, out of breath.*

Yvette   They'll only do it for two hundred. And we'll have to act quick, they'll not be in charge much longer. I better go and take One-eye to the colonel for the money. He's already confessed to the bank box, they've had the thumbscrews on him. He said he threw it in the river. But it's gone.

Mother Courage   Gone? How will I get my two hundred?

Yvette   So you thought you'd get it from the bank box. I'd've been a right mug. Look, you're going to have to shell out if you want Swisscheese back or shall we just forget it and you can keep your cart?

Mother Courage   Don't push me, Yvette. You'll get your cart. I've lost it already. Seventeen years. Just let me think for a moment, it's all going too quick, I haven't two hundred to give them, you should have bargained after all. I should always keep something back or any little shit can kick you in the gutter. Tell them I'll pay one-twenty or nothing. Either way I've lost the cart.

Yvette   He won't do it. He's almost had it as it is. You'd better give him the whole two hundred.

Mother Courage (*in despair*)   I can't. I've worked for thirty years. She's already twenty-five with no husband. I've got to think of her, too. Don't push me, I know what I'm doing. Tell him a hundred and twenty or the whole thing's off.

Yvette   It's your business.

She goes out quickly. **Mother Courage** *avoids looking at the* **Chaplain** *or her daughter. She sits down to help the* **Chaplain** *polish the knives.*

Mother Courage   Careful with those glasses, they're not even ours now. Swisscheese will be back, I'll pay the whole two hundred if it comes to it. You'll get him back. And for fifty guilders we could fill a case full of stuff and start from scratch.

Chaplain   The Lord will provideth.

Mother Courage   Just rub them dry.

They polish the knives in silence. **Kattrin** *suddenly runs in sobbing from behind the cart.*

Yvette *comes running back.*

Yvette   They won't do it. I told you. One-eye wanted to forget it. He said the drums would roll any minute. I offered a hundred and fifty, he just looked right through me. It was all I could do to let me come and talk to you again.

Mother Courage   Tell him two hundred. Run.

Yvette *runs off. They sit in silence. The* **Chaplain** *has stopped polishing the knives. In the distance is the sound of drums.*

Mother Courage   I think I bargained too long.

The **Chaplain** *gets up and goes to the back.* **Mother Courage** *remains seated. It grows dark. The drumming stops. It gets light again.* **Mother Courage** *hasn't moved.*

Yvette *appears, very pale.*

Yvette   That's what business gets you. Keep your cart. He got eleven bullets. I don't know why I'm even talking to you. They're saying they don't think the bank box is in the river, they think it's here, they think you know him after all. They're bringing him over. If you seem like you know him you've had it. They're right behind. What about Kattrin? Does she understand?

Mother Courage   Yes, she understands.

Yvette *gets* **Kattrin** *who goes to her mother and stands next to her.* **Mother Courage** *takes her by the hand. Two men bring on a stretcher with a body on it. The* **Sergeant** *walks beside it. They put the stretcher down.*

Sergeant   There's somebody here whose name we don't know and in the interests of our records we were hoping you could help us. He ate a meal at your canteen. Know him, do you? (*He takes the sheet away.*) Well?

Mother Courage *shakes her head.*

Sergeant   You've never seen him before in your life, have you?

Mother Courage *shakes her head again.*

Sergeant   OK, get rid of it. Looks like nobody knows who he is.

Scene Four.

1629. **Mother Courage** *sings the song of the Great Capitulation.*

Outside an officer's tent.

Mother Courage *is waiting. A* **Clerk** *looks out of the tent.*

Clerk   I know your face. You're the one who was with that paymaster, weren't you? I wouldn't be making any complaints if I was you.

Mother Courage   So what? They've slashed my cart to ribbons with their sabres and then fined me five guilders for absolutely nothing. What do you want me to do? Even if I let that pass you'll just assume I've got a guilty conscience about something.

Clerk   I'm warning you. Keep your mouth shut. The only reason you're trading is cos we're short of canteens. I'd pay up and puck off if I were you.

Mother Courage   See, I've got a good right to complain.

Clerk   Have it your way. You'll have to wait for the captain.

He goes back to the tent. A **Young Soldier** *enters.*

Young Soldier   OK! Where's that little twat of a captain. The thieving bastard's got my money, I bet he's pissing it up the wall with is cronies. Where is he?

An **Older Solider** *comes after him.*

Older Soldier   Shut up. Or they'll have you in the nick.

Young Soldier   Come out, you thieving turdsucker, or I'll split you into pieces. I swam a fucking river for that reward. And now I can't even buy a beer. Come on, I'll cut your spine off.

Older Soldier   Mary and Joseph! You'll end up in the fucking river.

Mother Courage   What's the matter? Didn't they give him his drink money?

Young Soldier   Let me go or I'll cut your spine off while I'm at it.

Older Soldier   He saved the captain's horse and he didn't get his money. He's a bit wet behind the ears.

Mother Courage   Let him go. He's not a dog to be chained up. I think it's perfectly reasonable to want his drink money. Why else should he exert himself?

Young Soldier   He's getting mortal in there. You drunken wankers. I'm a fucking hero so get me my reward.

Mother Courage   For God's sake keep your voice down. You're not the only one with problems, you want to save that voice till the captain comes or you'll be too hoarse to offend him. Shouters never last long, twenty minutes and you'll have to be sung to sleep.

Young Soldier   Oh shut up. Why should I be out here starving and he's in there whoring his way through my reward. It's not fair. And I'm not going to stand for it.

Mother Courage   For how long? An hour? Two hours? Twenty minutes? A week? You don't even know. It would be terrible, wouldn't it, to be locked up for a decade only to find out you could stand injustice after all?

Young Soldier   I don't know why I'm listening to this bollocks. Where is the captain?

Mother Courage   You're listening to me 'cos I'm right. Look, your anger's vanishing as we speak. Didn't last long, did it? I think you need a longer anger, my friend. Where will you get that from?

Young Soldier   Are you saying I'm out of order for asking for my money?

Mother Courage   Quite the reverse. All I'm saying is you haven't got enough anger to get what you want. Pity. If there was more in you then I'd stoke you up. 'Go on, son, cut his fat heart out of him.' But what happens when you bottle and I'm stood in front of him? I get it in the neck and it wasn't even my reward.

Old Soldier   You're right. He's only having a little strop.

Young Soldier   We'll see who's having a strop. When he comes out I'll hack his arms off.

Clerk   The captain will be out shortly. Sit down!

The **Young Soldier** *sits down.*

Mother Courage   I rest my case. They've got us sussed.
Sit and we are seated. There'll not be a revolution when
we're all sat on our bony arses. For God's sake don't stand
up again! You don't need to be embarrassed in front of me.
I'm just as bad as you are. They've bought us off, haven't
they? I'll tell you why we don't complain. It's bad for
business. Now let me tell you about the Great Capitulation.

> Once in the blossom of my youth
> As proud as proud could be

(Not just any peasant's daughter, I had looks, I had talent,
oh yes, my sights were set on higher things.)

> I made myself heard, forsooth,
> There were no flies on me
>> But a bird's twitter nears
>> 'Just wait a few years!'
>> You will march at last
>> To the beat, slow or fast
>> And your foot will tap
>> As it's caught in a trap
>> And you'll turn, to a man,
>> Convinced it's God's plan.
>> What a load of crap!
> And before the year was over
> Some medicine cured the disease.

(Two children round my neck, and the price of bread, I ask
you.)

> And when it was all over
> I was down on my hands and knees.
>> But a bird in a tree
>> Said: 'Just wait and see!'
>> You will march at last
>> To the beat, slow or fast
>> Come all melancholics!
>> Join humanity's frolics
>> And with your fellow man
>> Dance to God's plan
>> – Bollocks!

I've seen men storm the heavens above
No star was too big or too far.

(Where there's a will there's a way.)

But after a few little summits
They're at home lighting up a cigar.
    But a bird, up above
    Says: 'Hang on, luv.'
    To the chapel at last
    You'll march slow or fast
    So sound the advance
    And join in the dance,
    Don't think I'm kidding,
    It's all in God's bidding
    – Fat chance.

You should only be sitting here if you really mean it. If you
haven't got enough anger you should forget the whole thing,
honey.

Young Soldier   Kiss my arse.

He stumbles away. The **Older Soldier** *goes after him.*

The **Clerk** *sticks his head out.*

Clerk   OK, the captain's ready. You can make your
complaint now.

Mother Courage   Forget it. I've changed my mind.

Scene Five

1631. The War is spreading. **Mother Courage**'s *little cart
crosses Europe until it ends up in Bavaria. The victory of the Imperial
Commander Tilly costs* **Mother Courage** *four shirts.*

Mother Courage's *cart stands in a bombed-out village. From far
away we hear the hint of military music. Two* **Soldiers** *are propping
up the bar, served by* **Mother Courage** *and* **Kattrin**. *One of
them has a woman's fur coat draped over him.*

Mother Courage   Can't pay, eh? No money, no booze, mate. It's no use playing victory marches if they don't pay you your wages, is it?

First Soldier   I want a drink. It's not my fault I missed the looting. We were shat on, there was only half an hour's pillage, I reckon the general's on a back-hander from the mayor.

The **Chaplain** *stumbles in.*

Chaplain   There are still people lying out there in the yard. A family. Please help. I need linen for bandages.

The **Second Soldier** *goes with him.* **Kattrin** *gets very excited and tries to convince her mother to hand out some linen.*

Mother Courage   I haven't got any linen. I sold all my bandages to the army and I'm not tearing up good shirts.

Chaplain   I need linen.

Mother Courage *denies* **Kattrin** *entrance to the cart by sitting on the steps.*

Mother Courage   Don't give him anything. If they're not going to pay, they haven't got anything.

Chaplain (*to a woman he's carried in*)   Why didn't you run when you heard the battle?

Farmer's Wife   The farm.

Mother Courage   No, you won't give anything away but you expect me to give you handouts. Well, fuck that.

First Soldier   They're Protestants, aren't they, it's their own fault.

Mother Courage   Who gives a toss what religion they are. They've just lost their farm.

Second Soldier   They're not Protestants. They're Catholics.

First Soldier   Well, they all look the same with their guts hanging out.

A **Farmer** *is brought on by the* **Chaplain**.

Farmer   I've lost my arm.

Chaplain   Where's the linen?

They all look at **Mother Courage** *who doesn't stir.*

Mother Courage   I can't afford it. Not with duties and taxes and bribes I've got to pay.

Kattrin, *uttering gurgling noises, lifts a wooden plank and threatens her mother with it.*

Mother Courage   Put that down, you stupid cow, or I'll really give you something to squawk about. I'm not giving nothing. I've got myself to think of.

The **Chaplain** *lifts her from the steps, puts her on the ground then grabs some shirts and tears them into strips for bandages.*

Mother Courage   What are you doing? They're a guilder apiece.

A cry comes from the house.

Farmer   There's a baby in there.

Kattrin *runs in.*

Chaplain (*to the* **Farmer's Wife**)   It's OK. Someone's going to get it.

Mother Courage   Stop her, the roof'll fall in.

Chaplain   I'm not going in there again.

Mother Courage *is torn both ways.*

Mother Courage   Stop wasting it, for God's sake.

The **Second Soldier** *keeps her back.* **Kattrin** *brings a baby out of the ruins.*

Mother Courage   Satisfied you've got another hungry mouth to feed? Give it to its mother straightaway or I'll be hours trying to prize the bugger off you. (*To the* **Second Soldier**.) Stop gawping, you stupid idiot, go and tell them to stop that bloody racket, I think we've got the point. Some bloody victory – all I've gained is losses.

Chaplain   There's blood coming through.

Kattrin *is rocking the baby in her arms and humming a lullaby.*

Mother Courage   There she is, happy as a pig in shite. Give it back now, she's coming round again.

Mother Courage *discovers the* **First Soldier**, *who has got hold of the drinks, trying to make off with a bottle.*

Mother Courage   You pissy cullion grabber. Thought another victory was at hand? Well, this time you're paying for it.

First Soldier   But I haven't got anything.

Mother Courage (*grabs his fur coat*)   There. It's stolen anyway.

Chaplain   There's someone else still in there.

Scene Six

1632. Outside the town of Ingolstadt **Mother Courage** *goes to the funeral of the fallen Imperial Commander Tilly. Talk of heroism and the duration of war. The* **Chaplain** *complains and poor* **Kattrin** *gets a pair of red shoes.*

Inside a canteen tent. There's a bar towards the back. Rain. Drums and funeral music in the distance. The **Chaplain** *and* **Regimental Clerk** *are playing chess.* **Mother Courage** *and* **Kattrin** *are stock-taking.*

Chaplain   I think it's starting.

Mother Courage   What a shame for the poor old general, eh? Twenty-two pairs of socks – must have been a nasty accident. I reckon it was the mist. I mean, the poor fella'd just given the order to fight to the death and unfortunately retreated the wrong way. Four hurricane lamps. Terrible shame.

There's a whistle from the back. She goes to the bar.

Mother Courage   You should be ashamed of yourself, skiving off your dead commander's funeral.

Regimental Clerk   They shouldn't've paid them before he was actually six foot under, if you ask me. There's going to be nobody there.

Chaplain   Shouldn't you be there?

Regimental Clerk   What? In this rain?

Mother Courage   Oh God forbid that your uniform might get wet. I heard they wanted to ring the church bells, of course, but unfortunately he forgot to leave any churches standing, so they're going to fire a cannon instead. That'll make a nice change. Seventeen belts.

Customer   Oi! A brandy.

Mother Courage   Money first, top cat. And get out with those filthy boots on. You can drink outside, drizzle or no drizzle. (*To the* **Regimental Clerk**.) Officers only in here.

Funeral march. They all look to the back.

Chaplain   They'll be filing past the body.

Mother Courage   You have to feel sorry for him, don't you? All he wanted was to be remembered for some important event and the whole thing's buggered up by a lot of lazy wankers whose sole ambition is having a quiet beer with their mates. Tragic, isn't it? The best-laid plans ruined by the mediocrity of the common man.

Chaplain   I don't agree. You can always rely on a soldier so long as there's raping and pillaging and gratuitous acts of violence to be done. A hundred years war? You could have two hundred. No problem.

Mother Courage   So you don't think it's coming to an end?

Chaplain   One dead general?! Put it this way. We'll never be short of heroes.

Mother Courage   I'm serious. I don't know whether to stock up while the prices are low. But if it's over that's money down the drain.

Chaplain   I *am* serious. There's no reason it won't just go on for ever. Of course, there might be a little hiccup, nothing's perfect, it might have to stop for a breather. I mean, maybe it'll come a cropper because of some human error. It's like most things, turn your back for a second and the whole thing goes to rack and ruin, but you can be sure that the best minds in Europe, kings, popes, you name it, will be working on a way to jump-start it back to life. Stock up, Courage.

Soldier (*singing at the bar*)
    A schnapps, my man, make haste
    I've got no time to waste
    I've got to fight again for King and Country.
    Here. Make it a double. I'm celebrating.

Mother Courage   I wish I could be so certain.

Chaplain   Think about it. What's going to stop it now?

Soldier (*sings*)
    Tit's out, my girl, be quick
    I want to wax my prick.
    I've got to fight again for King and Country.

Regimenal Clerk   But what about peace? For Christ's sake, I'm from Bohemia, I want to go home eventually.

Chaplain   Would you indeed. 'What about peace?' What happens to the hole when the cheese is eaten?

Soldier (*sings*)
>   Throw your best card down
>   We're going into town.
>   We must join up again for King and Country.
>
>   Last rites, if you please
>   The moment you must seize.
>   I'm going to die right now for King and Country.

Clerk   You can't live without peace.

Chaplain   But war has peace. Special little places of serenity. War satisfies all needs, peaceful ones included, it wouldn't last a fortnight otherwise. You can stop for a crap, you can fight, have a beer, a nice little kip in a ditch if you fancy. Admittedly it's a bit tricky to get through a full game of bridge without interruptions, but let's face it, there's always that problem in peacetime. You might get your leg shot off and whatnot, but you soon get used to it, a few drinks of brandy and you'll be hopping about like a toad on a griddle. And, of course, there's no end of opportunities for procreation. Just grab a girl, nip behind a barn and Bob's your uncle. An entire new generation and so the whole thing can keep going indefinitely. No, the war will always win. Why should it ever end?

Kattrin *has stopped working and stares at the* **Chaplain**.

Mother Courage   I better stock up then, hadn't I?

Suddenly **Kattrin** *throwns down a basket full of bottles and runs out.*

Mother Courage   Kattrin. (*Laughs.*) The poor thing's waiting for peace because I promised her a husband.

Mother Courage *runs after her.*

Regimental Clerk   Checkmate!

Mother Courage *comes in with* **Kattrin**.

Mother Courage   We're only having a bit fun, it'll just go on for a little bit longer, we'll make a bit more money and peace will be all the merrier. Now you go down to the Golden Lion, just get the expensive stuff and we'll collect the rest with the cart later, it's all organised, he'll go with you. Don't worry, nothing'll happen, most of them are at the funeral. Just make sure they don't nick anything. Think of your dowry.

Kattrin *puts on a headscarf and goes off with the* **Regimental Clerk**.

Chaplain   Are you sure she'll be all right with him?

Mother Courage   Don't worry, she's not that good looking. It's still daylight outside.

Chaplain   You know, it's amazing how you keep this business going. It's no wonder they call you Courage.

Mother Courage   Oh yes, the poor need Courage. To get you up in the morning, to plough that field in wartime, to bring children into this cesspit of a world, to kill one another, oh yes, you need Courage to look another human being in the eye.

Mother Courage *sits, taking a pipe from her pocket.*

Mother Courage   Will you chop me some kindling?

Chaplain   I'm a shepherd of souls not a chopper of wood.

Mother Courage   Well, I don't have a soul. But I need some wood.

Chaplain   What's that chewed up old thing?

Mother Courage   It's just a pipe.

Chaplain   It's not 'just' any pipe.

Mother Courage   What're you on about?

Chaplain   That's the pipe of the cook of the General Oxenstijerna.

Mother Courage   Well, what the hell were you asking for?

Chaplain   How was I supposed to know, that you knew it was the pipe of the cook of the General Oxenstijerna? You might of thought it was any old pipe as far as I knew.

Mother Courage   It might be any old pipe.

Chaplain   No it isn't. You're smoking it deliberately.

Mother Courage   So?

Chaplain   I just have to say, even though with God's luck you'll never see the wastrel again, well, in my opinion he's a bit unreliable.

Mother Courage   Really? I thought he was a figure of great propriety, actually.

Chaplain   Great propriety? Don't get me wrong, I don't have anything against him personally, but I'd hardly call him a figure of propriety. He's a bloody Don Juan. Look at that pipe, for heaven's sake. It says everything.

Mother Courage   It doesn't seem to be saying anything to me.

Chaplain   It's nearly bitten in half. That's the pipe of a relentless man of violence, and if you had any sense of judgement it'd be as plain as day.

He wields a hefty blow to the wood.

Mother Courage   Watch what you're doing, Samson.

Chaplain   I already told you, I'm not a fucking lumberjack, I'm a saver of souls. I shouldn't be here doing this manual work, I should be using my God-given gifts of oratory. I should be preaching; with a single sermon I'd inspire a troop of pacifists to march into battle like a horde of barbarians, five minutes with me and their lives would seem as valuable as a rag to wipe their arse with. Oh I could preach you senseless if I only had the chance.

Mother Courage   I quite like my senses, thank you very much.

Chaplain   Courage, I often think that under that hard exterior of yours there's a soft heart. You're only human, you too need a little warmth.

Mother Courage   The only way you're getting warm in here is with some firewood, buster.

Chaplain   Please, Anna, I've been thinking what would happen if we formalised our relationship. I mean, now the whirlwind of war has thrust us together.

Mother Courage   I think it's formalised quite sufficiently, thank you very much. I run the show and you chop the wood.

Chaplain   You know very well what I mean. Don't let your heart turn to stone.

Mother Courage   Don't come near me with that axe, or you'll get some formalising round the jaw.

Chaplain   Stop it. I'm serious. I've thought this through.

Mother Courage   Face the facts, padre, I like you very much and I don't want to get angry with you. But all I'm concerned with is looking after my kids and my cart. I'm not my own woman. As we speak, my arse is on the line with all these supplies and all this talk of armistice. Where will you fit in when I'm ruined? Just cut some firewood so we'll be warm at night. I think that's formal enough for these times . . . What's that?

Kattrin *comes in, out of breath with a wound over her eye. She is carrying all kinds of things: leather goods, a drum.*

Mother Courage   What's happened? Did they attack you? She's been attacked. It must have been that bloke who was drinking here. I shouldn't've let her go. Put that stuff down. It's not too bad, just a flesh wound. I'll bandage it. It'll be fine in a week. They're born fucking animals.

Chaplain   No they're not. They didn't rape at home. It's the warmongers who bring it out of them.

Mother Courage   Didn't the clerk walk back with you? It really isn't so bad, you won't notice it in a while. I've bandaged it up nicely. Here, I'll give you something, that's it, calmly now. I've kept them specially for you. (*She pulls the red shoes out of a sack.*) Now there's a surprise, eh? You always had your eye on those, didn't you? They're yours. Try them on before I change my mind. You won't even notice the scar, even if you could, it's not a bad thing, it's the pretty little ones that spend the war on their backs. I've seen stunners end up with mugs that could frighten off wolves. So you never know, maybe it was all a stroke of luck. Not bad are they? I gave them a good polish before I packed them away.

Kattrin *leaves the shoes where they are and creeps into the cart.*

Chaplain   I hope she won't be disfigured.

Mother Courage   She's ruined. No point in waiting for peace any more.

Chaplain   She didn't let them take the stuff.

Mother Courage   Maybe I shouldn't have been so insistent. If I only knew what she was thinking. In all these years she's only ever stayed out once. Lord knows what happened. She just came back in the morning and worked harder than ever. I've never gotten to the bottom of it. (*She starts sorting out the things that* **Kattrin** *brought.*) That's the war for you. A very fine way to make a living.

We hear the sound of cannon fire.

Chaplain   There he goes. A historic moment.

Mother Courage   It's a historic moment for me, all right, they just punched my daughter's eye out. She'll never get a husband now, not with that and being dumb. And she's so crazy about kids. She's only dumb because when she was little some soldier stuck something in her mouth. God knows where Eilif is and I'll never see Swisscheese again. Damn the fucking war.

Scene Seven

1632. **Mother Courage** *at the height of her business career.*

A street in the country. The **Chaplain** *and* **Kattrin** *are pulling the cart. New goods are hanging off it.* **Mother Courage** *is wearing a chain of silver coins.*

Mother Courage   I'll not have anybody knocking war. They tell you that it crushes the weak. Well, they don't do so bloody well in peacetime, do they? No, the war will feed you just as well as the free market . . .

> War is just business, but by other means
> You trade bread, you trade bullets and cheese.
> It's just the weak-minded who can't stand the course
> And share in the great victories.

What's the point in settling down in one place? They're always the first to get it. Keeping moving that's what I say.

> Quite a few people want quite a bit
> But don't want to put in the graft.
> They dig an escape but they're digging their grave
> Believe me, I'm not that daft.
> War is just business but by other means
> So the real human way to behave
> Is to grasp on to all opportunities
> We're a long time poor in the grave.

Scene Eight

1632. Gustav Adolf, King of Sweden, falls in the battle of Lutzen. Peace threatens to ruin **Mother Courage***'s business. And her dashing son does one deed too many and meets a sticky ending.*

A camp. A summer morning. In front of the cart stand an **Old Woman** *and her son. The son drags a large bag of bed linen.* **Mother Courage***'s voice comes from the cart.*

Mother Courage   For Christ's sake, it's the crack of dawn.

Young Man   We've walked twenty miles and we've got to be back later today.

Mother Courage   What do I want with feather beds? People haven't got houses.

Young Man   Wait till you've had a look.

Old Woman   We're wasting our time. Let's go.

Young Man   And sell the roof over our head to pay for taxes. Throw in the necklace and she might give us three guilders.

Voice (*from behind*)   Peace! The King of Sweden has fallen!

Mother Courage *pokes her head out of the cart, she is unwashed and unkempt.*

Mother Courage   What they ringing bells for? It's the middle of the week.

The **Chaplain** *comes crawling from under the cart.*

Chaplain   What are they shouting?

Mother Courage   Don't tell me peace has broken out, I've just got a new load of supplies in.

Chaplain (*calls out at the back*)   Is it true? Is it peace?

Voice   It happened three weeks ago, news has only just got through.

Chaplain   Why else would they be ringing the bells?

Voice   A load of Protestants rode into town with the news.

Young Man   Mother, it's peace. What's the matter?

The **Old Woman** *collapses.*

Mother Courage   Jeez Mareez! Kattrin, get your black dress on. We're going to church. We owe it to Swisscheese. Do you think it's true?

Young Man   That's what they're saying. Can you stand up, Mother?

The **Old Woman** *stands up.*

Young Man   I'll start the saddle-making again. And we'll get Dad's bed fixed. It's all going to be fine. Are you all right? (*To the* **Chaplain**.) I think she fainted. On account of the news. Dad always said this would happen. I think we'll be off now.

They go.

Mother Courage (*off*)   Give her some brandy.

Chaplain   They're gone already.

Mother Courage (*off*)   What's going on in the barracks?

Chaplain   I think they're having a meeting. Shall I go? Maybe I should put my dog collar on.

Mother Courage   I'd go and find out what's going on first before you come out as the Antichrist. At least I got two kids through the war. I'll see Eilif at last.

Chaplain   And who should be coming down the alley by the barracks but the general's cook.

The **Cook** *comes on, very run down, with a bundle.*

Cook   My oh my. If it's not Mr Preacher.

Chaplain   Mr Cook, how lovely to see you. Courage, you have a visitor.

Mother Courage *climbs out.*

Cook   I said I'd drop back for a chat. Look, I've brought your brandy.

Mother Courage   Jesus, Cooky. After all these years.
Have you heard anything about Eilif?

Cook   Isn't he here? He set off to see you before I did.

Chaplain   Wait, I'm going to slip my cassock on.

Mother Courage   He'll be here any minute then. (*Calls
into the cart.*) Kattrin! Eilif's coming. Get a glass for the cook.
Just comb your hair over, no one will notice, Mr Lamb's a
friend anyway, no need to stand on ceremony. (*To* **Cook**.)
She doesn't want to come out. She's not too fond of peace,
you see, it took too long coming. Someone hit her over the
eye, you can hardly see it any more, but she's very self-
conscious.

Cook   That's the war for you.

Mother Courage   Well, you've caught me at a very bad
time, Cooky, 'cos I am ruined.

Cook   What do you mean?

Mother Courage   This peace will strangle me. I've only
just shelled out, on the chaplain's advice, for a load of new
supplies and now everyone's going to piss off leaving me
sitting on a fortune I can't sell.

Cook   Why did you listen to him? I should have warned
you about him years ago. He's a complete bag of wind. So
he's the big man around here, eh?

Mother Courage   He washes the dishes and pulls the
cart.

Cook   The only thing he pulls is the end of his tong. I
expect you've heard a few of his stories then by now. He's
got a very old-fashioned view of the sexes. I tried to put him
right on a few things but it was a total waste of time. I don't
think he has many morals.

Mother Courage   Are you moral?

Cook   I might be many things but I am totally moral. All the best!

Mother Courage   Well, fuck morality. Where will that get you when there's a run on the market?

Cook   That's what I like about you. Your endless concern for higher matters.

Mother Courage   I'm glad it was higher matters that came to mind when you thought of me.

Cook   So here we are, the church bells ringing, the brandy flowing. Happy days, eh?

Mother Courage   Well I could do without the church bells, thank you very much. They won't pay anyone's wages. And as for my famous brandy . . . Have you been paid yet?

Cook   Not exactly. That's why we left. Why stay there when I could be paying a visit to old friends?

Mother Courage   You mean you've got nothing.

Cook   I wish they'd shut up. I thought I might go into business. I've had it with cooking. Slaving away over tree roots and shoe leather only to get it thrown back in your face. No, if you ask me, cookery's a dog's life. I'd be better off as an ordinary soldier. But there's no chance of that now.

The **Chaplain** *files past in his clerical clothes.*

Cook   Anyway, more of that later.

Chaplain   It's still OK. Only a few moths.

Cook   I don't know why you're bothering. You're not going to get your old job back. Who's going to listen to your preaching about an honest life now? Anyway, Sunny Jim, I hear your latest advice was persuading this lady to buy a load of useless provisions.

Chaplain   What's that got to do with you?

Cook   Because it's immoral. What right have you got to go interfering with a business organisation with your unwarranted recommendations.

Chaplain   Listen, I'm not the one who's unwarranted. (*To* **Mother Courage**.) I didn't know you had to account to him for your every move.

Mother Courage   Oh calm down, for God's sake. But you can't deny this peace has turned out to be a dead loss.

Chaplain   Don't badmouth the peace. You're just a parasite of the battlefields.

Mother Courage   I beg your pardon?

Cook   If you want to insult her, you'll have me to deal with.

Chaplain   I'm not dealing with you at all. Your intentions are all too obvious. (*To* **Mother Courage**.) When you dismiss peace as if it were some old snot-rag my whole sense of humanity recoils. You don't want peace because you only want profit. Well, remember: 'He who sups with the devil needs a very long spoon.'

Mother Courage   I don't care nothing about the war, and it cares nothing about me. And let me tell you, I resent being called a parasite. Our paths separate here.

Chaplain   Why are you complaining when the whole of humanity sighs a relief? Because of an old pile of rags in your cart?

Mother Courage   I'll have you know they are not rags. They're my livelihood. And they were yours. But not any more.

Chaplain   Keep your trophies of war.

Cook   I thought you were old enough to know better than to give someone advice. (*To* **Mother Courage**.) Given the situation I'd try and get rid of all this before the prices fall through the floor. I'd get going if I was you, you haven't got a moment to waste.

Mother Courage   Now that's what I call good advice. And I think I'll take it.

Chaplain   Because 'Cooky' says so?

Mother Courage   Because you didn't say so. I'm off to the market.

She goes into the cart.

Cook   One nil to me, padre.

Chaplain   If you don't shut your Dutch trap I'll put my fist down it, cassock or not.

The **Cook** *takes off his boots and unwinds the bandages on his feet.*

Cook   If you weren't such a godforsaken bum you could've been in line for a nice little parsonage. They won't need cooks. There's bugger all left to cook. But people still keep on believing, nothing changed there.

Chaplain   Please, don't throw me out of here. Since I've come down in the world, I've become a better person. I've got nothing to preach any more.

Yvette *comes in, dressed in black with a cane. Older, fatter and very powdered. Behind her is a servant.*

Yvette   I say, you people, does this place belong to Mother Courage?

Chaplain   Indeed it does. And with who do we have the honour?

Yvette   With the wife of Colonel Starhemberg, my good man. Where is Courage?

The **Chaplain** *calls into the cart.*

Chaplain   The wife of Colonel Starhemberg to see you.

Mother Courage (*off*)   Coming!

Yvette   It's me. Yvette!

Mother Courage (*off*)   Yvette!

Yvette   Just thought I'd look you up.

The **Cook** *turns round and* **Yvette** *sees him.*

Yvette   Peter!

Cook   Yvette?!

Yvette   Stone the fucking crows. What brought you here?

Cook   A cart.

Chaplain   You are acquainted.

Yvette   Unfortunately. (*To* **Cook**.) You're fat.

Cook   You're not exactly fading away yourself.

Yvette   Well, nice to see you, you little shit. I've waited a long time to tell you what I think of you.

Chaplain   By all means go ahead, but for God's sake wait for Courage.

Mother Courage *comes out of the cart with all kinds of goods.*

Mother Courage   Yvettte! What are you doing in mourning?

Yvette   I think it rather suits me. The colonel, my husband, died a couple of years ago. Quite unfortunate.

Mother Courage   The one who nearly bought the cart?

Yvette   His older brother actually.

Mother Courage   Very nice for you. At least somebody did well out of the war.

Yvette   It's had its ups and downs, as they say. But now it's up again.

Mother Courage   Let's not talk badly of colonels. They make money like some people make enemies.

Chaplain (*to the* **Cook**)   I'd get them shoes back on if I was you. (*To* **Yvette**.) Madam, you promised to give your opinion of this man.

Cook   Yvette, don't mess about.

Mother Courage   This is a friend of mine, Yvette.

Yvette   This isn't a friend of anyone. This is Pete the Pipe.

Cook   I'll have you know I'm not Pete the Pipe or anything else. I am called Mr Peter Lamb, actually.

Mother Courage   Peter Piper. He who drives the ladies wild with his pipe. I've been looking after it for you.

Chaplain   And she's had it in her mouth.

Yvette   Count yourself lucky I was here to warn you. He's the dirtiest scab this side of Flanders. He's had more women than he's cooked hot dinners.

Cook   Now steady on. That was a long time ago.

Yvette   Stand up when you are addressing a lady. Oh I used to love you. And all the time you were nobbing some brandy-legged floosie who you dumped as well. You thought more of your gravy than you thought of any of us.

Cook   Well, it didn't do you much harm.

Yvette   Shut your trap, you pathetic little weasel. Stay away from him, he's still dangerous even in this state.

Mother Courage (*to* **Yvette**)   Come along, I've got to get rid of this stuff before it's too late. Maybe you have a few contacts in the army. (*Calls to* **Kattrin**.) Kattrin, forget the dress, bugger the church, I'm going to the market. When Eilif comes give him something to drink.

Mother Courage *goes off with* **Yvette**.

Yvette (*as she goes*)   What was I thinking? Thank my lucky stars I managed to rise above your level. And if I've managed to save one soul from your evil clutches, Peter Piper, I know I'll secure a place in heaven.

Chaplain   And so I conclude: 'The mills of God grind slowly.' Who said I had no sense of humour?

Cook   I'm not a bad man. I'm just unlucky. Everyone's got the wrong impression. I may as well take a hike before she gets back.

Chaplain   A very sound idea.

Cook   I'm bored of peace already. Mankind was made to go through fire and brimstone, why else would we be born in sin? I'd rather be roasting for the general wherever he is, than stuck here with you lenten fools. A nice fat capon with carrots and mustard, that's what I'd like.

Chaplain   And cabbage.

Cook   I know. But his nibs always asked for carrots.

Chaplain   Well, he didn't know anything.

Cook   It never stopped you stuffing your face.

Chaplain   But against my better judgement.

Cook   But those were the days, eh?

Chaplain   I'd probably have to agree.

Cook   You shouldn't have called her a parasite. Your days are numbered. What's up?

Chaplain   Eilif!

Eilif *enters followed by* **Soldiers** *with bayonets.* **Eilif** *comes near, his hands are tied. He is as white as chalk.*

Eilif   Where's my mother? What's the matter with you?

Chaplain   In town.

Eilif   I heard she was here. I came to see her one last time.

Cook (*to the* **Soldiers**)   Where are you taking him?

Soldier   Hell and back. And back again.

Chaplain   What has he done?

Soldier   Broke into a farm. Killed the man's wife.

Chaplain   How could you do that?

Eilif   I didn't do anything any different from before.

Cook   But it's peacetime.

Eilif   Shut up! Can I sit until she comes?

Solider   We haven't got time.

Chaplain   When we were at war they praised him for that sort of thing. Sat at the general's right hand. It was thought of as bravery then. Can we talk to an officer?

Soldier   Too late, mate. What's brave about killing an innocent woman?

Cook   You stupid fool.

Eilif   If I was stupid I would have starved, clevershite.

Cook   You're so clever you're going to be hanged.

Chaplain   We should get Kattrin.

Eilif   Leave her. I'd rather have some brandy.

Soldier   There's no time for that. Come on.

Chaplain   What will we tell your mother?

Eilif   Tell her the truth. Tell her lies. I don't know. Tell her nothing at all.

The **Soldiers** *lead him away.*

Chaplain   I'll come with you. It's a hard journey.

Eilif   I don't need a preacher.

Chaplain   Don't be so sure.

The **Chaplain** *follows.*

Cook   I have to tell her. She'd want to see him.

Chaplain   Don't say anything. Or just say he was here and he'll come again tomorrow. I'll be back, I should tell her myself.

He hastily departs. The **Cook** *watches them go. He walks up and down uneasily then approaches the cart.*

Cook   Hello there. Aren't you coming out? I hear you're hiding from peace. I don't blame you. I'm the general's cook, remember me? I wondered if you had anything to eat till your mum gets back. A bit of bacon. A bit of bread? Just to kill time. (*He looks inside.*) She's got a blanket over her head.

In the distance the sound of cannon fire resumes. **Mother Courage** *comes running back. She is out of breath and still has her goods.*

Mother Courage   It's all over. The war's been on for three days. Thank God I heard before I got rid of all this stuff. They're already shooting Protestants in town. We better get moving. Kattrin, start packing. Why are you upset? What's the matter?

Cook   Nothing.

Mother Courage   Your face. What is it?

Cook   It's the war. I'll not get a hot meal till tomorrow.

Mother Courage   You're lying.

Cook   Eilif was here. But he had to go.

Mother Courage   Here? We'll meet him on the march. We'll go with his side this time. How was he?

Cook   Same as ever?

Mother Courage   He'll never change that one. I knew the war couldn't take him away from me. He's far too clever. Will you help me with the packing? Is he on a good foot with the general? Did he tell you about his acts of heroism?

Cook   Oh yes. He's been heroic all right.

Mother Courage   Tell me about it later. We have to go.

Kattrin *appears*.

Mother Courage (*to* **Kattrin**)   Peace is over. (*To* **Cook**.) What are you doing?

Cook   Going to join up.

Mother Courage   Good. Where's the chaplain?

Cook   In town. With Eilif.

Mother Courage   Well, maybe you should stay with us for a bit of the way. I need a hand.

Cook   I hope you didn't take too much notice of Yvette.

Mother Courage   On the contrary. It seemed like a hearty recommendation. Where there's smoke there's fire, or so they say. Coming?

Cook   Why not?

Mother Courage   The twelfth moving on already. Get in the harness. Here's a bit of bread. If we get back behind the Protestant lines we might see Eilif this evening. He's my favourite of them all. Well, peace didn't last long, thank the Lord. Off we go again.

From Ulm to Metz, from Metz to Mahren
My cart goes, so pull it
The war'll stop you starving
All you need's a bullet
The war can't live by lead alone
It needs people too
Come on lads from every home
Join up or it's through.

Scene Nine

*1634. The war has lasted sixteen years. Half the population of
Germany has died. Epidemics kill those who survived the slaughter.
Famine ravages the countryside. Wolves scavenge the burned-out towns.*
Mother Courage *is in the German mountains with the Swedish
Army. It is bitterly cold. Business goes from bad to worse. The* **Cook**
gets a letter from Utrecht and is given his marching orders.

*In front of a wrecked vicarage. A grey early winter morning. Wind
howls.* **Mother Courage** *and the* **Cook** *in shoddy sheepskins are
pulling the cart.*

Cook   It's pitch black. Nobody's up yet.

Mother Courage   But it's a parsonage. He's going to
have to crawl out of his feather bed to ring the bells at some
point.

Cook   But the whole place is in ruins.

Mother Courage   Occupied ruins, I just heard a dog
bark.

Cook   If a parson's got anything to eat he won't give it to
us.

Mother Courage   Maybe we should sing some hymns
then.

Cook   Sod this.

He unharnesses himself.

Look, Courage, I've had a letter from my aunt in Utrecht.
My mother has died from cholera and the inn belongs to
me. Here it is, if you don't believe me. Read it. Not that it's
anything to do with you. But you see how it goes on about
the way I'm living.

Mother Courage *reads the letter.*

Mother Courage   You're not the only one who's
suffered. I can't take much more of this. Running myself
ragged like a butcher's dog with the meat and getting none

of it myself. Now I haven't even got anything to sell, and nobody's got anything to buy it with anyway. Last week someone tried to sell me an illuminated manuscript for two eggs, for a bag of salt they'd throw in their plough as well. Who'd want a plough? Nothing grows any more. In Pommerania they're eating their own children. Nuns were caught on the game.

Cook   The world's dying out.

Mother Courage   Sometimes it feels like I'm driving through hell selling bad luck or through heaven ladling brimstone to wandering souls. If I could only find a place with no shooting and have a couple of quiet years with the children.

Cook   What about the inn? Think about it, Anna. I've made up my mind. I'm going back today, whether you come or not.

Mother Courage   It's all a bit sudden. I'll have to talk it through with Kattrin. I don't usually make life-changing decisions in the freezing cold morning with nothing in my stomach. Kattrin!

Kattrin *climbs out of the wagon.*

Mother Courage   Kattrin, I have something to ask you. Cooky and I would like to go to Utrecht and run an inn that he's inherited. You'd have a roof over your head. You'd meet plenty of people. And an innkeeper's daughter is a very attractive proposition to a lot of people, not just alcoholics. Looks aren't everything, dear, and you'd meet a lot of people. I'd like it too. I get on with Cooky, and he's got a good head for business. We'd have regular meals and we'd all have our own bed. You'd like that now, wouldn't you? This is no life. We're dying here. You're covered in fleas. We need to decide. Either go east with the Swedes or to lovely warm Utrecht to live in an inn happily for the rest of our lives. That's decided then.

Cook   Anna, can I have a word? Alone.

Mother Courage (*to* **Kattrin**)   OK. Back in the cart now.

Kattrin *climbs back in the cart.*

Cook   I don't think you understand. I didn't think I'd have to spell it out. You can't bring her.

Kattrin *sticks her head out and listens.*

Mother Courage   You mean leave her behind?

Cook   What are you thinking of? You read the letter. We might just scrape by, the two of us, but three? It's out of the question. Give her the cart.

Mother Courage   I thought she might find herself a husband.

Cook   Don't be ridiculous. How's she going to find a husband. Dumb and disfigured at her age.

Mother Courage   Keep your voice down.

Cook   Listen, facts are facts whatever the volume. She can't come. Anyway, nobody wants to look at that over a glass of brandy. Would you?

Mother Courage   I said shut up!

Cook   There's a light!

Mother Courage   How could she pull the cart on her own? She's terrified of war. She can't bear it. She has nightmares. I hear her groaning. God knows what she sees, Cooky. She's sensitive. Last week she kept a hedgehog we'd squashed on the road.

Cook   But it's too small! Good sir, servants and all honest dwellers of the household. We are now about to sing you the song of Solomon and Julius Caesar and other great minds that did little to help them. So you shall see we are decent and diligent people and therefore have a hard time. Especially in winter.

You've heard of wise old Solomon
Who knew everything on earth.
Do you know what became of him?
He cursed the fact of his birth
He realised that it all meant nothing
He could see it all, all plain as day
His insight plagued him forever
And he cursed God who made him that way.

It's a fact. All virtues are dangerous in this world. What
about courage? Oh, I was a soldier, I had courage, but
where did that get me. Stuck outside of a freezing morning
with no hot soup for breakfast. I'd've been better off being a
coward hiding under the bed at home. Why?

You've heard of a great man called Caesar
Who sat on his throne like a god
He was at the height of his power
When they went and murdered the sod.
He shouted: 'Et tu, Brute'
As he saw it all, all plain as day
It was courage that had got him this far
And courage that put him away.

(*Under his breath.*) They haven't even looked out the window.
Good sir, the honourable servants etcetera. If you think
courage is a useless virtue. Let's try telling the honest truth.
See if that fills an empty stomach.

There was a fella, Socrates
The truth was all he could think
Don't suppose they thanked the poor bastard
They just gave him hemlock to drink.
But he reasoned about the decision
The truth was just truth, plain as day.
This honesty wasn't just justice
But he knocked back the drink anyway.

Yes, they say 'Be generous'; 'Share and share alike'. But
what if you've got nothing to share in the first place? Do-
gooders might not have it easy, but at least they've got

something to start with. I'll tell you why selflessness is a rare virtue, because it doesn't pay.

> There was a saint, name of Martin
> Who gave a poor man half his clothes
> But the poor lad came a cropper
> It was winter and both of them froze.
> He thought about this when he'd done it
> And there it was plain, plain as day
> And he wished he'd been less of a martyr
> As they silently shivered away.

And that's how it is with us. We're decent people. Don't murder, steal or start fires. And so we sink deeper and deeper. The song is true. We see no soup. If we were murderers and thieves we'd be overweight. Virtue doesn't pay. Vice does. And surely that's wrong.

> Here you see just, decent people
> Who live the Commandments ten
> But what good has that done us?
> Here we stand all hungry men.
> How virtuously we all started
> But it's become plain as the day
> There's no one to blame for our troubles
> It's our own fault for being this way.

Voice (*from upstairs*)   Hey. You. Come upstairs. There's soup.

Mother Courage   Peter, it's sticking in my throat. I'm not saying you're not being sensible. But is that your final word?

Cook   My final word. Think about it.

Mother Courage   There's nothing to think about. I can't leave her.

Cook   If you can't see sense, Anna, there's nothing I can do about it. I'm not a barbarian. The inn's just too small. We better go in or I'll've sung for nothing.

Mother Courage   I'll get Kattrin.

Cook   No. If they see three of us, they'll change their minds. We'll sneak her some down.

Kattrin *appears from the wagon with a bundle. She makes sure the other two have left and arranges a pair of trousers for the* **Cook** *and a skirt for her mother next to each other so they'll be easily spotted. Just as she's finishing.* **Mother Courage** *comes out of the house with a bowl of soup.*

Mother Courage   Kattrin. Stay there. Where are you going with that? What are you thinking of?

Mother Courage *investigates the bundle.*

She packed her stuff. You've been listening, haven't you? But I told him to stuff his stinking rotten inn in Utrecht. What would we want there. You and me don't belong in an inn. There's still life in this war yet.

She sees the skirt and trousers.

You are stupid, aren't you? What do you think I'd've thought if I came out and saw that and you'd gone?

She holds **Kattrin** *tight.*

I didn't give him his marching orders because of you. It was the cart, wasn't it? I couldn't leave the cart, where I lived, no, it wasn't you, it was the cart. Come on, we'll go now and leave his stuff for him, the stupid bastard.

She climbs up on to the cart and throws **Cook**'s *stuff down.*

That's him out of the business. And I'm never having anyone else in ever again. Just you and me, Kattrin, and the winter will pass like all the others. Come on, it looks like snow.

They hitch themselves to the cart and go. The **Cook** *comes out and looks uncomprehendingly at his stuff.*

Scene Ten

1635. For the entire year **Mother Courage** *and* **Kattrin** *pull their cart after the increasingly dishevelled army.*

Country road. **Mother Courage** *and* **Kattrin** *are pulling the cart. They pass a farm where a voice is singing.*

Voice (*sings*)
   In the garden's a rose
   In beautiful bloom
   We watch how it grows
   From winter to June.
   With a garden we're blessed
   by nature's bequest
   The beautiful bloom of a rose.

   When the cold winds blow
   At night through the pines
   We're safe from the snow
   In our house with the vines.
   In our warm little nest
   We are truly blessed
   When the cold, snow winds blow.

Mother Courage *and* **Kattrin** *have stopped to listen. Then continue their journey.*

Scene Eleven

January 1626. The emperor's troops bear down on the town of Halle. The stone begins to speak. **Mother Courage** *loses her daughter. The war is a long way from being over.*

The wagon, now very run-down, stands near a thatched farmhouse, which leans against a wall of rock. Out of the woods come an **Officer** *and three* **Soldiers** *heavily armed.*

Officer   No sudden noises, understood. Anyone yelps, they get it with a pike.

First Soldier But won't we have to make a noise when we knock to get a guide?

Officer That's not a 'noise', you buffoon, knocking is a perfectly natural sound. Could be a cow bumping against a fence.

The **Soldiers** *knock on the door of the farm. A* **Farmer's Wife** *answers. They put their hands over her mouth. Two* **Soliders** *go in.*

Man's voice (*within*) What's going on?

The **Soldiers** *bring out a* **Farmer** *and his son. The* **Officer** *points to* **Mother Courage**'s *cart from which* **Kattrin** *has appeared.*

Officer Look, there's another one.

A **Soldier** *drags her out.*

Who else lives here?

Farmer This is our son. That's a dumb girl. Her mother's in town doing business because people are fleeing and selling up cheap. They're hawkers. Travelling people.

Officer Keep the noise down. I'm warning you, any more of that racket and you'll get a pike through your throat. I need someone to show us a path to the town.

He points at the **Young Farmer**.

You. Over here.

Young Farmer I don't know a path.

Second Soldier He doesn't know a path.

Young Farmer I don't help Catholics.

Officer Show him your pike.

The **Young Farmer** *is forced to his knees and threatened with the pike.*

Young Farmer I won't do it even if you kill me.

First Soldier   I know how to deal with you.

He walks to the stable.

First Soldier   Either come to your senses or all this lot are for the slaughter.

Young Farmer   Not the cattle.

Farmer's Wife   Please, not the cattle. We'll starve.

Officer   It's his choice.

First Soldier   I'll start with the bullocks.

Young Farmer   What should I do?

The **Farmer's Wife** *nods.*

Young Farmer   I'll do it.

Farmer's Wife   Thank you for sparing us, Mr Captain, sir, forever bless you, sir, amen.

The **Farmer** *holds his wife back from further thanks.*

First Soldier   I knew that'd change his mind. I had him by the bullocks, so to speak.

The **Young Farmer** *leads the* **Soldiers** *on their journey.*

Farmer   What the hell are they up to?

Farmer's Wife   Maybe they're scouts. What are you doing?

The **Farmer** *puts a ladder against the roof and climbs up.*

Farmer   I want to see if they're alone. (*From the top.*) There's movement in the bushes. Right back to the quarry. Armoured men in the clearing. And a cannon. There's a whole regiment down there. God help anybody in town.

Farmer's Wife   Are there any lights in town?

Farmer   Nothing. They're all asleep. (*He climbs down.*) If they get in they'll slaughter everybody.

Farmer's Wife   The guards will see them coming.

Farmer   Obviously they've killed the guards in the tower already or they'd be blowing their horn, wouldn't they?

Farmer's Wife   If only there were more of us.

Farmer   More of us. There's just us and a cripple.

Farmer's Wife   So you don't think we can do anything.

Farmer   No. There's a whole bloody regiment down there.

Farmer's Wife   Couldn't we run down to town quickly?

Farmer   The hillside's crawling with them, you idiot. Maybe we could signal.

Farmer's Wife   Then they'd definitely kill us.

Farmer   You're right. There's nothing we can do.

Farmer's Wife (*to* **Kattrin**)   All we can do is pray. Come on, pray, poor creature, pray. You might not be able to speak, but at least we can all pray. The Lord will hear us if nobody else will.

They all kneel down, **Kattrin** *behind the peasants.*

Farmer's Wife   Our Father, who art in heaven, please hear our humble prayer and save all those poor souls which art asleep in the town and suspect none of the vicious slaughter which is about to happen. Please Father, waken them up so they can climb on to the walls and see all the pikes and cannons and suchlike shining in the moonlight in the valley below.

She turns to **Kattrin**.

Please watch over our poor mother and wake up the guard so he sees what's going on and it's not too late. And save our son-in-law who is sound asleep with the four young ones, please don't let them die as they are innocent and know nothing of this world.

Kattrin *moans.*

Farmer's Wife   One is only two and the other ones are all under seven, my Lord.

Kattrin *stands up disturbed.*

Farmer's Wife   Our Father, please hear this prayer, as only you can hear us. We would go down there ourselves except we don't have any pikes or anything, and us and our entire farm with the bullocks and everything are all in your hands. And the town is in your hands as well because the enemy is at the gates in great numbers.

Kattrin *has sneaked unnoticed to the cart. She has taken something out and slipped it under her apron. She has climbed the ladder to the roof.*

Farmer's Wife   And above all, forgive us our trespasses as we forgive those who trespass against us. Amen. There.

Kattrin *is sitting on the roof. She beats the drum she has taken from under her apron.*

Farmer's Wife   Jesus Christ. What's she doing?

Farmer   She's a fucking lunatic.

Farmer's Wife   Get her down.

The **Farmer** *goes for the ladder but* **Kattrin** *pulls it up.*

Farmer's Wife   She'll be the end of us.

Farmer   Stop that, you fucking cripple.

Farmer's Wife   You'll have the Catholics on to us.

Farmer   Get some stones.

Farmer's Wife   Haven't you got a conscience? Do you know what they'll do to us?

Kattrin *goes on drumming, staring into the distance.*

Farmer's Wife   I told you not to let that riff raff on to the farm. What do they care if we lose our cattle?

The **Officer** *comes running through.*

Officer   I'm going to cut you to bits.

Farmer's Wife   It's not us. We tried to stop her. We're innocent. We don't even know her.

Officer   Where's the ladder?

Farmer   Up there.

Officer   I order you to throw that drum down.

Kattrin *keeps on drumming.*

Officer   You'll all have to answer for this.

Farmer   They've been cutting down pine trees over there, let's get a trunk and knock her out of it.

First Soldier (*to the* **Officer**)   Permission to make a suggestion, sir.

He whispers something into the **Officer**'s *ear. He nods.*

First Soldier   Can you hear me? We wish to make you an offer, in your best interests. Come down now, and we will take you into town at the front of the batallion and you can point out your mother and she will be saved.

Kattrin *keeps on drumming.*

The **Officer** *pushes him aside.*

Officer   She doesn't trust you. No wonder, with a face like that. (*Calling up.*) Listen to me. I am an officer and I give you my word of honour.

She continues.

Officer   Is nothing sacred?

Young Farmer   Sir, it's not just because of her mother, sir.

First Soldier   We can't let this carry on. They'll hear it in town.

Officer　I know, let's disguise the drumming with another sound. Now what could that be?

First Soldier　But I thought we weren't supposed to make a noise, sir.

Officer　An innocuous noise, you idiot, not a military noise.

Farmer　Maybe I could chop wood or something.

Officer　Excellent. Get chopping.

The **Farmer** *gets an axe and starts chopping a tree trunk.*

Officer　Faster. More. You're chopping for your life, man.

Kattrin *drums less loudly as she looks around and then starts with more alacrity.*

Officer　For God's sake, how do you run a farm, you weakling? (*To* **First Soldier**.) You chop too.

Farmer　But there's only one axe.

Officer　Ah. Well, we'll have to burn the farm down. We'll smoke her out.

Farmer　No. Don't burn the farm down. They'll see it in town, captain.

Kattrin *has listened and is laughing as she drums.*

Officer　Look, she's laughing at us. I can't stand it any more. I'm going to shoot her and bugger the consequences. Get me a gun.

The two **Soldiers** *run off.* **Kattrin** *keeps on drummung.*

Farmer's Wife　I know. If we start to smash her cart up she'll sharp stop drumming. That's all they've got, that cart.

Officer (*to* **Young Farmer**)　You, man, smash that cart. (*To* **Kattrin**.) Listen, we'll smash your cart if you don't stop drumming.

The **Young Farmer** *gives the cart a few feeble whacks with a plank.*

Farmer's Wife   Stop it. You bitch.

Kattrin *utters some pathetic sounds as she looks at the cart. But she keeps on drumming.*

Officer   Where the hell are those cretins with the gun?

First Soldier   At least they mustn't have heard it in town. Or we'd have heard gunfire by now.

Officer   See. They can't even hear you. Now, for one last time. Either you stop drumming or we will shoot you.

The **Young Farmer** *throws down his plank.*

Young Farmer   Keep drumming! Or they'll all be killed. Keep drumming, keep drumming.

The **First Soldier** *knocks him to the ground and beats him with his pike.* **Kattrin** *starts to cry but she goes on drumming.*

Farmer's Wife   Not in the back. For Christ's sake you'll kill him.

The **Soldiers** *come running with a shotgun.*

Second Soldier   The colonel's going apeshit. We're all going to get court-martialled.

Officer   Set it up! Set it up! (*To* **Kattrin**.) For the very last time, stop drumming!

Kattrin *carries on as loud as she can.*

Officer   Fire!

The **Soldiers** *fire the gun.* **Kattrin** *is hit, but hits the drum a few more times before slowly sinking down altogether.*

Officer   Well, that put an end to that racket.

But **Kattrin**'s *last few beats are echoed by the sound of gunfire from the town. One can hear the tolling of bells and the thunder of cannons.*

First Soldier   She did it.

Before dawn. The sound of pipes and drums and soldiers marching.

In front of the cart **Mother Courage** *is crouched by* **Kattrin**.
The peasants are beside her.

Farmer   You have to go, woman. There's only one
regiment left. You'll never make it alone.

Mother Courage   I think she's asleep.

> *Eia popeia*
> What rustles the straw
> The neighbours' babes cry out
> While mine sleeps below
> The neighbours wear rags
> And you're dressed in silk
> From the skirt of an angel
> And drink heaven's milk.
>
> The neighbours are starving
> While you eat cake
> If it's too dry now
> No crying you make
> *Eia popeia*
> What rustles the straw
> One less in Poland
> The other, who knows?

You shouldn't have told her about your brother's kids.

Farmer   If you weren't in town doing business it wouldn't
have happened.

Mother Courage   She's asleep now.

Farmer's Wife   She isn't asleep. She's dead.

Farmer   You have to go. There are wolves and outlaws.

Mother Courage   Yes.

She gets a sheet from the cart and covers **Kattrin**.

Farmer's Wife   Don't you have anyone else to go to?

Mother Courage   Yes. I have one left, Eilif.

Farmer   You better find him. We'll see she gets a decent burial. You can be sure of that.

Mother Courage   Here's some money for the expenses.

She pays the **Farmer** *some money. He shakes her hand and carries* **Kattrin** *away. The* **Farmer's Wife** *shakes her hand too with a nod.*

Farmer's Wife   Hurry.

Mother Courage *buckles herself into the cart.*

Mother Courage   Hopefully I'll be able to manage on my own. There's not much left in it. I have to get back into business.

A regiment passes from behind with their pipes and drums. **Mother Courage** *starts pulling the wagon.*

Mother Courage   Hand on there, lads. Wait for me!

> With its fortune and its fears
> The war somehow pulls through
> It could last a hundred years
> And no man makes his due
> He eats dirt, he wears disgust
> His wages, they are sin
> But miracles happen, they surely must
> A new life will begin.
>> Spring is coming, Christian men arise
>> Snow is falling, dead are gone
>> And if you've not met your demise
>> You should be moving on.

Methuen Modern Plays

include work by

Jean Anouilh
John Arden
Margaretta D'Arcy
Peter Barnes
Sebastian Barry
Brendan Behan
Dermot Bolger
Edward Bond
Bertolt Brecht
Howard Brenton
Anthony Burgess
Simon Burke
Jim Cartwright
Caryl Churchill
Noël Coward
Lucinda Coxon
Sarah Daniels
Nick Darke
Nick Dear
Shelagh Delaney
David Edgar
David Eldridge
Dario Fo
Michael Frayn
John Godber
Paul Godfrey
David Greig
John Guare
Peter Handke
David Harrower
Jonathan Harvey
Iain Heggie
Declan Hughes
Terry Johnson
Sarah Kane
Charlotte Keatley
Barrie Keeffe
Howard Korder

Robert Lepage
Doug Lucie
Martin McDonagh
John McGrath
Terrence McNally
David Mamet
Patrick Marber
Arthur Miller
Mtwa, Ngema & Simon
Tom Murphy
Phyllis Nagy
Peter Nichols
Joseph O'Connor
Joe Orton
Louise Page
Joe Penhall
Luigi Pirandello
Stephen Poliakoff
Franca Rame
Mark Ravenhill
Philip Ridley
Reginald Rose
Willy Russell
Jean-Paul Sartre
Sam Shepard
Wole Soyinka
Shelagh Stephenson
Peter Straughan
C. P. Taylor
Theatre de Complicite
Theatre Workshop
Sue Townsend
Judy Upton
Timberlake Wertenbaker
Roy Williams
Snoo Wilson
Victoria Wood

For a complete catalogue of Methuen Drama titles
write to:

Methuen Drama
215 Vauxhall Bridge Road
London SW1V 1EJ

or you can visit our website at:

www.methuen.co.uk

The Scottsdale Pain Relief Program

ALSO BY THE AUTHOR

Fears and Phobias: Fighting Back
Depression
Phobia Free and Flying High
Power Over Your Pain Without Drugs

The
Scottsdale

THE REVOLUTIONARY SEVEN DAY DRUG-FREE PROGRAM TO REDUCE PAIN

Pain Relief
Program

Dr. Neal H. Olshan

Beaufort Books
Publishers
NEW YORK

MT

Olshan, Neal.
   The Scottsdale pain relief program.

   1. Pain—Treatment. 2. Autogenic training—Popular
works. 3. Relaxation—Popular works. I. Title.
[DNLM: 1. Pain—therapy—popular works. WL 704 052s]
RB127.039   1987   616'.0472   87-1103
ISBN 0-8253-0423-7

Published in the United States by Beaufort Books Publishers,
New York.

Designed by Irving Perkins Associates

Printed in the U.S.A.   First Edition

10 9 8 7 6 5 4 3 2 1

11/01/91

ACKNOWLEDGMENTS

"Thank you" is a phrase that barely scratches the surface when I think of all the people who helped the Scottsdale Pain Relief Program become a reality.

I am indebted to my wife, Mary, who provided constant support and critical insights during long hours of writing. Her ability to analyze and suggest alternatives was magnificent.

I am also indebted to Sandy Olshan for her emotional support: "How's it going, Dad? You're doing really good!" To Bob Olshan for his humor and art work. A citation goes to Maureen Olshan for her constant support although she was sometimes uncertain why I was writing until 2:00 A.M. and up at 6:00 A.M.

A special thanks to Andrew Wolin, M.D. and Lynda Wolin, R.N. for sharing their medical knowledge, giving support, and providing many moments of laughter.

A warm and special thanks to my publisher at Beaufort, Susan Suffes, whose expertise and professionalism were invaluable. She is the publisher all writers hope to work with but seldom meet.

To all people who suffer from pain

CONTENTS

PREFACE

Have you ever wondered how many people actually read the introduction to a book? I hope you won't skip this introduction because I have some very important items to discuss with you before you begin chapter one.

Prior to beginning the Scottsdale Pain Relief Program, you should have consulted with a physician regarding your pain problem. *Never* proceed with the Scottsdale Pain Relief Program for an undiagnosed pain. As an example, a person experiencing headaches never should begin this program unless he or she has been examined by a physician. The Scottsdale Pain Relief Program has been designed to be compatible with any ongoing treatment and should not be used as a substitute for appropriate medical care.

Most of you who suffer from chronic pain have either been on a medication merry-go-round or are still going in circles with a seemingly endless progression of pills for your pain. Because there are so many different types of pain medication, you will need to consult with your physician about an appropriate program for reducing your medication intake in the safest manner possible. If you are presently taking medication, do not feel that you have to stop all medication prior to the seven-day program. Your success at controlling pain once you have completed the seven-day program and begun the Lifetime Maintenance Program should increase your pain tolerance and decrease your discomfort to a level that will allow you to substitute your personalized pain relief formula for medication. It is important to remember that you should never stop your medication abruptly or reduce medication without your physician's supervision.

As you will learn in chapter one, I have experienced chronic pain, and thirteen years ago, out of my own discomfort, I began development of what is now the Scottsdale Pain Relief Program. Although I would like to, I cannot guarantee you total pain relief; but if you follow the seven-day program and use the Lifetime Maintenance Program, you will gain control over your pain.

There are no complicated instructions or special skills needed as you enter and progress through the seven-day program. The development of your personalized pain relief formula will be through your input.

Once you have learned your personalized pain relief formula and through practice can apply it to your daily life circumstances, then you will begin to reclaim all those parts of your life that have been taken from you by pain.

Throughout this book I will serve as an adviser and gatekeeper. The true measure of success will be based upon your commitment, dedication, and willingness to learn a new technique to control pain.

Once you have completed the seven-day program and are into your Lifetime Maintenance Program, then you will realize that the Scottsdale Pain Relief Program has become part of your life—a life that is no longer controlled by pain.

For all of you who have not yet found success in your search for pain relief or have not been able to afford to go on a search for pain programs, I present to you, for your private use, the Scottsdale Pain Relief Program.

Part One

Part one of the Scottsdale Pain Relief Program contains all of the information you need to begin the seven-day segment. As you read through chapters one, two, and three, don't hesitate to take as much time as possible, rereading when necessary. Having the proper information and understanding is essential to the success of the seven-day program and ultimately your continued progress through the Lifetime Maintenance Program.

Throughout the first three chapters I have provided you with quotes from people who have completed the Scottsdale Pain Relief Program—people like you who suffer from pain. I have inserted these quotes because I feel that it will be more significant for you to hear from other pain sufferers rather than from pain "experts." Statements made by people just like you may help you to understand better the commitment and understanding needed for successful completion of the program.

CHAPTER ONE

A Beginning and a Solution

Take a moment to answer these questions:

Do you have pain for more than thirty minutes at least three times a week?

Does pain control part of your life?

Have you been unsuccessful in the search for pain relief?

If you have answered yes to any of these questions, then you need the Scottsdale Pain Relief Program. In seven days, you will begin to take control of your pain.

The Scottsdale Pain Relief Program has been designed to provide help to anyone who is willing to commit his or her time and effort to completion of the seven-day program and daily use of the Lifetime Maintenance Program.

A Book for You

I have developed and written this book for only one purpose: to help you learn how to relieve *your* pain. Even the design and style of the book is for you. Notice the book isn't heavy, the type is easy to read, and explanations are nontechnical and straightforward. People with neck, shoulder, or arthritis pain shouldn't have to hold a heavy, cumbersome book that could actually cause an increase in their discomfort.

If you are experiencing pain right now, and I would assume, if you are reading my book, you are hurting, there is little need to force-feed you chapter after chapter of research studies, scientific mumbo jumbo, quotes from "leading authorities," and explanations that end in the statement, "Unfortunately you are going to have to live with the pain." That's not much of an alternative!

> *You want help and you want it right now—that's what the Scottsdale Pain Relief Program is all about: to show you how to reduce your pain.*

Types of Pain.

Below is a list of pain problems that have been treated with the Scottsdale Pain Relief Program.

Arthritis	Dental Work
Backaches	Diabetic Neuropathy
Burns	Herpes
Cancer	Irritable Bowel Syndrome
Causalgia	Menstrual Cramps
Cluster Headaches	Migraine Headaches
Crohn's Disease	Muscular Aches
	Neuromas

Neural Pain
Phantom Limbs
Postsurgical Discomfort
Raynaud's Disease
Sciatica
Sinus Headaches
Sports Injuries
Sympathetic Dystrophy

Temporomandibular Joint
  Syndrome (TMJ)
Tendonitis
Tennis Elbow
Tension Headaches
Tic Douloureux
Ulcerative Colitis
Ulcers

The Scottsdale Pain Relief Program has been successfully providing help to pain sufferers for over five years. Now you can have the complete program.

It's yours for the rest of your life!

Your Beginning

The mere fact that you are reading this book means that you have at least the initial desire to seek a solution to a pain problem. The answer doesn't lie in the thousands of research papers, studies, and clinical textbooks. The solution to pain lies within each and every one of you. No one has ever taken the time to teach you the skills needed to activate the process that lies within all of us to gain control over our pain and thus begin

living life rather than just existing from day to day.

My Start

For over thirteen years I have read all the studies and research papers and attended panel discussions with doctors, clergy, scientists, and people who suffer from chronic pain. As a program consultant for the Commission on Accreditation of Rehabilitation Facilities, I have journeyed to all parts of the United States with teams of professionals evaluating and accrediting inpatient and outpatient pain centers, which can now be found in most major cities. I have also developed major pain programs for outpatients and hospitals. At present, I treat and work with pain patients every day of the week. Through the sum total of my thirteen-plus years, I have been drawn inevitably to this point, where I hope to provide you with the means by which to take control of your pain, no matter who you are, where you live, or what type of suffering you experience.

> *"How can you keep treating pain patients?"*
>
> *"Don't you get tired of hearing them complain?"*
>
> *"I would have burned out years ago."*

These are all comments I have heard over the years. I admit to being discouraged and frustrated at times not to be able to help a greater number of people. Very seldom does a week go by that I do not receive letters from people, some living as far away as Puerto Rico, pleading for some type of help. These people have read about my program in articles, heard me on the radio, or seen me talk on television programs trying to present the idea of hope for the chronic pain sufferer through the Scottsdale Pain Relief Program. For most, the cost of coming to Arizona for treatment is prohibitive. Prior to writing the Scottsdale Pain Relief Program, I could only provide encouragement and hope that they would find help wherever they were. Frequently I would receive additional letters months later detailing their own frustration in seeking appropriate answers and alternatives.

Facts and Figures

Nearly every book on pain seems obsessively weighted with facts and figures. Granted, a large, continually growing segment of our population suffers from pain on a minute-by-minute, hour-by-hour, and day-to-day basis; but other than letting you know that you are not alone, facts and figures do little to help you relieve discomfort. They might even push you to increased frustration. Obviously, all of these enormous numbers of people experiencing pain get little solace in reviewing the latest statistics from various state and governmental agencies—in case you haven't heard, we're dealing with an epidemic, one that enslaves greater numbers of people each and every day, with no visible end in sight.

The Numbers, Please

I have always found it interesting and slightly amusing that the first thing I am usually asked on television talk shows is to recite the pain "numbers." There seems to be definite shock value in pain's daily toll. Here are some of the annual figures: one-hundred and fifty million-plus people in the United States suffer from pain, twenty-one million people visit doctors for back pain, fourteen million hours of doctors' time is spent on treating headaches, and there are seventy-five million arthritis sufferers, forty-two million people experiencing headaches, and over one hundred million dollars a year spent in the United States for pain medication, salves, ointments, and other over-the-counter products. Besides letting you know you are not alone, they do little to help you feel better.

The Beginnings of My Pain

I am a chronic pain sufferer, one of the statistics!

That's right, I suffer from chronic back discomfort. For years I had back pain due to a football injury in college, but by applying to myself the principles I now teach daily to others, I have been able to reduce what had been an often distressing and disabling pain to a dull ache, which at times I don't even notice.

Because I know what it's like to experience the unrelenting, throbbing, searing, pinching, stabbing pain day after day, I can easily identify with others who experience pain. I am cautious, however, never to make that fatal mistake, when talking to a patient, of saying in a very authoritative tone, "I know just how you feel."

No one knows exactly how you feel because pain affects each one of us differently. We can make certain assumptions about how someone in pain may feel, and we may draw parallels to other people we know or even ourselves, but you are the only one who truly knows what your pain is like, and what it has done to your life in the past, and what it is doing to your life now.

Most people who come to me for treatment are surprised to find that I have back "discomfort." When they come into my office, they may notice that the couch and chairs are firmer than usual and allow people to sit down and get up more easily without sinking into soft cushions. There are special pillows for back support. There is room in my office to stand up, stretch, and move about after sitting for long periods. The small pillow that I slip behind the base of my back when I sit down may be the first clue. I also get up and stretch or move every fifteen to twenty minutes.

I know what it's like to have wondered if tomorrow could be any worse. That was before I started searching for answers.

My Search

It's more the rule, rather than the exception, that people who come into my office are curious to know about my back pain. They are unaccustomed to meeting health care providers who are also chronic pain sufferers. I usually know they are wondering how it began for me.

As a second-string linebacker my playing time was usually limited to big wins or disastrous losses. During one of my shining moments I was blocked illegally. The pain was immediate, but I said nothing then for it was my chance to prove my worth as a football player. I continued to ignore the injury so that I could keep playing.

While in graduate school, I could stand it no longer. The pain was getting worse. It was difficult for me to sit for longer than twenty minutes without gritting my teeth. I went to neurologists, neurosurgeons, and orthopedic surgeons, who suggested various procedures from myelography (injecting special dye directly into the space around the spinal cord, followed by X rays which can reveal protruding disk matter) to laminectomies (surgery to remove the posterior arch of a vertebra). Medication was becoming a dark alley with no way out. If it was strong enough to deaden the pain, then I couldn't function in school. I was at Arizona State University studying psychology, and I felt there must be some other alternative rather than invasive (going inside the body) procedures or the medication merry-go-round.

I began to study pain and pain treatment, searching for answers. From those days at Arizona State University in the early 1970s, I knew that my professional and personal focus would be helping people who suffer from pain syndromes by developing new types of treatment.

Research, studies, and interviews all gave me the foundation of knowledge needed to gain a thorough understanding of the mechanisms involved in the pain response. I also learned that for every possible answer there were two or three unanswered questions that seemed to repeat year after year, with no one providing solutions.

The repeated questions involved the people who were not candidates for surgery whose medication wasn't working; or when they took enough to dull the pain, they could not function in any normal lifestyle setting. There was also the ever-enlarging group of people who had experienced failed surgeries. The common denominator among all these people, myself included, was the costly, time-consuming disappointment-after-disappointment "highway" we were instructed to follow to search for *someone* to take away our pain and suffering. I tried that route for five years with no results.

Finally, when I decided to get off the highway and search out an alternative, pieces began to fall into place. The answer seemed almost too simple: Develop a plan to teach people to control pain by using the body's built-in painkillers and at the same time help them to regain control of their lives.

I developed my first pain program in Scottsdale, Arizona, in 1975 at the first outpatient pain treatment center in the United States. Since that time, pain treatment centers have grown up faster than a group of well-fed bunny rabbits. Of course, along with the growth of pain treatment centers has been the appearance of pain experts. There are many scientists who are dedicated, hardworking professionals seeking answers to chronic pain, but, unfortunately, pain treatment has become a big-dollar item in the United States, with hospitals and clinics rushing to reap the burgeoning profits. As I worked into the late 1970s trying to develop and refine a workable pain program, I couldn't help but notice that every hospital of any size and stature had to have a pain program. These pain programs were usually four to six weeks in length and were inpatient (the person stayed in the hospital at least five days per week). During the course of treatment an individual would receive physical therapy, occupational therapy, recreational therapy, psychotherapy, biofeedback, and more. Usually these programs operated in a group format with anywhere from six to twelve pain patients being treated at a time. Costs ranged from 8000 to 18,000 dollars. The comprehensive programs were difficult to participate in for anyone who was employed either full or part time. Formats differed from program to program, but basically were multidisciplinary (a combined, coordinated thrust of numerous professionals). Some were good, some bad, and some just took the money and kept running.

In the early 1980s, the insurance industry suddenly awakened to the problem of pain treatment, panicked, and immediately began to place restrictions on reimbursement for pain treatment or pain management therapy. I found it quite astonishing, when interviewing several top executives of the major medical insurance companies, to be told candidly that they could not recognize pain as a problem that was amenable to treatment other than traditional (surgical, medication), because the cost to them would be phenomenal. At my first pain center I went head to head with insurance companies on more than one occasion. It was also frustrating to try to convince fellow members of the psychological and medical community that pain could be treated with alternatives to medication, prolonged physical therapy, or surgery.

Since I was experiencing pain, I had the opportunity to test all of my techniques on myself. Some worked, others held promise, and some were never to be tried again. I found that year after year my efforts seemed to focus more toward the body/mind connection and the brain's ability to develop systems to reduce and control discomfort along with the depression, anger, frustration, decreased self-confidence and irritability that all too often go hand in hand with pain.

The Scottsdale Pain Relief Program has been nearly ten years in development and implementation. What I present to you now is a program which may help you:

decrease pain

increase pain tolerance

increase self-confidence

reduce depression

reduce anxiety

regain control of your life

The Scottsdale Pain Relief Program is not a cure, and it is not a miracle. It is a very straightforward, honest, and reliable approach to gaining control of your pain. There are no shortcuts, magic pills, silver bullets, or enchanted wands—only application, dedication, and the true desire to be a victor in your daily battle against pain.

CHAPTER TWO

Getting Started

Take a deep breath in through your mouth, exhale slowly through your nose, and let your shoulders relax . . . release the tension . . . and let's go.

As with all things, there must be a beginning, and so we find ourselves in the starting block of a long-distance race: the Pain Relief Marathon. To qualify for this event, you must first be willing to look at your circumstances and reactions to pain in an honest and open manner. Take a few moments now and complete the form that I have developed for you.

This will be the first questionnaire presented to you in the book. The directions will be relatively similar for each:

1. Answer all the questions based on how you have felt during the past ten days.

2. Don't seek help from anyone else to answer the questions.

3. If the statement does not apply, leave it blank.

4. If you don't want to mark in the book, then number a blank sheet of paper from one to ten for use as an answer sheet.

5. Answer each question with yes or no.

Chronic Pain Qualifier

1. My pain has been present for more than four months.
2. I have been to at least two doctors for my pain condition.
3. I feel frustrated by my pain.
4. I am in pain at least fifty percent of my waking hours.
5. Sometimes, people don't understand my pain.
6. I feel as though the pain is controlling or beginning to control my life.
7. When my pain increases I become depressed and/or anxious.
8. I feel trapped by my pain.
9. Thinking about the future makes me nervous.
10. I am afraid the pain will increase.

If you have answered yes to five or more of these statements, then the pain is beginning to take control of your life, and the Scottsdale Pain Relief Program may be the answer you have been seeking.

Gaining Control

The story of Jim B. is sad and the all-too-often repeated testimony of the chronic pain sufferer. Jim suffered a back injury that eventually led to twenty-four years of nearly constant suffering. He has had a total of seven back surgeries. He has been addicted to pain medication (at one time as many as twenty Percodan per day). He has been treated over and over again with physical therapy and even has had age regression treatment supposedly taking him back to the time of his birth trauma.

When all of these treatments and therapies failed, leaving Jim a pain medication "junkie," he tried to commit suicide on two occasions. On the final suicide attempt, Jim sat in a bathtub with slashed wrists and ankles, watching his life's blood flowing down the drain. A doctor who realized he could help Jim no more recommended Jim see me for evaluation.

Jim completed the Scottsdale Pain Relief Program one-and-a-half years ago and now works every day at his Lifetime Maintenance Program. His battle remains a constant one, day in and day out. He strives to maintain control over the relentless pain.

This summer I received a card from Jim as he and his wife drove from Arizona to Minnesota.

Hi, Neal:

Had a good trip up to Minnesota. Staying with friends right on a huge lake—Fishing every day—boy—this is the life! Feeling just great—no pain! Praise the Lord! Thanks for making all this possible!

Jimmy

Jim, like so many others, regained control of his life.

False Expectations

The control of pain brings us to a very key issue. Many of you will have some discomfort for the rest of your life because of arthritis, injuries from accidents, or numerous degenerative types of diseases. Control *does not* imply an absence of pain. Although some people who use the Scottsdale Pain Relief Program will be able to completely short-circuit muscle contraction headaches, certain types of neuromuscular pain, and other pain conditions, the majority of you will have some residual discomfort. It should be so minimal, however, that it won't interfere with your life on a physical, emotional, social, occupational, educational, or personal level. Once you gain control, you need to maintain it on a consistent basis. You cannot experience a success and then turn away and expend no further effort. Because your efforts need to continue, I have included the Lifetime Maintenance Program.

Proof of Pain

I am going to ask you to do something from now on which may be difficult at first but is essential for your successful completion of the program.

> *From this moment on you do not have to prove your pain to anyone!*

I know this may be difficult, since anyone with a chronic pain problem experiences the trauma of pain proof.

How many of you have experienced a referral merry-go-round as you go from one doctor to the next and ultimately find yourself sitting in the psychologist or psychiatrist's waiting room, fully convinced (if not brainwashed) into believing that the pain may be a figment of your imagination? Obviously, the pain is a response to an inadequate childhood, some frustration with your job, an unhappy sex life, or all of the above. By the second or third doctor, you want to set a tape recorder on the desk and play back the information you have provided to everyone else. Meanwhile your anger builds inside, festering with a resentment nurtured in your belief that no one fully understands your pain and suffering.

Over the years there have been times when I have actually had to deprogram people to help them regain confidence in their own belief system, convincing them that pain proof is not essential to pain relief.

In the past five years the medical community has made positive steps toward identifying and appropriately diagnosing pain conditions.

Medical schools are finally realizing that the answer to pain is not a traditional doctor standing with a scalpel in one hand and a prescription pad in the other. Old traditions and institutions die hard, and unfortunately there are still too many medical personnel who will sit behind a large, protective desk, look over at a pain sufferer, and utter the infamous words, "You'll have to learn to live with it." You are then overcome with feelings of hopelessness and the belief that you have failed to prove your pain.

Friends and relatives are not exempt from this ordeal of proof. When nearly three-quarters of all pain sufferers find their marriages near or into divorce, they can usually look back to a spouse who really did not believe their pain.

The Proof Trap

When you allow yourself to be caught in the trap of proving your pain, the *what-if* statements follow:

> *"What if I were lying in a hospital bed with tubes sticking out of my body?"*
>
> *"What if my arm were in a cast?"*
>
> *"What if I had scars all over my face?"*
>
> *"What if I were dead?"*
>
> *"What if. . . ?"*

Along with the *what-if* statements are the projections, which sound like this:

> *"I wish my doctor could experience my pain for one day."*
>
> *"I wish my family knew how bad my head hurt."*

"I wish there were a way to measure the amount of pain I am in."

"I wish I were dead!"

The *what-if* and *I-wish* statements are all traps into which pain patients fall. All of us have at one time or another succumbed to some of these statements, which we utter in our own subconscious attempts at trying to prove that we are not imagining the pain but truly hurting.

Bill of Rights

Before you read this next section, I want you to get up from wherever you are sitting or lying and go to where there is a mirror. Stand or sit in front of that mirror, and as you read the Bill of Rights for People in Pain, I want you to stop after each sentence, look directly into the mirror, and repeat the sentence back to yourself five times. Each morning of the seven-day program, you are to repeat the bill of rights in front of the mirror, in the same manner, before you start your day. As you progress through the Scottsdale Pain Relief Program, you will learn to believe and trust in each of these statements. They will become *your* bill of rights, which you will earn through successful completion of the seven-day program and continued use of the Lifetime Maintenance Program. Like a bill of rights for any country or organization, they are only as potent as the people using them.

Over the years I have found that people who gain the most success from the program use and believe in their rights. To assert these rights in all situations is a matter of belief in yourself and your ability to control pain. Many people have taken these simple sentences and written them down on a piece of paper or a card to carry the bill of rights with them wherever they go. The card serves as a constant reminder and reinforcer.

The Bill of Rights for People in Pain

1. I have the *Right* to live a full and happy life.
2. I have the *Right* not to have to prove my pain.
3. I have the *Right* to control decisions regarding my pain.
4. I have the *Right* to demand appropriate medical attention.
5. I have the *Right* to be alone when I choose.
6. I have the *Right* to refuse requests that may increase my pain.
7. I have the *Right* to pain relief.

These rights are not to be taken lightly. They serve as the foundation for your Scottsdale Pain Relief Program and everything you build upon it through the Lifetime Maintenance Program.

The Emotional Side of Pain

Anyone who suffers from pain knows firsthand that pain can definitely affect your emotions. During the course of my practice I have always been amazed when people come into my office and talk about a pain condition they have had for three, five, or more years and then in the same breath tell me the pain has not in the least bit affected them emotionally or psychologically. We are not talking about pain that is psychogenic or caused by emotions but chronic pain, which inevitably leads to emotional fallout.

Admitting to yourself that the pain may be affecting you from an emotional standpoint can be the most difficult task. None of us likes to admit that we have emotional difficulties, especially when pain has already restricted our ability to enjoy life, maintain relationships, or work.

Emotional Fallout—A Closer Look

Take a few minutes and read through the descriptions of emotional difficulties that may be caused by pain. The number of problems and degree of severity may vary from person to person and are dependent upon type of pain, lifestyle, and basic personality structure.

Irritability.

"I can't be bothered with that now."

"Leave me alone and let me rest."

"Go ask your mother [father]."

Most people who suffer from a pain condition will recognize these statements. It is only natural that when you are in pain you will be more irritable. Noises, activities, conflicts, or even making decisions, which before the pain had presented little difficulty, now take major efforts and may cause you to feel on edge most of the time.

Depression.

"I don't have the energy."

"I just don't feel like doing anything."

"I just don't seem to be interested in anything."

Over the years depression has been given a connotation of severe mental illness, hospitalization, drug treatments, or electroshock therapy. There is no question that pain is depressing. It causes you to feel down, listless, and lacking energy. The longer the pain continues, the greater the possibility that depression will become a way of functioning and eventually a destructive coping mechanism. The essence of depression is nonactivity, and the factor of feeling sorry for yourself is a natural ingredient.

Increased Frustration.

"I don't have the patience anymore!"

"When is this going to end?"

"Why doesn't anyone listen to me?"

These statements are often made by pain sufferers. They are a direct result of the pain relief search ending in a blind alley. They are also found in the medication merry-go-round.

Anxiety.

"I feel jumpy all over."

"I feel shaky."

"I'm so nervous I can't think straight most of the time."

We are not talking about the anxiety that may be stereotyped on television or in movies. The anxiety that you experience with pain relates to how other people view you, whether they believe that you are in as much pain as you say, or your fear of what may happen in the future. When you look to the future, you wonder if it will be one where you are not constantly harassed by your pain. If the future looks bleak and your anxiety increases, then this creates what we call anticipatory anxiety. You are anticipating continuing pain fallout, and this creates a sense of anxiety, uneasiness, and shakiness, which may occur on a constant, once-daily, or even hourly basis. Worry about future pain long enough and you'll live in a constant state of anticipatory anxiety.

Anger.

> *"I feel like beating my head against the wall!"*
>
> *"I just want to scream!"*
>
> *"I want to hit someone or something."*

These are statements made by people who are angry—angry at the fact that they have to continue suffering from pain. They are upset at how the pain has restricted their lives either at home or at work. The anger may eat away at you in the same manner that a cancerous malignancy can gradually steal your life. Many times irritability, frustration, and anger go hand in hand and appear to be partners in a conspiracy to cause you increased discomfort beyond the pain.

Hopelessness/Helplessness.

> *"I feel like giving up."*
>
> *"I feel doomed!"*
>
> *"What's the use?"*

I've heard these statements over and over again from patients in my office. You may have heard them from friends or relatives, or possibly even yourself. The feelings of hopelessness/helplessness are generated as an outcome of any prolonged amount of pain. I talk to people every day who continually use the phrase, "I don't feel as though I have any control over my life with the pain." When there seems to be no solution to the pain, and day after day you suffer, then the feelings of hopelessness/helplessness begin to take seed.

Isolation.

"Just leave me alone."

"I just don't feel like going out of the house."

"No one understands how I feel."

You hurt both physically and emotionally. You begin to notice a lack of interest in being around people. Friends who normally called or came to visit seem to contact you less frequently. Even at work, you tend to isolate yourself from your coworkers, and they may ask you if something is wrong. Of course, there is the pain, but how do you tell them that you just don't feel like being around people?

Decreased Concentration.

"I read a page and then I can't remember what I have read."

"I can't seem to get into my work anymore."

"I keep asking people to repeat what they've told me."

People who suffer from headaches know full well the impact of their pain on the ability to concentrate and perform tasks that require them to focus their attention. A decrease in the ability to concentrate is not limited just to headaches but can affect you with any type of pain. The pain constantly interrupts your conscious focusing and is a negative distraction.

To Be Depressed or Not to Be Depressed?

That is the question. You are the only one with the answer. The pain-depression cycle is something you are going to overcome through the seven-day program. That sense of feeling down, blue, and fatigued can be alleviated through two steps:

1. Activation of the body's chemicals that are built-in antidepressants
2. Lifestyle changes that will halt the growth of depression and put you back in control of your emotions

The Pain-Depression Roller Coaster.

Some years ago a young woman sat in my office sobbing. She described her life as a mess. Two years before she had been rear-ended in an automobile accident and suffered a neck injury. No bones were broken, but the diagnosis had been severe cervical strain. Following her accident, her family doctor put her on muscle relaxants and pain medication. One month later she felt no better and in fact was now developing daily headaches. Her job performance was beginning to suffer because of the amount of time off from work she needed, and her social life was almost nonexistent. This was only the start. For the next two years she went to nine doctors, physical therapy, and various clinics. Her fiancé broke off their engagement, and her employer of five years threatened to replace her because of days missed for treatment and doctors' visits.

Every day she forced herself out of bed and tried to complete the duties of her job as secretary/receptionist. The pain continued unabated, and she noticed feelings of worthlessness, frustration, and a general sense of hopelessness. Her long-standing friendships began to crumble. There were feelings of confusion and anger, which fed directly into a quickly sinking self-worth.

Two-and-a half years after the accident, she was unemployed, living with her parents, and feeling as though life were not worth living. She not only had a chronic cervical pain syndrome, but she had also developed a depression that was slowly destroying her life.

She was on the pain-depression roller coaster, from which she felt there was no escape. She was certain that nothing could help.

Fortunately a friend of her mother's had been through the Scottsdale Pain Relief Program and suggested that the daughter come to see me.

After reviewing her case, it was obvious to me that all the professionals had focused on her pain, provided her only minimal relief, and then had branded her as a hysterical woman. As the doctors' reports followed her from one office to the next, she might have worn a red *H* (for hysterical) painted on her forehead signifying that she was not stable and exaggerated her symptoms.

Convincing her to begin the Scottsdale Pain Relief Program was a difficult task. Her faith in doctors had been shattered along with her confidence. She didn't believe she had within her the capabilities for learning to control her pain and restabilize herself emotionally.

She soon came to learn that there was within her a power to slow the roller coaster and allow her to jump off at an appropriate time.

Fortunately the woman I have just described is capable of using the Scottsdale Pain Relief Program. There are literally hundreds of thousands of people who do not know about the Scottsdale Relief Program. They continue to ride the roller coaster, with little or no hope of ever getting off.

Is There a Chronic Pain Personality?

The never-ending effort to classify and put everything in its own special little box has not omitted the person suffering from pain. As early as the seventeenth century, the physician Thomas Willis described diabetes as being caused by "an ill-manner of living, sadness, long grief." Passivity, depression, stress, sadness, and prolonged grief have all become viewed as components of a diabetic personality.

We have heard of the Type A personality, which is characterized by tense, aggressive, and always-on-the-go people who might be more prone to heart attacks and ulcerative diseases. In fact, the Type A personality has been so well publicized that new branches of therapy have been developed that are specially devoted to treatment of this problem.

Irritable bowel syndrome, which can become a chronic pain condition, has been associated with women who are high achievers and self-demanding with perfectionist qualities. Of course, the irritable bowel syndrome is not solely the province of women; it may be experienced by men, although statistics indicate that more women are sufferers from this condition.

The individual with arthritis has often been described as having a personality that involves depression, repression, stress, and anxiety. Quite obviously, the arthritic personality contains many of the attributes we find in chronic stress conditions.

Through the course of my own practice, I have seen the effects of chronic stress and tense and anxious personalities as they relate to skin disorders.

The physiological factors involved in headaches have been well known for years. People who are tense, driven, and unable to relax may be subject to muscle contraction or migraine headaches.

I could go on and on, citing quotes from as early as 1701 to the present day, from studies being conducted in major hospitals and research facilities throughout the United States.

Is there a chronic pain personality? I don't believe that there is a box that everyone who suffers from chronic pain can be placed into, but I have found certain psychological and emotional characteristics that appear to be prevalent in people who suffer from chronic pain. Whether or not we become involved in a chicken-and-egg (which came first?) discussion is of little consequence. The item of major importance is the identification of any characteristics you may have that could adversely be affecting your ability to control the pain.

Here is a summary of characteristics that I have found in chronic pain sufferers. Go through the list and evaluate how many of them might apply to you. The Scottsdale Pain Relief Program has been designed to help you remove as many of these negative characteristics as possible.

Depression
Repression
Anxiety
Self-demanding behavior
Tension
Dependency

Hostility and Your Pain.

"I sometimes get so angry!"

"I wish I could hit someone!"

"If I could break something, I would probably feel better."

"I feel like I'm going to explode."

Hostility will not only increase your pain but will also cause a decrease in your body's ability to control the discomfort. The link between unresolved hostility and physical illness has been well defined by the scientific community. In a scientific study conducted in North Carolina, 250 medical students were given psychological testing to measure hostility. Those who received the highest scores showed five times the number of heart problems than did those medical students with low scores on the hostility scale.

I could go on and on, citing studies that show a direct connection between hostility and increased physical dysfunction even in terms of the body's own immune system.

People suffering from pain conditions who are hostile not only experience greater increases in pain but also do poorly in pain treatment, whether it be surgery, medication, or teaching the body to produce its own built-in painkillers. As the director of a pain center in a major hospital, day after day I would see patients for evaluation and possible participation in the pain treatment program. When an individual would sit across from me and react in a very angry, hostile, and belligerent manner, I could with almost one hundred percent certainty predict failure for this person unless the individual identified and was willing to resolve the hostility, which otherwise would prevent him from ever controlling his pain.

If you consider yourself an angry or hostile person or have been told by other people that you are, take a look at the suggestions. Don't be afraid to try them. Losing some of your anger and hostility can be a definite boost toward success in the Scottsdale Pain Relief Program.

Suggestions:

> *When you feel the anger building, take an extra exercise/activity segment, leave the scene of the possible argument, or take a walk.*
>
> *When you feel the anger reaching a point of explosion, use the pain relief breathing, and then use the pain relief scan on page 112. With both of these techniques you can short-circuit the anger response and make a decision based upon the proper combination of intellect and emotion.*

Avoiding Pain Traps.

You are an explorer seeking out the mythical cave in which the secrets to pain control may be found. As you begin this difficult journey, I must warn you of the traps and pitfalls that threaten to slow and stop you in your search.

Fortunately there are rules to follow that will increase your chances of entering the cave and learning the secrets. Some of the traps are slight and only temporary, yet some of the pitfalls are fatally deep.

Carefully follow each of these suggestions as you begin your journey, and you may be able to avoid the traps.

> *Don't make your pain the center of every conversation*
>
> *Don't use your pain as an excuse to get out of recreational or work activities*

Don't use your pain to gain sympathy

Don't exaggerate your pain to control or punish others

Since we are all human, there is little doubt that no one can avoid all pain traps, but with a careful, concerted effort you will be able to insure that any pitfalls are only ankle deep.

You already know some of the methods for avoiding the traps. The program will teach you the rest.

Help! Can Anyone Hear Me?

I have always found a curious phenomenon surrounding people who have chronic pain. It doesn't matter whether that pain is from arthritis, headache, or a low back injury. After a certain amount of time, people around you become somewhat deaf. You get a sense of them hearing you but not listening to you.

I have to assume that you are not a constant, nagging complainer but simply a person who suffers pain, which becomes evident through facial expressions, certain comments, or gestures. People ask you if everything is all right or you are uncomfortable. When you answer them for the first time there is curiosity; up to the eighth time, sympathy; and then, without warning, they start to become deaf.

You may have already noticed this phenomenon with your doctor. In your quest for a solution to the pain, I am confident that you have encountered medical care providers who listen to you but don't hear what you are saying. Fortunately there are changes evolving within the practice of medicine, and additional emphasis has been placed in medical schools, internships, and residencies that will help doctors not only to listen, but actually to hear what their patients are trying to tell them.

The selective deafness syndrome may also apply to relatives or friends who turn a deaf ear to your continuing problem. They don't know what to say or do, or how to react to your complaints of pain.

They may feel inadequate to deal with your call for help and therefore try to pretend that the problem does not exist by refusing to hear it.

Experiencing selective deafness among friends, associates, or relatives can be devastating for someone experiencing chronic pain. Most of you have already experienced this to one degree or another, and the experience may have left you with a bitter taste in your mouth.

Helping People to Listen and Hear You

Here are some hints to help you overcome the problem of selective deafness:

1. When you talk, strive to maintain eye contact.
2. Slow your speech, applying appropriate pauses.
3. Keep your sentences shorter and allow for responses.
4. If you are going to talk to a physician, write down your questions or comments in advance, and go through them one by one to seek answers.

Putting an End to the Emotional Fallout

If pain is a black cloud hanging over your head and you're constantly being rained on by the emotional fallout, then it's time to move out from under the shadow of your pain. As you progress through the seven-day program and into the Lifetime Maintenance Program, you will be excited as each drop of the fallout begins to disappear.

The Two Faces of Pain Relief

Pain relief can be a two-sided coin. When pain has been with you for an extended period of time, you may have some confusion when you experience pain relief. Being aware of the ways you might react will help you to deal with success in the most appropriate manner.

Sometimes the Last to Know

"I am afraid of success."

"If I begin to change, everyone will expect a miracle."

"If my pain is lessened, then people may expect more of me."

"I am afraid to believe in my good days."

Would you believe me if I told you about some people, who—although their pain is destroying their life—have become so accustomed to the discomfort that the thought of being without pain is extremely frightening?

Remember the last time you had a good day, a time, although brief, when the pain seemed to be less? Your excitement was soon sabotaged by the thought, "Don't allow yourself to hope, since the pain will probably be back tomorrow." So instead of enjoying your freedom from pain, you waited complaisantly for the return of your nemesis.

The False Positive

Some people don't become pessimistic when they experience pain relief—rather they blast off into the outer space of uncontrolled positivism.

"My pain is a lot less today so by tomorrow it will be gone forever!"

Of course, the crash comes when tomorrow their pain has returned, leaving them depressed and feeling cheated. When people become so blindly positive that they forget the nature of their pain process, then they become very vulnerable to disappointment, which leads to an extra heavy cloudburst of emotional fallout.

A Matter of Balance

As on a teeter-totter, there has to be a proper balance between the fear of pain relief on one side and blind positivism on the other.

Striking the proper balance is a matter of continual practice and adjustment. As your pain never remains static, so, too, your emotional fallout may vary from day to day or week to week. Upon completion of the seven-day program, you will have balance.

Defining Pain:
Is It Chronic or Acute?

Acute.

You are hanging a picture on the wall and the hammer slips off the nail and impacts your thumb. There is an instantaneous response of pain as nerves are compressed in the area of your thumb by the head of the hammer, a signal is shot to the brain that is reinforced visually as you look at your injury. The signal in your brain has been interpreted as pain; within a matter of microseconds you feel the pain exploding in your thumb. After a grimace, or possibly some well-chosen words, you might continue hanging the picture, revert to childhood behavior and suck on your thumb while throwing a temper tantrum, or even choose the wisest course of action and soak it in a glass of ice water.

Whichever method you've chosen, unless there has been nerve damage or bone broken, your pain should decrease in a matter of hours, with some residual soreness perhaps lasting several days. A week following the episode, there should be almost no discomfort and the memory of the pain will probably only occur next time you have to hang a picture.

This is an example of an acute pain response. All of us experience acute pain responses almost every day of our lives, whenever we bump a knee on the edge of a table or stub a toe.

A Tale of Chronic Pain.

Let's move past your sore thumb, which of course no longer bothers you since it has been a week since your picture-hanging incident. It's

Monday morning and you're at work, minding your own business, when Harry asks you to help him move the copy machine to the other side of the room. He assures you that between the two of you, it will be a snap. Well, it does turn out to be quite a snap because as you bend over and begin lifting your corner of the machine, Harry decides to look at the new office assistant as she walks by and shifts the weight of the machine to your side. You're in a bent-over position with your legs straight. As you struggle to catch the machine, there is a searing pain that shoots across your low back. Gritting your teeth, you struggle to maintain balance while Harry senses your predicament and regains his share of the load. The copy machine is now moved, but you spend the rest of the day taking aspirin and walking as though you're still trying to lift the copier. You tell yourself that the pain will soon disappear and that all you did was stress your back.

The day after the copy machine incident, the development of chronic pain begins. If you were to write a diary, here's how it would look:

Day after went to family doctor—painkillers and muscle relaxants—stay home rest of the week.

Four days later—not any better—called doctor, who said to come in.

Saw family doctor—he seemed perplexed but gave me some medication to help me sleep better and told me to continue taking the muscle relaxants and pain pills.

Went back to work but by eleven o'clock in the morning the pain was in my back and left leg.

Called family doctor and he referred me to an orthopedic surgeon friend of his.

Could not get in for an appointment for four days.

Saw orthopedic surgeon, who took X rays and examined me—said I had low back strain and to take muscle relaxants—I told him that I was already taking muscle relaxants and he gave me a different kind—said to "take it easy on my back."

Now two weeks after hurting my back and it feels worse.

Becoming frustrated and angry.

Have not been able to play tennis since the injury.

Trying to work but it's hard to sit for long periods of time.

Went back to orthopedic surgeon and he prescribed different medication.

Heard about a physical medicine and rehabilitation doctor from a friend and made an appointment to see him.

Saw new doctor and was given new medication plus physical therapy five times a week.

Three months later, still going to physical therapy, now three times per week—job interrupted all of the time.

Have tried nine different kinds of medication.

Cannot sleep during the night.

Feeling depressed during the day.

. . . and on, and on, and on.

You have just witnessed the typical development of a chronic pain condition affecting the low back. This scenario is repeated with thousands of people each and every day to varying degrees as we become a population plagued by chronic pain problems.

You could probably write your own diary regarding your specific pain, whether it be headache, arthritis, or back pain.

Pain Anticipation.

Ask anyone who suffers from chronic pain, and they will tell you of their constant fear: "I wonder how I can live when the pain gets worse." Most pain sufferers live in dread of "the big one," with a constant level of anxiety and stress. Spending your time wondering and anticipating the next increase in pain sets the stage for pain anticipation.

An Unconscious Trigger.

If you consciously spend time focusing on the next attack you may have or an increase in pain due to other circumstances, then inadvertently you may be setting yourself up for "the big one." Focusing on the possibility of increased pain creates a chronic stress situation that serves as a trigger for increased muscle tension, muscle spasms, and decreased production of internal pain-controlling and emotion-stabilizing chemicals.

The triggering does not happen immediately, but given enough time and repetition of thoughts regarding a fear of pain increase a domino principle will take effect, triggering the increase in pain. When the pain does increase, the little voice inside you says, "See, I told you so." Once that little voice has spoken, the emotional dominoes (anxiety, depression, decreased self-image, decreased self-esteem) begin to fall.

Pain Pumpers.

Pain pumpers are behaviors or conditions that are directly under your control. The greater the number of pain pumpers, the more chance there will be of an increase in your pain and a possibility of sabotaging your efforts to control and reduce discomfort. See how many of the pumpers on the list are familiar to you, and use the Scottsdale Pain Relief Program to reduce as many as possible:

Stress
Anger
Anxiety
Overweight condition
Poor eating habits
Smoking (nicotine addiction)
Misuse of pain medication

Pain anticipation
Pain manipulation
Poor sleeping

Before You Start the Program

In chapter four you will actually begin the Scottsdale Pain Relief Program by preparing for the seven-day program. You may be surprised to learn that you have already progressed through very important aspects of the Scottsdale Pain Relief Program just by coming this far.

As chapter two ends, you need to become aware of the three types of people who start the Scottsdale Pain Relief Program. If you find yourself in any one or a combination of these types, then be honest enough with yourself to admit the fact and allow for any changes before day one.

Harry Have-A-Look.

Harry figures that he is going to take a look at the program. He doesn't want to commit himself at this point, but he plans to read through the seven-day program and see if it suits his needs. He has also made a decision that if he does not like the program, he can stop at any time he wants. The Harry Have-A-Looks need to make a definite commitment before even beginning the next chapter. If you have a habit of starting projects and never completing anything, then you may be a Harry. If you are, your first step will be to recognize the problem and make the commitment to start the seven-day program. Constantly be alert to the possibility of slipping back into the Harry Have-A-Look condition.

Mary Maybe.

Mary is similar to Harry Have-A-Look, but Mary usually completes whatever she begins, although never in a comprehensive manner. She is committed to completing what is started, but she tends to perform on only a superficial level. "Maybe it will work and maybe it won't" are her guiding words. Mary Maybe's need is to start the program with the conviction of obtaining success.

Jerry Joiner.

Jerry will join almost anything. He has been known always to complete applications that are addressed in the following manner: "You have been selected." Usually Jerry has heard about the Scottsdale Pain Relief Program from someone else or heard it mentioned on the radio or television. Jerry tends to buy the book and read the first several pages before putting it down on the coffee table and returning to his favorite television program—which will soon be interrupted by his chronic pain problem. If you're a Jerry, ask yourself if you have anything more important to do than spending seven days with a chance of gaining control over your pain.

Just One Minute: Before You Go Any Further

Before you proceed to chapter three, take this brief test, answering each question with a yes or no:

1. I have read chapters one and two completely.
2. I understand how the emotional fallout from pain may affect my life.

3. I am willing to go back and reread any areas that I don't thoroughly understand.

4. I am committed to continuing my search for relief from my pain.

5. I am beginning to feel there is hope.

If you have been able to answer yes to all of these questions, then it is time for you to move on to chapter three.

Part Two

If you are like most chronic pain sufferers, it has taken years to reach the point you are at today. All the frustration, misinformation, depression, anguish, and—most important—pain are going to be changed forever with your commitment to begin day one of the intensive seven-day program.

A Design for You.

By now you may have come to the realization that although I do not know you personally, it sounds and feels as if the Scottsdale Pain Relief Program was designed specifically with you in mind. It is my hope that you have this feeling, since the program was developed and modified through input, practice, and experimentation by people just like you.

CHAPTER THREE

The Pain Segments

Pain Segment Particulars.

As you go through this section, normal curiosity will probably lead you to look at other segments besides the one for your specific pain. You will notice that some segments are not very large while others encompass numerous pages. This is not to say that one pain problem is greater than another; it only indicates that certain pain conditions may affect a greater number of people in our population.

Crossover.

After reading your pain segment, you should look at other types of pain and suggestions that have been provided. There is a significant crossover effect; for example, certain suggestions found in the back pain segment regarding posture and sitting can be and should be applied by everyone whether or not they have a back injury. In fact, I encourage every patient who goes through the Scottsdale Pain Relief Program to read the other pain segments and utilize the suggestions as a preventative medicine technique. Performing some of the exercises found in the back segment will help you to prevent future back difficulties, and you will benefit from overall neuromuscular fitness (flexibility, endurance, and strength). Don't be afraid to cross over.

Using the Pain Segments.

The pain segments should be referred to for your specific type of pain or condition. Each pain segment will describe briefly the type of pain and present helpful suggestions, which may include:

Exercises
Alternative treatments
Activities: do's and don't's

Your specific pain segment should be read and thoroughly reviewed prior to your beginning the seven-day program.

The Pain Relief Statement.

The pain relief statement is to be inserted into your personalized pain relief formula on day six of your seven-day program. The pain relief statement will serve as a mental trigger to activate further the body's built-in ability to reduce pain.

The Foundation.

The use of a pain relief statement is based on research with autogenic therapy (a method of self-control through repetition of body/mind phrases). In use since the early 1900s, autogenic therapy can be found at almost all major pain centers in the United States. My doctoral dissertation from Arizona State University was on the use of autogenic therapy for the treatment of anxiety and stress conditions. At the time I wrote my dissertation, there were over two thousand scientific articles worldwide relating to the benefits of autogenic therapy, and only twenty of these were in English. Times have changed, and since then autogenic therapy has been accepted universally as a technique for the following:

Anxiety reduction
Pain reduction
Increased body/mind interaction
Stabilization of emotional difficulties (anxiety, depression, phobias, etc.)

Autogenic therapy in its traditional format may take as long as from three to four months for full training and activation of the formulas. When I first began using autogenic therapy in the treatment of pain patients, I would follow the prescribed length of treatment but found it to be cumbersome, frustrating to the patient, and too long. Over several years, I worked to modify the formulas without losing their inherently beneficial effects. Although the pain relief statements appear to be quite simple, within their basic nature lies their success. Unlike other treatments, pain relief statement utilization does not demand anything from your body/mind interaction; rather you make a passive, yet assertive, statement. If repeated in conjunction with your personalized pain relief formula, this statement will direct the appropriate body/mind interaction. Since you will be providing the statement to yourself, the control remains totally within you.

Repetition of the Statement.

When you are asked to repeat silently the pain relief statement (autogenically), you should bear in mind some very specific do's and don't's.

Do take your time

Do repeat the phrase silently in a rhythmic and paced manner

*Do modify the statement to the extent of providing the best possible
description of your condition or pain site*

Don't force the statements

Don't modify the statement to make it a demand

*Don't be fooled by the statement's simplicity and forget to include
it as part of your personalized pain relief formula*

Headaches

Wherever I go I ask the question, "What comes to mind when I
mention the word *pain?*"

Eight out of ten times the response is:

HEADACHE!

The number of people suffering from headaches and the costs of this
type of pain are staggering.

*Headaches are the most common ailment in our country, affecting
ninety percent of all Americans.*

*From ten to twenty percent of the American population suffers from
recurrent migraine and cluster headaches.*

*More than forty-two million Americans are treated for headaches
each year.*

*An estimated 126 million sick days are lost each year for
headaches.*

*The cost to employers for sick days as a result of headaches is
estimated at six billion dollars.*

Less than ten percent of all headaches is caused by disease.

If you experience headaches, all of the statistics in the world are not going to make them go away or help decrease either the pain or how much it devastates your life.

Different Types and Causes.

Headache sufferers find little comfort in knowing that over forty-two million other Americans have frequent headaches and that seventy percent of all households have at least one person who is headache prone.

Most pop aspirins and comfort themselves with the knowledge that headaches, though painful, are not usually indicative of serious illness.

Whether you have a muscle contraction headache or a migraine headache, I am sure that well-meaning friends and physicians have all jumped at the opportunity to inform you of the latest cure or diet.

Why is it that a headache sufferer will eat a piece of chocolate and soon after develop a headache but several weeks later ingest the same amount of chocolate and experience no headache?

Why on one Friday night might you have four or five drinks and wake up the next morning with a horrible hangover but the next weekend repeat the same drinking and have no headache?

Both male and female bodies go through monthly cycles that determine whether or not you may get a headache. Women are more sensitive to headache food triggers around the time of their menstrual periods. Men have similar cycles, but these are harder to predict.

The body and mind work together to regulate body cycles. Dips and swings in the body's chemistry create either a friendly or a hostile ground for headaches to develop.

(Note: If you experience recurring headaches, you should have them evaluated by a qualified physician prior to beginning the Scottsdale Pain Relief Program to rule out their being the result of some ongoing disease process, such as tumors.)

This section will cover each of the major types of headaches: tension, migraine, cluster, and sinus. You probably already know which particular type you suffer from, but I've presented all of them. Before you go any further, just spend a few minutes and read through all the different types to make sure that what you think you have is what you really have.

Headaches in Review.

Each type of headache will have characteristics that are used to make a diagnosis. Some of these may be common to more than one type of headache. Read over the lists, especially the one for your headache. If you have been told that you have one particular type of headache but the description does not match up, then you should seek a consultation with a doctor specializing in the diagnosis and treatment of headache conditions.

Tension Headaches

Steady pain
Pain on both sides of head
Pain may last for days or weeks
Feels like band around head
Direct link to emotions (stress)
May occur day or night
May increase during the day

Migraine Headaches

Throbbing, recurrent pain
Usually on one side of head
May be felt around one eye
May have visual distortions (scotoma)
Increased irritability
Pallor
Dizziness

Sweating
Strange hearing and taste sensations
May occur without warning
Lasts from several hours to days
Nausea and possible vomiting
May have loss of speech or motor coordination
May start around menstrual period
May see glittering or scintillating forms
Sensitivity to light (photophobia)
Nose may run

Cluster Headaches

Little or no warning
May last from minutes to several hours
Usually last between thirty and ninety minutes
Flushing
Behind one eye
Tearing from affected eye
Nostril on affected side congested, may run
More common in males age twenty to forty

Sinus Headaches

Pain increases in head-down position
Dull, deep, pressurelike pain
Pain increases with bending or stooping
Pain starts above eyes
Pain may spread to forehead or cheeks
Nasal congestion
Gradually increases during the day
May follow infection
May occur seasonally (peak allergy times)

Stress and Your Headache

To Stop Before They Start

You will soon be using the Scottsdale Pain Relief Program on a daily basis along with the pain relief statement. Your personalized pain relief formula should be used daily and whenever you feel the beginning of stress or tension. Don't wait until after you already have the headache.

Finding the Stress Around and Within You.

You're going to be a detective. As the famous stress sleuth, your job will be to search out all those parts of your environment that lead to a stress response and ultimately your headache. Now take a sheet of paper. On it list everything you can think of that causes stress in your life. Once you have made this list, take out a second sheet of paper and make two columns. In the first column list all the items you could possibly change that are within your control.

An example of such an item was found by Linda, who seemed to develop a headache every morning after her fourth-grade–level daughter had left for school. Linda identified the stress as the tension created trying to select her daughter's clothes in the morning amid the constant arguments about what she was going to wear. This was a stress within Linda's control. She had her daughter pick out the clothes the night before. Another example would be that of Richard, who found the traffic so congested on the way to work that by the time he sat at his desk, he had the beginning of a headache. Richard evaluated the stressor and when he found the traffic to be a major cause he planned an alternative, less congested route that would allow him to arrive at work early, less stressed.

Now take your list of stressors, and in the second column list all of the items that are not under your control to change. An example of something not under your control would be the condition of the street in the middle of your town, the Internal Revenue Service, or the disposition of your boss.

Now develop a plan to reduce the stressors that are under your control. Do this slowly, picking first the easiest to change. Take your time as you slowly move through the list. Each item you remove adds increased control into the arsenal in your battle against the effect of stress on all types of headaches.

Your Pain Relief Statements

Your pain relief statement should be used on day six of the seven-day program.

Tension Headaches.

I am in control of my tension headache and stress.

Migraine Headaches.

I am in control of my migraine headaches and my hands are warm.

[Increasing hand warmth has been found to be an effective technique to short-circuit the beginning of a migraine headache.]

Cluster Headaches.

I am in control of my cluster headaches and stress.

Sinus Headaches.

I am in control of my sinus headaches and my forehead is pleasantly cool.

[The use of coolness has been shown to be effective in the reduction of pressure and swelling in sinus headaches.]

Back Pain

"Low back pain is the price we pay for upright posture," explains the neurosurgeon James Campbell of the Johns Hopkins Medical Institution in Baltimore. Gravity and the mechanics of the spine make low back pain commonplace: According to Dr. Campbell, an estimated eight out of ten people will have at least one significant episode of low back pain during their lifetimes.

There it is. You wake up in the morning and your back is so stiff, you can't even get out of bed. Maybe you bend over to pick up a piece of paper—and can't straighten up again. Your car is rear-ended, and several days later your back pain is beginning to drive you crazy.

On any given date, 2.4 million Americans are disabled by back trouble. That works out to approximately ninety-three million workdays lost each year.

A New Diagnosis.

During the course of my professional career treating pain, I have been aware of changes within the medical profession regarding how back pain is viewed. Surgical procedures appear now to be considered as a court of last resort. I have found doctors slightly more hesitant to begin treatment by immediately prescribing antiinflammatory or narcotic pain medication. The medical profession is definitely becoming aware of the role played in back pain by tension and stress. (The diagnosis of stress-caused back pain and stress-caused increase in the severity of a preexisting back condition is now being considered more thoroughly by doctors.) Doctors are becoming aware of the need for a method to break the back pain stress cycle.

Back Pain → Stress → Increased Muscle Tension → Increased Pain →
Increased Stress → Emotional Fallout → Increased Pain →
Increased Stress → and on and on

The Scottsdale Pain Relief Program will be used to interrupt the pain stress cycle.

Three Major Causes: Sleeping, Sitting, and Standing on Your Back Pain

The Seat of the Problem.

What type of chair you sit in can play a very important role in your battle against pain. Although you may be using your pain relief imagery formulas on a daily basis and have just achieved excellent results from the seven-day program, your sitting in a chair that causes microscopic reinjuries to your back on a minute-to-minute basis will destroy much of the good work you have done.

If you have the type of job that requires you to sit for long periods of time, don't put off getting the proper chair. If your employer isn't convinced, then you may need to return to your physician and request a note or prescription from him specifying that you need a chair correct for your back.

Before you buy any chair for your personal or business use, consult the following recommendations:

> A chair should provide correct support for the spine in every sitting position. To support the lower back and check the effect of the pelvis tilting forward, the bottom half of the back rest should have extra padding.
>
> The top of the backrest should reach your shoulders so that it will support the spinal column.
>
> The angle between the seat and the backrest should adjust automatically when you are either leaning forward working or leaning backward relaxing, as well as when you are sitting upright.
>
> The seat height also should be adjustable, with the seat raised or lowered so that your feet rest comfortably on the floor. Look for a seat that slopes downward at the front edge and curves upward at the back. This feature, in conjunction with the backrest, insures proper back support. It also reduces pressure on the thighs, which insures adequate blood flow in the legs and feet and minimizes fatigue.
>
> The chair's operating controls should be unobtrusive and easy to manipulate.

A good chair can be a definite asset in pain relief and your Lifetime Maintenance Program.

Standing Up to the Pain.

"I stand at my job all day as a checkout clerk, and I'm lucky if I can sit down during lunch."

"I'm on my feet all day at the post office and by ten-thirty in the morning, my back is already beginning to kill me."

"Standing at the sales counter for an eight-hour day leaves me with so much pain that when I get home in the evening, the only thing I can think about is lying down and not being bothered by my family."

If some of these statements ring true, then it is about time you took some steps to modify your standing behavior and begin to reduce the stress on your low back. Standing for prolonged periods of time fatigues the muscles in the hips, low back, and abdomen, which tends to pull the pelvis forward, causing strain on the low back muscles.

If you must stand for long periods of time, definitely try these suggestions:

Using a small stool, put one foot on the stool, alternating every few minutes. This technique will relieve some of the strain on the low back muscles, allow for better blood flow to the affected areas, and help return the spine to a more natural curve.

Don't stand in one position for prolonged periods of time, even if you only have a small space in which to work. Move every few minutes or so.

Don't be rigid. Flex your knees, and if possible do some minimal stretching movements several times every hour.

Putting Back Pain to Sleep.

The worst enemy of your back, guaranteed to leave you waking in the morning with increased pain, is a poor mattress. I know of very few doctors who, even though they know the importance of an appropriate mattress, will take the time to explain why having the right kind of mattress may not only prevent a continuation of your back pain, but may also aid in the overall healing process. Without the right kind of mattress, this prayer is usually repeated each night:

> *"Now I lay me down to sleep, my back pain I will surely keep."*

For my back condition, I prefer a firm mattress. Many of my patients have found the waveless type of water bed to be excellent for a good night's sleep with a minimal amount of awakening discomfort. If you have difficulty obtaining a new mattress or a water bed, then a three-quarter-inch-thick piece of plywood inserted under your mattress may provide enough additional support.

Without the proper mattress, the following chain reaction will occur:

> *Back pain—poor mattress—poor sleep—increased fatigue—microreinjuries while sleeping—leads to increased pain, stiffness, and fatigue upon awakening.*

Although the Scottsdale Pain Relief Program may be used with any type of mattress, why not take the time and get the best mattress for your particular back problem?

Sweet Dreams.

When you have back pain (or any other pain), getting a good night's sleep is difficult enough even without causing microscopic reinjury to your back when you are lying in bed. We have already discussed the need for an appropriate mattress or bed, but how you position yourself down to sleep makes a big difference to the way you are going to awaken in the morning.

> *"What's the big deal with how I sleep? I just lie down and finally the pain eases slightly and I fall asleep. So what's the big deal? I'll wake up in the morning feeling lousy anyway."*

Comments like that have been made to me over and over. Again, we return to the basic concept that the Scottsdale Pain Relief Program will provide you with a method for using pain relief imagery to facilitate the body's production of built-in painkillers. You don't live in an isolated cocoon, though, and so you need to evaluate other aspects of your lifestyle based upon what type of pain you may suffer. If having the right type of bed or mattress possibly can reduce your overall discomfort by from one to one-and-a-half percent, and using the proper sleep position can further reduce this by another one percent, then before you know it, you have just decreased your pain by approximately from two-and-a-half to three percent. All these small bits help to reinforce the basic pain relief imagery and *do* add up to pain relief.

Here's how to sleep and allow your back to be in the best position for continued self-healing. (These suggestions may be used with any pain condition.)

> *Bend your knees, unlocking your spine into a neutral position, to relieve muscle and ligament stress.*

Lie on your side with the hips and knees bent toward the chest and the head on the pillow.

Many times a small pillow between the knees will support the upper legs so circulation in the lower legs is not blocked.

A small pillow between the legs may prevent the lower back from twisting.

If you must lie on your back, then place a pillow under your knees to prevent a swayback position.

Do not use an extremely fluffy pillow.

Changing positions frequently while you sleep is not bad.

Now, have a good night's sleep.

The Best Little Back Exercises in the World.

Exercise, stretch, and *strengthen* are the key words for anyone with a bad back. Having a bad back has qualified me to try most of the exercises that seem to find their way into doctors' offices, magazines, and popular books devoted to the back. Everyone seems to have their own little special exercise that is guaranteed to help decrease back pain and prevent reinjury.

Total Agreement—Unbelievable.

Experts, including orthopedic surgeons, specialists in physical rehabilitation, neurologists, neurosurgeons, physical therapists, and exercise therapists, are in agreement about certain exercises that are essential for anyone experiencing back pain. Your physician should be able to provide you with the appropriate exercises for your condition.

Summary.

Coping with back pain is never a single-item endeavor. Exercise, proper diet, appropriate body weight, and your personalized pain relief formula will all help you to deal with it.

Your Pain Relief Statement

Your pain relief statement for back pain will contain an emotional component. Use the complete statement on day six.

I am in control of my back pain and stress.

Arthritis

What do the following people all have in common?

Neanderthal man
Alexander the Great
Julius Caesar
Henry VI
Benvenuto Cellini
Egyptian pharaohs

All of these people suffer from arthritis, along with over seventy-five million people in the United States.

Arthritis is basically an inflammatory process by which the body's own immune system turns against its host and begins to attack the body's own tissues.

There are over one hundred forms of arthritis, including rheumatoid arthritis, gout, systemic lupus erythematosus, osteoarthritis, ankylosingspondylitis, polymyositis, tennis elbow, and fibrositis.

In the United States, seventy-five million people experience arthritic-type symptoms in their joints and muscles on a repeated basis. Of the approximately one hundred types of arthritis currently known, there are eight major categories: synovitis, attachment arthritis, crystal arthritis, joint infection, cartilage degeneration, muscle inflammation, injury conditions, and other general conditions.

Synovitis.

This condition indicates that the lubricating fluid in our joints has become inflamed. The joint may feel warm or swollen and have red skin. Synovitis may occur at any age. It appears mostly to strike women. A more common name for synovitis is rheumatoid arthritis.

Attachment Arthritis.

Attachment arthritis causes the ligaments (which are attached to the bone) to become inflamed. Attachment arthritis appears mostly to affect men and appears usually between the ages of fifteen and forty. The condition is most commonly known as ankylosingspondylitis. It is sometimes referred to as *poker spine*.

Crystal Arthritis.

The most common form of crystal arthritis is gout. As the name implies, chemical crystals develop and are then found in the joint fluid. This condition may also be known as microcrystalline because the crystals formed in the joint space are very small. As with attachment arthritis, crystal arthritis appears mostly to affect men. It has an onset between the ages of thirty-five and ninety.

Joint Infection.

In this condition, bacteria invade the joint fluid and infections occur, which are commonly known as staphylococcus or gonococcus infections. This type of arthritis may affect any individual, at any age, and usually is treated effectively with antibiotics.

Cartilage Degeneration.

Whenever there is a breakdown in the joint cartilage the condition is known as osteoarthritis or osteoarthrosis. It may affect equally men or women, but it usually does not set in until after the age of forty-two. Due to the constant use of joints, which results in wear and tear over a period of time, this type of arthritis occurs in almost every individual, if the person lives long enough.

Muscle Inflammation.

As the name implies, this type of arthritis is found not in joints but in muscles. The muscle tissue becomes inflamed, causing pain and difficulty in movement. Muscle inflammation does not show any preference to sex or age. It is known more commonly as polymyalgia rheumatica, polymyositis, and dermatomyositis.

Injury Conditions.

This type of arthritis results from injury or irritation. It may be caused by back strain, tennis elbow, or shin splints.

Other Arthritic Conditions.

Systemic lupus erythematosus is considered a form of arthritis. At one time it had a mortality rate of from thirty to forty percent within five years. Development of new treatment techniques has reduced significantly the death rate, but the crippling effects continue. Additional conditions that are classified in the general category are: fibrositis and rheumatism associated with psychological conditions such as depression.

Summary.

There is no question that arthritis is a frightening, painful, crippling disease process that strikes a high number of our population. Many people with arthritis go on with their daily lives, but some suffer such severe crippling effects that they are bedridden and eventually become so disabled that they cannot care for themselves.

Your Pain Relief Statement

The pain relief statement for arthritis will include an emotion-stabilizing part. Insert the pain relief statement on day six.

I am in control of my _____ [pain site, pain condition] and my _____ [the word for the emotion or condition].
Example: I am in control of my hand pain and my depression.

Muscle Pain

The area of muscle pain contains probably the largest number of people suffering discomfort. Muscle pain can range from certain arthritic conditions to muscle damage caused by improper jogging shoes. Classified under muscle pain are the following categories: low back pain, neck pain, temporomandibular disorder joint dysfunction (TMJ), tension headaches, and various sports injuries.

You can see that the area of muscle pain is quite large. Actually there is some crossover between various conditions.

In this part of the chapter, I have tried to include some of the more prominent muscle pains, including symptoms. At the end of each description, I have provided you with the pain relief statement to be inserted on day six into your personalized pain relief formula.

If Yours Is Not Included.

If your specific muscle pain condition has not been included in this section, don't worry. You will still be able to insert this pain relief statement on day six.

I am in control of my _____ [insert pain site or pain condition] and _____ [response].
Example: I am in control of my shoulder pain and stress response.

Neural Pain

The category of neural pain describes conditions that directly affect the nerves of the body. Examples of neural pain are: trigeminal neuralgia, tic douloureux, postherpetic neuralgia, sympathetic dystrophy, neuromas, causalgia, and sciatica. All neural pain conditions involve damage, pressure, or inflammation that adversely affects the nerves and creates pain signals. The causes of neural pain may be viruses, trauma, infection, or damage to an associated structure. Whatever the cause may be, the pain is initiated directly by nerve damage. The pain may range from stabbing bursts to a constant burning sensation.

Trigeminal Neuralgia and Tic Douloureux.

Many times these two conditions are considered as one since they both affect the trigeminal nerve found in the face. The pain from these conditions can be excruciating. The discomfort may be constant or occur at intervals. For some people who suffer this type of neuralgia, the pain may be set off by vibration, air movement, or contact with the skin over the nerve.

Postherpetic Neuralgia.

Postherpetic neuralgia is a very painful condition resulting directly from the aftermath of herpes zoster. This is the same virus that causes chicken pox in children; but in adults, collagens may occur under the skin, damaging nerves. Although lesions on the skin may disappear, the nerve damage remains. Nerve fibers may be destroyed (mostly large nerve fibers), but damage to the smaller nerve fibers (those that carry pain messages) continues through the course of the disease.

Sympathetic Dystrophy.

Sympathetic dystrophy may be caused by trauma, surgery, or degenerative diseases. This condition is sometimes difficult to diagnose since the pain may not occur at the site of the original injury; for example, following a hand injury a person may develop a sympathetic dystrophy that causes constant pain in the arm, shoulder, and neck.

Neuromas.

Neuromas are globes (tumors) that form on nerve endings and lead to intense chronic pain. Whenever you have a nerve damaged by trauma, there is a possibility that a neuroma tumor will grow at the site of the injury. People who have nerves severed due to an accident may be more prone to forming neuromas. Some people have been shown to have a tendency toward neuroma growth.

Causalgia.

Causalgia is the general term used to describe various types of nerve damage where the pain occurs as a burning sensation.

Sciatica.

Sciatica has been associated with low back injuries. The pain is usually described as constant and going down the leg and ending in the foot. Sciatica usually increases with prolonged sitting, especially since the chair may press against the sciatic nerve in the back of the leg.

Summary.

From all the examples I have given to you, it is quite easy to see that neural pain accounts for a significant number of chronic pain syndromes. Neural pain may be combined with muscle pain to form a pain complex. Unfortunately, most cases of nerve damage will remain with an individual for the rest of his or her life. The Scottsdale Pain Relief Program's Lifetime Maintenance Program will be essential not only for initial pain relief but also for the possibility of continued pain relief in the future.

Your Pain Relief Statement

Your pain relief statement will be inserted on day six and is to be used with your personalized pain relief formula. Your statement should be as follows:

I am in control of my _____ [pain condition or pain site] and
my [emotions].
Example: I am in control of my facial pain and my anxiety reaction.

Temporomandibular Disorder Joint Dysfunction (TMJ or TMD)

Of all stress-related disorders, TMJ syndrome possibly may be the
most misdiagnosed and most controversial. Even the name *TMJ* has
recently (in 1983) been changed by the American Dental Association
to *TMD*, standing for *temporomandibular disorder*.

Estimates of the number of people suffering from TMD have gone
as high as seventy-five million Americans. Most specialists agree that
women appear to make up the majority of sufferers.

Symptom Complex.

TMD pain is usually accompanied by ringing or buzzing in the ears,
worn-down teeth, sinus problems, or pain in the areas of the jaw,
face, and neck. In forming a diagnosis of TMD, most specialists will
look for a clicking sound when the mouth is opened or closed, which
is caused by the late slotting of a disk into position within the joint of
the jaw.

Stress Related.

There is almost total agreement that chronic stress plays a definite
and detrimental role in the development and continuation of TMD
pain. Nighttime bruxism (teeth grinding) has been related directly to
a person's inability to deal appropriately with stress. The tension is
carried into his or her sleep cycle. This has been identified with
TMD symptoms.

Have you ever seen anybody who has a tight-jaw personality? These people usually are anxious, overstressed, and easily angered. The dysfunctional emotions are translated into increased muscle tension, which keeps the muscles of the jaw in a constant state of muscle contraction. This possibly leads to a TMD condition. Most people can experience briefly what TMD is like by playing a reed instrument for a prolonged period of time, snorkeling, biting on a pencil, or cradling the telephone between shoulder and ear. These activities may irritate the temporomandibular joint and associated musculature, which can lead to pain.

Summary.

TMJ or TMD is a difficult pain condition to diagnose since it may duplicate the symptoms of dental problems, neck irritations, or head injuries. The causes of TMD include misalignment of the jaw due to: hereditary factors, accident, missing teeth, or stress. Additionally, the syndrome may be the result of teeth grinding (bruxism) or daily activities such as the way you use the telephone or continuous gum chewing.

Your Pain Relief Statement

We have established a definite connection between stress and TMD. The personalized pain relief formula, which includes the pain relief statement, will prove to be beneficial both in reducing the muscle tension behavior and overall discomfort and in short-circuiting your stress response.

This pain relief statement is to be inserted on day six into your personalized pain relief formula.

I am in control of my pain and stress.

Abdominal Pain

Abdominal pain may show itself through various conditions or diseases. Some of these are listed below:

Crohn's disease
Irritable bowel syndrome
Menstrual cramps
Ulcerative colitis
Ulcers

The list is not by any means complete. In many abdominal pain conditions, stress plays a significant role in the development and continuation of the pain. Ulcers and colitis are two of the more common conditions directly related to a person's inability to deal with stress appropriately.

(Note: If you have any sudden, incapacitating pain in your abdomen for more than thirty minutes or abdominal pain that awakens you at night, or if you experience any rectal bleeding, seek medical advice immediately.)

It's Stress Related.

If your physician has informed you that your abdominal pain, whether it be from ulcers, colitis, or irritable bowel syndrome, has its roots in your stress response, then you definitely need to use the Scottsdale Pain Relief Program for reducing the pain response and short-circuiting stress. Some of the conditions causing abdominal pain may disappear completely after appropriate use of the Scottsdale Pain Relief Program, especially if they are stress related.

The Stress Connection.

If you have been told that your pain is related directly to stress or that stress is increasing your pain, then you need to follow several steps to reduce and, in many cases, extinguish your pain.

Evaluate which stresses in your present environment may be reduced.

Complete the Scottsdale Pain Relief Program and utilize the Lifetime Maintenance Program.

Check with your physician about possible changes in your diet.

Become involved in an appropriate activity/exercise/program that will serve as an excellent means for preventing buildup and releasing stressful reactions.

Your Pain Relief Statement

The pain relief statement should be inserted on day six. Do not forget to include the emotional part of the statement.

I am in control of my abdominal pain and emotions. (You may state specific emotions for further emphasis.)
Example: I am in control of my abdominal pain and anxiety.

Burns

Burns can be the most devastating and pain-producing conditions known. Some of the most difficult and heart-wrenching times in my professional practice have involved working with burn pain patients, especially when pain medication had little or no effect on their suffering.

Patients suffering from burns have used the Scottsdale Pain Relief Program successfully as a means of coping with the constant, sometimes unbelievably severe pain following the initial burning and during the numerous medical procedures that are performed directly on the burns themselves. When you suffer from burns, it is always difficult to find a comfortable sleeping position. Burn patients have found that the Scottsdale Pain Relief Program has helped them control the devastation of their pain and allowed them to get more sleep and rest.

Emotional Benefits of the Program.

Besides the pain relief aspects of the Scottsdale Pain Relief Program, burn patients have used the personalized pain relief formula to help regain emotional control of the severe depression that often accompanies burn rehabilitation.

Your Pain Relief Statement

Your pain relief statement should be inserted on day six in your personalized pain relief formula.

I am in control of my pain and my body and my mind work together in the healing process.

Cancer Pain

In chapter four I will mention the work and study I have participated in with Dr. Carl Simonton. Some of my early ideas regarding pain control were stimulated by the teachings of Dr. Carl Simonton and Stephanie Mathews Simonton since these ideas they related to their work with cancer patients.

Numerous forms of cancer can be extremely painful, and over time traditional medications begin to lose their effectiveness. Patients with cancer who have used the Scottsdale Pain Relief Program not only use their pain control object for pain relief but also incorporate the concept of their white blood cells destroying the cancer and combine this with their mental imagery.

(Note: The Scottsdale Pain Relief Program and mental imagery for cancer should not be used as a substitute for appropriate medical diagnosis and treatment. They can serve as an excellent companion to therapy for anyone who experiences the devastation of cancer.)

Your Pain Relief Statement

The pain relief statement for cancer pain will be somewhat different from the other pain relief statements. The pain relief statement should be inserted into the personalized pain relief formula on day six.

I am in control of my _____ [pain site, pain condition, or cancer site] and my body attacks the cancer.

Sports Injuries

Ever since we have become a jogging, walking, bicycling, fitness-minded population, there has been a significant increase in sports injuries. Five years ago one would be hard-pressed to find a listing for a sports injury clinic in the physicians' section of the phone book, but that has changed in direct proportion to the numbers of people who have taken on repetitive activities and exercises as part of their life-style.

Not Without Injuries.

The numbers and types of sports injuries appear to be increasing each year. Here is a list of just a few:

Backache
Exertion headaches
Tension headaches
Tendinitis
Neck injuries
Bone and joint injuries

You will notice immediately that many of the sports injuries are mentioned in other sections of this chapter. There is a significant degree of crossover.

You should never self-diagnose or self-treat a sports injury. Consult a qualified physician who specializes in them. If you find that even with appropriate medical treatment you still have the pain and discomfort, then you may want to use the Scottsdale Pain Relief Program.

Your Pain Relief Statement

Your pain relief statement for conditions related to sports injuries will be as follows:

I am in control of my _____ [pain site or pain condition] and my emotions are calm.

Additional Pain Segments with Pain Relief Statements

I have tried to present you with a variety of pain segments. Here are some additional pain conditions and situations along with pain statements.

Dental Pain.

I AM IN CONTROL OF MY _____ *[pain site or condition]*.

Example: I am in control of my tooth pain.

Phantom Limb Pain.

I AM IN CONTROL OF THE PAIN IN MY _____ *[pain site]*.

Example: I am in control of the pain in my arm.

Postsurgical Pain.

I AM IN CONTROL OF MY _____[pain site] AND MY BODY
AND MIND WORK TOGETHER TO HELP THE HEALING PROCESS.

Example: I am in control of my shoulder pain and my mind and body
work together to help the healing process.

Raynaud's Disease.

I AM IN CONTROL OF MY _____ [pain site] PAIN AND MY
_____ [affected areas] ARE WARM.

Example: I am in control of my hand pain and my fingers are warm.

If you are experiencing any pain that has not been discussed, and
you have been evaluated by a physician, then follow these instructions.

Using the standard pain relief statement, insert your pain site or
pain condition along with one of the following emotional control
inserts:

Stress	Frustration
Depression	Fear
Anxiety	Emotions
Anger	Self-confidence
	Self-worth

Here is the pain relief statement to complete:

I AM IN CONTROL OF MY _____ [pain site or condition] AND
MY _____ [emotional control insert].

Example: I am in control of my back pain and my depression.

When You Should See a Doctor Regarding Your Pain

You should call a doctor when:

The pain is new and you have never experienced it before.

There appears to be no explanation why the pain started.

Your usual pain has worsened progressively and continues to increase in intensity.

You are having a fever with the pain.

You cannot urinate..

You have bowel dysfunction.

The pain appears to be out of proportion to the injury or reason for discomfort.

Selecting an Appropriate Doctor.

We do it numerous times during our lives, but usually on the basis of family tradition or friends' recommendations. I'm talking about the selection of a doctor to evaluate or treat your pain condition.

I always tell my patients that the process of selecting a physician should be approached from a consumer's standpoint. Recommendations of friends or family should be an important part of the overall selection process, but you need to consider the physician's training, treatment philosophy, and willingness to be an active member of your treatment team. This team might be just yourself and the doctor, but it could include other specialists. There are three very important steps in the selection of a physician:

1. Checking his or her credentials, training, recommendations, and references from former patients

2. Determining his or her willingness to answer your questions
3. Listening: Does the doctor hear what you are saying?

Always remember that you are a consumer and there is absolutely nothing wrong with interviewing a prospective doctor who might play an important role in your medical care.

CHAPTER FOUR

The Scottsdale Pain Relief Program

The Basics.

At last, here you are.

The tantalizing concept of controlling your pain—the main reason you are reading this book—is now within reach and yours for the taking. Like anything else that is achieved in life, there is hard work needed to develop the skills by which you, like so many others, will be able to gain control over your pain.

The basic program covers seven consecutive days and must be completed in the proper order. Following the end of the basic program, you will be directed to segments designed for your specific pain problem. These segments will provide you with more methods and suggestions for relief of your pain.

On day eight, you will begin the Lifetime Maintenance Program.

I have attempted to make all directions and instructions simple, straightforward, and easy to apply. There is no need for elaborate, expensive equipment or devices. The Scottsdale Pain Relief Program is not like that Christmas bicycle you struggled to assemble on December 24 with the instructions reading "Simple Assembly—Only Screwdriver Needed." After numerous skinned knuckles, curses under your breath, and confusion over those "simple" instructions and diagrams, you neared the end of your task only to find the most vital part *missing*.

I will guarantee you that nothing is missing from the Scottsdale Pain Relief Program—since the single most important ingredient is *YOU!*

Using the Scottsdale Pain Relief Program.

To help you better understand and more fully use the Scottsdale Pain Relief Program, I have included the most common and frequently asked questions along with my answers.

Question: "Will the Scottsdale Pain Relief Program take away all my pain?"

Answer: The program is designed to teach you how to control pain. The program in itself cannot reduce any pain but is simply a vehicle to be used by you for pain reduction and control.

Question: "What if I don't have any built-in painkillers?"

Answer: Everyone has natural painkillers within their body. These painkillers are called *endorphins* (for *endogenous morphinelike substances*) and are produced by the brain.

Question: "Can I start the program and then finish it at another time?"

Answer: No. The program should not be started unless you are committed to completing the full seven days without interruption.

Question: "How much time a day will I have to spend during the seven-day program?"

Answer: Usually everyone's time varies, but the minimum amount of time for successful completion of the program appears to be approximately sixty minutes per day.

Question: "Do I practice the program once a day?"

Answer: The more you practice, the greater the effectiveness of the pain relief formula. There will be a morning session and an evening session with daily practice. After you have developed your custom formula, it should only take you less than a minute to use the formula. You should practice as many times a day as possible, making pain relief a habit.

Question: "Will I have to practice for the rest of my life?"

Answer: Yes, but once your pain relief formulas become a habit, you may only have to devote several minutes a day to it.

Question: "Are there any harmful side effects to the program?"

Answer: No. If you have obtained approval from your doctor regarding any physical restrictions, then there are no detrimental side effects from the Scottsdale Pain Relief Program.

Question: "Can the program be used with any type of pain?"

Answer: The Scottsdale Pain Relief Program has been designed to be capable of providing pain relief for any type of pain condition. Of course, you should have any pain condition diagnosed by a physician first to insure that the condition is not life threatening!

The Body/Mind Connection

The Body's Built-In Painkillers.

The nineteenth century provided us with the first glimpse of man's attempt to identify the body's built-in ability to conquer pain. The physicist James Clark Maxwell dabbled in many diverse areas, one of them being the athlete's endurance of pain. He was intrigued by the seemingly endless stories of top athletes performing to and beyond points of pain. Why could they keep going even when the very fibers of their exhausted bodies were trying to scream out in pain? What mechanism within them was activated to block this pain and allow them to continue?

The Brain Connection

The body is a tremendously complicated electrochemical system that is controlled significantly by your emotions, your outlook on life, and your ability to counteract the effects of stress, tension, anxiety, depression, and pain.

It is quite amazing to realize that the brain contains over one hundred billion nerve cells and even though almost none of these actually touch each other, they carry messages back and forth across gaps known as synapses. The degree to which messages are transported between nerve cells in the brain can be linked to neurotransmitters, which either slow down, block, or allow the messages to pass from one cell to another. Pain is one of these messages. It can be stopped or reduced by altering the brain's ability to pass a pain impulse from one cell to the next. Since the mid-1970s and the discovery of endorphins (the body's naturally produced painkillers), we have understood better some of the functioning that occurs with pain and the decrease of pain when these internal chemicals are produced. The simplest explanation of why endorphins work is that by slowing down the transmission of data (pain information), endorphins actually facilitate a decrease or block in our perception of pain.

The Automatic Response.

Although we can be certain the automatic response occurred before written history, we only have to go back through the course of recorded human existence to find examples of an inborn response for short-circuiting pain in survival situations.

Here are two modern-day examples of the automatic response.

CASE ONE.   The late-model sedan careened out of control on the icy highway, slewing from side to side until crashing broadside into a utility pole. Mrs. Cramer was thrown from the wreck and lay dazed on the gravel shoulder of the road. As consciousness gradually returned to her cloudy thoughts, she heard her eight-year-old daughter's screams coming from the shattered car. Somewhat unsteady at first, she stood up and ran toward the car as the first flames burst from underneath the engine compartment. She could see her daughter screaming and staring at her out the window on the driver's side. She reached the car and pulled open the door, lifting out her daughter in one swift motion. She ran as fast as she could and fell exhausted by the side of the road as the car erupted in flames, sending waves of blistering heat into the freezing night.

When the ambulance attendants checked the mother, they found that she had what appeared to be a severe fracture of her right forearm and a severely swollen ankle. She reported having felt no pain when she pulled her daughter from the car and raced to safety. Somehow her mind had produced painkillers that allowed her to save her daughter's life. She did not experience the excruciating pain of her injuries until safely in the ambulance.

CASE TWO.   It was third down and the home team needed eight yards in a game marked by mud, rain, and thudding impacts which could be heard all the way to the press box. Tom had played the whole game at defensive tackle. Through his exhaustion, he realized that if their defense could prevent the other team from gaining a first down, then his team could protect their slim lead and win the game. He focused his mind away from everything else and on the man in front of him. He prepared to summon every last ounce of strength for the charge into his opponent, which would lead him into the backfield and the opposing quarterback. All fatigue and exhaustion were pushed aside, and the mental picture of him pulling the quarterback into his grasp flashed through his mind. As if in a trance, his body exploded forward at the snap of the football, stepping left, moving right, and shouldering the blocker out of his way. Time seemed to elongate as he raced into the opponent's backfield with his only thought to reach the quarterback before he could throw the football. As the quarterback's arm pulled back, Tom lunged forward, driving his arms and shoulders into the quarterback's side and causing the ball to burst from his hand.

Tom ran to the sidelines with the cheers of the crowd ringing in his ears. He sat on the bench, took off his helmet, and reached for a squeeze bottle of water. The gun sounded.

They had won. Tom now allowed himself to feel an overwhelming sense of fatigue and exhaustion. It was not until he was removing his shoulder pads in the locker room that Tom found that two of the fingers on his left hand had been broken sometime during the game and only now throbbed as if they were on fire.

CASE THREE. Kate had been playing outside with several other seven-year-olds from the neighborhood. She knew that her mother didn't want her to stand on her brother's skateboard, but she tried anyway. On the smooth driveway surface the skateboard shot out from under her, and she fell backward, scraping her elbow along the rough surface. There was sudden shock and pain, which increased as she looked at her arm and saw a beginning droplet of blood forming within the abrasion. Tears swelled in her eyes as she ran to the house calling for her mother. In the bathroom her mother washed the wound, put antiseptic on it, and applied a bandage. The scrape now hurt worse than when she had first injured the arm. The stinging and burning wouldn't go away, and Kate continued to sob. Her mother sat Kate on the couch and turned on the television. Through her sobs and pain, Kate heard familiar voices, and looking up she saw a Chip 'n' Dale cartoon. Within thirty seconds, Kate no longer felt the pain in her arm but was totally preoccupied with her favorite cartoon characters.

In each of these cases a mechanism within the body and controlled by the brain blocked the individual's pain. The length of time and the circumstances differed, but the basic fact remained the same: Each of us has the capability of blocking, reducing, and controlling pain. This is possibly a survival response passed on from our cavemen ancestors and nearly lost from thousands of years of disuse.

Threshold versus Tolerance.

The point at which anyone becomes aware of pain is called the pain threshold or recognition level. This is the body's method for warning us of some malfunction or injury within our systems. The recognition level may vary from person to person. One individual might feel a paper cut on the finger as a minor discomfort, while another with a lower pain threshold experiences the injury as a more significant pain. The difference in each individual's perception of pain is known as the pain tolerance, which indicates how much pain someone can tolerate. We all know people who can withstand greater or lesser degrees of pain than we can.

One major objective of the Scottsdale Pain Relief Program is to increase your pain tolerance through production of the body's built-in painkillers. An advantage to this system lies in the fact that although someone's tolerance for pain might be increased, the pain threshold remains constant and therefore the body's warning signal will continue to effectively alert you to malfunctions or injuries.

If the body's built-in pain system were to cancel out automatically any pain within the body, then your safety would be in jeopardy. The only time the body appears to block out pain totally is during extreme trauma, in life-threatening situations, and only for a short amount of time.

Pain is very much like the horn on a car: It warns of impending problems and helps you avoid accidents. If the horn becomes stuck, then it no longer serves its warning purpose but becomes an irritant. The same applies to pain. When it continues on after the initial warning and results in chronic discomfort, then it becomes like a stuck horn.

It's in the Blood.

What better system is there within the body to transport the body's built-in painkillers? The blood travels to virtually every area of the body, from the tip of your tiniest toe to the top of your head. This miraculous transport system has been found to be the main carrier of the body's naturally produced opioids. Beta-endorphin was reported discovered in the circulation as early as 1977. The source of this opioid is believed to be the anterior and intermediate lobes of the pituitary gland. It is carried in the blood via the plasma. Enkephalin, also a circulating opioid, finds its source in the adrenal medulla of the brain.

From the beginning of my work with pain, I was aware of a phenomena that occasionally took place in doctors' offices and hospitals. A patient, experiencing significant pain from a surgical procedure, was administered a shot of demerol every four hours. After several days of injections, the doctor decided to stop them in favor of a weaker medication. The patient continued to complain of pain, and so the doctor decided to conduct an experiment. When the next shot was ordered, the doctor had the nurse administer a syringe of saline water instead of the demerol. The nurse proclaimed to the patient that the shot would take effect in just a few minutes. Sure enough, upon the nurse's return, the patient commented on the wonderful pain-relieving qualities of the injection. In many cases the patient would then fall asleep, relaxed and in significantly less discomfort.

The use of saline injections, sugar pills, and other substitution devices has been known for many years to create an effect known as the placebo response. The patients think they have received something to reduce the pain, and their belief systems transmit that message to the brain, which in turn responds by producing the body's built-in painkillers. The patients mistakenly think the relief is due to the medication.

When Are the Opioids Produced?

Stress

Under severe stress, both physical and emotional, the body will automatically produce the opioid peptides (painkillers) and dump them into circulation, thus producing pain-killing effects. Rarely does a day go by that we don't read in a newspaper of some traumatic incident such as the mother, critically injured in a car accident, who walks four miles to summon help for her unconscious child. The article goes on to state that the mother felt little pain, only numbness, as she struggled to save her daughter. We often hear a sports story like that of the professional football player who broke two fingers in the championship game but didn't notice the pain until the final gun sounded and he was sitting in the locker room, staring at his throbbing fingers.

Physical Exertion

Runner's High is a term that Wide World of Sports has popularized through their coverage of long-distance running events ranging from the Boston Marathon to the Iron Man Triathlon in Hawaii. Commentators, many of whom are former top athletes, will note during the middle and later stages of a race that the runners are experiencing a second wind or a runner's high. What does this phenomenon create for the runner? Many report a feeling of well-being, a sense of floating, and an ability to go beyond physical limitations. How does this mechanism occur? Study upon study has shown that under continued physical exertion the brain sends signals to opioid-producing stations within the body and there is a dramatic increase in blood plasma levels of beta-endorphin. Additionally, other circulating hormones and chemicals are produced that have been linked directly to reducing depression and anxiety.

Many of the world's top athletes actually train the body to the peak of conditioning. Besides gaining muscular strength and cardiovascular endurance, they are also training the body to produce its own built-in painkillers and emotion stabilizers on demand.

Acupuncture

Known for thousands of years throughout the Far East and China as a procedure for the elimination of pain, acupuncture is now gaining wider acceptance in the Western world. What mechanism within the body is activated through the skillful use of the acupuncture needle? Scientists seeking an answer to this question have found that plasma levels of opioids appear to increase with certain types of acupuncture. Medical researchers in China and other Eastern countries have written and talked of the body's ability to suppress pain. To them the notion is not new, but rather it is an accepted fact of life.

Their culture has always looked to mechanisms within the body to heal, to increase the body's tolerance to pain, or actually to diminish pain. Our culture has developed around the notion that the body is healed by medication, surgery, radiation—essentially everything outside of the body.

Sexual Activity

The feelings of ecstasy and pleasure experienced during intense sexual activity may be more than a product of one's fantasy, since the level of the body's built-in painkillers (beta-endorphins) increases dramatically with sexual behavior. This ability of the body is not limited just to one specific age group.

And All the Others

Hypnosis, self-hypnosis, trances, TM, food deprivation, pregnancy, isolation, hibernation, suggestion, and the placebo effect have all been shown to increase the body's tolerance to pain.

Your Built-In Painkillers

The Scottsdale Pain Relief Program will teach you how to develop the ability to activate your own built-in painkillers to decrease your specific pain. Once you have completed the seven-day program, then all of the skills needed to customize the formulas for your specific pain will be at your disposal.

Pain Control Imagery

The use of mental imagery as a technique for facilitating the combined efforts between mind and body has been well documented for years. Between 1975 and 1976, I had the opportunity to be in the first group of professionals training in a special program under the guidance of Carl Simonton, M.D. in Fort Worth, Texas. Dr. Simonton is an oncologist who, after years of using the traditional methods including radiation and chemotherapy to treat his cancer patients, became concerned that there was no alternative that involved the individual's own ability to fight cancer. He noted that some people would have "miraculous" remissions from what were considered fatal tumors, and he began to study the differences that might exist between these people and people with similar cancers who succumbed. His research led him back to the late 1800s when physicians had already begun to explore the relationship between the mind and the body and how an individual's thought process could affect his or her physical health. Once Dr. Simonton had established the link between the mind and body, he set about with coworkers to develop a program that could teach terminally ill cancer patients how to activate their immune system to destroy cancer cells. This involved the teaching of deep relaxation techniques combined with specialized mental imagery. Some patients imagined their white blood cells as Pac Man–like creatures traveling through the body to the site of the tumor and gobbling up the cancerous cells. Dr. Simonton's research indicated that patients who were capable of developing this type of mental imagery had a higher rate of remission than patients with similar conditions who were being treated through traditional means.

When I studied in Fort Worth, Texas, with Dr. Simonton, I had just established a pain center in Scottsdale, Arizona. I was treating cancer patients for their pain, but I felt that more could be accomplished. Unfortunately, the techniques used by Dr. Simonton at that time and further developed since lay somewhat dormant in my mind and in dusty notes in my office until about three years ago. Then a patient told me that during a deep relaxation session, she would imagine a big sponge traveling inside her body to the site of the pain. The pain was a green liquid that the sponge could soak up. The pain would decrease, and she would feel better. After she made these remarks, I went back to my notes and spent a considerable amount of time in the library researching the latest documents regarding the use of imagery. I concluded that this could be the missing link needed to help the pain sufferer activate, on a consistent basis, the body's built-in painkillers, the endorphins.

It took me almost a year to develop the specific formulas for teaching someone how to activate the body's built-in painkillers through the use of mental imagery. I will provide you with examples from some of my patients of how they applied their particular type of mental imagery to a specific pain problem. Of course, your mental imagery will be designed by you, for you. Because it will be customized to your circumstances, you will gain the greatest benefit.

Finally: The Formulas

By combining the use of autogenic therapy and mental imagery, I was able to complete the pain relief formulas. With the help of hundreds of patients, the program I am about to present to you represents the summation of research and trial and error, a product that has been proven to provide not only temporary pain reduction but also a plan to regain the ability to enjoy life through a Lifetime Maintenance Program.

Starting the Program.

Starting the Scottsdale Pain Relief Program is not merely a matter of reading the book and saying, "Well, I guess I'll start tomorrow." Preprogram preparation will be one of your keys to success.

Most people have found the best starting day to be a Saturday. This allows them Saturday and Sunday for adjustment to the routine. The following Saturday, you will begin the Lifetime Maintenance Program. The final choice as to starting day will be up to you, but allow at least a full day prior to day one for completion of the program setup.

All of the instructions in the preprogram should be followed carefully and completely. Completing the preprogram will take approximately two hours of uninterrupted time.

The Old Do's and Don't's.

Do follow the programs exactly from day to day

Do take your time

Do read through the entire program before beginning

Do practice the exercises and activities exactly as they are presented

Do involve your spouse or significant other if you desire

Do make sure you congratulate yourself for successes

Do discuss any physical changes that may occur with your physician

Don't skip any of the days

Don't get ahead of yourself

Don't expect too much, too soon

Don't expect the pain to disappear totally after seven days

Don't intermix any other techniques with this program

Don't plan any trips, vacations, or other significant activities during the seven-day program

Don't become frustrated

Don't change your practice times from day to day

Don't use this program as a substitute for proper medical care

What You Will Need.

Here's your list of items you will need prior to beginning the program. These should be available to you during the preprogram.

Two pencils

Colored markers or crayons

An 8″ × 10″ notebook or at least fifteen sheets of notebook-type, lined paper

Ten 5″ × 7″ index cards

One roll of cellophane tape

Optional: *A portable cassette tape recorder and two blank cassettes*

All of these items should be placed in one location along with your book.

A Place to Practice.

You will need to practice the morning and evening segments of your program at the same location, which should be a room that will provide you with a quiet, undisturbed environment. The room you select should have either a bed or lounge chair for your use. During practice sessions, any telephones in the room should be unplugged.

Insuring a quiet, undisturbed environment for your morning and evening segments is absolutely essential. If there are family members in your house, you will need to have a meeting with them prior to starting your program. By now, your spouse should be aware of the Scottsdale Pain Relief Program and you both should have taken time to review chapters one through four. This will have given you specific ideas for how to tell your family about the program and how to request their cooperation in an assertive manner. If you have prepared your family members properly, then their cooperation will help you to be successful. You don't have time in your program to be interrupted constantly with requests that could wait until after you have finished your practice.

Day by Day.

Day one of the Scottsdale Pain Relief Program will establish the routine that will be followed on days two through seven. Each daily program has been divided into three segments.

The Morning Program

This segment will take approximately twenty minutes for completion. It is to be performed while you are still in bed, at the same time each morning. The night before, you will review the next day's program and plan the coming day. The morning segment will consist of the pain control imagery and specific assignments that are to be completed during the day whether you are at home or at work.

The Day Program

Special practice assignments will be given during the morning segment that *must* be completed during the day (prior to 6:00 P.M.). These special practice assignments are to be performed once hourly for the first four days and twice hourly during days five through seven. Each practice segment will take no longer than twenty seconds for completion and during an average nine-hour day will require no more than six minutes of your time. The day program is designed not to interfere with any of your normal activities. Each of the seven day programs will differ slightly in content and direction, although the focus remains constant toward the development of a pain self-regulating system through repetition and constant reinforcement.

The Evening Program

The evening program will be performed just prior to your going to bed but should be at the same time each evening. This segment will take twenty minutes and will serve as a summary of the morning and day segments. Each evening program will be completed by a review of the next day's activities.

Pain Control Imagery

Putting It Together.

We've waited long enough. The time has now arrived for you to take the first step toward successful completion of the Scottsdale Pain Relief Program. Before beginning the seven-day program, you will need to develop some basics for your pain imagery.

Here is an outline of what I'm going to ask you to do and why.

1. *Pain Diagram.*
   The pain diagram will help you define more accurately the exact areas of your pain. The diagram will be used in your mental imagery as a targeting device. The diagram and pain areas will be used to provide target areas for your endorphins.

2. *Pain Color.*
   The pain color will be used to represent your discomfort. The most popular colors to describe pain appear to be red, black, and dark blue (or purple). You will learn how to develop your own color, which from this point on will represent pain.

3. *Pain Object(s).*
   Selecting your pain object or objects is an extremely important aspect of your total pain control imagery program and the development of your personalized pain relief formula. When you combine your pain object with the pain color, you will have your personalized representation of what pain would look like in your body. Be as graphic and detailed as possible. Once you have combined the pain object and the pain color, you will have the pain target for your built-in painkillers (endorphins).

4. *Pain Control Color.*
   The pain control color should be powerful. It is your representation of what color the endorphins are within your body. Some choices for the pain control color have been yellow, light blue, orange, and green.

5. *Pain Control Object(s).*
   The pain control object or objects will also be part of your personalized representation of the body's built-in painkiller system. The pain object will be attacked by your pain control object. Make sure your pain control object is your own creation; don't rush or take someone else's suggestion. Take all the time you need and make sure that your pain control object is a product of your own imagination and thought process.

(Note: If you have any difficulty imagining the color of either the pain object or the pain control object, don't become discouraged or try to force the imagery. If you are not successful on your first attempt, take a short break and then come back to try again. Mental imagery is a technique that all of us used as children, but unfortunately much of this ability was put to the wayside as we grew older. You never lost the ability, but it may take some effort and patience on your part, so don't be discouraged.)

Pain Diagram.

Using the figures provided in this book, you may mark your areas of pain by shading in pencil or tracing the diagram onto another piece of paper to complete your pain diagram. Do not throw this away for we are going to refer to it during the program.

Take a look at your diagram and evaluate it. Is this the area or areas where you are experiencing the most pain? If the site of your pain changes, then pick the most frequent area. Ask yourself the question, "If someone else were to look at my drawing, would they be able to describe where my pain is?" If your answer is yes, then you have successfully completed your pain diagram.

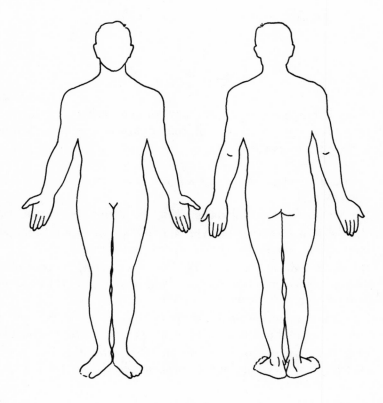

Pain Imagery.

For this exercise you may follow the same direction as the pain diagram either using the book or paper. Please do this alone, without the help of others, since the pain imagery has to be developed by you—to be used by you—to be effective for you.

Pain Color

For all you budding artists, we are now going to pick a color to represent your pain. This exercise will take approximately five minutes. Follow the directions carefully.

1. Find a quiet place where you will not be disturbed for at least five minutes.
2. Lie down or sit in a comfortable chair, whichever is more convenient.
3. Take a deep breath in through your mouth and let it out slowly through your nose, closing your eyes as you exhale.
4. Breath in and out nice and easy five times, taking in your breath through your mouth and exhaling through your nose. Count silently to yourself as you exhale each breath.
5. Now use your imagination and picture in your mind that you are standing in front of a blackboard with a piece of chalk in your hand.
6. Once the image of yourself standing in front of the blackboard is firm, take the chalk and write on your imaginary blackboard the word *pain* in large letters.
7. When you have completed the word, write the name of the first color that comes to mind below the word *pain*.
8. Now imagine yourself away from the blackboard, and in front of you on a table there is a large sheet of white paper.
9. Picture yourself writing on this large sheet of paper the word *pain* in the color you selected on the blackboard.
10. Picture the word *pain* in the color you selected clearly in your mind.
11. Open your eyes, and you now have your pain color.

You are now through the first exercise. If your family has been quiet and has not disturbed you, please don't forget to thank them. If they ask what you have been doing, share your exercise with them. By keeping them informed of the different exercises you do in the program and of your progress, you will allow them to become a positive factor in your Scottsdale Pain Relief Program rather than disinterested or confused observers.

The color you have selected to represent pain will now be used in all of your pain relief formulas to represent your particular pain. Once you pick the color, stick with it. Don't change once you start the program.

Pain Object(s).

To select your pain objects, you don't need to go through the same procedure that you did for your pain color. The pain objects will be used at the site of your pain and will be *your* pain objects. These objects are developed as part of your imagination, and they should be a visual imagery representation of what your pain means to you. To give you a few ideas, I have included some pain objects that people have used:

Tiny creatures with big claws and sharp teeth

Spiders

Crabs with big claws

Groups of X's

Clusters of dots

Worms with teeth

Fungi

Because the pain object should be the visual representation of your pain, if your pain is pinching, your objects may have claws. If your pain is stabbing, your objects may have spears or sharp claws.

Take a few minutes to think about your pain, referring to the information sheet where you described how your pain felt, and try to apply the characteristics to the pain objects you have selected.

Now take a sheet of paper and on it draw your pain objects. *(Note:*

Use a pencil first to draw your pain objects and make any changes until they look like *your* pain. You will not be graded on your artistic ability. You should never have anyone else draw your pain objects since this has to be the representation you will use in the pain imagery.)

Pain Controllers

Pain Control Color.

To develop your pain controllers, you will need to make a return visit to that quiet place where you selected your pain color. Let anyone around know that you will be busy for approximately five minutes and not to interrupt you. Use the following procedures:

1. Find as comfortable a position as possible, whether lying down or sitting.
2. Take a deep breath in through your mouth and let it out slowly through your nose, allowing your body to settle as much as possible.
3. Take five deep breaths, inhaling through your mouth and exhaling through your nose. As you exhale through your nose, silently count to yourself for each deep breath.
4. Try to clear your mind of any thoughts you might have as if you were painting over a window with white paint.
5. Now picture the most pleasant scene you possibly can, whether it be at the park, beach, countryside, or mountains. Fill in the scene with relaxing sights and sounds. This scene may represent a place where you have been before that you found to be very relaxing and enjoyable.
6. Place this scene firmly in your mind. Let your mind and body enjoy the serenity of the surroundings.
7. Now silently ask yourself what your favorite color is.

8. Picture this color in your mind. Notice how you get the same feeling as you do in your favorite scene. Open your eyes and sit up slowly, taking time to stretch your arms and legs gently.

Your favorite color is now your pain control color. This will be the color of the pain control objects you use in your pain relief formulas.

Pain Control Object(s).

If you have been following along carefully, you will know what we are going to do next. It's time to decide on the characteristic of your pain control objects. The pain control objects will be in your pain control color.

To help you, I have included a list of some pain control objects that have been selected and developed by people who have successfully used the Scottsdale Pain Relief Program. Remember, the objects have to be of your choice and should not be drawn or suggested to you by anyone else. The examples are only to serve as stimulus for your own imagination.

Tiny Pac Men (Women) that gobble up the pain objects

Cats that eat the pain objects

Tiny painters that paint over the pain objects with pain control colors

Sponges that absorb the pain control objects

Go now to the sheet of paper on which you drew your pain objects. Take a pencil and draw your pain control objects. Remember the standard practice in this book: No one's art is ever graded.

Congratulations. You now have your pain color, pain objects, pain control color, and pain control objects.

Pacing Yourself.

Slow and easy wins the race.

Haste makes waste.

These are statements familiar to all of us that are important in daily life. For someone experiencing a chronic pain condition, taking the time to plan ahead and pace yourself has an extra degree of importance. Whether you are a high-powered executive or a laid-back teacher, you will need to learn the basics of appropriate pacing.

The Pacing Commandments.

Read over the Pacing Commandments and think about how you might apply them to your specific work, recreational, or home situation. If you find yourself thinking, "Well, I'm sure that's very nice, but they really don't apply to me and I don't see any need to use them," then think about whether or not you would like the following statement to apply to you:

> *The use of appropriate pacing techniques will help to prevent reinjury or exacerbation of existing pain conditions and will allow for the maximum benefit of the Scottsdale Pain Relief Program.*

Need I say more? Here are the commandments:

> *Never ride in a car for more than from forty-five to sixty minutes without stopping for a five-minute break to stretch and use your pain relief formulas.*

Never sit in one position for longer than from thirty to forty-five minutes without using your pain relief formulas.

Break difficult tasks into smaller segments, especially if they involve repetitive bending, lifting, stooping, or twisting.

Be assertive; don't accept tasks or assignments that you know will lead to possible reinjury or exacerbation of your pain.

Always use the intermission at movies, plays, or concerts to your best advantage—by using them.

Don't feel obligated to keep up with someone else; go at an appropriate speed for you.

Probably the most important commandment is not even listed as one but is simply this statement:

Always listen to what your body is trying to tell you and then act upon its advice.

Optional Activities

Throughout development and use of the Scottsdale Pain Relief Program, I have strived constantly for simplicity. Busywork in filling out numerous forms will only sidetrack you from your purpose, which is completion of the seven-day program and learning how to use the Lifetime Maintenance Program.

Some people who have used the Scottsdale Pain Relief Program find the use of a diary to rate and graph their pain helpful, and therefore I have included it as an *OPTIONAL* part of your seven-day program. Additionally, patients have commented that the use of audio cassette tapes (self-recorded) were helpful during the morning and evening practice sessions. I have included some instructions regarding the recording of your own tapes, but making audio recordings of the practice session is an *OPTIONAL* part of the seven-day program.

Music to Your Pain.

The saying that music soothes the savage beast holds a higher degree of validity than most people realize. For years I have had quiet, relaxing music playing in the background in my office while treating patients. After a few moments, they consciously do not notice the music, but the relaxing quality of the sounds seems to enhance all of their treatments for pain.

Most of us have had the experience of listening to comfortable music and feeling a heightened state of relaxation or calmness.

The brain, through your sense of hearing, will utilize appropriate music to further a state of well-being, which is generated through production of the body's internal chemicals, especially painkillers and emotion-stabilizing substances.

Selecting Your Music.

If you plan to use music as part of your seven-day program, and I strongly recommend it, take some time to determine what sort of music gives you the greatest feeling of peace, tranquility, calmness, and overall sense of well-being. Most of my patients have preferred instrumental music, often with flowing rhythms that duplicate the heartbeat of the human body while at rest.

Once you have selected the appropriate music for you, you will need to place a tape recorder or record player in your private practice area to use for morning and evening practice sessions. While you are practicing, play the music as background sound, with the volume low. Playing music while you are practicing also serves to block extraneous noises or sounds that may interfere with your concentration.

Making the Final Selection.

The best way to make your final selection of music is to gather together the tapes or records (they should be at least thirty minutes in
length) and go to your private practice area, lie down or sit in a
comfortable chair, and listen to each one of your selections. Listen to
your inner voice and evaluate how you are feeling physically and
emotionally while you are listening to the music. The selection process should be relatively easy. If you find several pieces of music (at
least thirty minutes in length) that provide you with feelings of well-
being, then you may select them all and alternate their playing during your seven-day program.

Optional Pain Relief Formula Practice Tapes

Throughout my years of working with pain patients, I have tried constantly to design more effective ways to help people practice
independently. The seven-day Scottsdale Pain Relief Program was designed for independent use. Although the program may be completed
without recording any audio cassettes, people have reported that making the tapes facilitates practice and that using the tapes is easy and
convenient.

I want to provide for every contingency that might enhance your
success with the pain relief formulas. Therefore I have developed for
the program an option of making audio cassettes of each day's practice sessions.

You may record the pain relief formulas in your own voice or that
of a friend. Small cassette tape recorders are found in nearly every
household or may be borrowed from a friend or neighbor. Using the
tape recorder as a reinforcement device becomes another step toward
increasing the probability of success.

In my own treatment I record pain relief imagery sessions and give the tape to the patient for practice until the next appointment. When my patients use the tapes, there is a noticeable improvement, especially in terms of utilizing the formulas as accurately as possible.

If you decide to record the pain relief formulas, then I strongly recommend that all recording be completed prior to your beginning the seven-day program. You will need seven blank cassettes with approximately thirty minutes on each side. Number the tapes from day one to day seven. Write on the tape the exact name of the pain relief formula.

(*Note:* Never listen to the audio cassettes while driving, operating machinery, or experiencing a hazardous situation.)

Tips on Making Your Own Tapes.

1. Carefully read over the complete script for each exercise before you record. The scripts are designed for direct reading into the tape recorder, so you should read them aloud several times before making the final recording.

2. Choose a spot and a time where you will have absolute quiet. Distracting noises such as a telephone ringing, a child yelling, or a dog barking will interfere with your concentration when you listen to the tapes for practice.

3. Take your time! Read the sentences in a relaxed voice. Try to develop a rhythm in your speech.

4. Be careful not to speak too close to the microphone, as this might garble your voice and result in static. Run through a test session to see how far away from the mike you should speak.

5. After you have completed a tape, listen to it and compare it with the script.

6. If the tape is satisfactory, then punch out the tiny plastic tab in the back of the cassette. When this is done, the tape cannot be recorded over by accident. The tab on the right is for side one and the one on the left is for side two.

Pain Relief Reminders

"I just forgot."

"I was so busy, I forgot."

"I could remember if someone set an alarm for me or reminded me."

"I was so mad when I realized that two hours had gone by without practicing."

These are common statements made to me by people going through the seven-day program. As a natural consequence of human nature, we all can become distracted and preoccupied. Unfortunately, missing several of the daily practice sessions, especially toward the end of the seven-day program when they become more intense, can lead to a decrease in the program's potency. The pain relief reminders have been developed as one technique to help you be consistent and punctual in your daily practice.

Rubber bands around wrists, strings around fingers, notes in pockets and purses, and even writing on your hands have been techniques used by people to remind them of something that has to be done. Pain relief reminders are simply what their name implies. They are little tricks you may use as reminders for your daily practice. Each individual's lifestyle is different, and their home and work situations will demand different types of reminders. When you see one of *your* reminders, there will be an immediate recognition and stimulus provided to remind you of the practice sessions required for each day of the program. Don't think the reminders are for the seven-day program only, for I'm going to ask you to continue using them even into the Lifetime Maintenance Program.

Be innovative and creative in the development of your pain relief reminders. After you use one reminder for a while, don't hesitate to change to another. If you find a reminder not working so successfully as you would like, don't hesitate or delay in changing it.

The following list represents a sampling of reminders used successfully by people in the Scottsdale Pain Relief Program.

Colored adhesive dots that can be placed on objects like telephones, desks, refrigerators, watch dials, daily calendars, and clocks

Special markings made at the appropriate times in appointment books

Asking your secretary, spouse, or coworker to help remind you, especially during the first several days (but do not rely on other people totally for your reminders; the interpersonal reminder should be combined with at least one other type of pain relief reminder)

Rubber bands on wrists

Reminder cards placed on everyday objects like desks, calendars, and car seats

The Day Before.

You start the seven-day program tomorrow. All the information and facts that you will need for successful completion of the program have been presented to you in chapters one, two, and three. By coming this far, you have shown a definite commitment, so don't turn back now. You should already have reviewed day one and taken a brief look at days two through seven. You have allotted time for the morning and evening sessions, and you have selected a pain relief reminder to help with the hourly practice sessions during the day from 9:00 A.M. to 6:00 P.M.

Everything is at your fingertips. Now all that remains is for you to begin the program.

If you are feeling a slight bit of nervousness along with hopeful anticipation, these emotions are quite normal.

I wish you the best and smoothest of journeys as you embark upon your final expedition in search for pain relief. Your reward is now coming into sight.

I have said it before, and I'll probably say it again and again throughout the book, don't be afraid to go back and review, spending all the time you need to understand fully each one of the chapters.

What You Will Do Each Day.

Each day of the program you will be presented with specific tasks to complete and formulas to practice. Don't let the simplicity and ease of directions fool you—the program has been designed for maximum impact on your specific pain problem.

Each day you will be required to do the following:

Morning practice (twenty minutes)
Daily practice (twenty seconds or less every hour until 6:00 P.M.)
Evening practice (twenty minutes)

There is definitely a necessary time commitment for each day of the seven-day program. You have to decide for yourself whether a commitment of approximately sixty minutes total time per day for participation in a program that will teach you how to obtain relief from your pain is worth the time. Let me give you a little hint and, possibly, a slight nudge. Recent time management studies indicate that all of us, whether at work or at home, waste approximately two-and-a-half hours per day that could be used for productive endeavors. The bottom line is that even with participation in the Scottsdale Pain Relief Program, you will still have one-and-a half hours per day to waste if you so desire. After giving you this information, and if you were sitting in front of me, I would now challenge you to tell me that you don't have time during your day to participate in a program that has the potential of changing the rest of your life.

Most people who have participated in the Scottsdale Pain Relief Program have little problem committing to twenty minutes in the morning and twenty minutes in the evening for practice, but they do experience some difficulty, at least in the beginning, remembering to practice the pain formulas on an hourly basis. The pain relief reminders will help you by insuring consistent practice during the day.

Preprogram Checklist.

Step by Step: At this point you are ready to begin the seven-day program. Please review the steps to make sure you have completed each one before starting day one.

1. Read chapters one through three.
2. Discuss program with family or significant others.
3. Develop pain color and object(s).
4. Develop pain control color and object(s).
5. Obtain all materials needed for the seven-day program as listed on Page 92.
6. Review day one.

If you have completed all of the steps, then it's time to begin controlling your pain.

Day One

Introduction.

Day one is about to start. Chapters one, two, and three gave you the basics, but now comes the true test of your commitment. Although I have suggested that you review the complete program prior to starting, don't get ahead of yourself. Take each day one at a time with occasional glances to the future.

Daily Review.

On each of the seven days, the daily review section will go back to highlight important aspects of the previous day's program. The review will be presented in a checklist format, and you will be asked to read each statement and answer either yes or no. If you should answer no to any question, go back to the prior day and reread that material or redo the assignment until you can answer yes to the statement. When you answer yes to all the statements, then continue to the day's pain relief formula.

Here is your first day's review. Answer yes or no to each statement.

1. Is the body capable of producing its own painkillers?
2. Do I understand the connection between emotions and pain?
3. Have I set aside special times in the morning and evening for practice?

If you have answered yes to all the statements, go on to today's pain relief formula. If you have answered no to any statement, then go back to review that area until you can answer the statement with a yes.

Today's Pain Relief Formula.

The Pain Relief Scan

The Basics.

One of the best ways for you to begin short-circuiting the pain is with the pain relief scan, which combines a specialized breathing technique with a method for reducing muscle tension or bracing.

Think back to the last time you were frightened, angry, stressed, or in severe pain, and remember how you were breathing. Most of the time your breathing changes under stress or with pain. Breathing becomes rapid, with high-in-the-chest inhalation and exhalation patterns. This type of breathing sends a message to the brain, which interprets it as danger or the fight/flight response (the extreme anxiety response that is triggered when danger or overwhelming stress is perceived and activates processes such as increased respiration, increased heart rate, and decreased blood flow to the extremities). The way you short-circuit this response is to learn a method to control your breathing and send a message to the brain that you are relaxed and in control.

The second part of the formula is the scan. When you are in pain, the muscles of the body become tense and tight, reducing the body's ability to transport fuel (oxygen, nutrients, and essential chemicals) to the muscles and carry away the waste products of muscle contraction.

Relaxed breathing and muscles enhance the body's ability to produce and use effectively its built-in painkillers.

Goals.

The pain relief scan will accomplish the following:

It will stop the stress/pain breathing response.

It will reduce muscle tension.

It will reduce pain.

Instructions.

The pain relief scan will be used to start all of the pain relief formulas. Follow the instructions carefully, reading them over completely several times before you begin.

Close your eyes.

Inhale deeply through your nose.

Hold the breath for a silent count of six.

Exhale slowly through your mouth.

(Repeat five times.)

With your eyes still closed, start at the top of your head and imagine as if someone had just begun to pour pleasantly warm water on your hair and the warmth was beginning to gently glow down your body. Picture in your mind's eye (mental imagery) the warm liquid slowly moving down your body and relaxing all the muscles it passes over.

Stop at any muscles that seem tense or tight or where you are having any pain.

Don't rush; take your time.

Keep your breathing calm and regular.

(When you reach your feet, there will be a general sensation of heaviness in the body and you may feel some warmth in your arms and legs.)

Repeat the breathing part of the formula five more times, silently counting to six while you hold your breath and then exhaling slowly through your mouth.

Take one deep breath, letting it out in a regular manner. Open your eyes, gently stretch your arms and legs, and get up slowly.

(*Important* Note: Never stand up quickly or jump up following the practice of a formula—you could become faint or dizzy and fall!)

Today's Practice

Morning Session.

TIME =   Twenty minutes

REPETITIONS =   Twice

FORMAT: Perform the complete formula while lying down or sitting in a comfortable chair. Use your private practice setting.

Daily Sessions.

TIME = Twenty seconds

REPETITIONS = Once every hour from 9 A.M. until 6 P.M. Don't forget to use the Pain Relief Reminders.

FORMAT:

Take one pain relief breath.

Hold the breath for a silent count of four.

Exhale slowly through your mouth.

Mentally picture your body and see any area where there is tension, tightness, or pain.

In your mind's eye gently pour the warm water on the areas.

Feel the relaxation.

Take one regular deep breath and let it out slowly.

(Note: This formula may be practiced with eyes open or closed. Use it both ways since it will be important to be able to activate the formulas with your eyes open under certain circumstances where it would be inappropriate to close your eyes such as driving, in a meeting, at work.)

Evening Session.

Repeat the twenty-minute morning session, in its entirety, twice.

Day One in Review

You have now completed the first day of the seven-day program, and you should congratulate yourself. Don't rest on your laurels too long, though, for we have more work to do. Go back through the day's activities and see if there were any problem areas. If you had difficulty using your practice area for the morning and evening sessions, then plan for any needed changes now—don't wait until tomorrow. If you missed an hour during the daily practice, don't despair or become discouraged; do something about it. Plan ahead for tomorrow.

Remember to go back to any of the previous chapters for review if you have any questions.

Today you have learned:

The first pain relief formula

The pain relief scan

How to practice hourly during the daily practice sessions

Day Two

Introduction.

Today we are going to learn basic imagery. This will be the starting point for your personalized pain relief formula. Like any other technique in the Scottsdale Pain Relief Program, basic imagery will take practice, commitment, and your willingness to try something new.

Daily Review.

Your daily review for today will cover day one. Please answer yes or no to each of the following statements.

1. Will proper breathing short-circuit the emotional response to pain?
2. Am I able to visualize my pain areas?
3. Is my location for morning and evening practice sessions adequate?
4. Are my pain relief reminders working?

If you have answered yes to all of the statements, go on to today's pain relief formula. If you have answered no to any statements, then go back to review that area from day one until you can answer the statement with a yes.

Today's Pain Relief Formula.

Basic Imagery

The Basics.

This pain relief formula is designed specifically for you to use as the first step toward development of your personalized pain relief formula. Basic imagery must be accomplished prior to your use of the pain objects and pain control objects.

The use of mental imagery (basic imagery) will allow you to create scenes and situations through your imagination. If this is performed with enough clarity, your brain will activate an emotional and physical response that will be compatible with your imagery.

Mental imagery is not automatic and needs to be practiced and refined to reach its peak of effectiveness. Whenever you practice your imagery, strive for the clearest, most vibrant picture. Use colors and movement if possible. It may take practice before you will be able to use color in your imagery.

Goals.

Basic imagery will accomplish the following:

It will help you mentally to define your pain areas.

It will reduce muscle tension.

It will reduce pain.

Instructions.

Basic imagery will follow the pain relief scan. Follow the instructions carefully, reading them over completely several times before you begin.

Close your eyes.

Inhale deeply through your nose.

Hold the breath for a silent count of six.

Exhale slowly through your mouth.

(Repeat five times.)

Clear your mind of any extraneous thoughts.

Count silently to yourself from twenty to one, repeating each number as you exhale.

When you reach the number one, mentally picture in your mind the most comfortable, enjoyable, relaxing scene that you possibly can. This scene may be in the countryside, by a running stream, or on a sunny, deserted beach with the sounds of waves in the background.

Try to picture your scene as completely as possible.

(*Note:* As you mentally imagine your scene, don't be afraid to put yourself into that scene, sensing smells and sounds, as if you were actually there.)

See yourself in this scene.

Notice how relaxed and completely at peace you are.

Stay in this scene for as long as you would like but with increasing clarity imagine as though you were an artist filling in a beautiful painting.

Keep your breathing calm and regular.

Repeat the breathing part of the pain relief scan five times, silently counting to six while you hold your breath, and then exhaling slowly through your mouth.

Take one deep breath, letting it out in a regular manner. Open your eyes, gently stretch your arms and legs, and get up slowly.

Today's Practice

Morning Session.

TIME =   Twenty minutes

REPETITIONS =   Once

FORMAT: Perform the complete basic imagery.

Daily Sessions.

TIME =   Twenty seconds

REPETITIONS =   Once every hour from 9:00 A.M. to 6:00 P.M.

FORMAT:

Take one pain relief breath.

Hold the breath for a silent count of four.

Exhale slowly through your mouth and allow your shoulders and arms to relax and sag slightly.

Using your basic imagery, place yourself in your favorite scene.

Picture the scene as vividly as possible for ten seconds.

Sense the calm and peaceful control.

Take one regular deep breath and let it out slowly.

(*Note:* As with day one's formula, I would like you to practice your basic imagery with your eyes open at least twenty-five percent of the time. I know this is difficult, and the first time you practice the basic imagery with your eyes open, you may only be able to develop a partial scene. This is all right. It will improve as you practice.)

Evening Session.

TIME = Twenty minutes

Repeat the morning session in its entirety, but this time try to picture your scene more quickly (without rushing too much) and spend more time placing yourself within the imagery. Be aware of what you are doing and try to sense the deep, controlled relaxation you should feel in that scene.

Day Two in Review

Day two has been demanding. Basic imagery requires you to use skills that you once had as a child and may have been forced to give up in the face of the sometimes harsh realities of life. You have not lost these skills. All of us have them within our reach, although it may take some effort to regain their use after many years.

If you would like to practice an additional twenty-minute segment after your evening session, please feel free to do so, but follow the exact procedure that you used during the day. At this point in the program do not attempt to change any of the formulas, for this may reduce their effectiveness and adversely affect your progress later in the program.

Today you have learned:

Basic imagery

How to combine the pain relief scan breathing technique with basic imagery

Day Three

Introduction.

As you enter day three of the program, you are starting to develop good practice habits and your body and mind are being trained to help you learn to control your pain.

Daily Review.

Although the daily review may seem rather simple and uncomplicated at times, never skip answering the statements.

Here is your third day's review. Answer yes or no to each statement.

1. Have I been able to develop my scene through mental imagery?
2. Is the breathing segment of the pain relief scan, which is used to begin each practice session, becoming more automatic?
3. Have I evaluated my pain relief reminders?

Today's Pain Relief Formula.

Pain Control Imagery

The Basics.

The time has arrived finally for you to use your pain control object(s). At this time go back and take a look at the section on your pain control object(s). Today we are going to take that pain control object and integrate it into your basic imagery. The integration of your pain control object into *your* favorite scene will present your first big challenge. You will be successful if you follow these simple guidelines:

> *Do not force yourself or become angry if you have difficulty with your imagery.*

If you become distracted, gently bring yourself back to your scene.

Insure during your morning and evening session that you are not interrupted.

By now you should have noticed that each formula builds upon the previous day's work, as we gradually but steadily move toward the development of your personalized pain relief formula, which will be developed fully on day five. Your progress will improve if you maintain your natural rhythm and listen to your inner pacing.

Goals.

The pain control imagery will accomplish the following:

It will improve your skills in mental visualization.

It will begin the integration of your pain control object into your favorite scene.

It will improve your ability in the twenty-second practice sessions.

Instructions.

The pain control imagery will utilize a combination of your favorite scene and your pain control object. Review your pain control object before beginning this session.

Follow the instructions carefully, reading them over completely several times before you begin.

Close your eyes.

Inhale deeply through your nose.

Hold the breath for a silent count of six.

Exhale slowly through your mouth.

(Repeat five times.)

Use the second part of your pain relief scan and allow the sensation of warm water to flow from your head to your toes.

Clear your thoughts.

Using the basic imagery, develop your special scene, putting yourself into the scene as much as you possibly can.

Focus on yourself within the scene.

Visualize that your hand is opened, palm up.

Place your pain control object in the palm of your hand.

Notice that the palm of your hand and your arm feel comfortably warm and relaxed.

Sense how comfortable you feel holding the pain control object in the palm of your hand.

Visualize the pain control object in its pain control color.

Notice how the warmth increases when you picture the pain control object in its color.

Notice how the pain control object appears to radiate a pulsing, vibrant sensation.

Now visualize that the pain control object, in its color, is becoming absorbed into the skin of your hand.

As the pain control object is absorbed, notice that your hand feels warmer, just as if you were placing it near a warm light bulb.

When the pain control object has disappeared into the skin of the palm of your hand, take one deep breath, letting it out in a regular manner. Open your eyes, gently stretch your arms and legs, and get up slowly.

Today's Practice

Morning Session.

TIME =   Twenty minutes

REPETITIONS =   Once

Daily Sessions.

TIME =   Twenty seconds

REPETITIONS =   Once every hour from 9:00 A.M. to 6:00 P.M. You may practice more than once an hour if you desire.

FORMAT:

> *Take one pain relief breath.*
> *Hold the breath for a silent count of four.*
> *Exhale slowly through the mouth.*

Use your visual imagery to picture your pain control object in the palm of your hand. You do not need to place yourself in your favorite scene, but instead look at your hand and visualize the pain control object, in its color, sitting in your palm.

Visualize the pain control object being absorbed into the palm of your hand.

Feel the increased warmth and relaxed sensation as the pain control object is absorbed into your hand.

Take one regular deep breath and let it out slowly.

Evening Session.

TIME = Twenty minutes

REPETITIONS = Once

Repeat the morning session in its entirety, concentrating on the absorption of the pain control object into the palm of your hand and always being aware of the pleasant sensation occurring as this process takes place. With increased practice, the warm, pleasant sensation you experience as the pain control object is absorbed into your hand will begin to spread up your arm and to other parts of your body.

Day Three in Review

For many this has been a difficult day. I am asking you to reach deep inside yourself and explore the limits of your mental imagery abilities although you are only three days into the Scottsdale Pain Relief Program. Before I developed the Scottsdale Pain Relief Program, I would have had to spend from one to two weeks just learning the basics and then up to four or five weeks training in an elementary type of pain control imagery. Times have changed, and I am sure you do not want to wait five weeks to get into your pain relief formula. Don't be discouraged. Keep practicing and moving forward!

Today you have learned:

Pain control imagery

The first step in learning your pain control imagery

The first step in using your pain control object

The use of mental imagery in a present-tense situation (the daily practice sessions)

Day Four

Introduction.

As we move into day four, there may be a slight frustration on your part, especially if you are pushing too hard. As I've said previously, sit back, take your time, don't rush, and pay close attention to your natural pacing. The feelings and sensations you experience following a good meal, an enjoyable movie, or a walk on a beautiful day will activate a calm inner pacing.

Today we are going to take your pain control object on a trip in your body. For the first time, you will meet up with your pain object(s).

The time has come for your pain control objects to earn their pay and go to work providing you with pain relief.

Daily Review.

The review of your first three days will be slightly more comprehensive. Answer yes or no to each statement.

1. Am I capable of visualizing my pain control objects?
2. Am I capable of visualizing my pain control object in (pain control) color?
3. Upon exhaling the first pain relief breath of any practice session, am I beginning to feel a greater sensation of overall body relaxation?
4. Has my practice schedule become automatic?

If you have answered yes to all the statements, go on to today's pain relief formula. If you have answered no to any statement, then go back to review or practice that area until you can answer the statement with a yes.

Today's Pain Relief Formula.

The Beginning Journey

The Basics.

The belief in your ability to activate your built-in painkillers should be something you never doubt. At times during the seven-day program you may question it, but never doubt the capability of your own body to control pain, as long as you are willing to provide the time and practice.

In today's formula, your pain control object will be going on a journey to one of the most exclusive destinations in the world: the inside of your body. In the course of its journey, it will come into contact with the pain object.

Goals.

Pain relief formula four—the beginning journey—will accomplish the following:

>*It will begin the built-in painkiller activation process.*
>
>*It will allow your pain control object to move within your body.*
>
>*It will develop the visualization of your pain object.*

Instructions.

Today's formula will be your most challenging endeavor, and therefore I suggest you read it a minimum of three times before attempting the practice sessions.

Follow each of the instructions carefully and do not move any faster than your normal, relaxed rate of breathing (inner pacing).

>*Close your eyes.*
>
>*Inhale deeply through your nose.*
>
>*Hold the breath for a silent count of six.*
>
>*Exhale slowly through your mouth.*
>
>*(Repeat two times.)*
>
>*Perform your pain relief scan, starting at the top of your head.*
>
>*Place yourself in your favorite scene.*
>
>*Visualize your pain control object, in its color, resting in the palm of your hand.*

Visualize and sense the increasing warmth and vibrancy of the pain control object as it begins to dissolve into the palm of your hand.

Notice the warmth as the pain control object disappears.

With your visualization, see the color of your pain control object faintly as it moves up your arm and begins to spread throughout your body.

As your pain control object travels throughout your body, feel an increase of warmth, heaviness, and general well-being.

Now move away from the scene of yourself and picture the pain object, in its color.

Notice that when you visualize the pain object the feeling of well-being that you had previously begins to disappear.

Again, visualize yourself in a favorite scene.

Think where you are experiencing the most pain or discomfort at this moment.

Picture your pain object in that part of your body where you are having the most pain or discomfort.

Notice how the pain object's color shows through the skin where you are experiencing pain.

Notice how the pain increases slightly as you focus on the pain object.

Visualize your favorite scene and place yourself there.

Imagine your whole body and see the pain object at its location.

Now picture in your mind's eye your pain control object in the palm of your hand, warm and vibrant.

Visualize the pain control object dissolving into the palm of your hand and beginning to move on a journey throughout your body toward the pain object.

Feel a sensation of warmth, relaxation, and well-being as the pain control object spreads and moves towards the pain object.

Take one deep breath, letting it out in a regular manner. Open your eyes, gently stretch your arms and legs, and get up slowly.

Today's Practice

Morning Session.

TIME =   Twenty minutes

REPETITIONS =   Once

(Note: If you want to spend additional time in your morning session, please do not restrict yourself to the twenty-minute schedule.)

FORMAT: Perform the complete beginning journey formula.

Daily Sessions.

TIME =   Twenty seconds

REPETITIONS = Once every hour from 9:00 A.M. to 6:00 P.M. I recommend practicing more than once per hour if possible, but this does not have to be accomplished consistently.

FORMAT:

Take one pain relief breath through your nose.

Exhale slowly through your mouth.

Visualize your pain object(s) at the site of the pain you are experiencing.

(*Note:* If you are not experiencing pain at the time of your practice session, then visualize the pain object at the usual site of your pain.)

Picture in your mind's eye the pain control object dissolving quickly into the palm of your hand and spreading throughout your body.

Picture the pain control object at the site of your pain object.

Take one regular deep breath through your nose and exhale normally through your mouth.

Evening Session.

TIME = Twenty minutes

REPETITIONS = Once

Repeat the morning session in its entirety, but try to visualize the pain control object entering the body more quickly and spreading throughout the body at a faster rate. At this point, the pain control object is still not to come into contact with the pain object.

Day Four in Review

You are now over halfway through your seven-day program. I know it has been demanding, but the rewards are yours for the rest of your life.

Tomorrow you will gain the final ingredient prior to the full development of your personalized pain relief formula. Once you have your personalized pain relief formula, you will find the hourly practice sessions to be more productive. Most people start practicing their personalized pain relief formulas more than once per hour.

Today you have learned:

The beginning journey

How to spread your pain control object throughout your body

The placement of your pain object at your pain site

Day Five

Introduction.

Today is a big day. You will be given the final ingredients for your personalized pain relief formula. At this point in the program, I would like you to go to chapter three and read the segment that relates to your specific pain. In each pain segment, there are suggestions relating to the customized aspect of your personalized pain relief formula.

Daily Review.

The daily review for today will be short and to the point. By this point in the program, you should be reviewing on a daily basis those items that are still somewhat unclear or trigger further questions. Most people would find it difficult to progress this far in the program without a good foundation of knowledge gained in the first three chapters and the first four days of the Scottsdale Pain Relief Program.

Here is your review for day five. Answer yes or no to each statement.

1. Does the pain relief object serve as an automatic activating device for the body's built-in painkillers (endorphins)?
2. Will the reduction in size and number of the pain objects be related directly to decreased pain and increased pain tolerance?

If you have answered yes to both these statements, go on to today's pain relief formula. If you have answered no to either statement, then go back to review that area until you can answer the statement with a yes.

Today's Pain Relief Formula.

Your Personalized Pain Relief Formula—Part One

The Basics.

Your personalized pain relief formula—part one is the initial step toward the finalization of a formula that has the capability of being activated fully, anywhere, anytime, and under any circumstances, in less than thirty seconds.

Although the previous four days of the program have been extremely important, I cannot overemphasize the need for you to become completely and totally absorbed in today's lesson along with days six and seven.

By now many of you have already begun to experience some pain relief along with beneficial emotional consequences such as less depression and anxiety and a more positive attitude toward yourself and your environment. Do not let your successes lull you into complacency. The most difficult and demanding three days of the program are ahead of you, so take a deep breath, let it out slowly, and let's begin.

Goals.

Your personalized pain relief formula—part one will accomplish the following:

> It will allow direct interaction between your pain control object and the pain object.

> It will be the first of three parts to your finalized personalized pain relief formula.

It will allow continued pain reduction.

It will provide improved psychological and emotional functioning and coping.

Instructions.

Your personalized pain relief formula—part one will be shorter in overall length than yesterday's formula, but you will be required to practice it more times during your morning and evening sessions. The shorter formula and increased practice sessions begin a conditioning process designed to develop your capabilities for activating your personalized pain relief formula in the shortest period of time possible with the highest degree of effectiveness.

Follow the instructions carefully, reading them over *twice* before you begin.

Close your eyes.

Inhale deeply through your nose.

Exhale slowly through your mouth.

Using your mental imagery, visualize the pain control object, in its color, resting in the palm of your hand.

Picture through mental imagery the pain object in its color, at your pain site.

Take a deep breath in through your nose and slowly let it out through your mouth, and as you do so, visualize the pain control object dissolving into the palm of your hand.

Visualize the color of your pain control object moving to all parts of your body, initiating a warm, heavy, and peaceful feeling and sensation.

As if you were a movie camera zooming in for a close-up, mentally picture your pain object.

(Note: If you have more than one pain site, visualize the most severe pain site at this time.)

> Visualize the pain control object beginning to interact (eat, dissolve, cover, attach) with the pain object.
>
> Visualize the pain object becoming slowly smaller.
>
> Take one deep breath, letting it out in a regular manner through your mouth. Open your eyes, gently stretch your arms and legs, and get up slowly.

(Note: If you are going to repeat the formula or continue with the visualization, do not take this final step. Perform it only at the conclusion of your session.)

Today's Practice

Morning Session.

TIME =   Twenty minutes

REPETITIONS =   Once, but the imagery should be continuous until the end of twenty minutes.

FORMAT: Perform your personalized pain relief formula—part one for a full twenty minutes. Some people will find the process of removing the pain object to be quite difficult and at the end of fifteen minutes may have only removed, destroyed, or dissolved a portion. This is perfectly all right because you may never totally or completely rid yourself of the pain object. Remember, our purpose is to reduce the pain object to a point where it is no longer adversely affecting your physical or emotional well-being.

In the morning session, when you reach the interaction point between the pain control object and the pain object, continue with that part of the visualization if you have additional time. Do not complete the entire exercise and then start again.

Daily Sessions.

TIME = Twenty seconds

REPETITIONS = Twice every hour (every thirty minutes) from 9:00 A.M. to 6:00 P.M. Practicing on a twice-hourly basis will be difficult; I fully understand this, but if we are going to make the kind of progress I am sure you want, then there has to be a commitment to twice-hourly practice. If you should feel the desire and have the time to practice more than twice an hour, please do so. Remember that even if you were to practice three times per hour, the total time used would only be *one minute*.

FORMAT:

Take one pain relief breath and exhale slowly through your mouth.

Mentally visualize your pain control object(s) attacking the pain object(s).

Take one regular deep breath and let it out slowly through your mouth.

Evening Sessions.

TIME =   Twenty minutes

REPETITIONS =   Once

Use the daily practice technique for initiating the visualization process. Then begin your visualization of the pain control object destroying the pain object. If you should become fatigued or notice that you are being distracted, switch visualization to your favorite scene, allow yourself to relax fully, and once you feel reenergized, then begin visualizing the pain control object destroying the pain object once again.

(Note: If you want to go longer than twenty minutes, I would recommend that you do not. Instead of going longer in the evening session, I would rather that you use the daily session technique and practice using a twenty-second time span.)

Day Five in Review

You have now completed part one of your personalized pain relief formula. Increased practice is going to be extremely important. I would rather you practice with twenty-second segments instead of long, intensive sessions. Your intentions at this point are twofold:

1. To activate the pain relief formula as quickly as possible
2. To develop the activation of the pain relief formula as an unconscious habit

Earlier in the day you read your pain segment in chapter three. Now I would like you to read tomorrow's program and learn how you will be applying the pain segment to your personalized pain relief formula—part two.

Today you have learned:

To begin the destruction of your pain object(s)

To initiate the beginnings of your personalized pain relief formula

To begin using the personalized pain relief formula on an unconscious-habit basis

Day Six

Introduction.

As you enter day six of the Scottsdale Pain Relief Program, you are one step away from your personalized pain relief formula in its final form. Today you will be shown how to incorporate the pain segment into your personalized pain relief formula. I do not recommend that you review day seven until you have completed today's program. There is always a tendency to go slightly faster than is recommended, especially when you are probably beginning to experience pain relief benefits from the first five days.

Daily Review.

This will be your last daily review, since on day seven I'm going to be presenting you with something different. By now you should be answering yes to all of the statements with almost no need for review.

Here is your final review. Answer yes or no to each statement.

1. Does the pain control object have to be used over and over to maintain control of the pain object?

2. Am I capable of using the personalized pain relief formula to reduce and control the pain?

At this time I am going to ask you to go back to the first five days and repeat the daily reviews. I have full confidence that you have been able to answer most or all of these questions with a resounding *yes!* But if any statements are unclear, reread that section, and change the no to a yes.

Today's Pain Relief Formula.

Your Personalized Pain Relief Formula—Part Two

The Basics.

Only one more day to go and you will have your finalized personalized pain relief formula. You have worked hard up to this point, so don't get ahead of yourself. Slow, steady, and even pacing will always be to your benefit.

Your personalized pain relief formula—part two will incorporate for the first time your pain segment. At the end of each pain segment is a formula statement which is to be included in your personalized pain relief formula. In today's instructions you will be given the appropriate place for insertion of your formula statement.

I suggest that you write your formula statement on a piece of paper and then commit it to memory, since you will be using it throughout today's sessions.

Goals.

The personalized pain relief formula—part two will accomplish the following:

It will intensify your pain control skills.

It will combine pain relief imagery with your formula statement.

It will shorten the activation time to under thirty seconds.

Instructions.

Follow today's instructions carefully, reading them over at least twice prior to beginning. At this point you should have your pain relief formula statement memorized.

With your eyes open, inhale deeply through your nose and exhale slowly through your mouth.

Visualize your pain control object destroying your pain object.

(Note: Always make sure to use the pain control color and pain color.)

Repeat your pain relief statement silently to yourself five times.
Example: I am in control of my _____ (insert pain site or description as found in the pain segment)

Again, visualize your pain control object attacking the pain object.

Repeat your pain relief formula statement five times to yourself silently.

Continue alternating your mental visualization with silent repetition of your pain relief formula statement.

Take a deep breath, let it out slowly, and stretch your arms and legs.

Today's Practice

Morning Session.

TIME =   Twenty minutes

REPETITIONS =   Repeat formula in four complete segments during this twenty-minute session. Start and terminate your personalized pain relief formula—part two with the pain relief formula statement every five minutes (four complete segments during your twenty-minute session).

FORMAT: Perform your personalized pain relief formula—part two with the pain relief formula statement.

Daily Sessions.

TIME =   Twenty to thirty seconds

REPETITIONS = Twice every hour from 9:00 A.M. to 6:00 P.M. Try to practice more than twice an hour but do not abbreviate the formula. Because you are going to use your personalized pain relief formula—part two with the pain relief formula statement, allow thirty seconds to complete the entire formula. Do not cut it short or modify it.

FORMAT:

With your eyes open, take one pain relief breath.

Visualize your pain control object attacking the pain object.

Repeat your pain relief formula statement silently to yourself twice.

Visualize your pain control object attacking your pain object.

Take a deep breath, let it out slowly, and gently stretch your arms and legs.

Evening Session.

TIME = Twenty minutes

REPETITIONS: See below

For this evening session, your time will be approximately twenty minutes; but during that time period you are to practice the daily session format just presented under the heading *Daily Sessions*. I realize you will not be able to complete the personalized pain relief formula—part two with the pain relief formula statement every thirty seconds for twenty minutes. This would be tremendously fatiguing and very difficult to accomplish. When you practice for tonight's session, keep each complete segment to thirty seconds or less and take a short break (approximately two minutes) between each.

Day Six in Review

You are now at a point where your formula is completed in thirty seconds or less. I do not expect that you will be completely proficient in its execution, nor will you find each thirty-second segment to be an improvement upon the last. You can only move just so fast.

Following completion of your evening session, try to continue practicing in thirty-second segments at least twice every hour, with your last thirty-second segment performed while you are in bed, just prior to falling asleep.

Today you have learned:

To integrate your pain relief formula statement with your personalized pain relief formula—part two

To utilize the complete formula in thirty seconds or less

A Preview of Day Seven.

Day seven is just around the corner, and with it the final building block of your seven-day pain relief program. Tomorrow's design and requirements will be different from those of the previous six days, and therefore I advise you to take the time now to review day seven.

Day Seven

Introduction.

Today is the last day of the intensive seven-day part of the Scottsdale Pain Relief Program. Tomorrow you will begin the Lifetime Maintenance Program, and the excitement has just begun. At this point I think it is important to let you know that if you are reading these sentences after completing six days of the program, then you need to congratulate yourself on a task that has been difficult, demanding, and possibly frustrating at times. If you can complete the six days (there is no reason why you can't) by using your personalized pain relief formula, then you can continue to improve and expand your ability to gain pain relief, retake control of your emotions, and begin enjoying life.

At this point in the program, you should also be noticing some of the positive factors that your emotions are beginning to create. People may comment to you that you seem like a changed person, or that something is different about you. Don't be bashful and deny yourself these compliments. Take them; you earned each and every word of praise.

Daily Review.

Your daily review for today will consist of rereading your pain segment in chapter three and completely reviewing the Lifetime Maintenance Program in part three.

Today's Pain Relief Formula.

The Personalized Pain Relief Formula

The Basics.

Today's formula represents a culmination of all six days of intensive application and practice. The personalized pain relief formula combines pain relief breathing, the pain relief scan, pain control objects, pain control color, pain objects, pain color, and your pain relief formula statement. All of these techniques are now combined into one simple, effective, and powerful formula.

You have yet to reach a point where your body and mind work together automatically to initiate the formula, and therefore you will have to continue practicing on a daily basis throughout the course of the Lifetime Maintenance Program. This may seem like a never-ending task, but once you have become proficient at using your pain relief formula, you will only be using minutes each day for continued pain relief and emotion-stabilizing benefits.

Goals.

Today's goal can be simply stated:

To activate the complete personalized pain relief formula anytime, anywhere, and under any circumstances

Instructions.

As a little surprise for you, today there will be no morning session, daily session, or evening session. You are to begin using the personalized pain relief formula on a twice-hourly basis from the time you awaken to the time you go to sleep. This might seem like a tremendous amount of practice, but at this time in the program, you should be prepared for a commitment of this magnitude and encouraged by the fact that each practice session will take no longer than thirty seconds for completion.

If you awaken at 6:00 A.M. and go to sleep at 10:00 P.M., this represents sixteen hours of twice-hourly practice, or thirty-two sessions. The total required practice time during one complete day will be *sixteen minutes*. One minute per hour, sixteen minutes per day, is not an exorbitant price to pay for pain relief and emotional stability.

Follow the instructions carefully, and read them over twice before beginning your day.

Take one pain relief breath.

Visualize your pain control object attacking your pain object.

Silently repeat your pain relief statement (once).

Take a deep breath, and let it out slowly, flexing your arms and legs.

At this point in the program, you will have the choice of practicing with your eyes open or closed. Most people find it preferable to practice with their eyes closed while lying in bed or just prior to going to sleep. In fact, most patients report an enhanced ability to sleep with a prolonged and deeper sleep pattern if they practice their personalized pain relief formula just prior to attempting sleep.

Today's Practice

TIME = Thirty seconds per session

REPETITIONS = Twice every hour from awakening in the morning until going to sleep at night

FORMAT: The complete personalized pain relief formula

The Final Day in Review

Twice an hour every hour seems like a lot, but in reality it's a small price to pay for lifetime benefits, some of which you have already begun to experience. Whenever you practice your personalized pain relief formula, use it completely. Do not abbreviate it or take any shortcuts.

If you want to use the formula more than twice an hour, please do so. Be innovative and experiment with its use. For instance, if you are feeling stressed by a particularly difficult meeting, then use the formula with your eyes open to reduce stress and prevent a stress/pain buildup. No one will realize you are using the formula. The more you experiment with its use under varying situations and circumstances, the more proficient you will become, with a proportional gain in confidence as you experience the positive results.

The Final Assignment.

The final assignment for the seven-day program will be to read part three of the book.

Part Three

The seven-day program is finished but not forgotten. I strongly encourage you to refer to any part of the seven-day program as often as you feel the need to review. This also applies to any of the sections in part one. Since you are not an inanimate object but a constantly changing organism within an ever-changing environment, you will need to refresh your memory at times or reread parts of the book and apply them to new situations.

Part three will contain your Lifetime Maintenance Program and the chapters *Eat, Sleep, Be Merry, and Control Your Pain* and *A Prescription for Living.*

When you suffer from chronic pain, it affects your entire lifestyle. Because you are not just a back injury, a migraine headache, or an arthritic hand but a fully functioning individual who has a chronic pain problem, the Lifetime Maintenance Program has been designed specifically to have a spillover effect. Typical patient responses best demonstrate how the Scottsdale Pain Relief Program will affect positively all areas of your life.

"When I finished the seven day part, I was flying high. For the first time in three years I could sit long enough to go to the movies with my family. They said I was not a stranger anymore."

—BILL P.

"Everyday I was depressed by the thought of another day of headaches. I know people didn't like me anymore and I didn't like myself. The program taught me how to stop the headaches and I can now look at myself in the mirror and smile."

—LINDA M.

"Some days I would sit and plan how to kill myself. The pain was like a gun pointed at my head all the time. I went through the pain program. The pain is still there but much less and I don't feel like killing myself. I'm even thinking about the future. I didn't think I had one before."

—GARY K.

You can see from these comments that the techniques you have learned and the foundation of knowledge you have gained will be a very powerful tool to help you improve the quality of your life. As with any tool, it has no function unless you pick it up, learn how to use it, and actually apply it. As you move through the chapters in part three, constantly challenge yourself by asking how the information presented to you may be applied to you as a whole, fully functioning person.

CHAPTER FIVE

The Lifetime Maintenance Program

In the Scottsdale Pain Relief Program there are three distinct points of celebration: the first, when you successfully complete the intensive seven-day program; the second, when you begin the Lifetime Maintenance Program; and the third, the continuous celebration each and every day you use the pain relief formulas to regain dignity in your life.

By now you have proven your commitment and desire for pain control to a very important person: yourself. If you let that commitment waiver for even one day, you will pay a price.

> *"I was so busy today I completely forgot."*
>
> *"I had the flu. You can't expect me to practice."*
>
> *"I was doing so well, a few days off seemed like an appropriate reward."*

If you were with me, I would ask you what is wrong with the statements you have just read. I hope you would look concerned and note how the people behind the statements were deceiving themselves. Your comment would come out this way:

> *When I started the program, you let me know right off about the commitment needed to be successful. I remember that every day of the seven-day program you reinforced the idea of a maintenance program only being as good as an individual's ability to practice every day; and I remember the two enemies—discouragement, which could lead to prematurely stopping the program, and overconfidence, which could lead to the erroneous conclusion that once you experience successful pain relief, practice is no longer necessary.*

If you have come this far, why ruin your achievements by becoming overconfident, lazy, or procrastinating?

Help! I'm Being Held Prisoner by My Pain.

There are no bars, no guards, and no high walls with spotlights, but just as surely as if you were in prison, you could experience your pain becoming a life sentence with no parole. You've already gone past the stage of expectation (that your pain will disappear) and into the stage of despair (thinking, I may have to live like this for the rest of my life).

Although the pain is the gatekeeper, you may now make the decision to apply for a lifetime parole. The seven-day program was simply the parole application process; now that you have successfully completed that test, it will be up to you to make a decision regarding the Lifetime Maintenance Program. Once you make the decision to leave your pain prison, you will only return if you stop practicing and working every day toward pain relief. Unfortunately, your cell will never be occupied by anyone else and will always be awaiting your return should you fail in your Lifetime Maintenance Program.

The comparison might sound somewhat drastic, but for anyone who has suffered from a chronic pain syndrome for more than nine months, it can feel as though you are a prisoner of your pain.

Strength in Numbers.

Yes, you can form a maintenance group. There are times when several people independently have completed the seven-day program and, for additional support, have developed a group approach to implementing the maintenance program. You do not have to begin a group that only sticks to the maintenance design I will present here.

Not everyone in the group needs to have the same type of pain, but it might help, especially when identifying with each other's special needs or difficulties.

Here's an example of how one person developed and implemented a maintenance group.

Sharon's Group

Sharon M. suffers from rheumatoid arthritis. Her story was the same as literally millions of others, until she participated in the Scottsdale Pain Relief Program. When she completed the program, she was not pain-free, but she had reduced certain aspects of her discomfort to a tolerable level. She had increased her daily activities and was now doing volunteer work. She was challenging life again.

As she began the Lifetime Maintenance Program, Sharon decided to contact other people who had just completed the seven-day program. Since Sharon had first heard about the program during a seminar I gave to an arthritis self-help group, she knew at least six other people at approximately the same stage of the Scottsdale Pain Relief Program.

She took the risk and called the people, inviting them over to her house on a Tuesday night with the idea of discussing their progress and exchanging ideas. To her surprise and pleasure, five out of the six attended the first meeting. After getting to know each other, they proceeded to have a lively discussion regarding their experiences with the program. Each person told a similar story, with some variations. Soon it was late and they decided to meet again in two weeks at one of the other people's house.

Two years have passed since the initial meeting at Sharon's house, and the group still meets on a monthly basis. They have become more than good friends, for they share the continued dedication never to letting pain ruin their lives again. I have been invited to speak to their group informally on at least three occasions, and each time I have come away with excellent ideas and suggestions. Whenever people contact me about starting a group, I give them Sharon's name and the next thing I know, I'm being invited to speak to a new group. To watch the beginning of a new group is an exciting experience.

Why Form a Group?

Several important growth factors may be germinated through maintenance groups. The fellowship, support, and caring provided by these groups can be immensely helpful when a member's condition deteriorates even while they are using the program to control the pain.

STARTING A GROUP. If you want to start your own maintenance group, follow these simple suggestions and you may find a very pleasant and enriching experience just around the corner.

> Contact the prospective people for your group and arrange for the first meeting.
>
> Try to limit your group size to six or less.
>
> Be sure all group participants have completed successfully the seven-day program.

The Lifetime Maintenance Program Explained.

The Lifetime Maintenance Program is exactly what its name implies. This is the program to follow for the rest of your life. Before proceeding any further, you need to do two things:

1. Thoroughly read chapter six.
2. Go to chapter three, pick the pain segment that applies to your specific discomfort, and review that segment completely.

In chapter seven, you will be given a prescription for living.

By completing both of these requirements, you will gain a better understanding of additional methods for controlling your pain. All of the techniques and suggestions that are presented to you are extremely important and should not be taken lightly. Although your personalized pain relief formula will be the most powerful tool in the ongoing effort to maintain pain relief, the suggestions provided to you in chapter six and the pain segment will add to your success.

Why Activities?

During the course of your seven-day program, you will expend significant effort toward reeducating your body/mind connection to decrease pain, increase pain tolerance, and help you obtain an emotional face lift.

Activity and exercise on a daily basis send a message to your brain that is positive in nature. It will respond with the production of natural chemicals that serve as antidepression and antianxiety substances. The runner's high is not the sole property of world-class athletes. Research has shown that any activity that elevates the heart rate and lasts for from twelve to fifteen minutes will cause the production of these internal emotion stabilizers.

Your Benefits.

By participating in a daily activity program, you will soon begin to experience these very pleasant, rewarding benefits:

Increased muscular strength

Increased muscular endurance

Increased flexibility

Increased blood flow to the muscles

Increased elimination of waste materials from the muscles

Increased ability to deal with stress

Increased positive self-image

Increased capacity for stretching

Increased cardiopulmonary fitness

Increased self-confidence

Increased energy

Of course you will not benefit from all of these positive results the first time you participate in your daily activity. It usually takes at least two or three weeks before you begin to notice significant, positive changes, but you have to start the ball rolling on day one of the seven-day program.

The Best Five Exercises

Before I determined the top five exercises for people with chronic pain problems, I consulted with exercise physiologists, physicians of all and varied specialties, physical therapists, and physical fitness coaches.

Each specialist was asked to rate the activity based upon several factors: potential for injury, potential for reinjury, cardiovascular benefits, ease of application, cost effectiveness, and musculoskeletal benefits. After compiling all of the data, the top five factors were:

Walking

Stationary exercycle

Low impact aerobics

Swimming

Biking

In your search for the appropriate exercise, please consider one of the above as a possible first choice.

(*Note:* After you choose any activity, be sure to consult your physician and obtain his approval.)

Setting Up the Exercise/Activity Program

After you have approval from your physician, it is time to begin your exercise/activity program. Whichever exercise/activity you select, there are some ground rules you should always observe:

1. Participate in your exercise/activity program at least once a day. Twice a day will not hurt, but you should be careful not to overdo it. *Never* sacrifice other parts of your seven-day program for an extra exercise/activity period.

2. The exercise/activity program should be performed *every* day. No excuses!

3. When you perform any stretching exercise, use a firm yet comfortable surface.

4. Pay careful attention to your body position at all times.

5. Pace yourself correctly. You should never be in a race to finish.

6. Clothing should be loose and comfortable. If your exercise/activity program involves walking or use of an exercycle, invest in a good pair of jogging, walking, or aerobic shoes.

7. Do not continue your exercise/activity periods if you experience a steady increase in pain.

Exercise/Activity Pitfalls to Avoid.

1. Pick an exercise/activity program that is compatible with your age, physical capacities, and pain situation. Refer to the section in this chapter on making your exercise/activity choice, which will provide you with a list of recommended activities for various physical conditions.

2. Start slowly and increase gradually. If you choose a walking program, for example, don't become involved with a neighbor who has been walking for three years and invites you out for a three-mile journey on your first attempt.

3. Don't hesitate to change any activity that prompts an increase in your pain response or that you find unsatisfactory for other reasons such as weather or safety.

4. Don't vary your exercise/activity times. Be consistent. Let a positive habit form by setting aside a specific time each day.

High-Risk Activities

If you have a muscle, ligament, or bone condition, then it will be important for you to avoid certain types of activities. Although you might have participated in these activities before your injury occurred or your condition began, you will no longer be able to pursue them safely without significantly increasing the risk of reinjury or even new injury due to your present physical condition. Use common sense, and if that voice inside tells you not to participate, by all means *listen*. I have listed some of these activities with a brief explanation:

1. *Football, basketball, and baseball.* Because they involve twisting, jarring movements, jumping, bending, and contact with other players, these sports are potentially hazardous for a weak back or neck.

2. *Bowling.* This activity can easily aggravate back or neck problems, since you lift a heavy weight while twisting and bending your upper body.

3. *Weight lifting.* Lifting free (loose) weights can put tremendous amounts of stress on the musculoskeletal system. If you exercise at a health spa with Nautilus-type equipment, it is absolutely essential that you make sure the person designing your exercise program is aware of your pain problem and is qualified to design a program that will not reinjure you.

4. *Tennis and Other Racquet Sports.* These sports can strain the back because of their twisting and quick stop-go movements added to the pounding shock of the hard court.

5. *Golf.* A recent survey found that twenty-five percent of all golf pros suffer from low back injuries. The twisting movement of the swing, constant bending to tee the ball or remove the ball from the cup, and prolonged putting or driving practice may lead to a back reinjury.

Activities Your Body Will Like.

Just because you have an injury or pain condition, there is no reason why you cannot participate in enjoyable activities. Certain activities not only provide excellent cardiovascular conditioning, muscle toning, and positive emotional responses, but they are also excellent for anyone with a pain condition.

1. *Swimming.* This is the best sport for relieving musculoskeletal pain, since the water supports the spine, thus relieving pressure on it. It also helps tone and stretch key muscles. The backstroke and the sidestroke are best for the back, legs, arms, shoulders, and hips. Avoid the butterfly and the breaststroke, which cause you to arch your back.

2. *Cycling.* This is excellent aerobic exercise if you have pain problems,

provided you maintain an upright position. It is not recommended for arthritis, however, so instead use a stationary exercycle.

3. *Walking*. This is the perfect exercise for promoting a healthy body/ mind. According to the Swedish back expert Dr. Alf Nachemson, walking puts less strain on the spine than does unsupported sitting, and only a little more than plain standing. You may begin a walking program with no practice, and you need no special equipment except for good shoes.

Your Personal Activity Program

Repetitive daily activity is an integral part of the Scottsdale Pain Relief Program. You need to perform your personal activity program at least once a day, every day. To break up any boredom, I always recommend at least two activities that can be alternated or varied.

(*Note:* Prior to beginning any physical activity program, you should obtain the approval of your physician. Your doctor may provide you with suggestions for various activities based upon your physical condition.)

Exercise/Activity Program.

You are to continue your activity on a once-daily basis. Maintain a schedule that allows you to participate in the activity at the same time each day. Consistency leads to increased chances for success.

If you begin to tire of your activity/exercise, then begin developing a substitute for your primary interest. For example, many of my patients begin a walking program and after several months substitute a few times a week with swimming. This provides for an extremely well-rounded approach to your exercise/activity program. The program may be divided in the following manner:

Walking—Monday, Wednesday, Friday, Saturday, and Sunday

Swimming—Tuesday and Thursday

You may alternate among two or three activities, just as long as you perform them on a daily basis, without fail.

Your Personalized Pain Relief Formula.

On day seven of the program, you developed your personalized pain relief formula. This short version allowed you to complete the entire formula in from thirty to forty seconds. I asked you to practice on an every-thirty-minutes basis. The every-thirty-minutes practice schedule will be continued, but within three weeks you will already begin to notice definite changes. As you use the pain relief breathing, your mind will begin to activate the personalized pain relief formula before you can actually begin to use the autogenic pain relief phrases or the pain control imagery. A positive habit of pain relief will be formed and begin to be activated on an automatic basis.

Once the pain relief reaction becomes automatic, you will find it being activated not only for your pain but for any part of the emotional fallout, which has been discussed earlier. When the personalized pain relief formula is activated automatically for emotions, it becomes an emotion-stabilizing formula. The diagram below presents the chain reaction that occurs with continuous practice during the Lifetime Maintenance Program.

Pain → Personalized → Decreased → Activation → Decreased
Pain Relief   Pain   of Automatic   Emotional
Formula   Emotion-   Distress
                                   Stabilizing
                                   Formula

Summary.

You know how to use your personalized pain relief formula not only for pain but as an emotion-stabilizing formula. In chapter six you are going to learn how food and sleep can affect your pain. Read the chapter carefully, for the information contained within it is absolutely essential for continued success in the Lifetime Maintenance Program.

CHAPTER SIX

Eat, Sleep, Be Merry, and Control Your Pain

Your body is a tremendously complicated electrochemical machine that needs to be fueled. I have already shown you how stress can affect directly your pain by increasing it and decreasing your emotional resilience. What we have not discussed is the fact that chronic pain, through its stress response, can cause the body to burn a significant amount of energy, thus creating a very high demand for the proper intake of food. A balanced diet is extremely important for anyone who is suffering from pain.

During the past several years, there have been reports of special diets that cause a decrease in pain. When most of these diets are explored in depth, however, I have found that the major component is a healthy balance between proteins, carbohydrates, and fats.

There are certain foods that may contribute to your discomfort through allergic or physiological reactions. This problem has been dealt with in the section on how foods feed your pain in this chapter.

(*Note:* Maintaining a correct balance of proteins, carbohydrates, and fats in your food intake is of extreme importance. Check with your physician about the correct combination for you.)

Serotonin—A Crucial Link.

Serotonin is manufactured naturally within the brain and serves as a neurotransmitter, facilitating the flow of messages within the body's network of nerves. The appropriate production of serotonin has been linked to better sleep, calmer moods, increased energy levels, and control over appetite. It is a key ingredient in the pain response mechanism.

Before delving more completely into serotonin and its link to pain, let's take a moment and discuss exactly what serotonin's function is within the human body. Serotonin, which has been classified as a neurotransmitter, is released at the neurons (nerve fiber endings) and helps the nerve impulses cross the synaptic gap between two neurons.

Serotonin is a neurotransmitter that is derived from the essential amino acid tryptophan and is found in the blood, most nerve cells, and other body tissues. Tryptophan is a specific nutrient that is derived from certain protein foods; it may be purchased over the counter in tablet form. If you follow any good, healthy diet that allows for a proper balance of proteins, carbohydrates, and fats, you will help to insure that an adequate level of tryptophan is produced by the brain and therefore provide for adequate levels of serotonin.

Serotonin and the Pain Threshold.

Recent scientific studies have indicated that decreased levels of serotonin in the blood and tissue can cause people to have a lower tolerance for pain. When their serotonin level is appropriate, people will have an adequate ability to utilize the body's built-in painkillers, allowing them to work adequately toward decreasing the body's pain. When the body's serotonin level is low or depleted, pain you normally would have been able to ignore becomes greater both in terms of when you notice it and when it becomes intolerable.

(*Note:* Lower levels of tryptophan lead to decreased serotonin production within the brain and cause an increased sensitivity to pain and decreased ability to produce the body's internal painkillers.)

Maintaining Serotonin Levels.

We have seen that the body's production of serotonin is linked directly to the production of the amino acid tryptophan. Remember that amino acids occur naturally in plant and animal tissues and serve both as a built-in block of protein molecules (serotonin) and as some of the body's built-in painkillers (endorphins, enkephalins). Amino acids must be obtained from foods or supplements. The human body synthesizes many amino acids from the food sources in your diet.

If serotonin is responsible for endorphins and enkephalins, which are found in the brain areas and produce analgesia (pain relief), and it acts to switch on and off neurons involved in pain control, then having appropriate levels of serotonin to insure the proper transmission of signals that increase the body's production of natural pain killers is obviously essential.

Increased Pain Threshold—A Partial Answer.

If we are able to increase our pain threshold, then the point at which we will notice pain is increased and we are able to tolerate greater degrees of pain without the devastating physical and emotional after-effects. Increased pain threshold is only one part of the answer, but it does play a role in the total Lifetime Maintenance Program. By eating correctly through a well-balanced diet, we can insure an adequate production of tryptophan and thus create an environment for appropriate serotonin production. Some scientists and doctors have advocated the supplementation of tryptophan through tablets. I would recommend consulting your physician before trying this. Although tryptophan has been judged safe enough for over-the-counter administration, it is always best to check with your physician. Serotonin cannot be obtained in supplemental form, so don't go to your favorite pharmacist and ask him for a serotonin pill.

Scientific research has shown one other way in which serotonin production is increased within the human body, and that is through exercise. Earlier we discussed the beneficial aspects to exercising and elevating the heart rate and, therefore, increasing the body's production of serotonin which not only affects the body's level of pain threshold but serves as a natural antidepressant (the runner's high).

Keeping You Safe.

It is interesting to note that serotonin, endorphins, and enkephalins all serve to increase our ability to withstand pain and help achieve a greater degree of emotional stability without removing pain perception. Since pain is the body's warning signal, it would be detrimental to our health if the body could no longer provide us an alarm system indicating a body malfunction.

None of the internally produced painkillers will remove the body's ability to signal the alarm relating to body malfunction.

A Stuck Signal.

Unfortunately, anyone who experiences chronic pain has a horn which is stuck and, therefore, the warning signal actually becomes an irritant. The body's built-in chemicals that are facilitated through proper diet and appropriate food intake will facilitate natural chemical balance and enhance your internal abilities to obtain control over your pain through the Scottsdale Pain Relief Program.

The Proper Food Intake.

Obtaining information regarding the appropriate intake of protein, carbohydrates, and fats is a simple matter of contacting your physician, the American Heart Association, the local YMCA, or numerous other organizations who will gladly provide you with appropriate diets. If you have any difficulty obtaining this information, go to your local hospital and ask to speak with the nutritionist. I am sure he or she would be happy to provide you with additional sources regarding safe and appropriate diet information.

The Pain of Eating Poorly.

A report in the June 1983 issue of the *Journal of Surgery* directs attention to a correlation between good nutrition and increased functioning of the body's immune, healing, and pain reduction systems. Since we know that pain can suppress the body's immune system (the ability to fight disease and repair itself), we must not allow a suppression in the immune system by insuring proper nutrition to maintain the body's ability to tolerate pain as effectively as possible.

How Food Feeds Your Pain.

Pain has a voracious appetite and likes to be fed. We have seen how we might feed pain from a physical and emotional standpoint. Now you will learn how not to help your pain by eating foods that may cause an increase in discomfort.

Before telling you what you should or should not eat, I need to emphasize the importance of eating meals at regular times and not overeating—especially when you're experiencing pain or the emotional fallout from pain increases.

Pain Triggers.

Most research regarding the role of certain foods, liquids, and chemical substances as triggers for pain has been limited to headaches. I have found during the course of my practice that making anyone who suffers from pain aware of food triggers often will have a beneficial effect upon the individual's particular pain response.

If you suffer from headaches, absolutely avoid the triggers. If you are experiencing other types of pain, try eliminating these substances and judge for yourself whether or not they have an effect on your pain response.

Pain Triggers

Cheeses, such as a Brie, Gruyère, and cheddar (natural and aged and high in tyramine content which may cause vascular changes and trigger headaches)

Chocolate milk

Smoked and processed meats such as hot dogs, bologna, and sausage

Peanut butter

Beer

Seeds such as sunflower or pumpkin

Monosodium glutamate (MSG) flavoring (found in meat tenderizers and Chinese cooking)

Soft drinks containing caffeine

Chocolate

Coffee

(In excess) bananas, citrus fruits, and yeast extracts

Pickled and marinated food

In the list of pain triggers I have tried to include the major offenders and instigators of pain. In the past whenever I have presented such a list to patients, I could have almost guaranteed that someone was going to come up and say something like "lamb chops caused my joints to ache." Because each of us is an individually functioning system in our environment, certain foods or substances not listed may cause you an increase in pain or may actually trigger the onset of discomfort. If you notice that each time you eat a particular food it is followed by either the onset of pain or increased pain, then by all means eliminate that item to determine if you have a pain trigger I have not discussed. You should also be aware of the fact that since we are constantly changing systems, a pain trigger that did not bother you five years ago may become a pain trigger now or in the future. Your constant evaluation of possible pain triggers will be a necessity for your Lifetime Maintenance Program.

Pick and Choose.

Controlling the amount that we eat is difficult enough, but trying to eliminate all of the items listed at one time would be very difficult. While trying to avoid most items on the list, be aware of any changes in your pain patterns that may occur when you eliminate a particular item (especially if you are a headache sufferer). If you go to a Chinese restaurant, ask for dishes without MSG. Be aware that eliminating these items from your diet should take place over an extended period of time. Stopping your intake of peanut butter for two days, for instance, is likely to have little effect upon your pain. Common sense will also tell you that if you only eat chocolate once every three weeks and you have headaches four times weekly, the chance that the chocolate is a trigger for your headaches is slight.

Sleep—A Crucial Element.

"Ah, ah, if only I could get a decent night's sleep. I can't remember the last time I slept through the whole night."

"I can't seem to turn off my mind when I try and go to sleep. All that happens is that I lie there and toss and turn, and toss and turn."

For anyone who has experienced pain, obtaining a good night's sleep is a goal worth its weight in gold. During sleep the body rebuilds, recuperates, and prepares you for the following day. If your sleep cycle becomes disrupted for even two or three days, the body's ability to produce its own built-in painkillers becomes impaired. Additionally, when you lose sleep there's a greater susceptibility to depression. If you don't believe me, take a look at how you or anyone you know reacts when not sleeping well for two or three days. You will notice the appearance of depressive-type symptoms.

I mentioned earlier in this chapter the beneficial effect that proper diet will have on the production of tryptophan, which in essence will help facilitate increased levels of the neurotransmitter serotonin. We took a look at serotonin's beneficial effect of increasing your ability to withstand higher degrees of pain. Besides its effect on pain, the production of serotonin is an ingredient to facilitate quicker and longer sleep patterns.

The Warm Glass of Milk.

Most of us remember grandmother talking about having a warm glass of milk before bedtime to insure a good night's sleep. Well, this wasn't just an old wives' tale; research has found that having a warm glass of milk actually stimulates increased tryptophan production in the brain and thus enhances the use of serotonin.

Do's and Don't's.

Here are some do's and don't's to help you obtain a better night's sleep and awaken more refreshed and better able to use your personalized pain relief formula.

Don't's

> *Don't eat a large meal within three hours of planning to go to sleep*
>
> *Don't perform your exercise/activity program within an hour of going to sleep*
>
> *Don't take over-the-counter sleeping medications*
>
> *Don't take anyone else's sleep medication without first checking with your physician*
>
> *Don't lie in bed trying to organize your tomorrows*
>
> *Don't concentrate on disturbing thoughts prior to attempting sleep*

Do, Do, Do . . .

> *Do make sure that your bed is appropriate if you have a neuromuscular pain problem*
>
> *Do use your personalized pain relief formula once you are lying in bed, as a method for relaxing your body and inducing sleep*
>
> *Do use the pain relief scan when you first lie down in bed to insure the release of muscular tension*

Do consult your physician if your sleep difficulties last longer than one week

Summary.

I have found, through my years of care and treatment involving pain, that one of the key statements of advice I can give is to use common sense at all times. Don't become involved in fad diets or remedies. A good, nutritious diet and appropriate sleep will serve as important ingredients for your success within the Lifetime Maintenance Program.

CHAPTER SEVEN

A Prescription for Living

Although each chapter of the Scotts-
dale Pain Relief Program is of equal importance, this chapter will
help you to set and firm your course of success in utilizing the Lifetime Maintenance Program.

Read each section carefully (reviewing the chapter more than once
will be beneficial). If you are not sure whether a section applies to
your pattern of behavior or coping style, ask your spouse or another
person who knows you to give you his or her honest opinion. Before
asking for anyone's opinion, let the person read this chapter in its
entirety.

A Word Before You Start.

Always be open to discovering and learning from all aspects of your
emotional and physical behavior. Remember, the main objective of
this chapter is to help you extinguish the behaviors that might reinforce your pain and prevent success in the Lifetime Maintenance
Program.

Daily Exercise/Activity.

Keep up the good work. If there has been any difficulty in performing your activity, evaluate your daily schedule and make any appropriate adjustments. Don't wait until tomorrow.

Pain Relief Thinking

As you think, you are. Never has a truer statement been spoken. If all you think of is pain and if your past, present, and future revolves around pain, then your pain will be reinforced. The more you focus on your pain, the less effective the pain relief formulas will be in utilizing your body's built-in painkillers to provide you with relief.

As with everything in the Scottsdale Pain Relief Program, pain relief thinking will take practice, but after a relatively short time the habit pattern will be formed. Follow these simple instructions and by the end of day seven pain relief thinking will have become an important tool you can use for success in your battle with pain.

> *Whenever you have a negative pain thought (thinking about pain while using the pain relief formula or pain relief breathing should not be considered negative) consciously think to yourself the words* I am in control.
>
> *The words* I am in control *repeated silently to yourself will block the pain thought and will become an appropriate linking mechanism for automatic activation of your personal pain relief formula.*
>
> *At first you will have to repeat the phrase* I am in control *from three to five times to block effectively the negative pain thought. After practicing, you will find that the phrase* I am in control *will become automatic, short-circuiting the negative pain response.*

Here are some samples of negative pain responses that need to be removed.

"I am getting discouraged about my pain."

"My pain will probably be worse tomorrow."

"The weather is making my pain greater."

"I don't think I'll be able to go because of my pain."

"My pain will probably be worse today."

"I'll never feel better!"

Mind Over Emotions

As you are now aware, your emotions play a significant role in your chronic pain complex. The mind-over-emotions part of the pain relief statement is designed specifically to help you gain the greatest degree of control over emotions such as depression, anxiety, frustration, irritability, and anger, which all serve to pump up your pain. You are going to be requesting your mind and body to work together as a team not only to identify but also to control any emotions that interfere with your ability for pain relief.

Always include the pain relief statement as part of the personalized pain relief formula. You may want to use some of the other pain relief statements found in chapter three.

Sexual Activity and Pain.

"Not tonight, I've got a headache."

How many times have we heard that famous statement on television or in the movies? It's the age-old excuse. It never seems to go out of style.

Participating in sexual activity is of great concern to anyone who has suffered a back injury. Most of the time, advice is very short, nondescriptive, and possibly damaging ("If it hurts, stop."). So what happens to the person with a back injury? The first time sexual relations are attempted and pain is experienced, activity has to stop. A man will develop secondary impotency due to the anxiety and anticipation about the increase in pain. This scenario is similar to the one experienced by post–heart attack victims, when the doctor tells them that sexual activity is just fine ("but don't get too excited.").

Not an Excuse.

Don't allow your pain to be an excuse for avoiding sexual activity. If you develop an excuse mechanism by blaming your pain, then you may find your body and mind working together to increase pain and thus present you with a more justifiable excuse.

Pain Relief.

Recent studies have both indicated and verified that the body increases the production of endogenous circulating opioids (including endorphins) as a result of sexual stimulation. During the past several years, for example, articles have appeared in newspapers and magazines relating to research that suggested that sexual activity could modify the pain of arthritis.

Common Sense.

When in doubt, use common sense.

Be open to discussing any fears or apprehensions you may have with your sexual partner. Openness and honesty will go a long way toward the development of gratifying sexual activity that will not increase significantly your level of discomfort and, in fact, may actually aid in your pain relief.

Positive Pain Relief Addiction

*"I'm pleased to inform you of your pending addiction to the
Scottsdale Pain Relief Program."*

Sound strange? Of course it does, especially since anyone who has
been on (narcotic) pain relief medication is keenly aware of that devastating word *addiction*. Heroin users become addicted; cocaine users
become addicted; alcoholics become addicted. All of these addictions
have negative consequences.

Now I'm telling you about the *positive* addiction to the Scottsdale
Pain Relief Program.

I'm sure many of you have experienced the frustration of sitting in
your doctor's examining room with continuing complaints of pain
and hearing him say, "I really can't give you any more medication
because I think you are becoming addicted." Unfortunately no alternative is provided, which leaves you in a situation where you are
counting your pills, going to other doctors for medication (doctor
shopping), or even showing up at your local emergency room and
presenting the right number of symptoms to get the right medication.

Are You Positively Addicted?

You know you are positively addicted when the following events
happen:

You look forward to your exercise/activity program.

*Your postactivity glow (feelings of well-being and calmness) lasts
for more than twenty minutes.*

You practice your pain relief formula more than required.

The major drawback to positive addiction can be found if you miss more than one day of activities. The withdrawal symptoms that you will experience are similar to those of nicotine, caffeine, or even medication. Once your body becomes accustomed to the natural chemical production fostered by consistent activity, then you are hooked on positive addiction.

Stress

The time has come for me to tell you about a very serious topic and something that needs to be dealt with immediately. Now that you have completed the seven-day program, you probably will have experienced positive outcomes to pain relief and increased emotional control. You will have attained your personalized pain relief formula and be able to activate it in thirty-to-forty-five seconds or less any time or any place you desire. You have worked extremely hard and made a commitment for those seven days; but upon completion of the program, some people fall into a trap of becoming complacent. I have been providing you with information every day that I am going to ask you to rely upon in the Lifetime Maintenance Program. There are several factors that may cause problems or interfere with successful maintenance. Stress is one of them, and so you need to start developing the ability to cope with it.

What Is Stress?

Think for a minute about what the word *stress* means to you. What I know for certain is that no matter how many people I ask about stress and what it means to them, I may get many different answers. Most people will be consistent in one response: Stress isn't good for you, but it's a fact of life. Stress has become the buzzword of the 1980s and in all likelihood will continue that way into the 1990s. This infamous word has been blamed for everything from the sinking of the Titanic to tension in Soviet-American relations—rigdtly so, since stress does play a significant role in all of our daily lives and—most important—our health.

Stress, in its most basic form, is the way you react—physically and emotionally—to pain.

Positive and Negative Stress.

Stress comes in two varieties: positive and negative. Not all stress is bad, but some stress can be linked directly to devastating diseases such as cancer. The body's immune system becomes depleted or reduced when you are under chronic or constant stress. Recent studies have indicated that people who have a history of cancer in their family (an example being breast cancer) may be more susceptible to the development of malignancy if they remain in a chronically stressful condition.

Positive Stress

Getting that income tax return in on time, cramming for a test, and performing physically beyond normal capabilities are all aspects of positive stress responses. Some people claim that they work better under stress; this may be a real consequence with positive results, but only if people do not place themselves in constant (daily) stressful situations. We have all known people who respond with bursts of energy, increased concentration, and creative ideas when they are put under stress, but afterward such emotional reactions to stress drain off. In between, these people tend to rest and relax, and so they are ready for the next stressful event.

Wouldn't it be wonderful if we could all react in that manner?

Negative Stress

I am talking about negative stress with a capital N. Stresses that hit at you on a daily basis are unrelenting and have an intensity that leaves you in a state of upheaval both physically and emotionally. Your body is like the engine on a car. Most cars are capable of driving at maximum speed for short periods of time if you press the accelerator to the floor, but after you've passed the car in front of you or averted some precarious situation, you let up on the accelerator and the engine returns to normal. A negative stress situation is as if you pressed the accelerator of your car all the way to the floor and kept it there. Even the newest, most well-tuned car will soon begin to break down if subjected to the unrelenting stress of maximum performance. Some engines cease completely or blow up (as in a heart attack or a stroke), while some others experience a breakdown of a particular part or system (as in a decreased function of the human body's immune system or its development of ulcers). In many cases, especially if the car is not new, the stress focuses on a weak link like a previously damaged drive shaft or carburetor, and that part of the engine becomes the first to break down. The same holds true with the human body. We can all cope with brief periods of acceleration, but under the constant pressure of unrelenting stress (like constant acceleration), we tend to suffer a massive breakdown or the malfunction of a previously weakened link. The body's weak links may be caused by inheritance, genetic predisposition, previous injury, or ailment.

If you suffered a back injury like the one I did playing college football, whenever you allow yourself to be overstressed, the stress goes directly to the low back and may appear as increased discomfort. Fortunately, I have learned to recognize and resolve stressful complications in my life. This has helped me to eliminate one of the factors that could adversely affect and increase my back pain. I am not perfect, of course, and there are times when I tend to forget or become complacent in the knowledge that I know how to control stress and its relation to my back pain. I spend time on a fairly regular basis reviewing my reactions to stress to insure that stress does not affect my damaged back.

A Two-Edged Sword.

The sword of stress cuts both ways and, unlike the finest broadswords, becomes sharper with usage. Chronic stress may attack you physically or emotionally and many times in both ways.

A Fact of Life.

Stress is a fact of life. You couldn't avoid all stress even if you were to go live in a cave as a hermit. There would always be the stress of something like bears coming in to live with you or dropping rocks. No one is capable of insulating himself or herself from stress. Even knowing its potential for doing damage to the body and mind, some people do not want to make the effort to learn effective stress-reducing techniques. There are few guarantees in life, but one of them is that if you are a pain sufferer, prolonged chronic stress will cause an increase in your pain.

Managing Stress.

Learning to deal with stresses in your environment and the stresses you create within yourself is a matter of identification, practice, and lifestyle change.

You will never learn to deal effectively with your stress if you are not willing to examine which types of stresses are affecting you. You will need to look at your job, home, and relationships and examine how you feel about yourself in all of these situations. Try to identify the situations in your life that make you feel tense, jumpy, or nervous. Try listening to your body and letting it become a barometer for stressful reactions.

Spend some time examining the stressful events in your life, and use this stress reduction miniprogram as a way of identifying and dealing appropriately with stress responses.

The Pain Relief Formulas and Stress.

Upon your completion of the seven-day program, you will have at your disposal one of the most effective methods known for dealing with chronic stress. You will still be able to gear up for the IRS or that report your boss wanted finished by Thursday morning, but without the adverse chronic stress reactions that would cause an increase in your pain.

The method is simple: Whenever you have identified a stressful event and cannot change the cause of the stress, use your personalized pain relief formula to short-circuit the body's (physical and emotional) negative reaction to the stressful event. If you use the personalized pain relief formula as a method for short-circuiting a stress response, after enough practice it will become an automatic habit and allow you to deal effectively with any stressful situation. Additionally, by learning to deal with stress, you will be eliminating one of the major causes of pain increase.

Reinforce, Reinforce.

Whenever you positively reinforce an event, the chances of that event occurring again are increased. We spend much of our lives looking for all reinforcement from outside of ourselves. From the time we are small children, this reinforcement is provided by parents, teachers, and friends. Much of how we view ourselves becomes dependent upon positive or negative reinforcement. If someone is reinforced negatively over and over, then the person will eventually view himself or herself as negative. Tell yourself enough times that you are worthless, and soon you will truly believe that worthlessness is your main characteristic. In fact, you may believe this so strongly that as a result of your actions other people begin to take this same view.

When you reinforce the positive nature of the Scottsdale Pain Relief Program, your body and mind gradually begin to believe that you can actually perform and take control of your pain relief. No one can reinforce positive thoughts continually without an occasional negative response sneaking into the mind. Make an effort to reinforce on a constant and consistent basis the belief in your ability to obtain pain relief. Do it well and do it often. Your body and mind will then work together to fulfill the prophesy you have created.

Overcoming Your Pain—Depression Cycle.

Since we have already established that pain and depression go hand in hand, you need to do something about taking charge of your depression and removing as much of it as possible from your lifestyle. Read over these suggestions, determine which ones apply directly to you, and begin to take control of your depression.

Develop a sense of order in your life.

Try to be on time for appointments, answer your mail, balance your checkbook, have food in the kitchen, eat regular meals, and obtain enough sleep. Developing order in your life will simplify your existence and allow you enough leftover energy for activities such as the Scottsdale Pain Relief Program, hobbies, and achieving your overall goals. When you organize and accomplish, you reinforce your sense of worth and confidence.

Don't dress depressed.

You should pay careful attention to both your dress and your personal grooming. Depressed people tend to dress emotionally. They may look unkempt or unshaven and tend to put off paying any attention to their personal appearance. Try dressing in brighter colors and spending time on your appearance.

Don't be a giver-upper.

Even when you're down and blue, don't give up on activities. Don't quit school, change your job, or stop an uncompleted project. Major decisions should not be made while you are depressed.

If a project appears to be overwhelming, then break it into smaller segments, completing each segment as you go forward.

Use an emotional release.

The best emotional relief will result from a combination of the personalized pain relief formula and the exercise/activity portion of the Scottsdale Pain Relief Program. This will allow you to dissipate some of your internal feelings of frustration or anger.

Treat each day as a new challenge.

Don't spend your time bogged down in past failures. Treat each new day as a challenge, plan for that challenge, and accept any successes you may achieve. If you are not able to accomplish all you hope to, then analyze why you have not met your expectations and then set a new course of action.

Don't talk about your problems.

Try to spend at least one day not talking about your problems either to yourself or anyone else. If you can be successful for one day, then try two and then three. The more you focus on and talk about your problems, the greater will be the chance that you are actually reinforcing your depression.

Eliminate Depressing People.

It would be virtually impossible to eliminate all people who have problems or are depressed from your life, but you can go a long ways toward identifying those people whom you associate with on a daily basis who are generally up individuals and experience less depression. If you spend all of your time around people who are down, then it will be quite easy for you to slip into the quicksand of depression and make it a group experience.

Dumping Your Negative Emotions.

If you are going to learn how to control your pain, then you will have to *dump* your negative emotions. These emotions are usually shown through pessimism, feeling down, never being able to find anything good in anything or anybody, and a general Scrooge-like outlook on life.

If you are a negative thinker, then you are going to have to force yourself to begin looking on the bright side of things. You cannot hope to convince your brain to produce its own built-in painkillers if you spend the majority of your time brainwashing yourself into looking at the negative, unsuccessful side of your existence.

Your Prescription for Living.

Your prescription for living will be to utilize the Lifetime Maintenance Program as a method for living life to its fullest. Here's your prescription:

> *Practice your personalized pain relief formula as often as possible and under varying situations and circumstances.*
>
> *Keep up with practice, for the more you practice your personalized pain relief formula, the greater its effectiveness will be.*
>
> *Through constant practice, allow the personalized pain relief formula to become an automatic habit.*
>
> *Maintain an appropriate exercise/activity program.*
>
> *Through the advice of your physician, maintain the most nutritional diet possible.*
>
> *Accept the challenge to be evaluating constantly your emotional reaction to others and the environment.*

Be aware that you are an ever-changing organism in an ever-changing environment and therefore be willing to facilitate and accept change.

The most important part of this prescription: Believe in yourself and your ability to control your pain.

My Final Comments for You.

Most people report that upon completion of the Scottsdale Pain Relief Program there is a slow, but steady, continuation of their success in reducing pain and the associated detrimental psychological consequences.

Although I can't be with you to provide congratulations upon successfully completing the Scottsdale Pain Relief Program, I still would like to give you a sincere "well done." But in the same breath, I have to caution you against becoming complacent and forgetting that the Lifetime Maintenance Program needs to be performed every day and under varying situations and conditions.

The book has come to an end, but you are only beginning to use the power within you to control pain and gain positive emotions. Your future is now up to you.